UNDER THE EDITORSHIP OF

Wayne C. Minnick   THE FLORIDA STATE UNIVERSITY

Improving
VOICE AND

Houghton Mifflin Company · Boston

Hilda B. Fisher

NORTHWESTERN UNIVERSITY

ARTICULATION

ɑ r t ɪ k ju l e ʃ ə n

EW YORK · ATLANTA · GENEVA, ILL. · DALLAS · PALO ALTO

Preface

THE STUDENT WHO ENROLLS in a voice and articulation course is essentially a pragmatist. He evaluates the course not so much by what he learns about speech in general as by his own speech improvement. This text is equally pragmatic: its primary purpose is to provide practical methods of achieving the greatest improvement in speech in the shortest possible time.

I have observed that the most lasting improvement in voice and articulation results from speech exercises which involve maximum conscious control of speech functions, through heightened sensory awareness of one's performance. I have also observed that the intelligent student derives the greatest benefit from exercises whose rationale he understands and accepts, and that this understanding depends on basic knowledge of the physiology of voice production, the acoustics of speech, and linguistic structure. Consequently, this text puts heavy emphasis on exercises *in context*, not on rote practice or practice in a vacuum.

In many ways, the exercises are the heart of the text. Designed primarily to correct particular problems in phonation, resonance, vocal variety, and articulation, they have one primary goal: to help the student develop objective self-awareness. Not only is the operation of sensory feedback in habit formation explained; it is applied countless times in carefully directed exercises. Special attention is given to auditory training — to discrimination, negative practice, and spontaneous and second judgments from tape recordings. The student is also alerted to significant kinesthetic, tactual, and visual cues to the proper control of speech functions. The exercises have been thoroughly tested in university classes over the past several years. In fact, their content and organization have been dictated largely by students' questions or demonstrated needs.

All original exercises were created with careful attention to phonemic content and grammatical structure. To test the carry-over of acquired vocal skills, each section contains literary excerpts for reading practice. In keeping with students' tastes and interests, most of the excerpts are from prose selections, and many are from contemporary writing. Such material has the added advantage of being closer to actual speech than much-anthologized archaic poems.

Since theory and practice are presented in this book as closely integrated units, the student can proceed immediately with intelligent practice and not delay the application until all the scientific and theoretical matter has been mastered. As soon as he receives his instructor's initial voice critique, he can turn to those sections of the text particularly useful to him and begin work.

Information relating to anatomy and physiology, the physics of sound, phonetics, and the psychology of learning is presented in enough depth to support practical application. Original illustrations, simplified and extremely functional, help to clarify the scientific data presented in the text. Though such technical material does not pretend to be exhaustive, it does, I believe, serve two important purposes: to relieve the beginning student of the burden of collateral readings, so that he may give first attention to personal improvement; and to reduce the need for lectures, so that most of the time in class can be devoted to exercises and criticized performances. It goes without saying that each instructor may decide for himself how much scientific data the student must learn and be responsible for.

This text is designed for a course in voice and articulation, or for any course concerned with improving the speaking voice. It is so arranged that Part One may be used alone for a course in voice improvement, while Part Two, with Chapter One as an introduction, may be used alone for a course in articulation.

I wish to express my gratitude to the thousands of students who served as the proving ground for this manuscript in its various stages; to my teaching staff in voice and articulation for testing, challenging, and corroborating the methods of this text; to my teachers, who helped to mold my thinking; to my colleagues for their inspiration; to my family for their patience. Finally, my particular thanks go to Miss Jerilyn Logemann for the art work and endless hours of typing and proofreading the manuscript, and to Mr. John W. Poindexter and his secretary, Miss Severn B. Alnutt, for exceptional editorial help.

Hilda B. Fisher

Contents

Part One

VOICE

CHAPTER 1

A Rationale for Speech Improvement

PART ONE • Your Goals and Attitudes in Speech Improvement

THE IMPORTANCE OF GOOD SPEECH

Effective speech is a goal worth pursuing. The one faculty which sets man apart from all living organisms — which makes him unique — is his ability to think and communicate in language. The one form of communication which man uses most effectively in interpersonal relationships is speech. With it, he gives form to his inmost thoughts — his dreams, ambitions, sorrows, and joys; without it, he is reduced to animal noises and to empty gestures. In a real sense, speech is the key to human existence.

The superiority of human intelligence is most clearly shown in the use of language. Even the smartest animal cannot postulate philosophical theses, sell life insurance, design bridges, or manufacture automobiles. All these complicated activities depend on the uniquely human ability to put ideas into words. It is not surprising that psychologists use language tests to measure individual intelligence, or that we evaluate our associates' ability largely in terms of their use of language. For language is the principal medium for determining human intelligence, interpreting human experience, and advancing human knowledge.

But language — speech — is more than an index of human intelligence. It fulfills a human need. It bridges the differences and distances that separate human beings; it helps to give meaning and purpose to their lives. One of the common complaints of lonely people is that they have no one to *talk* to — no one with whom to share their essential humanity. Perhaps even more important, speech is indispensable in problem-solving. How often do you think or say, when confronted with a difficult decision or anxiety over some problem, "I will talk to my (friend, husband, wife, mother, etc.) about it," or "If I could only talk this thing out, I could solve the problem." Psychiatrists apply this principle in their therapy, for a great deal of their treatment consists of letting the patient talk his way through his confusions to a solution. The greatest achievement in marriage counselling is often the reopening of speech channels between a husband and wife whose communication has broken down. The most significant contribution of labor unions is that they provide a climate for airing grievances and for open discussions between labor and management. At all levels of interpersonal relationships, human beings need to talk — for personal expression and for problem-solving.

Through speech, we control our environment or adapt to it satisfactorily. The more skillfully we use speech, the more successful we are at dealing with people. Consider your own interpersonal relationships. How could improving *your* speech habits help you? Might speech improvement further your professional goals? Your social goals? Or your personal goals?

Professional success and advancement often depend greatly on the individual's speech. For instance, consider the man who has worked long and well for his company but is bypassed for promotion to a management position — because of his speech. Perhaps he is told that the men might not respect him, that he does not sound like an educated man, or that his speech suggests lack of personal discipline. Or think of a girl who wants to be an executive secretary and believes she has the intelligence and skill for the job, only to learn that her speech does not project the "company image" to the clients, or that she does not sound as poised, mature, or well-mannered as she should. Or think of a young man who would like to be a teacher but cannot pass the oral examination required for certification in the school system where he wants to teach. And, of course, think of the "professional" speaker, such as the radio announcer or the actor, who depends on his speaking ability for his livelihood and whose success is directly related to his skill in speaking. No matter what the job is, good speech can be an important factor in professional success and advancement.

Speech also helps to determine the individual's social success. In America, where class structure is less rigid than in Europe, a man is accepted more at face value. No one denies him the right to better his position as his talent and opportunity permit. Even so, society applies certain standards before admitting him to the inner circle. One of them is how well he speaks. The person who constantly uses "fractured" speech — whose grammar is poor, whose pronunciation is careless, and whose vocabulary is largely slang — will find many doors closed. Leadership, even acceptance, in social organizations depends on how compatible the individual is, how clearly he expresses his opinions, how well he gets along with people in the daily interchange of ideas — in short, on his habits of speech.

Finally, speech directly affects the individual's personal adjustment. We size up a new acquaintance largely on the basis of his speech. For instance, a coed, talking to familiar friends, might describe her new roommate, whom she has barely met, as if she had made a detailed character analysis. On what basis except speech could she say that the girl is "lovely," "very sweet," "a snob," "grouchy," "sour on the world," "nice," "a drip," or "a kook"? These are inferences, made from a very few impressions. One of the most significant is the girl's speech, not only *what* she says but also *how* she says it. Even our evaluation of the personality of a friend or relative is based to a large extent on how he speaks. A certain woman said of her husband, "He never appreciates anything I do for him. I can work for hours preparing a special dinner, and he doesn't even know the difference." The husband says, "I tell her the dinner's fine. What more does she want?" What she wants, probably, is for him to say it with sincerity and enthusiasm, as if he really means it. A boy and a girl have an argument. He says he is sorry. She says, "You're not *really* sorry." Why isn't she convinced? Perhaps his manner of speaking is not convincing. Or the husband complains that his wife isn't really interested in his job. Every night when he comes in from work, she says, "Well, how did it go at the office today?" He says she doesn't *really* want to know, that her question is perfunctory. It is probably *how* she says it that matters. We tend to forget how important speech is in establishing and maintaining amicable relations with our closest friends and relatives — that we foster or damage interpersonal relationships more with our speech than with any other single factor.

SPEECH HABITS CAN BE CHANGED

How many times have you heard someone say enviously, "Oh, how *lucky* she is to have such a lovely voice!" or "Isn't he *lucky* to talk so distinctly?" Have you, too, been tempted to think that some fortunate people — not you, of course — were *born* excellent speakers? If you have, remember that good speech habits are less likely to result from luck than from pluck. With few exceptions, the person who speaks well does so because he wants to speak well, and because he has worked at it.

Speech is a learned skill; it is not a gift or an accident. If you have observed children learning to speak, you know how much practice and how many errors precede fluent use of language. Every normal individual is born with a remarkably complex nervous system which enables him to produce the sounds that comprise spoken language. And he is born with the capacity for abstract thinking which permits him to formulate language. Yet he must learn the form of an individual language, with all the intricacies of its communication system, as he grows up. There is no other way.

As you learned to speak more proficiently, your speech gradually became automatic. Now you probably think of your speech habits as "natural." If they were literally natural, you would be able to speak only the way you do, and you could not improve. The truth is that your speech habits seem to be an integral part of you because you have had them so long and are so used to them. But remember that if a habit can be formed, it can also be changed. Remember, too, that you can improve your speech only by changing your speech habits.

ATTITUDES THAT RELATE TO SPEECH IMPROVEMENT

To ask if you want to improve your speech may seem ridiculous. You would not be reading this chapter now if you were not interested in speech improvement. But interest and personal involvement are not necessarily the same thing. For example, many overweight people are interested in reducing but are not willing to follow a strict diet. So, too, some people are interested in improving their speech *if* someone else will do all the work — if they do not have to involve themselves or be inconvenienced.

Motivation, the impelling inner urge which spurs you to reach a goal, is crucial in speech improvement. If you are really motivated to improve your speech, you will not give up until you reach your goal. Only the wishful thinker believes that someone else will improve his speech — by hypnotism, osmosis, or touching him with a magic wand. The realist knows that changing any habit requires self-discipline, determination, and stamina. Consequently, whenever you are tempted to compromise your goals, or to find excuses for neglecting required speech exercises, remember your primary motivation — why you want to improve. Only with proper motivation will you succeed.

Objectivity is necessary in appraising your own speech. In its truest sense, objectivity is the capacity to view a thing with reason rather than emotion — without personal feeling, prejudice, or bias. Obviously, none of us can be completely objective about our own behavior. We are too much involved in creating and maintaining a good self-image to be thoroughly detached emotionally. Yet if we are to improve, we must accept the idea that some aspect of our behavior needs changing. In short, if we are to be able to evaluate our own achievements, we must be able to look at ourselves objectively.

One barrier to such objective self-analysis is rationalization. We rationalize when we explain our behavior in terms of motives which we approve in order to conceal our real motives. If our motives represent emotional needs which seem personally or socially unacceptable, we resolve the conflict by attributing our actions to other motives. For instance, the overweight person who feels unloved and rejected might be ashamed to recognize that his overeating makes him feel more secure; therefore, he rationalizes his overeating by attributing it to a glandular disturbance, the threat of stomach ulcers if his stomach is empty too long, or some other physical condition.

In much the same way, a person might rationalize that his poor articulation is caused by frequently recurring head colds, rather than recognizing that he has ignored the demands of good speech and has aimed at lower standards of social acceptance than he wants to admit. Rationalizing allows us to excuse behavior of which we disapprove. As long as we excuse poor speech habits, we can be free of anxiety about them, and also be absolved of doing anything about them. Stripping away rationalizations and seeing your motives as clearly as possible will help you use your time and energy more productively.

Another barrier to objectivity is defensiveness. To defend oneself against attack is, of course, quite normal. No person with a healthy self-image would allow himself to be abused and vilified without fighting back. But to react aggressively to all criticism is not normal. The secretary who calls her supervisor "a nosy old crone" because she pointed out some typing errors is reacting defensively, not objectively. So is the student who, having been criticized for nasality, snaps, "Your voice isn't so good, either!" The mature, self-assured person accepts objective criticism and uses it to his advantage. The immature, defensive person reacts with anger instead of reason.

In a class where all the students are attempting to improve their speech, criticism is necessary. How else is a student to find out how good his performance is, or gauge accurately what remains to be done? From the criticism of his classmates and his instructor, he learns to evaluate his own performance realistically. Class criticism should, of course, be fair and objective. If it is adverse, it should not be barbed or destructive. If it is complimentary, it should not be empty or fatuous. It should, in short, be an objective evaluation of the performance, not an attack on the person speaking or thinly veiled flattery. The ideal climate for speech improvement is one in which no student criticizing another in class ever feels constrained to cushion the blow of his criticism with, "I liked your speech, but . . . ." In such a climate, each student expects his criticism to be accepted as he himself accepts criticism, recognizing it as a measure of his progress.

PART TWO • Appraisal of Your Voice and Articulation

BASIC ELEMENTS OF VOICE AND ARTICULATION

Speech in all its aspects includes a number of factors. Some of them, which have great significance in determining the overall effectiveness of speech, have been deliberately omitted since they lie outside the scope of this book. One such factor is speech composition, which pertains primarily to public speaking courses and has to do with choosing a subject, organizing one's ideas, and composing a speech with meaningful phrases, sentences, and paragraphs. Another, which pertains to a course in semantics, is the careful choice of words to express precise meanings and to avoid ambiguity and vagueness. Still another, more often presented in an English course, involves grammar and syntax. All of these factors are important in their own right, but they are not the province of this book.

This book is concerned with the elements of speech which are basic to any use of voice: (1) *loudness* of the voice, (2) *quality* of the vocal tone, (3) *pitch* of the vocal tone, (4) *rate* of speaking, (5) *clear articulation* of the sounds of speech, and (6) *acceptable pronunciation* of English words.

Loudness of the voice, the power or intensity of the vocal tone, is in many respects the most basic element. If a voice cannot be heard, its message cannot be understood. Furthermore, variations in loudness in successive spoken syllables contribute to emphasis in speech. For any communication to occur, signals of some kind must be transmitted from the sender to the receiver. If speech is the mode of communication, audible signals must be transmitted; otherwise, there is no communication. On the other hand, excessive loudness can be annoying, socially offensive, or physically painful. The ideal, obviously, is neither too little nor too much.

Quality of the vocal tone, or *timbre* as it is sometimes called, enables you to identify a particular voice. No matter what words are being spoken, no matter what the pitch, loudness, or rate at a given moment, you can recognize the voice of someone you know well by its quality. A person's voice quality may be an asset or a liability, depending on whether it facilitates listening or distracts from what is being said.

Pitch of the vocal tone refers to its place on the musical scale. Children normally have higher-pitched voices than adults; men normally have lower-pitched voices than women. Movements from one pitch to another contribute to vocal variety, which, in turn, clarifies and emphasizes meaning.

Rate of speaking is a time factor of speech. In its broadest sense, it is a measurement of the number of words or syllables an individual speaks per minute. Components of rate are: (1) the relative duration of successive syllables in an utterance, (2) the number of pauses in an utterance, and (3) the duration of individual pauses. Rate greatly affects listener comprehension.

Articulation involves the movements of the tongue, jaw, lips, and soft palate to shape the individual sound segments of language, and the transitions between those sounds in spoken words and phrases. Next to loudness, clear articulation is the most basic element of speech. Speech is made up of auditory signals transmitted to the hearer — sound segments of language joined together into comprehensible words and phrases. Articulation produces speech signals which can be understood. *Enunciation* and *diction* are other terms sometimes used to refer to clear articulation.

Pronunciation involves the choice of particular vowel or consonant sounds to be used in a specific word and the syllable to be accented. It is not a matter of which sounds the speaker *can* produce but of the ones he uses by choice or habit. If a student asks, "Do you begin **chiropodist** with the consonant in **share** or in **care**?" he has proved that he can *articulate* both the consonants in question, but he is not sure how to *pronounce* the word. The change of syllabic accent from the noun **present** to the verb **present** is also a matter of pronunciation.

WHAT IS GOOD SPEECH?

The question "What is good speech?" has been the subject of endless controversy. Practically everyone has an opinion on the subject, and likes to express it. It might be interesting for you to stop here and jot down your own ideas about what good speech is, and then to compare what you wrote with what you are about to read.

Before stating the general characteristics of good speech, it seems appropriate to discuss briefly how standards of speech are established — why one way of talking is considered better than another.

Common acceptance within a social structure is one realistic basis for a standard. If most people approve, the custom, action, or attitude must be approvable. For instance, Americans use a fork to convey food to the mouth. The Muslims of North Africa, on the other hand, prefer their fingers, and the Chinese, of course, chopsticks. Americans wear shoes, the Japanese a special kind of elevated sandal, and certain South Sea islanders no shoes at all. Yet each custom is perfectly acceptable in its own environment. When asked what social usage is "right" or "proper," one inevitably has to counter with "Where?" Within a given social framework, certain forms of behavior are approved which might be frowned on elsewhere.

It is impossible to define good speech in all particulars, universally. Cultural, regional, and occupational differences work against a unitary definition. Japanese exchange students in America, for example, have resisted attempts to make them talk louder, because the level of loudness we consider good is in poor taste in Japanese society. A Japanese girl also found it difficult to open her mouth to articulate English sounds as we think appropriate, because, she said, "If one of us girls opened her mouth like that at home, my father said he would put a hot coal from the hibachi in it." By the time of the Revolution, the British were criticizing "Yankee" (New England) voices as having a "twang," and they still note the differences in our voices and theirs. We, in turn, think many British speakers sound as if they have enlarged adenoids. The differences in pronunciation and word choice in England and America prompted Sir Winston Churchill to quip, "Isn't it a pity that two nations having so much in common don't speak the same language?"

Even within the United States there are some differences in popular standards of speech. If you have traveled widely or have had other opportunities to compare speech from various sections of our country, you have probably noticed the differences. You may have observed that the rate of speech in Minnesota and Alabama is not the same. Or you may have noticed that pronunciations in Boston, New Orleans, and San Francisco differ. If you live in a cosmopolitan area, you have undoubtedly observed differences in speech in various parts of your city. From all the varieties of speech we hear, is there a *best* form for us to choose?

Even the experts differ widely about what is "best." According to some, good speech should be evaluated wholly on the esthetic level. Thus, to improve his speech, one should develop a "pretty," varied voice (without particular regard for conveying meanings), adopting a particular pitch level whether he can produce it well or not, and avoiding certain vowel sounds because they are inherently unpleasant. This kind of advice could lead to an "arty," affected speech which would certainly attract attention but would not improve communication. At the opposite extreme are those who say, "Leave your speech alone." They consider it dishonest to improve, as if you were a leopard trying to change his spots. According to this advice, if people can't understand what you say or cringe at the sound of your voice, let them adapt to you and accept you as you are or reject you, but don't change — unless, of course, you don't mind being insincere.

Between these two extremes is a standard which seems realistic for our society. Good speech, as we define it, is (1) *easily understood*, (2) *unobtrusive*, and (3) *appropriate*. Let us consider each of these characteristics individually.

Good Speech Is Easily Understood

The basic requirement of speech is that it communicate. The better speech is, the more easily the listener understands. But what is involved in being easily understood?

1. *Adequate loudness* of voice is necessary. Your words must impinge on the listener's ear for communication to occur. Speech should be loud enough — neither too soft nor too loud.

2. *Clear articulation* prevents many confusions in meanings. An artificial separation of words which calls attention to itself is not recommended, since it would detract from what is being said. Articulation at its best is precise and distinct while appearing so effortless that the listener finds it easy to understand what is said and is not conscious of how it is said.

3. *Precise use of words and correct grammatical forms* greatly affect ease of understanding. If a word is to convey an idea, it must be used according to its commonly assigned definition. If you use words because they sound impressive, though their meanings are not clear to you, or if you arbitrarily extend the meaning of a word so that you can use it loosely for many purposes, your audience may be more confused than informed. Words should increase the clarity of your speech and make your communication more effective; they should not merely decorate or gild.

Grammar must conform to standards of accepted usage if words are to make sense to the listener. Do you string together an endless progression of clauses connected by **and** or **so**? Do you use "which" clauses which do not have clear antecedents? Do you sometimes confuse adjectives and adverbs? If you do, you should consult one of the excellent review grammars or handbooks of English usage in the bookstores.

4. *Phrasing and emphasis*, if well used, increase understanding. Unfor-

tunately, some speakers seem to feel that variations in vocal pitch, loudness, and rate are mere embellishments (like frosting on a cake) and are not basic necessities of communication. Nothing could be farther from the truth. Phrasing groups words into idea-units. If compared to eating, it is like feeding a baby the size bite he can chew and swallow before putting another bite in his mouth. We put words into "bite-sized" phrases so that the listener receives the information of one phrase, evaluates it, compares it with what he has just heard and remembers from previous experiences, and stores it in his memory for recall and association when he receives successive "bites" of information. Without phrasing, words become a confusing jumble.

Emphasizing words vocally gives them greater prominence, just as italicizing or color-printing does words in type. Because words which are emphasized strike the listener's ear with greater force, their meanings have more impact. Wise use of emphasis makes speech easier to understand.

Intonation (pitch change) at the ends of phrases aids understanding by signalling the speaker's intention. If the pitch drops at the end of a phrase, the listener assumes that the sentence is ended and "closes the door" on that train of thought. If the pitch rises, the listener usually interprets the phrase as a question. Pitch changes help the listener interpret what the speaker means by what he says.

Good Speech Is Unobtrusive

It does not attract attention to itself. If the listener cannot help wondering what is wrong with the speaker, where he came from, or what his self-concept is, that speaker's speech is not unobtrusive. To rephrase an old saying, "The *way* you talk screams so loudly I cannot hear *what* you are saying."

We normally think of obtrusive speech as poor or careless use of voice and articulation. Over-carefulness and artificiality can be obtrusive, too. Obviously working hard at shaping the lips and positioning the tongue, or drawing the face into grimaces and contortions to speak, is obtrusive. Sounding prim and pedantic, over-pronouncing consonants and cutting every word apart from the next with artificially precise care, is obtrusive. Using excessively wide sweeps of intonation which resemble singing more than speaking and sound patently insincere is obtrusive. Whatever interferes with the listener's concentration on the content of speech is obtrusive.

Most listeners are able to adapt to distracting speech characteristics, especially if the speaker has enough assets to balance the distraction. Even a speech problem as irritating as a lisp or severe hoarseness can fade in the audience's consciousness if the speaker has excellent speech otherwise. Bear in mind, though, that an excellent speaker with hoarseness or a lisp would be even better without it. Furthermore, during the initial period of auditory adaptation, such a defect is quite noticeable and distracting. If such a speaker's interpersonal contacts were all brief ones, his defects would affect his communication more than if he talked daily to the same audience. A speaker should never excuse himself for a speech problem just because his good friends seldom comment on it. He should remember that they have become accustomed to it. He is no better speaker; he simply has more indulgent listeners.

One important consideration is that we accept many things socially which are not necessarily commonplace to us. For instance, the common American custom in eating meat is to shift the fork to the right hand after cutting a bite and to convey the bite to the mouth with the right hand. Yet most of us do little more than casually observe a person who, in European manner, keeps the fork in his left hand to put the meat into his mouth. If he appears to have generally good table manners, we accept this variation in detail. In much the same way, we accept variant pronunciations and become critical only when the variations are flagrant or inconsistent. Very few people, for instance, pay much attention to whether the **r** in **park** or **after** is pronounced, but many notice an **r** added to **Cuba** enough to tell about that mispronunciation long after they have forgotten what was said about Cuba at the time. The fact that the audience's attention was drawn from what was said to the way it was said makes such an error significant.

Students trying to improve their speech are often concerned that they will sound "different," "unnatural," or "affected" when they begin to change their speech patterns. They *will* sound affected as they are consciously changing their speech. They will *be* affected until the new way of speaking becomes a habit. But such a feeling is not peculiar to speech. Girls will remember feeling distinctly ill at ease when they first tried walking in high heels, but few of them let that temporary awkwardness deter them from mastering the technique. They became graceful after the art of walking in heels became a habit. As long as you have to exercise conscious control over a function, it is somewhat unnatural. When the function becomes a habit, it operates automatically, without conscious control, and feels entirely natural.

Serious speech students frequently ask, "Should I try to use my 'new' voice all the time?" Perhaps you think the answer should be "Yes." Let us think about this for a moment. When you say that the more you exercise a function, the faster it becomes a habit, you are right. There is another side to the picture, however. Let us suppose, as an extreme example, that you are asking your boss for a raise. Will it increase your self-assurance to be consciously trying to control vocal characteristics which have not yet become habits? Can you devote your whole attention to the sparring demanded by the situation if you must also think consciously about how you are talking? There are some situations, to be sure, where you could safely combine vocal practice with conversation — situations where what you are saying is not very important and the person to whom you are talking is permissive and preferably forewarned that you will be practicing speech. Certainly you should practice all you can, but you should not jeopardize important occasions with simultaneous speech practice. Your obvious self-consciousness might be even more obtrusive than your errors in speech.

Sometimes a student resolves to be constantly aware of his speech problems and to try at all times to control them rather than plan to practice particular exercises in particular practice periods. Since "just being careful" is not an adequate substitute for speech exercises, he is simply deceiving, and punishing, himself. In the first place, his attempt to be careful of his speech all day every day is gruelling and nerve-racking. If he relaxes his vigilance, he feels guilty. If he is eternally conscious of his speech, he damages his effectiveness in numerous speech situations by his obvious concern with speech controls. Finally, his reward is disappointment, because he accomplishes less than if he had practiced prescribed exercises at scheduled practice sessions.

Good Speech Is Appropriate

Propriety has several dimensions.

1. *Appropriate to the speaker* means that speech characteristics should be compatible with the general image the speaker projects. A minister should not sound like a circus barker, or a professional athlete like a twelve-year-old boy. Neither, for that matter, should a well-dressed, obviously poised woman have a voice like a harpy, a professor speak unintelligibly, or a doctor sound unsympathetic.

2. *Appropriate to the subject* means that the various elements of speech should be suited to the occasion or the topic being considered. The way a person speaks in a serious discussion should be different from his casual conversation. Explaining a difficult or complicated procedure necessarily differs from describing something simple and familiar. The voice itself should reflect the speaker's varying emotions or attitudes.

An individual may have several levels of speech, each suited to different purposes. His colloquial speech (suited to informal use) may have less precise articulation and even a different vocabulary from his more formal speech. Teenagers often use colloquial speech (even slang) with their peers but more formal speech with adults.

3. *Appropriate to the audience* means meeting the demands of the listeners. It means talking loudly and clearly enough to be understood no matter what the size of the audience. It means talking more simply to children than to adults, being careful at the same time not to insult the children by patronizing them.

4. *Appropriate to social demands* means conforming to the level of speech correctness required within a social structure. Although American society is not rigidly stratified, there are several levels of social decorum. Speech which is entirely adequate in one environment might be criticized in another. At the lowest level, less attention is given to the social niceties, average educational attainment is minimal, and formal training in language is virtually unknown. At the opposite end of the continuum, where families have for generations paid careful attention to etiquette, culture, and formal education, there is closest adherence to language "correctness." The higher one moves up the social ladder, the more stringent the rules of usage become, and the higher the acceptable speech standards.

Each individual, consciously or unconsciously, decides what speech standard he demands of himself. It goes without saying that no single standard is suitable for everybody. A young woman doing personnel work in a large office felt the need of speech improvement to qualify her for her varied contacts. She was also concerned about her mother's speech, which she described as a "thick Polish accent." What kind of work did her mother do? She was a housewife. Where did she live? In a Polish community. Who were her friends? People of Polish extraction like herself, with Polish accents. The daughter was advised to leave her mother's speech alone. Her "audience" was entirely happy with her speech. As long as she remained where she was and talked to the people she knew, her speech was entirely appropriate.

Students who feel defensive about their speech sometimes contend that their particular pronunciations are "new developments" in the language. They support their argument by saying that all their friends pronounce a word the way they do, and therefore the pronunciation must have changed to their new standard. It is a very persuasive argument, particularly since change does normally occur with time in all social practices. Though language used to change rather rapidly, most linguists think, the rate of change has been retarded since the invention of the printing press and the advent of universal education. The popularity of a new form in a particular environment does not guarantee its adoption in general preferred usage. If enough people change to your pronunciation, especially those who influence social standards most, it will become standard. But it is not standard simply because you and your close associates say it that way.

Innovations in language usually originate in the lowest echelons of society, where there is less attention to the niceties of form. Simplification of grammar is a vivid example, as in "He done it" and "I seen it." Slang flourishes in such an environment, so much so that speech may become practically unintelligible to listeners from another environment. Lazy articulation results in such slurring and eliding of consonants and distortion of vowels that speech begins to sound like a foreign patois. Viewing the development of the English language, we conclude that new usages, either new words, new grammatical forms, or new pronunciations, normally meet one of three fates:

(1) *The new form may eventually replace the older form.* For instance, **them** has now replaced the older **hem** by analogy to the word **they**; **pianoforte** has been clipped to **piano**; the final /g/ in words such as **sing** and **wrong** has been lost. Since the ninth century, when our earliest English literature was written, a number of vowel sounds have shifted radically (the vowel in **goose** once sounded like **oh**, the word **mouse** like modern **moose**, **sea** like modern **say**, and **mice** rhymed with modern **fleece**).

(2) *The new form may never become accepted in standard usage*, either continuing at substandard levels or gradually dying out. Though –**ing** endings have been pronounced **in** (**comin** for **coming, doin** for **doing**) since the seventh century, such pronunciation is still not considered standard. The contraction

ain't from **am not**, though of long standing, has never been completely accepted in careful usage. Most of our slang vocabulary flourishes briefly and dies.

(3) *The new form may rise to standard usage alongside the old form,* coexisting with but never replacing the old. By this method we acquire synonyms in our language. This accounts also for alternate standard pronunciations, e.g., the spelling pronunciation of **often** with the /t/ pronounced, alongside the older **often** with a silent **t**.

Conservative linguistic usage has the twofold advantage of the widest acceptance and the greatest permanence in our social structure. The student who seriously desires a type of speech which is least open to criticism and attracts least attention should choose those usages and pronunciations which are most widely accepted and most firmly established.

One fairly frequent question has to do with whether a speaker should attempt to imitate the actual or imagined imperfections in the speech of a person or group to whom he is talking. Particularly, the question revolves around a well-educated person speaking to those less well-educated. Disregarding for the moment the snobbery implied by the question, one point should be made clear. A listener in such a situation would probably detect the artificiality of deliberately "incorrect" diction and interpret it as insincerity. Since he would suspect that the speaker was attempting to ridicule him rather than adapt to him, his natural reaction would be suspicion and hostility. Good speech, like good manners, is never out of place unless so flagrantly displayed that it becomes obtrusive.

5. *Appropriate to the geographical area* means using the accepted dialect of your part of the country. Though the word *dialect* is sometimes used to mean quaint, colorful pronunciation — like that of a Texas cowboy, a Maine fisherman, or an Irish policeman — as linguists use the term, a dialect is any form of speech with distinctive characteristics. The speech of any group of people in one place who talk essentially alike, and whose speech differs in recognizable particulars from speech elsewhere, is a dialect. The United States has a tremendous number of dialects.

As linguistic researchers have shown, dialects embrace wider areas at higher social levels than at lower ones. This means that the most acceptable types of speech have wider geographical spread than the less acceptable. Speech at lower levels of society differs in many respects in Chicago and Cleveland, but the differences reduce markedly at high social levels.

A dialect which reflects the common features of the most acceptable speech throughout a large geographical area is called a *standard dialect.* The United States has three standard dialects, each differing from the others in some significant matters of pronunciation yet each representing predominant cultivated usage within its own area. All are equally "good" varieties of English pronunciation and are entirely acceptable elsewhere in the United States or abroad.

(a) *Eastern* is the standard dialect most common among cultivated speakers of eastern New England. New York City and Philadelphia may be loosely included in this dialect, though their speech differs somewhat from Boston's.

(b) *Southern* is the standard dialect most common among cultivated speakers in the Southern states from the Atlantic Ocean westward to Texas — roughly the area of the Confederacy.

(c) *General American* is the standard dialect which represents the common features of cultivated speech in the remainder of the United States, including those geographical areas usually called Northern and Western.

Since the boundaries between two standard dialects are not as clearly drawn as state boundary lines on a map, there are fringe areas, sometimes a few miles wide and sometimes much more extensive, where two dialects mix.

Each standard dialect area contains many *sub-dialects*. If a sub-dialect represents less socially acceptable pronunciations, we call such speech *substandard*. As a rule, when we talk about highly distinctive (and often objectionable) characteristics of speech in New York, Chicago, New Orleans, or some other area, we really mean the substandard speech. Standard speech is seldom the object of ridicule, because, while it may not sound entirely familiar, it does sound cultivated and correct. Substandard pronunciations which are acceptable in a small geographical area but which attract adverse attention outside that area are called *provincialisms*.

Using a dictionary for guidance in pronunciation sometimes poses a problem. When more than one pronunciation is given, which is correct? If you use a reputable dictionary, any pronunciation it lists is acceptable. Normally, the editors recommend the first-listed pronunciation as having a higher level of acceptability. In many cases, however, the various pronunciations represent usages in different standard dialects. Make certain that you become familiar with your dictionary's system of representing pronunciations. Most dictionaries use a few symbols that are intentionally ambiguous in order to allow for dialectal latitude in pronunciation. Unless you understand the value of sounds the dictionary indicates, you will not pronounce the word as suggested. Remember that the function of a dictionary is not to prescribe pronunciations, but rather to report what linguistic research shows the usage of the majority of cultivated speakers to be. When several pronunciations are listed, make sure you know how each sounds and then choose the one most familiar to you. In all likelihood, it is the preferred pronunciation in your standard dialect.

INITIAL RECORDING AND CRITIQUE

Now that you understand the elements of voice and what good speech is, do you know how your speech needs improving?

Though many speech exercises are generally beneficial, it is difficult to become a better speaker unless you know in some detail which characteristics of your speech need attention. The purpose of your first critique, then, is to identify your speech problems, or the areas in which you need improvement.

A recording of your voice, either a disc or a portion of tape, will serve as an excellent basis for your first critique. When you receive your instructor's criticism, listen to your recording as objectively as you can, attempting to recognize the characteristics mentioned in the critique. When you listen to your subsequent practice recordings and a final class recording, you will be able to make comparisons with this first recording and note your progress in correcting the items on which you were criticized.

In the next two sections you will find an explanation of the terms which might appear on your initial critique. In subsequent chapters you will learn why your problems occur and how to correct them. Your first task is to understand what you need to improve.

TERMS USED IN VOICE ANALYSIS

The terms which may be used in a criticism of voice are listed in outline form for easy reference:

A. Loudness of voice

1. *Too loud* means your loudness is excessive for the situation and space. It may interfere with intelligibility, be annoying, or even be painful to the listener's ears.
2. *Too soft* means your voice is not loud enough. It may be difficult to hear or even inaudible.
3. *Fading* normally means a noticeable drop in loudness toward the ends of sentences, though the fade could occur at any point. When the voice fades, speech becomes unintelligible.

B. Quality of voice

1. *Harsh* quality sounds hard, low-pitched, strained, flat. It suggests a personality which is unsympathetic, aggressive, overbearing, cold.
2. *Hoarse* quality has the sound of strained or gargling breathiness — as if the speaker has laryngitis, or the production of voice is painful and difficult.
3. *Glottal fry* sounds like ticking or noisy scraping — a little like a small boy imitating a motor boat, or like fast-popping popcorn. Glottal fry usually occurs at the ends of sentences, only rarely throughout a person's speech.
4. *Glottal shock* sounds like a small, dry cough, or as if you held your breath and then let it burst out at the start of a word. It usually occurs only before a word beginning with a vowel sound, like **I, always, eat.** It makes speech sound quite emphatic and staccato.
5. *Breathy* quality sounds like breath escaping with the tone, as if the speaker were half-whispering. It sometimes suggests a sultry or over-

relaxed type of personality, or a person who is out of breath from running.

6. *Nasal* quality has a whining, honking sound. It may sound complaining, or like some of the singing of "country" music.
   a. *Phonemic nasality* occurs only on certain vowel sounds, e.g., the /æ/ vowel in **class**.
   b. *Assimilation nasality* occurs only on a vowel sound which is next to a nasal consonant in a word, e.g., **me, came, no, can, sing.**
   c. *Nasal emission* is the release of breath through the nose while articulating a consonant other than a nasal consonant, e.g., **keep, put, fish.**

7. *Denasal* quality is a stuffy-nose sound. It sounds cottony and dull. Comedians use this voice in impersonating a "punchy" fighter or a child with enlarged adenoids.

8. *Strident* quality sounds sharp, screechy, metallic, and high-pitched. It is the voice normally associated with a busybody or a quarrelsome person.

9. *Throaty* quality sounds hollow and heavy, as if you are talking into a barrel or a cavern, or are half-swallowing your tongue.

10. *Thin* quality sounds childish and small. It often suggests a weak, meek, or infantile personality.

11. *Muffled* quality sounds thick, indistinct, and mush-mouthed, as if your teeth are clenched, you are talking with food in your mouth, or your articulatory organs are over-relaxed.

C. Pitch

1. *Too-low modal pitch.* Modal (moe-d'l) pitch is the pitch you use most often, except for strongly emphasized words or at the ends of sentences. Any of the following voice characteristics *might* indicate too-low modal pitch:
   a. If your pitch does not drop at the ends of sentences, it may be because you cannot produce a lower pitch than your modal pitch. In that event, your modal pitch is too low.
   b. If your quality is glottal fry or harsh at the ends of sentences (when your pitch drops), it may indicate that you have to strain too much to reach those low notes. If so, your modal pitch is too low.
   c. If your quality is harsh or hoarse generally, it could relate to your using too-low modal pitch.
   d. If you are a female to whom strangers on the telephone say, "Yes, sir," your modal pitch *may* be too low.

2. *Too-high modal pitch.* Beware of applying this criticism to yourself on an esthetic basis without regard to the proper functioning of your voice. The problems related to too-low modal pitch listed above occur all

too often because individuals consciously lower their modal pitch in a mistaken notion that it will improve their voices. Though too-high modal pitch does not occur as often as the beginning speech student would suspect, the following vocal characteristics may be related to it.

   a. If the pitch you use for strongly emphasized words in a sentence is no higher or barely higher than your modal pitch, you may be unable to produce pitch high enough to contrast with modal pitch. If so, your modal pitch may be too high.

   b. If your voice is weak or has thin quality, your modal pitch may be too high. At optimum pitch both the tone production in the larynx (voice box) and the amplification of the tone by resonance are more efficient.

   c. If your voice quality is nasal or strident, you may be using modal pitch which is too high.

   d. If you are a male to whom strangers on the telephone say, "Yes, *ma'am*," or an adult female to whom they say, "May I speak to your mother, dear?" your modal pitch may be too high.

3. *Narrow range* refers to the extent of pitch change used to reinforce meanings. When you emphasize a word strongly, you raise the pitch on that word. When you complete a statement, you lower the pitch to indicate that you have finished that idea. If your high pitch (for emphasis) is not high enough in relation to your modal pitch, or if your low pitch is not low enough in relation to modal pitch, your range (the number of notes from highest to lowest which you use in speaking) is too narrow.

4. *Monotone*, which is actually quite rare, is an extreme manifestation of narrow range. It means literally that your pitch never changes, that it stays at modal pitch all the time.

5. *Stereotyped intonations* are monotonously repeated patterns of pitch change which are not related to and fail to reinforce meanings. Starting each sentence on a high pitch and drifting downward in pitch during the sentence is stereotyped intonation. So is ending each sentence (even positive statements) on rising pitch. Though your emphasis on important words may be quite good in other respects, unless your pitch changes reinforce your meanings, your intonations are stereotyped.

D. Rate

1. *Poor phrasing* means that you do not properly group your words into units of thought. Since a pause of varying length occurs between each two phrases, poor phrasing means inappropriately placed pauses. You may be crowding too many words into a phrase, producing a jumble of unintelligible syllables. Or you may be interrupting phrases with pauses more out of concern for catching your breath than for maintaining thought units.

2. *Too-long pauses* destroy the relationships of successive phrases, with the result that your listener loses the train of thought.

3. *Clipped syllables* produce a staccato effect and are difficult to understand. If combined with inadequate phrasing, they produce extremely rapid and unintelligible speech. If combined with too-long pauses, however, the overall rate may be no faster than a better speaker's rate, but it is still difficult to follow.

4. *Prolonged syllables* produce a tiresome, dragged-out type of speech which is annoying to the listener. Excessive prolongation produces speech which is difficult to understand, because the listener forgets the beginning of a sentence before it finally ends. Combined with too-long pauses, prolonged syllables can be quite boring.

5. *Hesitancies* include vocalized pauses (**er** or **ah**) or the repetition of one or more syllables at the beginning of a new phrase. This habit has been described by a student as "keeping your motor running while you decide where you're going." The hesitant speaker has no difficulty producing the sounds in the words he is about to say, but having failed to organize his sentences in advance, he reaches an impasse where he is not sure what to say next or whether what he planned to say is appropriate. Confronting a large audience or a single listener, he is appalled at the prospect of an honest pause and feels impelled to fill the space with vocal static.

E. Vocal Variations for Reinforcing Meaning

Vocal variation involves three different elements of voice which combine for vocal emphasis: loudness, rate, and pitch. When you stress a syllable, you say it louder and more slowly than another syllable in the same phrase, so that it strikes the ear of the listener more forcefully and seems to carry more important meaning. If that same syllable is spoken at a pitch level higher than modal pitch, the emphasis is further increased and results in *heavy stress*. Stress can occur on several syllables in a phrase; heavy stress occurs only once in each phrase.

1. *Inadequate stress* is the use of stress on fewer words than necessary to reinforce meanings. Sometimes this means disregarding all stress except heavy stress. If you said, "I have to take all these books back to the library before I can go to the house for dinner," with no stress except where the underlining occurs, the meaning other than **library** and **dinner** would be practically lost.

2. *Overstressing* involves using heavy stress too frequently, i.e., changing pitch on every stressed word.

3. *Stereotyped stress* may consist of regularly stressing the last word of every phrase, whether that word is most important to meaning or not. Or it may be a singsong kind of stress which suggests scansion of poetry.

In any event, it is a repetitive pattern of stress which violates meanings more than it reinforces them.

F. Clarity of Articulation

Any error in articulating a vowel or a consonant sound may be represented as a substitution of an incorrect for a correct articulation. Insofar as practical, your articulatory substitutions will be indicated in phonetic symbols, since these symbols have specific values you may check in Chapters 5 and 6. Each error will be written as a formula. When the sign / is used between two phonetic symbols, it means "substituted for." Thus if you said /d/ when you should have said /t/, the substitution is indicated by the formula d/t.

You must realize that a particular error in articulation applies to many other words than the specific one on which the error is marked in your first critique. Your errors in the initial recording are typical of your habits, not isolated "slips of the tongue." If you omit a /t/ in **first**, you probably omit any /t/ which follows another consonant at the end of a syllable, as in **act** or **lift**. If you distort the vowel /æ/ in **class**, you probably distort /æ/ in any word, but especially when /s/ ends the syllable where it occurs. As you study your critique, you should make a list of specific errors and include as examples the words in which they occurred. Then you should locate the exercises for your errors in Chapters 5 and 6 and mark them for regular, concentrated practice.

1. *Substitution of one phoneme for another.* A phoneme is a segment of spoken sound which differentiates meaning. The /s/ of **sick** and the /θ/ of **thick** are different phonemes. If you say /θ/ in **sick**, you are substituting one phoneme for another, and the error is written thus: θ/s. The vowel /ɛ/ in **ten** is a different phoneme from the vowel /ɪ/ in **tin**. If you say /ɪ/ in **ten**, you are substituting one phoneme for another, and the error is written thus: ɪ/ɛ.

2. *Substitution of an unacceptable allophone for a phoneme.* An allophone is a variety of a phoneme. Minor variations in phonemes which are essentially unnoticed are acceptable allophones. When a variation of a phoneme is noticeably "off-color" or distorted, though the substituted sound is not another phoneme, it is a substitution of an unacceptable allophone. The vowel /æ/ belongs in **bag**; the vowel /ɪ/ belongs in **big**. If you say **bag** with the diphthong /æɪ/, it is a substitution of an unacceptable allophone, and the error is written thus: æɪ/æ. Faulty placing of the organs of articulation to produce consonant phonemes can be "described" by special allophonic symbols. For instance, a /t/ is formed with the tongue tip touching the gum tissue behind the upper front teeth. If you make a /t/ with your tongue tip touching the teeth instead of the gum tissue, we indicate the faulty articulation with a symbol beneath a /t/ which looks like a small tooth, written thus: t̪/t.

3. *Substitution of nothing for a phoneme.* This error is omitting a phoneme which belongs in the word you are saying. For instance, if you say **lists** without the /t/, we write it thus: –/t. The dash means "nothing." Or suppose you say **visitor**, leaving out the /ə/ vowel which the second **i** spells. You have substituted nothing for the vowel, and we write it thus: –/ə.

4. *Substitution of a phoneme for nothing.* This error is adding a phoneme where it does not belong. Suppose you do not realize that the first **e** in **bracelet** should be silent and pronounce it /ə/. You have inserted /ə/ where it does not belong, and we write it thus: ə/–.

General problems in articulation. The kinds of errors we have been discussing involve individual phonemes. There are some problems involving groups of phonemes with common features which you should also be aware of. For example, if your lips are generally over-relaxed, any phoneme involving lip movement will be affected. You may not touch the lips together firmly enough for /p/ and /b/, or touch your lower lip to your upper teeth precisely enough for /f/ and /v/, or round your lips enough for /w/ and /ʍ/ (**wh**), or round them enough for the vowel phonemes /u/ as in **food**, /ʊ/ as in **foot**, /o/ as in **foe**, /ɔ/ as in **fought**, /aʊ/ as in **found**, and /ɔɪ/ as in **foil**. If this is your problem, as you study you should keep alert for phoneme descriptions involving the lips, concentrate on those phonemes, and pay more attention to your lip movements for speech generally.

G. Acceptable Pronunciation

Errors in pronunciation are usually much more specific than errors in articulation. A mistake in pronunciation means that you have learned that particular word incorrectly. You correct the error by memorizing the acceptable pronunciation. If you frequently mispronounce words, you should give more time to vocabulary study and make a habit of consulting your dictionary when in doubt. Mispronunciations fall into three categories:

1. *False analogy.* An analogy infers a similarity between two things. When you pronounce a new word, you probably observe how that word is *like* certain other words. If you make a false analogy, you assume a similarity between two words which does not exist. For instance, if you assume that the **ch** in **chaperone** represents the same consonant sound as the **ch** in **chair**, you are wrong, because the **ch** in **chaperone** actually sounds like the **sh** in **ship**. Or if you assume that the **s** which ends **Illinois** is pronounced like the **s** at the end of **boys**, your analogy is false, since the **s** in **Illinois** is preferably silent. A false analogy is usually a "spelling pronunciation," since it results from mistaking the sounds which the letters in the word represent. Another example is a word borrowed from England, along with the excellent wool material to which it refers. **Worsted** tricks many an unwary shopper, who, seeing the word on a suit tag, assumes a pronunciation analogy to **worse**, when the correct

pronunciation of the vowel is like **oo** in **wool** (the **r** is completely silent).

2. *Faulty memory* accounts for many errors in pronunciations, and not only in bizarre or uncommon words. For instance, it is apparently easy to confuse words spelled **er** with those spelled **re** or **ro**, etc.: **childern** for **children, hunderd** for **hundred, apern** for **apron, prespiration** for **perspiration, perscription** for **prescription, pre cent** for **per cent, pervent** for **prevent**. When to pronounce an /r/ is sometimes difficult to remember, especially if you live in a dialect area where /r/-dropping in certain positions in words is acceptable. For instance, in words like **mother, after, summer, winter,** the **r** may be dropped finally or if a consonant sound begins the next word, but it is still pronounced when the following word begins with a vowel. If a person forgets which words are spelled with **r**, he may say things like **sofer and mirra, staminer and vigah,** or **Florider and New Hampsha.**

3. *Faulty patterns* produce errors in pronunciation. One person says a word the way he heard it, but the person he heard say it was wrong. This is a sort of "secondhand" false analogy. Some examples are **caramel** pronounced like **car** instead of **care, chiropodist** beginning with the consonant of **she** instead of **key, chaise longue** pronounced like **chase lounge** instead of **shays long, maraschino** with **a-sheen** in the middle instead of **us-keen, on** pronounced with the vowel of **loan** instead of **lawn**.

   Change of stress (accent) on a word belongs to this category of errors also. A person who says **hótel** instead of **hotél** is not likely to have made it up; he probably heard someone else say it. Some of the mistakes in word stress involve moving the stress from the end of the word back to the beginning, as in **chástise** for **chastíse, búffet** for **buffét, débutante** for **debutánte, ídea** for **idéa, cígar** for **cigár, cígarette** for **cigarétte**. Sometimes, too, the stress is moved forward, as in **gondóla** for **góndola, cupóla** for **cúpola, absolútely** for **ábsolutely,** or **impótent** for **ímpotent**. Many stress errors occur in words which have been borrowed from another language, e.g., French, Spanish, Italian.

4. *Affectation* accounts for some errors in pronunciation. We use the term *affectation* here to mean a pronunciation consciously adopted because it sounds more genteel, elegant, or beautiful, without regard to preferred usage in one's environment. To pronounce **either** and **neither** with the vowel of **I**, when most good speakers around you say them with the vowel in **eat**, is an unwise affectation. A particular English teacher who had studied in England was unwise to require her students to imitate British pronunciations **libry** for **library** and **dictionry** for **dictionary,** particularly since she was not consistently British in saying **militry** for **military, cemetry** for **cemetery, secondry** for **secondary,** etc. Other pronunciations which Americans sometimes copy from the British are **ahnt**

for **aunt, cahnt** for **can't, tomahto** for **tomato** (but seldom **banahna** for **banana**), and occasionally **gárage** (rhyming with **carriage**) for **garáge**. Perhaps a strong reaction against an error like **pitcher** for **picture** produces an artificial and obtrusive pronunciation like **pick-tour** instead of the normal **pick-cher**, or **ed-you-cation** for **ed-ju-cation**.

PART THREE • Means of Re-forming Your Speech Habits

SPEECH LEARNING AND HABITS

Speech improvement is essentially the relearning of certain aspects of speaking. Knowing what is involved in learning to speak initially can throw light on your own speech deficiencies and help you decide what type of training you now need.

Initial speech learning is stimulated by the need to communicate. Because the child is surrounded by spoken language, some directed at him, some overheard, he becomes aware that language is a system of communication. When he discovers that a word is more effective than pointing, grunting, or whining, he learns to fulfill his needs and wants by using language. Normally, he learns to produce intelligible words; otherwise he may not achieve his purpose. Some environments are more stimulating than others and demand a higher level of achievement. Since the child speaks only as well as he must, his level of speech achievement during this learning period is determined by the demands of his environment. (See Figure 1 on facing page.)

SENSORY CHANNELS IN SPEECH LEARNING

The basis for the child's speech learning is the *input* (reception) of information about the speech of other people and his own speech. Input is channelled into the individual's brain by four sensory receptors: *audition*, the sense of hearing; *vision*, the sense of sight; *tactition*, the sense of touch; *kinesthesia*, the awareness of muscle tension and the movement of joints. Sensory stimuli come into his brain. He *hears* what other people say and what he himself says. He *sees* how other people move their lips, their jaws, and, to some extent, their tongues, in forming words. He *feels* his own organs of articulation make contact as he forms a word and can imitate the feel of the word he produced yesterday, or adjust his articulators if the word comes out wrong. He *feels tension* in particular muscles as they move to produce the sound segments of speech, or control his breathing or the pitch of his voice. These sensory stimuli coming into his brain are *input* signals which enable him to govern his speech *output*.

HEARING AND THE NATURE OF SOUND

The most important sensory channel in speech learning is auditory. In fact, hearing is such a critical factor that a child deafened before he learns how to speak will find mastery of intelligible oral language extremely difficult or impossible.

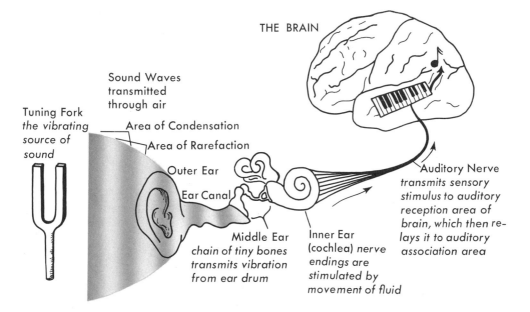

THE BRAIN

Sound Waves transmitted through air

Tuning Fork *the vibrating source of sound*

Area of Condensation

Area of Rarefaction

Outer Ear

Ear Canal

Middle Ear *chain of tiny bones transmits vibration from ear drum*

Inner Ear *(cochlea) nerve endings are stimulated by movement of fluid*

Auditory Nerve *transmits sensory stimulus to auditory reception area of brain, which then relays it to auditory association area*

Fig. 1 The Process of Hearing

(schematic representation)

Since sound is the fabric of speech — without it the act of communication cannot take place — a brief explanation of the nature of sound and the process of hearing seems in order.

Sound originates in the vibration of some object. If you slap your hand against the surface of your desk, you produce vibrations in the desk which you hear as sound. If you strike a key on the piano, the vibration of a string inside the piano produces a sound. A vibration is a movement back and forth, an oscillation. The movement may be so slight and so fast that it is not perceived visually, but it is perceived in audition.

Two basic characteristics of sound need clarification: *frequency* and *amplitude*. *Frequency*, the number of vibrations per second, is a physical characteristic of vibration. When you hear the sound, you identify the frequency as pitch. When you play Middle C (C_4) on the piano, the string which is set into vibration (by impact of the small hammer attached to the key) has a particular length and size (mass), and is tuned to a certain degree of tension which makes it vibrate at 256 cycles per second. (A cycle is a movement or vibration to one side, then to the other side, and back to dead center again.) When the frequency of that vibration is 256 c.p.s., the pitch we hear is Middle C. The smaller, shorter, and more tense a string is, the faster it vibrates (increased frequency) and the higher the pitch we hear.

Amplitude is the excursion of vibration — how far from side to side the vibrating element moves. Like frequency, it is a physical characteristic of vibration. The strength or force of the sound produced, its *intensity*, is determined by the amplitude of the vibration. When we hear the sound, we identify intensity as loudness. The greater the amplitude of the vibration, the greater the intensity, and the louder the sound.

Sound is usually transmitted to the ear through air. Because air is normally invisible, we tend to forget that it is substance. Though air is gaseous matter, like solid substances it is made up of molecules. There are, in fact, about four hundred billion billion molecules in every cubic inch of air. Molecules of air are constantly moving about and bumping into one another; they are highly mobile.

When a source of sound vibrates, the movement of the vibrating body (for instance, the piano string) "pushes against" air molecules, which in turn push against other molecules, and those in turn against still others, until the molecules are "piled up" in an area of condensation, or increased density, in the air. As the source of vibration swings back in the opposite direction, molecules are pushed before it, leaving an empty space, or area of rarefaction, following the area of molecular condensation. Thus, a trough of rarefied molecules follows a crest of condensed molecules. A crest and a trough together comprise one sound wave (cycle). The number of sound waves in air passing a given point per second exactly equals the frequency of vibration at the source of the sound.

The phenomenon of hearing involves three processes within the listener's hearing mechanism. The first, *reception of sound waves*, is purely mechanical. Successive sound waves (condensation-rarefaction patterns in air molecules) enter the ear by the auditory canal and push against the ear drum, causing it to vibrate at exactly the same frequency as that of the sound wave striking it. A chain of tiny bones in the middle ear, to which the ear drum attaches, conveys this vibration to the fluid inside the cochlea, a snail shell-shaped bony housing for the auditory nerve endings in the inner ear. Within the cochlea there are minuscule nerve endings, arranged like hairs along a membrane which coils upward through the "snail shell" like a winding staircase. According to a popular theory, nerve endings at the lower end of the cochlea are excited by high frequencies, those toward the upper end of the spiral by successively lower frequencies.

Faulty functioning of this mechanical apparatus is the most frequent cause of deafness or reduced hearing acuity. The chain of small bones in the middle ear may become inflexible and thus fail to transmit the pattern of sound waves to the cochlea. Or the nerve endings in the cochlea may be damaged so that they cannot receive the pattern of sound waves.

The second stage in the hearing process is the *perception of sound* in the brain. When the minute nerve endings in the cochlea are excited, a nerve impulse is transmitted to an area of the cerebral cortex (the surface of the brain) especially designed to receive such impulses. Neurologists have demonstrated that this auditory reception area is made up of points, matched to the pitch-sensitive areas of the cochlea, which receive specific pitches. Even so, if the process stopped here, you would know you had heard something, but you would not know what you had heard.

The third step in hearing is *auditory association.* Nerve impulses are relayed from the auditory reception area to the auditory association area of the cortex, where each incoming nerve impulse is compared with a memory file of what that person has heard before. The new stimulus is identified by being matched to a previously learned identification.

Obviously, then, the whole process of hearing is ineffective unless auditory association functions well. When a student has difficulty identifying sounds correctly or distinguishing between sounds, he may suspect that he is "hard of hearing," meaning that his ears are malfunctioning. In some rare cases his hearing mechanism may be faulty, but it is much more likely that the fault lies in his auditory association.

THE FEEDBACK LOOP

Feedback is the back-flow of sensory information which enables a person to control and adjust his speech. As he talks, he hears himself (audition), he feels his tongue against his palate, his lip touching his teeth, etc. (tactition), and he feels the location and amount of muscle tension or joint movement (kinesthesia).

Feedback operates in any controlled activity. When you are driving, for instance, you use feedback to keep the car in the correct traffic lane. You continually notice how close your car is to the curb, the lane divider, the stripe of paint along the street, or the other cars (visual feedback). In your arm and shoulder muscles you feel the wheel pulling in one direction or another (kinesthetic feedback). If you become a "lane straddler," the horn of another car gives you a warning (auditory feedback). Clearly, without feedback information driving would be haphazard at best, fatal at worst. Since speech is an infinitely more complicated function than driving and requires a more intricate feedback operation, learning how to use feedback for speech is crucial.

Feedback involves three factors: *inspection, comparison,* and *correction.* When driving, you observe the position of your car in relationship to stationary objects beside the road and to other cars. This is *inspection.* From experience, you have established an ideal relationship of your car to other objects, which is the position your car should occupy. When you measure the position of your car against the ideal position, this is *comparison.* If your car has drifted a bit too far to the right, you pull the steering wheel toward the left. This is *correction.* Thus by a series of minute corrections you keep your car in a straight path. If your inspection is inaccurate (suppose you are quite nearsighted), your control of the car is unsure. If your comparison is faulty (suppose you have borrowed a car which is much larger than yours, so that your points of comparison are thrown off), your correction may be inadequate or excessive.

Feedback is essential to speech control. In the adult, whose speech functions have been habituated, the operation of feedback changes somewhat, as we shall see presently. In the initial language-learning period the process is most clearly demonstrated.

Inspection is the first stage in the feedback loop: as the child says a word, information about how he said it feeds back to him through sensory channels. The most important of these is audition, illustrated in the feedback loop in Figure 2. Tactile and kinesthetic feedback occur simultaneously. Suppose, for example, the child wants a piece of cake, and instead says **take**. The segments of sound in **take** are conveyed as patterns in a sound wave to his ear. (The sound is chiefly airborne, though sound waves are also conducted to his inner ears by the vibration of bones in his head.) The nerve impulses in his ear are transmitted to an area of his brain where awareness of the sound of his spoken word occurs. Inspection involves listening to the sounds he actually produced (audition), noting the points where his tongue touched in producing the word (tactition), and being aware of the amount of tension in muscles involved in the articulation (kinesthetic sensation).

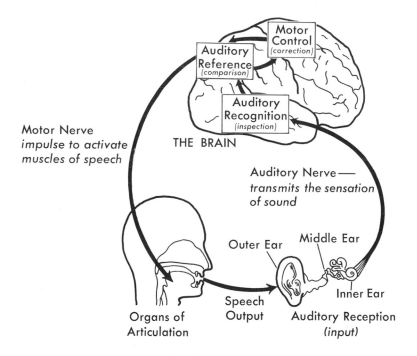

Fig. 2 The Auditory Feedback Loop

(schematic representation)

Comparison comes next. Perhaps just before asking for **take** the child heard his mother say **cake**. At least he must have heard **cake** a number of times before attempting to say it. The pattern for the way **cake** usually sounds, which he has stored in his auditory memory, is his *auditory reference* for the word. It is like a target he is shooting at. He has just asked for **take**. His auditory reference is **cake**. He makes a point-to-point comparison. Everything is "on target" except the first consonant, which is wrong. How much is it wrong? How much adjustment for error is required to make it right? While this auditory comparison is occurring, the child also makes tactile and kinesthetic comparisons. He remembers that the consonant used to begin **cookie** or **cat** sounds the way **cake** should. He also remembers that at the start of **cookie** or **cat** he felt contact on the back of his tongue and felt his tongue drawn back in his mouth, but for **take** he felt contact at the tip of his tongue and his tongue thrust forward in his mouth. In short, he "measures" the extent of his error and estimates the amount and kind of correction needed. This is comparable to the comparison technique in rifle practice. If you discovered your shots were hitting four inches to the right of the bull's-eye, you would aim your rifle a bit more to the left. In speech, comparison of the actual speech output with the stored reference makes accurate correction of error possible.

Correction is the final stage in the feedback loop. The child who said **take** for **cake** has now inspected his speech output. He has compared it, bit by bit, with his stored reference. He has discovered the nature and extent of his error. Now he corrects his error. Corrective data are relayed to the motor area of his brain, which is the origin of nerve impulses to muscles. From the points of the motor area controlling muscles which lift the back of the tongue go nerve impulses to stimulate the muscles to perform the needed activity. The child repeats the word with this corrected adjustment of the tongue, and this time he says **cake** correctly.

Pre-correction prevents errors before they occur. It would be cumbersome and irritating to go through life having to resay every word in order to correct the errors made the first time. We need to be "on target" with the first shot. If you were target shooting, with practice you would learn to correct the error in your aim before firing the shot. As you aimed the rifle, you would inspect (observe the relationship of your gun sight to the target), compare (recall the required aim to hit the bull's-eye), and correct your error before firing. So it is with speech. With growing proficiency, the child *presets* his speech apparatus. Drawing on his stored reference points for the sound of the word, he pre-hears the word he is about to speak. He inspects the set of his muscles as they are about to produce the word, checks his reference points for producing that word, and makes required corrections in his muscular control as he says the word. Obviously, this entire process operates with phenomenal speed. Pre-set is useful not only in controlling sound segments of words, but also in controlling vocal loudness, pitch, quality, and rate — all the elements which contribute to a synchronized production of speech.

The Development of Scanning Feedback

During the period of initial speech learning, the child's feedback is intensified. He learns to make point-to-point inspection of his vocal output. He gives careful auditory attention to detailed characteristics of the segments of sound which comprise words. He experiments and compares the tactile sensation of different articulations. He uses auditory and kinesthetic feedback as well as audition to monitor his control of vocal loudness, quality, pitch, and rate.

Once the child has learned the basic speech code and has acquired a workable system of communication, he shifts his attention from the hyper-attentive, point-to-point type of feedback to a more cursory type of speech inspection — to rapid acquisition of words, grammar, and syntax. He inspects his own speech output in a more general fashion, scanning only the dominant features rather than the minutiae. To a large extent, his feedback channels close off after he learns to speak.

If this process seems strange, remember how your use of feedback has changed from the time of your first driving lessons. Can you remember how straight you sat, stretching your neck tensely to see better, gripping the steering wheel tightly with both hands? Your visual awareness was so keen that you literally inspected each foot of the highway ahead of you, and at the end of a half-hour's lesson you were exhausted. After years of driving experience, you are probably totally unaware of inspecting your driving. You see without looking, and if you are a well-trained driver, that is enough. However, if you needed to learn to drive a new type of vehicle, or revise your driving habits, you would once more have to pay attention to feedback information — *to reopen your monitoring channels.*

Reopening Feedback Channels

As an adult, you do not monitor your speech as carefully as you once did. Over the years you have stored in your memory whole patterns of articulatory movements for words, and even whole phrases as units. You produce them automatically, without planning how to speak each sound. The muscular adjustments for controlling the loudness, quality, pitch, and rate of your speaking are largely automatic and require little conscious thought. Your auditory, tactile, and kinesthetic feedback channels operate only at the broad-scanning level. To be sure, if you get a "frog" in your throat or get your tongue "twisted" when you start to say a word, you suddenly become sensitive to your own speech. But as long as nothing unusual occurs, you could talk just about as efficiently with your ears plugged or with novocaine injected in your jaw. Such a relaxed approach to feedback is not alarming; in fact, it merely shows that yours is typical adult behavior. Furthermore, broad-scanning feedback is a remarkably convenient technique, because it permits you to give your thought and attention to the content of your speaking.

A problem arises only when you decide to do something to improve your speech. Then you must reopen your feedback channels of sensory perception in order to exercise conscious control over your speech functions. When you make your new speaking techniques a habit, you may "turn down" your monitor again.

CAUSES OF UNDESIRABLE SPEECH CHARACTERISTICS

What causes speech errors? How did they occur and why have they persisted?

Social conditioning accounts for most "bad" habits. In the first place, childhood standards of speech may have been too low. If a child gets what he wants or wins approval in his environment in spite of speech errors, he has little incentive to improve. If he is allowed to "talk baby talk," articulate carelessly, or use poor voice quality without correction, he assumes that what he does is good enough.

Furthermore, the child's speech models may have been poor. If everyone in his environment set a poor example, he probably simply conformed to this low level of performance. A child's speech is largely an imitation of his parents' speech, especially in his early years. Later he may conform somewhat to other speech models, for instance, his playmates and teachers. But the parents' influence is strong in the most formative stage of his speech learning.

Negative conditioning sometimes occurs. If a child is noticed primarily when he is naughty, he clings to any behavior which is rewarded with scolding or punishment. He may cling to a speech problem because it directs attention toward him, just as he might deliberately annoy his mother until she spanks him. Sometimes punishment and ridicule merely reinforce speech problems.

Residual habits from physical problems account for some speech errors. A child whose front teeth were missing for an unduly long time, or who had wide spaces between his teeth, might continue to say **th** for **s**, even after his teeth are normal. Or one who frequently had a cold and a sore throat which made talking painful might continue to use a weak, nasal voice developed during his illnesses.

Nervous tension can interfere with control of speech functions. A dry throat, an excess of saliva, difficulty in controlling the rate of speech, tremor in the voice, elisions in articulation — any of these may be the result of nervousness, as are shaky knees and moist palms. Even if you are normally calm and unexcitable, you know how difficult it is to control speech functions when you are under nervous tension.

Fortunately, in a particular speech situation there are tried-and-true methods of dissipating stage fright. Physical activity will consume some of the excess energy which makes you tremble or feel panic. Walk several steps before you start talking, use your hands and arms in gestures, avoid standing stiffly while you talk. Regulate your breathing to reduce tension. Breathe more slowly and less deeply. When you practice speech exercises, concentrate on auditory feedback; but when you are talking to an audience, concentrate on getting your ideas across and making your talk enjoyable. Remember, too, that some feeling of exhilaration and excitement is good. It helps you project your voice and makes you more dynamic and forceful.

Organic causes (physical deficiencies or impediments) underlie some speech problems. Some of them, by no means an exhaustive list, are: hearing impairment, paralysis of muscles which control speech functions, dental irregularities which interfere with good articulation. If you think you have an organic problem in speech, you should consult a physician; and you may need corrective work in a speech clinic. However, beware of imagining some physical basis for your poor speech habits and absolving yourself of the responsibility for improving them. Some people find it almost irresistible to identify with any problem they hear described. They read about the symptoms of heart attacks, liver ailments, or arthritis and immediately begin diagnosing their own aches and pains. The chances of your having an organic speech problem are very slight. In all probability, your real problem is simply the force of habit.

HOW TO IMPROVE YOUR SPEECH

CHANGING HABITS. Basic to any speech improvement is the changing of speech habits. You now have firmly established habits of speaking. As a result, you speak almost automatically, with only casual and subconscious attention to how you produce speech. To change a habit, you must first become conscious of what you are doing and what you should be doing. In a regimen of exercises you must consciously use feedback to control your speech output. When you have exercised conscious control until your feedback loop regulates your output as you wish it to be, reliably and automatically, your new habit will be established.

BASIC INFORMATION. Intelligent adults profit more from procedures when they understand the elements and principles involved. You have encountered in this chapter, or will find in the chapters which follow, explanations of physiological processes of the human body, principles of the physics of sound, information about the structure of the English language, and information from psychology. What you are asked to learn is germane to your goals. You will achieve best and most lasting results from your exercises if you understand clearly the physical structures with which you are working, their inherent capabilities, what you are trying to achieve, and how you can achieve it. But make no mistake: learning *about* speech is no substitute for doing something about it. No matter how much you know about the processes involved, your speech will be little changed unless you practice exercises.

A PRACTICE REGIMEN. If you seriously intend to achieve something personally in this course, you must establish a program of practice. To use an old analogy, this course demands the dogged, continual progress of a tortoise. Jackrabbit spurts of energy, interspersed with long naps, will not change your habits. Habit-changing requires constant attention and exercise. You need an established routine of practice.

How much practice do you need? Enough to change your habits. If you have used feedback to control your speech, you will know when your new habits are reliably established. How many days or weeks of practice you need depends on a number of factors: how many habits need changing, how intelligent and aware you are in practice sessions, how much you practice daily.

How often should you practice? The more frequently the better. The more often you direct your attention to the problem and exercise feedback control over it, the more you will be aware of this aspect of your speech between practice periods. Which is the better way to maintain typing skill, for instance — typing several hours a day or once a month? One speech student with a severe lisp corrected her problem in two months. How? Chiefly, by practicing every hour on the hour for about two minutes — usually between classes. But, you may say, you cannot get away by yourself to practice except in your room in the evenings, and perhaps even there you are interrupted by conversation, television, or the radio. Have you overlooked other opportunities for practice? Some exercises can be performed while you are dressing, driving a car, on a coffee break, or working at your desk. Memorize the steps in a particular exercise so that you can perform it without the book. Find time or make time for it, but by all means practice often if you want results.

How long at a time should you practice? As long, and only as long, as you can maintain a high level of concentration. Speech practice is no time for halfhearted, absentminded ritual. Merely reciting words or going through bodily motions accomplishes nothing worthwhile. The overall purpose of any speech exercise is to establish feedback controls. Unless there is continuous sensory awareness, you cannot adequately monitor your performance. Without monitoring, the exercise is useless. At first, your useful practice period may be only five minutes. As you get used to the demand for heightened concentration, you will be able to attend to sensory stimuli for increasingly longer periods, perhaps even an hour.

How many of your problems should you start correcting at once? One at a time, normally. The person who tries to travel all directions at once goes nowhere. When practicing, you need to concentrate as fully as possible on one particular speech function, such as voice quality. If at the same time you try to concentrate on whether you pronounce all the /t/'s, distort the /æ/ vowel, or drop your pitch too often, your attention will be so fragmented that it will be inadequate for any control. During a half-hour's practice, give close attention to one aspect of control at a time, for five or ten minutes each. You will accomplish much more this way than by dividing your attention among five problems simultaneously for the same total time.

EAR TRAINING

Auditory feedback is of prime importance in changing speech habits. Using your hearing to monitor your own speech, however, will probably require training. Most adults do not listen to their own voices critically. In fact, many do not even listen critically to the speech of other people.

Ear training involves a great deal more than simply listening to people talk. All of us do that daily, but primarily at the semantic level — for meaning. To be able to use hearing to monitor our speech, we need to learn to listen critically.

AWAKEN YOUR HEARING.   Analyze the speech of other students in your class. Compare your criticism of them with your instructor's criticism. Analyze the speech of your daily associates, of public speakers you hear, of television actors and announcers. It is important that you hear varieties of speech, good and bad. You need to make comparisons, to identify what is good about one voice and bad about another. When you are able to listen so intently to how people talk that you hardly hear what they say, your hearing has awakened.

CONCENTRATE ON SELF-HEARING.   It is especially difficult to hear yourself objectively. The first time you hear your recorded voice you will undoubtedly be astonished. "Is that really my voice?" is the normal reaction. You hear yourself both by airborne waves, as other people do, and also by conduction of sound waves through the bones of your head. The result is that your voice sounds slightly different to you than to other people. A good recording sounds more like you than you sound to yourself.

The ego-protective mechanism, which we discussed earlier, interferes with accurate self-hearing. All of us have self-images which we cling to — sometimes in spite of contrary evidence. We tend to confuse our intention with our performance. We try to be careful; consequently, how could we omit all those consonants? We are warm and compassionate; how could we have harsh voices? It is impossible to use auditory feedback for speech control unless you can accept the reality of what you hear in your own voice. Many of us who are quite critical of other people's speech are functionally deaf to our own speech errors.

The criticism of your instructor and your fellow classmates can be most valuable in helping you to learn to hear yourself objectively. But do not simply acquiesce in their criticism. This is not an exercise in being a good sport. Learn from their criticism what you should hear in your own voice. Then listen to successive recordings of your voice until you are able to identify the characteristics which have been called to your attention.

When you practice exercises, listen to yourself intently. Examine every segment of your speech bit by bit. During a particular practice session, you will be concentrating on one particular voice characteristic. Disregard every other aspect of your speaking, good or bad, and bend your energies to a thorough examination of that one characteristic. As you become adept at listening to individual aspects of your speaking, you will gradually learn to listen critically to several characteristics simultaneously.

BE SURE OF YOUR AUDITORY REFERENCE. Except by sheer chance, you cannot hit a target unless you can see it. Neither can you compare your vocal output with the way it should sound unless you know how it should sound. For instance, suppose you distort the vowel /æ/ as in **hat**. Unless you remember how /æ/ should sound, how can you compare your distortion with the correct sound? How will you know that the sound you are producing is wrong, or how much correction is needed to make it right?

One way to establish an auditory reference is to listen to another person's voice producing the sound you need to remember. This is especially helpful in articulation practice. If you hear a well-produced vowel sound and say the same vowel immediately afterward, you can compare yours with the correct one. In establishing an auditory reference for pitch, you may listen to another voice at the desired pitch or play the note on a piano or a pitch pipe. When using another person's voice to establish an auditory reference, however, be sure to listen to the particular aspect of voice you are trying to identify. If you need a pitch reference, be sure to listen only to pitch and not become confused by voice quality, pronunciation, and the like.

Ideally, your auditory reference should be established from your own voice. If you imitate another person's pronunciation accurately, and then use your own corrected pronunciation for repeated auditory stimulation, you will establish a more reliable auditory reference. Or you might select from a recording of your voice words or phrases which were good in a certain particular, and save that sample to play back repeatedly for ear training. If your voice is often nasal, let us say, you would select (possibly with your instructor's help) the parts of your recording which are least nasal to use in establishing an auditory reference.

NEGATIVE PRACTICE. Deliberately contrasting the "wrong" way and the "right" way of an aspect of voice or articulation provides valuable ear training. For instance, if you habitually stress too few words to reinforce meaning, you would read a sentence as you normally do and then reread it with stress on a greater number of meaning-carrying words, to hear the difference. Or if your voice quality is breathy, you would read a sentence first with a deliberately breathy tone, perhaps even exaggerated, and then with as little breathiness as possible to produce an audible contrast. In articulation, negative practice also has tremendous value. You say a word with your "wrong" vowel and then with the "right" vowel, or with the "wrong" consonant (or omitting the consonant) and then with the "right" consonant. Juxtaposing incorrect and correct productions enables you to make auditory discriminations which would be impossible if you tried to say only the correct form; furthermore, it enables you to compare the tactile and kinesthetic sensations of the two articulations.

Auditory comparisons are best made in short samples of speech. It is much easier to evaluate your voice in a single word or a phrase than in a long paragraph. You will derive much benefit from repeating the same sentence a number of times, evaluating each reading of it, and then attempting to correct your errors in the next reading. When you practice with a tape recorder, record a sentence, replay and evaluate it, then record again. For best ear training, evaluation should follow performance as closely as possible. The shorter the sample to be evaluated, the more intensive auditory comparison can be.

Team practice is extremely beneficial in establishing an auditory reference and in learning to make accurate comparisons between a particular characteristic of your voice and the auditory reference. If you practice with another student who has your same problem, you share experiences and help each other identify what you hear.

Learn what adjustments in your voice controls are necessary to correct your error. Voice production which is good occasionally, almost by chance, is not worth much. You need reliable controls of your speech musculature which enable you to speak well all of the time. You need to store up in your memory the correct tactile and kinesthetic references of good speech performance. Auditory evaluation of your speech enables you to identify correct muscular controls when you achieve them. When you perform an exercise that produces good control, which you recognize by auditory feedback, try to remember the tactile or kinesthetic sensations you had. This is the essence of learning to make the necessary corrections in your speech controls on the basis of your auditory feedback.

CHAPTER **2**

Improving the Quality and Intensity of Phonation

The Physiology of Vocalization

The vocal tone is the basic acoustic substance of speech. As such, it deserves careful consideration. The amplification of the vocal tone, which is resonance, will be discussed in Chapter 4. Shaping of the vocal tone into identifiable segments of language, which is articulation, will be discussed in Chapters 5 and 6. Our present concern is with the initial production of the vocal tone.

THE RESPIRATORY MECHANISM

The anatomical mechanism used for the production of voice is the same one which has the more vital purpose of respiration to maintain life. On inhalation, oxygen enters the mouth or nose and passes through the pharynx, the trachea, the bronchi, and bronchioles to the air sacs of the lungs, where it is absorbed by blood circulating in capillaries within the walls of the air sacs (Figure 1). From the first inspiration at birth to the last expiration at death, the life of a human being depends on the exchange of gases in his lungs. Oxygen, which is carried by the blood stream from the lungs to all the tissues of the body, is required to convert food into energy and to maintain the life of tissue cells. Waste gases of metabolism, chief among them carbon dioxide, are carried back to the lungs by the blood stream and expelled on exhalation.

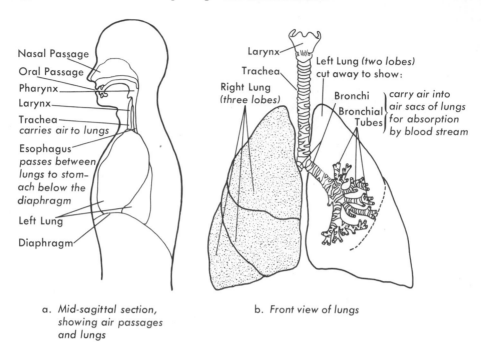

Nasal Passage
Oral Passage
Pharynx
Larynx
Trachea
carries air to lungs
Esophagus
passes between
lungs to stom-
ach below the
diaphragm
Left Lung
Diaphragm

Larynx
Trachea
Right Lung
(three lobes)
Left Lung (two lobes)
cut away to show:
Bronchi ⎞ carry air into
Bronchial ⎱ air sacs of lungs
Tubes ⎰ for absorption
⎠ by blood stream

a. *Mid-sagittal section,*
   showing air passages
   and lungs

b. *Front view of lungs*

Fig. 1   The Mechanism of Breathing

The average adult's rate of respiration is sixteen per minute, but may increase to thirty per minute during strenuous exercise. If breathing stops for more than a very few minutes, death ensues.

Respiration to maintain life is a reflex activity. Both the continuation of breathing and the depth and rate of breathing at any particular time are regulated by internal (automatic) stimuli, such as the level of oxygen or carbon dioxide in the blood and the activity of breathing muscles.

The larynx is the topmost part of the trachea. The trachea (windpipe) is a tube, made semi-rigid by C-shaped rings of cartilage within its walls. (The open side of the C-ring is toward the back of the trachea, against the muscular wall of the esophagus, which carries food to the stomach.) The two rings of cartilage at the top of the trachea are larger than the others and specialized in shape (Figures 1 and 2). These large cartilages comprise the housing of the larynx, sometimes called the "voice box."

Within the larynx (Figure 3) are the two vocal folds, made up of muscle tissue covered by mucous membrane with an edge of white ligament. During respiration, the vocal folds are pulled apart to allow unimpeded passage of air into and out of the lungs. If a foreign particle or an accumulation of mucus irritates the lining of the trachea, the vocal folds are automatically pulled tightly together while adequate breath pressure beneath them is built up to expel the unwanted substance in a cough. The vocal folds must also

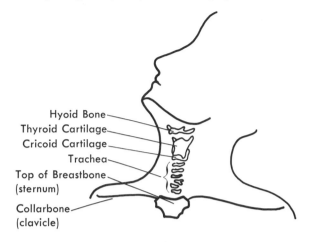

Hyoid Bone
Thyroid Cartilage
Cricoid Cartilage
Trachea
Top of Breastbone
(sternum)

Collarbone
(clavicle)

Fig. 2 Position of the Larynx in the Neck

(viewed half-front)

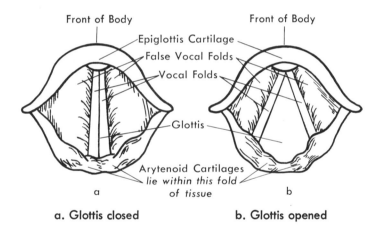

Front of Body   Front of Body

Epiglottis Cartilage
False Vocal Folds
Vocal Folds

Glottis

Arytenoid Cartilages
lie within this fold
of tissue

a   b

a. Glottis closed   **b. Glottis opened**

Fig. 3 The Larynx as Seen from Above

close together in order to hold the breath, as when a person is lifting a heavy object, swimming underwater, or "bearing down."

The same respiration mechanism in man can be regulated with such delicate control that it produces vocal tones. What is more, control is so discrete that attributes of the vocal tone — quality, intensity, and pitch — can be regulated. To produce voice at all requires that the muscles which control the various parts of the breathing mechanism be subject to voluntary control, in addition to the autonomic (involuntary) control which operates to maintain the more basic life-function of breathing. Skillful modulation of the voice, to suit it to esthetic standards of intensity, quality, or pitch, is a remarkable refinement of basic functions of respiration. Such modulation must reflect considerable attention to social standards of good speaking and conscious care in establishing habits of effective phonation.

This last point has been the subject of some contention, because of the fact that almost everyone knows at least one superior speaker who claims to be completely unaware of his techniques of effective speaking and totally untrained. Training is not necessarily a matter of attending a class in voice improvement. Good models of speech in one's early environment teach good vocal habits by example. Most adolescents have heroes or heroines whom they emulate — in voice, often, as in other attributes of social behavior.

This chapter concentrates on re-forming habits of breath control for the improvement of voice quality and intensity. For an adult, such new habits require conscious evaluation of vocal habits and a program of well-directed exercises.

THE PHYSIOLOGY OF PHONATION

A vocal tone is produced by the operation of two opposing forces. The first is a column of air moving upward in the trachea. The second is the pair of vocal folds which are pulled together to interrupt the air flow. The essence of efficiency in phonation is the delicate balance between these two forces. The synchronization necessary to regulate voice quality and intensity requires a skillful control of function in opposing musculatures.

PART ONE • Control of Breathing for Vocalization

BREATH SUPPORT

Breath support is control of the force and duration of exhalation. Stated in slightly different terms, it has to do with the time during which a single exhalation is extended, and the quantity of air being exhaled at any given moment in time. These are the chief aspects of breath support with which we shall be concerned, because they are the variables which affect quality or intensity of the vocal tone.

Breath support, then, is an aspect of exhalation. Since speech is normally produced on exhalation, this phase of the respiratory cycle is of primary concern. The nature of inhalation, however, has a direct bearing on the speaker's ability to control his exhalation. Therefore, we shall examine the entire respiratory function as it relates to speech.

RESPIRATION

Respiration is the operation of air flow to equalize pressure in a cavity of changing size. The thorax (chest cavity), containing the lungs, is roughly conical. The volume of a cone increases as its height or the diameter of its base increases (Figure 4). On *inhalation*, muscular action causes the floor of the thorax to lower, increasing the height of the "cone," and the walls to

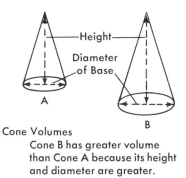
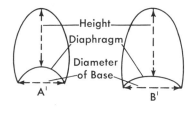

Cone Volumes
    Cone B has greater volume
than Cone A because its height
and diameter are greater.

Thorax Volumes
    Thorax B' has greater volume than
Thorax A' because its height and
diameter are greater.

Fig. 4 Volume Increase in the Thorax

move outward, increasing its diameter. When the resultant increase in volume causes the air pressure in the lungs to drop, air rushes in to equalize the pressure inside and outside the chest. *Exhalation* is produced by decreasing the height and diameter of the thorax, thus decreasing the volume and raising the air pressure, so that breath is expelled to equalize air pressure inside the lungs and outside the chest.

This mechanical process is controlled by certain muscles which are attached to the bony framework of the body trunk. In order to analyze your own breathing habits as they relate to speech, you should examine your respiratory functions as you study the physiology of respiration.

CHARACTERISTICS OF MUSCLE TISSUE

Before discussing muscle activity, we should note briefly the characteristics of muscle tissue. If you have seen a beef roast or barbecued spareribs, you have seen muscle tissue. When you cut the red meat of a steak "across the grain," you are cutting across the fibers of a muscle. Human muscles do not differ greatly in appearance from beef muscles.

The problem in any exercise is to know the capabilities of the specific muscles you are using. You may not produce muscle strain by misusing breathing muscles, as you might sprain an ankle or get a "charley-horse" in your leg. But you can defeat your purpose in breathing exercises if you expect muscles to perform in ways they cannot perform.

Tension of a muscle involves a tightening or stiffening of the individual fibers which are collected into a bundle or sheath. When a muscle is relaxed, it is flabby and soft. When it is tense, it is more rigid and stiff. You can observe this in your upper arm if you bend your elbow and "flex your muscle" (the biceps).

Contraction of a muscle means drawing up or shortening its fibers. A muscle normally contracts when it tenses. Its length during rest is normally greater than its length under tension.

Varying degrees of tension are possible and usual in muscle activity. Depending on the motor nerve impulse which activates muscle fibers, a given muscle can be only slightly tensed or increasingly tensed by gradual or quick stages. A muscle is seldom totally tense, nor is it often completely relaxed.

Tone or *tonus* of a muscle is just adequate tension to maintain posture (if it is a skeletal muscle) or the proper positioning of the structures to which it attaches. A person who looks "droopy" in posture has poorer muscle tone than one who looks lively and capable of easy movement.

Muscle attachment may be on bone, cartilage, ligament (a tough whitish tissue), or fascia (the inelastic tissue which covers muscle bundles or sheaths). When a muscle contracts, it pulls one point of attachment closer to the other, unless the structures to which it is attached are braced against that pull by tension of other muscles.

One-way activity is a law of muscle tension. A muscle can only pull. It cannot push. Furthermore, it can pull only in the direction in which its fibers run.

Voluntary activity is muscle tension subject to conscious or volitional control. All of the muscles with which we are concerned in voice control are of this type. Involuntary muscles, such as those in the intestinal walls, operate without our thought or intention. Muscles of posture and purposeful movement, including the muscles of breathing, are voluntary muscles. They can operate at the automatic level in habituated movements. They can also operate at the conscious level in response to thought and intention.

Muscle antagonism is the working of one muscle in opposition to another. For instance, the muscles which extend your finger are antagonists to those which clench your fist. Muscles which move your leg forward are antagonistic to those which move it backward. Skillful use of antagonistic muscles controls the smoothness of many physical movements. If you extend your arm to the side at shoulder height, you can make it a jerky movement by using only the muscles which move it to that position. But if you "hold back" somewhat with the antagonistic muscles — the ones which would lower your arm to your side or pull it out in front of you — your movement can be as graceful as a dancer's.

The Physiology of Inhalation

Inhalation, or inspiration, is the act of drawing breath into the lungs by increasing the volume of the thoracic cavity. Most physiologists agree that this action requires active contraction of certain muscles. Inhalation does not "just happen." We make it happen through tension of muscles which move either or both of two structures: (1) the floor of the thoracic cavity, downward; (2) the bony framework of the thorax, outward.

Which specific muscles contract for inspiration at any particular time depends on the breath requirements of the body at that time. During rest, inhalation requires the least muscular activity. For strenuous exercise inhalation involves the greatest number of muscles and the greatest contraction of those muscles. Speech requirements vary greatly, all the way from extremely relaxed conversation to vigorous, loud public speaking.

TYPES OF INHALATION

Three criteria determine the types of inhalation: (1) the muscle groups actively engaged in producing inhalation; (2) the area of the body which shows the greatest expansion with inhalation; and (3) the situation in which a type of inhalation would be adequate. One point must be made emphatically: there is no way for an individual to channel his breath into a particular part of his lungs. Since the three lobes of the right lung and the two lobes of the left lung are connected by continuous airways to the trachea, when air enters the trachea it distributes generally throughout the mass of spongy lung tissue. Note, also, that the following classifications are seldom exclusive; one adds on to another when increased volume of inhalation is needed.

Diaphragmatic Breathing

Diaphragmatic breathing is so named because the muscle which controls this kind of inhalation is the diaphragm. Because the area which shows the greatest resultant expansion is the abdomen, it is also called abdominal breathing (Figure 5). Exclusive use of the diaphragm for inhalation is not common,

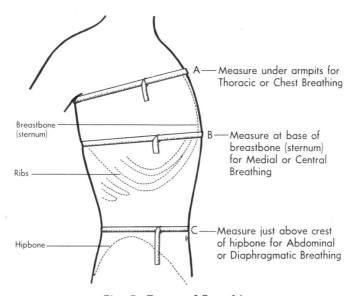

Fig. 5 Types of Breathing

To check the predominant breathing type: Measure in each area, both at the end of exhalation and at the end of inhalation. Whichever area shows the greatest variation in measurement is the predominant type of breathing.

except in infants (before the nerves to other muscles of inhalation are capable of conveying stimuli). In quiet breathing, at rest, action of the diaphragm accounts for approximately half the breath intake in the average adult, men normally showing slightly more abdominal expansion than women.[1]

[1] Philip Bard, *Medical Physiology*, 10th ed. (St. Louis: C. V. Mosby Co., 1956), p. 289.

The diaphragm is a muscle sheath which separates the thorax from the abdominal cavity. Shaped like a double dome, its fibers radiate outward from a central tendon just below the heart to attach to the tip of the sternum, the lowest six ribs on each side, and the lumbar section of the spinal vertebrae on the back. When relaxed, the diaphragm bulges upward, with the stomach and liver nestled beneath it (Figure 6). When it contracts, it pulls down and forward, pressing down on the viscera which tend to be displaced forward and to cause the abdominal wall to bulge. When the diaphragm tenses, it increases the height of the thoracic cavity and thus increases the cavity volume, so that breath is drawn in.

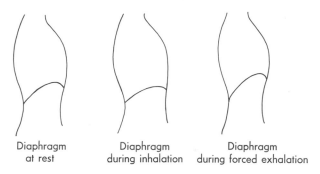

Diaphragm   Diaphragm   Diaphragm
at rest   during inhalation   during forced exhalation

**Fig. 6 Schematic Drawing of the Thorax
Showing Action of the Diaphragm**

(side view, facing right)

Quiet Costal Breathing

Quiet costal breathing involves minimal costal (rib) movement. It is also called lower thoracic breathing because it involves the greatest expansion in the lower part of the thorax, or medial breathing because the area of greatest expansion is about the middle of the trunk (Figure 5). In quiet breathing, at rest, lower thoracic expansion accounts for about half the volume of inhalation in the average adult.[2]

Each rib is curved, not only around the chest but also downward on the sides like a bucket handle (Figure 7). Rib attachments to spinal vertebrae are flexible to allow for an oblique rotation. They attach to the sternum (breastbone) by cartilage which is somewhat flexible. From the lower edge of each rib to the top edge of the next lower rib run muscle fibers in a downward-forward direction (Figure 8).

In quiet breathing, when these muscles contract, each rib is pulled upward a bit toward the next higher rib, much like the slats in a venetian blind. Because each rib has a bucket-handle shape, it also swings outward as it moves upward, thus increasing the lateral diameter of the chest. Since the lower end of the sternum is pulled outward by ribs attached to it, the front-to-back diameter of the thorax also increases.

[2] Bard, p. 288.

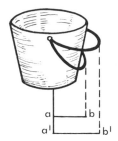

In the lifted position, the handle swings
farther out from the bucket (a¹b¹) than
when it is lowered (a b).

**Fig. 7   The Bucket-Handle Principle of Chest
Expansion through Rib Elevation**

At rest, most people use a mixture of diaphragmatic and lower costal breathing. Though it does not produce a great intake of air and is not suited to the best control of exhalation, many individuals use this type of inhalation for relaxed, quiet speech, especially for short utterances.

Active Costal Breathing

Active costal breathing is normally used during physical activity, where the need for oxygen increases, or for speech, where a greater volume of breath flow on exhalation is needed. It is also called *upper chest breathing*, or simply *chest breathing* or *thoracic breathing*, because the area of greatest expansion during inhalation is the upper chest (Figure 5).

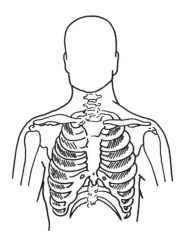

Fig. 8   External Intercostal Muscles (front view)
When they contract, they pull ribs upward and outward.

Deep inhalation involves two groups of active muscles. Muscles of the back which run from the spinal vertebrae to ribs (Figure 9.2) pull upward, rotating the ribs on their spinal axes. Muscles at the front of the chest which run from ribs upward to the shoulders (Figure 9.1) pull ribs upward, and because the upper ribs attach to the sternum (breastbone), pull it upward also. These latter muscles are effective for breathing, however, only if certain muscles of the back (antagonists) pull against them. If *only* the forward pull from shoulders to ribs were exerted, the result would be stoop-shouldered posture. The antagonists of these active muscles fall into two groups. One group (Figure 9.3), which runs between the shoulders and the spine, keeps the shoulders stabilized against the pull of muscles on the front of the chest (Figure 9.1). Another group (Figure 9.4), the long muscle fibers connecting at various points from the head all along the spine to the hip bones, keeps the back erect and acts as a brace for other back muscles (Figure 9.2) that pull ribs upward toward the vertebrae. This type of breathing increases the diameter of the thorax front to back and side to side, thus increasing its volume for inspiration.

Upper costal breathing rarely occurs alone, and certainly should *not*. If this were the only muscular activity, i.e., if the diaphragm were relaxed, the contents of the abdominal cavity would be sucked up into the thorax, causing the diaphragm to bulge upward and greatly reducing the intake of breath. Normally, when a person needs a larger volume of breath, he uses upper costal breathing *in addition to* increased activity of the diaphragm and the lower thoracic musculature. This combination facilitates deep breathing, which is required for strenuous activity but not necessarily for speech. The important consideration for speech is that this type of inhalation allows for maximum control of exhalation.

Clavicular Breathing

Clavicular breathing, or *shoulder breathing*, or *extreme upper chest breathing*, involves active lifting of the shoulders. (The clavicles are the collarbones of the shoulders.) Muscles which run from each clavicle and the sternum to the head (Figure 10) are active in clavicular breathing. Tension of these muscles raises the shoulders and upper chest, providing additional volume in the chest by increasing its vertical dimension.

Clavicular breathing is useful under some circumstances. In sports performed at maximal effort, such as the fifty-yard dash or speed swimming, clavicular breathing is often *added* to diaphragmatic, lower costal, and upper costal breathing to provide even more oxygen. Swimmers who use a crawl stroke find that clavicular and upper chest breathing combined are useful to coordinate with necessary arm movements. An opera singer is likely to use clavicular breathing in addition to the other three types, especially when singing across a loud, brassy orchestra, or when the musical passage to be sung on one exhalation is particularly long or loud. Physicians occasionally recommend clavicular breathing as an extreme measure for a patient with distressed breathing.

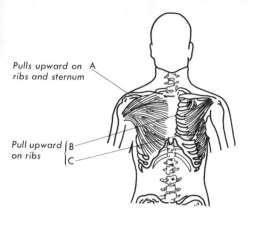

Pulls upward on A
ribs and sternum

Pull upward { B
on ribs { C

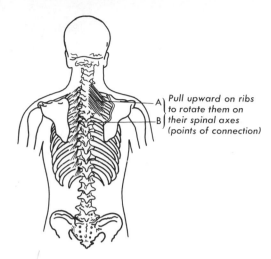

A } Pull upward on ribs
B } to rotate them on
their spinal axes
(points of connection)

9.1 *Upper Chest Muscles Active*
in Inhalation

A. Right Pectoralis Major (Paired)
B. Left Pectoralis Minor (Paired)
C. Left Serratus Anterior (Paired)
(B lies on top of C)

9.2 *Back Muscles Active*
in Inhalation

A. Right Serratus Posterior
Superior (Paired)
B. Left Levatores Costarum
(Paired)

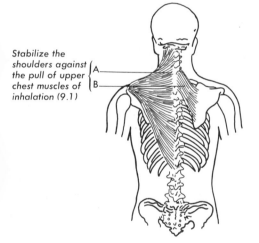

Stabilize the
shoulders against { A
the pull of upper {
chest muscles of { B
inhalation (9.1)

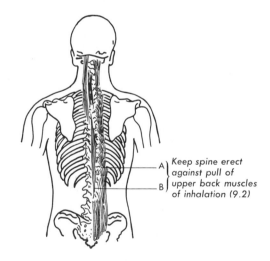

A } Keep spine erect
B } against pull of
upper back muscles
of inhalation (9.2)

9.3 *Back Muscles Antagonistic*
to Upper Chest Muscles
of Inhalation

A. Left Trapezius (Paired)
B. Right Rhomboid (Paired)
(A lies on top of B)

9.4 *Spinal Muscles Antagonistic*
to Upper Back Muscles
of Inhalation (9.2.)

A. Right Sacrospinalis (Paired)
B. Left Erector Spinae (Paired)
(A lies on top of B)

Fig. 9 Muscles of Deep Inhalation

47

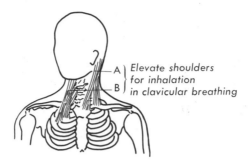

A. Left Sterno-cleido-mastoid (Paired)

B. Right Scalenes (Paired) (A lies on top of B)

Fig. 10 Neck Muscles Active in Clavicular Breathing

Despite this, clavicular breathing is *not* recommended for speech. First, it makes control of exhalation difficult. About the only way the shoulder and upper chest can return to normal position, when tension of the elevating muscles relaxes, is by dropping with the pull of gravity. Second, the increase in neck tension causes constriction and crowding of the larynx during phonation, and the shortening of the neck has an adverse effect on the pharynx as a vocal resonator.

The Physiology of Exhalation

PASSIVE EXHALATION

The movement of breath out of the lungs is an entirely passive process in a state of quiet rest. At rest, exhalation requires no active contraction of respiratory muscles. Whatever muscles are tensed to produce inhalation relax for exhalation. When the diaphragm relaxes, negative pressure causes the viscera of the abdomen to push it back up into a position of rest. The ribs, which were elevated by muscle tension, drop by the pull of gravity when that tension is released. As the volume of the chest decreases, the elasticity of the air passages in the lungs causes them to shrink and expel breath. The entire exhalation mechanism is triggered by a reflex and requires no thought or volition. Nor does it require any muscle tension.

ACTIVE EXHALATION FOR SPEECH

The need for regulated breath pressure for speech requires *conscious* control of exhalation. Part of this control is exercised in the larynx, which is, after all, a sort of valve. We shall discuss laryngeal function in more detail later. But first, what other controls are possible and practical?

In the abdominal walls there are three layers of muscle sheath, with fibers running in different directions from the lower ribs to the crest of the hip bone, and a fourth powerful muscle which runs from the sternum and ribs all the way down to the pubic arch of the pelvis (Figure 11.1). These four muscles,

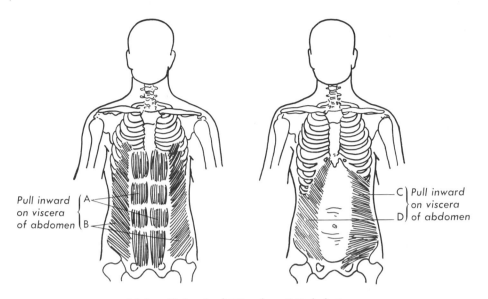

11.1 *Abdominal Muscles of Exhalation*
(B, C, D form successive layers from outside in.)

A. Rectus Abdominus, left and right

B. External Oblique, left and right

C. Left Internal Oblique (Paired)

D. Right Transverse Abdominal (Paired)

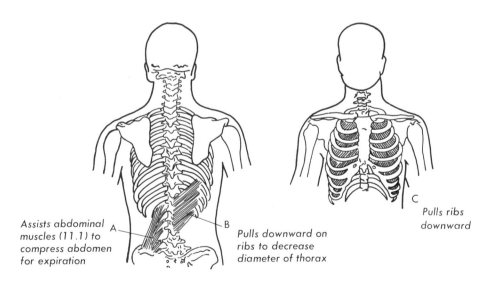

11.2 *Back and Chest Muscles of Exhalation*

A. Left Quadratus Lumborum (Paired)

B. Right Serratus Posterior Inferior (Paired)

C. Internal Intercostals (viewed from front)

Fig. 11 Active Muscles of Exhalation

which form the abdominal wall, act in concert, assisted by a fifth muscle of the lower back (Figure 11.2-A). When contracted, they pull inward against the contents of the abdomen like an elastic girdle, or, more properly, like several girdles worn at once. The compressed viscera of the abdomen push against the diaphragm, forcing it upward against the lung sac. With very forceful exhalation, the diaphragm is pushed up even higher than when in its state of rest (Figure 6). Forcing the diaphragm upward shortens the vertical dimension of the thorax.

Between each two ribs run short muscle fibers in a downward-backward direction (Figure 11.2-C). Contraction of these muscles draws the ribs down. On the lower back are muscle fibers which run from the lower ribs downward to the spinal vertebrae (Figure 11.2-B). When they contract, they draw the ribs downward also. Even tension of the muscles in the abdominal walls (Figure 11.1) exerts some downward pull on the ribs. You will remember that during inhalation the ribs are pulled upward and swung outward because of their bucket-handle shape, thus increasing the diameter of the thorax. When the ribs are pulled downward for exhalation, the "bucket handle" returns to its original position and the diameter of the thorax decreases.

Now, suppose a sudden strong burst of breath is needed for blowing out the candles on a birthday cake or for shouting very loudly. A forceful quick exhalation is required. To exhale maximum breath in the shortest time is simple. Relax all of the muscles which tensed for inhalation quickly and completely; at the same time, tense the muscles of exhalation as much and as fast as you can. If you need to become acutely aware of your exhalation musculature, this is a good exercise. If your exhalation muscles tense well, you should feel your abdomen jerk inward sharply.

Speaking, however, is not easily accomplished in a series of lusty, staccato shouts. Normal speaking requires a sustained exhalation of longer duration than in quiet breathing, and should be discreetly regulated in degree of force.

The average time of expiration in quiet breathing approximately equals the time of inspiration; the ratio is 1:1. The average ratio of expiration to inspiration in speaking is 5:1. Bear in mind that an average (the statistical *mean*) is arrived at by adding actual scores, often widely distributed, and then dividing by the number of scores. The *average* exhalation in speaking consumes five times as much time as inhalation. Some speech exhalations are obviously much shorter, since some utterances are quite short. Therefore, some speech exhalations must be considerably longer in duration than the average. In actual speech situations the ratio may rise as high as 10:1 or 15:1. An actor may need to increase the ratio even more. A speaker should pause for an inhalation only where a pause is needed for the separation of the idea-units he is expressing. If he has to interrupt a phrase to inhale, his control of the duration of an exhalation is faulty.

Force of exhalation increases as loudness increases. As Black and Moore observe, "The greater the exhalatory rate, the more intense the tone." [3] In

---

[3] J. W. Black and W. E. Moore, *Speech: Code, Meaning, and Communication* (New York: McGraw-Hill Co., Inc., 1955), p. 47.

most voices, the actual gain in loudness is greater than the increase in breath pressure, since intensity is affected by two additional factors; the nature of the breath release from the larynx, and the amplifying effect of the resonating cavities above the larynx.[4] The control of expiratory force is the most basic factor in vocal intensity.

The essence of breath control is the skillful balancing of the tension of antagonistic groups of muscles. The balance of force and antagonism may be illustrated (Figure 12) with your two hands. Place the palms together and push with equal force; the hands remain immobile. Now with palms still together, push hard with the right hand while relaxing the left; your hands will move *suddenly* to the left. Try pushing with the right hand while resisting with a gradually diminishing force from the left; your hands will move in a smooth, controlled motion to the left. The rate of movement is determined by the amount of force and the amount of resistance.

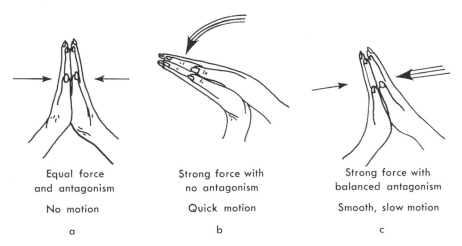

Equal force and antagonism	Strong force with no antagonism	Strong force with balanced antagonism
No motion	Quick motion	Smooth, slow motion
a	b	c

Fig. 12 Balance between Force and Antagonism

How does this apply to the force of exhaled breath? Unhappily, some students assume that all they need to do to control exhalation is to apply force to the outgoing breath. The active force consists of the tension in muscles of exhalation — those which pull inward against the abdominal contents to force the diaphragm upward, and those which pull downward on the ribs. If this were the entire control of exhalation, the breath would rush out too abruptly to be useful for speech.

There are two muscular systems which can resist this quick out-running of breath. One is obviously the system of muscles which pulls the vocal folds together in the larynx. This laryngeal valve is a strong enough sphincter to hold back the breath completely. Muscles of the larynx, as we shall see later, can be delicately regulated to govern the rate and force of exhalation. The

[4] J. W. van den Berg, "Physiology and Physics of Voice Production," *Acta Physiologica et Pharmacologica Neerlandica*, Amsterdam, V, No. 1 (1957), pp. 40–55.

other muscles which can be used to resist the quick discharge of breath are the muscles of inhalation. As long as they are tense, the breath will not leave the body. What if tension of the inhalation muscles — the diaphragm and the thoracic muscles which lift the ribs and sternum — is gradually released? If inhalation muscles gradually reduce tension while exhalation muscles gradually increase tension, breath will be exhaled slowly and smoothly enough and with adequate pressure to sustain phonation.

The question of deep breathing and its usefulness to speech inevitably arises. There was a time when most people assumed an automatic correlation between a speaker's chest expansion and the excellence of his voice, both the vocal loudness and the quality. As a matter of fact, by an extension of this notion anyone with a robust chest was presumed to have exceptional vocal potential. This fallacy was so widespread that even today people marvel that certain singers can produce strong, beautiful vocal tones despite their slender figures. Actually, the production of a steady, strong vocal tone does not require more breath than the average person can manage; it simply requires good breath support.

A physical education instructor directing breathing exercises who intoned, "In with the good air; out with the bad," was entirely wrong, especially if this principle were applied to speech. In the first place, no one ever breathes out *all* of the air in his lungs. Respiration is not a process of depleting and replenishing. The lungs remain somewhat inflated all of the time, with *residual air* (Figure 13). Suppose you inhaled as much as you possibly could, and

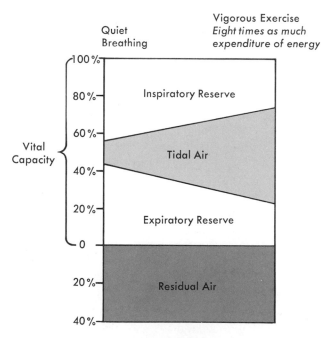

Fig. 13 Relationship of Tidal Air to Vital Capacity

then exhaled as much as you possibly could; that maximum exhalation could be breathed into a spirometer and measured as your *vital capacity* (Figure 13). The quantity of air which you inhale and exhale in normal (not forced) respiration is called *tidal air*, because it flows back and forth like the tide. The difference between normal inhalation and maximum inhalation is the *inspiratory reserve*. The difference between normal exhalation and maximum exhalation is the *expiratory reserve*. As shown in Figure 13, tidal air averages approximately 12 per cent of vital capacity in healthy young males at rest, in a sitting or standing position. With light activity, the volume of tidal air does not change significantly. When energy expended is eight times as great, tidal air is only four times as great, or 50 per cent of vital capacity. (The additional oxygen needed for heavy work is provided by increased rate of respiration as well as increased depth.) Tidal air used for speech would correspond with the smaller percentages on this graph, probably not exceeding 20 per cent of vital capacity in most speech activities.

Practical Inspiratory Controls

Good posture for inhalation varies somewhat with the body build of the individual. In general, however, stooped shoulders force the sternum and ribs downward, essentially preventing any type of costal inhalation. If stooping is severe enough to crowd the abdominal cavity, even the action of the diaphragm for inhalation will be limited. On the other hand, the muscles which maintain an erect spine and normal shoulder posture are the same ones that act as antagonists to brace against the contraction of muscles of inhalation. Check your own posture. Stand with your back against a wall, touching the wall all the way from heels to head. Is it difficult for you to touch the back of your head to the wall in this position? If so, look at your posture in profile in a full-length mirror. Are you stooped? What happens when you pull your shoulder blades closer together in back? Stiff elevation of the shoulders, like old-fashioned "military" posture, is not recommended for speech either. Your shoulders should be erect but not tense. Is your head balanced upright on your neck, or inclined forward as if you are "leading with your chin"? Good head posture will help relieve excessive tension in neck muscles.

If your posture leaves something to be desired, try improving it as you practice the exercises at the end of this chapter. One good device for aligning your body frame properly is to pretend that someone is pulling you up from above like a puppet, with a string tied to the top of each of your ears (*not* your nose!). Do you feel your head and shoulders coming into good alignment with your spine? Do you feel a lengthening of the space between your bottom ribs and the crest of your hip bones, as if you were stretching upward? Try speaking with this posture and see if your control of breathing is easier.

Quick inhalation is usually necessary for speech, if you are to avoid overlong pauses. Ideally, the listener should not even be aware that the speaker is breathing, and certainly should not be aware of breathing as a prominent interruption of speaking.

Inhale through the mouth during speech. Some people use too much time for inhalation because they have the erroneous impression that they must always inhale through the nose, even during speech. How much easier and more natural it is, with the mouth open for speaking, to inhale through the mouth between phrases!

Avoid over-breathing. Untrained speakers often breathe too deeply. They take in much more breath than they can use efficiently for speaking. Besides, deep inhalation consumes too much time and attracts too much attention. It is better to take quick, smaller breaths more frequently (at appropriate pauses between thought-units of your speech) than to try to fill up your lungs for a nearly interminable exhalation. Inhaling too deeply is often followed by a sigh (voiceless expiration) before speech resumes, or by very breathy speech. Trying to use your inspiratory reserve for speaking makes control of exhalation doubly difficult.

Keep inhalation free of excess tension. If your inhalations for speech are quite labored, you are probably trying to breathe too deeply or are not synchronizing the activity of inhalation muscles adequately. Reexamine the way you breathe, giving particular attention to how much your ribs and breast bone move. If your chest heaves and your shoulders lift with every inspiration, you are creating excessive neck and shoulder tensions. In that event, try keeping your chest and shoulders reasonably still (but erect) while expanding the lower chest and abdomen for inhalation. Take a quick gulp of air instead of trying to fill your lungs to maximum capacity. Inhale more frequently and less deeply.

Silent inhalation is necessary if breathing is to be unobtrusive. A wheezing or hissing intake of air sounds strained. Noisy inhalation *is* strained, since it involves tension in muscles which should be relaxed during phonation. The vocal folds should open widely for inhalation. If they are held almost closed, inspiration will be noisy. If the tongue crowds back into the throat during inhalation, the rush of breath through this narrow passage will be noisy. If the teeth are held together, the breath will hiss as it is drawn between them, rather like saying an /s/ on inspiration. Learn to relax the muscles of articulation and phonation quickly for a silent inhalation.

Inhale at sense pauses. Obviously, no one can talk indefinitely without inhaling. Some speakers attempt it. When they do, either their compulsion to get the idea expressed or their urgent need for oxygen will triumph. If they continue to speak until they are forcing out their expiratory reserve or even the residual air, the effect will not be good. Fading of intensity is almost inevitable, and tone quality is likely to deteriorate into glottal fry. On the other hand, if the need for oxygen becomes compelling, the speaker will have to pause to inhale, even though his pause interrupts the idea he is expressing. The solution is to *inhale before you must.*

Practice reading selections which you have marked with a / at the end of each sense-unit. You need not even wait until the end of a sentence to inhale, if you inhale quickly. A quick inhalation at the end of any phrase is entirely appropriate. Many small inhalations are much better than a few large ones. Always inhale *before* you have a desperate need for breath, at a natural sense-pause in your speech.

Practical Expiratory Controls

Since exhalation is the basis of vocal tone, it is important to consider the controls in the respiratory musculature which are significant to good tone quality and intensity. After discussing the physiology of the larynx, we shall consider certain problems of synchronizing the respiratory and laryngeal muscles.

Exhale economically. Learn to "spend" your expiration wisely. If you waste breath (unphonated), either before phonation begins, between words, or within words, you will exhaust your breath supply too soon. If you waste breath early in a sentence, you will have inadequate breath support later in the sentence.

Resist the out-rush of breath by gradually releasing tension in the muscles of inhalation. Counting aloud is an excellent exercise for observing or developing this control. Watch your chest and abdomen in a mirror, and try also to perceive kinesthetically the areas of muscle tension in your chest and abdomen. How far you can count on one breath depends, obviously, on how fast you count. As a pacesetter, count your own pulse. After a quick, moderate inhalation, practice counting: 1–2–3–4–5, *inhale*, 1–2–3–4–5–6–7, *inhale*, 1–2–3–4–5–6–7–8–9–10. Be careful not to force exhalation beyond normal tidal air. You should not feel "out of breath" or "caving in" when you reach 10, unless you wasted breath along the way. This is not a deep breathing exercise, but a breath conservation exercise. In successive repetitions, time your inhalation before each counting so that it consumes only the time of one pulse beat. Use this time-ratio of inhalation to exhalation as a desirable rhythm for speaking. Learn the kinesthesia of respiratory muscles working in correct antagonism to release breath at the rate needed for speech.

Suspend and resume expiration without wasting breath. We have observed that inhalations should not occur except at sense-pauses between phrases. Yet we do not inhale at every pause. A pause is a hiatus, an open space in speech, which serves the useful purpose of dividing the flow of words into comprehensible phrase groupings. If every pause involves wastage of breath, the supply of breath is soon exhausted. To help you perceive the kinesthesia of arresting the outflow of breath, try the following exercise.

Again you will be counting, which you can do so automatically that you can center your whole attention on your controls for breathing. Again, use your pulse rate as a timer. Each / indicates a pause. Use the time of one pulse beat for each pause or inhalation. Be careful not to inhale or exhale when you pause. Count: 1–2–3–4 / 5–6 / 7–8–9, *inhale*, 1–2 / 3–4–5 / 6–7–8–9, *inhale*, 1–2–3 / 4–5–6–7 / 8–9. At pauses you should feel the arrest of breathing not simply in the larynx but also in the thoracic muscles and diaphragm holding back in antagonism to the abdominal muscles of exhalation.

Regulate general loudness of the voice to suit the situation. It is a truism that a speaker should adapt his vocal intensity to the needs of the speaking situation, increasing it with greater distance or larger space. You are probably quite aware of excesses or inadequacies in the vocal loudness of other people. Are you as accurate and sensitive in appraising your own?

Psychologists explain that poor control of loudness sometimes reflects the way an individual feels about talking and the people he is talking to. They say that an aggressive personality is often revealed in too-loud speech and an inhibited one in too-soft speech. On the other hand, there are certainly many normal individuals whose vocal intensity fails to suit the situation simply because they have not learned to monitor their speech for loudness or have misgauged the demands of a new speaking experience. Even if your voice is too loud because you are hyper-stimulated, or too soft because of stage fright, these problems can be corrected in large measure by reliable self-monitoring.

Monitoring your vocal intensity is primarily auditory. It also involves kinesthetic awareness of the increased tension in muscles of expiration as you exhale more air for greater loudness, or less tension in these muscles with decreased exhalation for a quieter voice.

1. *Establishing memory of loudness levels.* To help you respond to auditory and kinesthetic feedback, stand or sit near one wall of your room and speak a sentence aimed at various distances, first to a point four feet away, then to one ten feet away (across the room), then to one twenty feet away (probably out in the hall). For instance, say the sentence, "I am talking just loudly enough to be heard distinctly." Avoid over-tensing your throat and raising the pitch when you increase loudness. Articulate clearly, but do not become objectionably pedantic. Get a friend to tell you whether your loudness is exactly right for each distance. Listen carefully to yourself and pay attention to the amount of tension you feel in breathing muscles for each degree of loudness. Repeat this exercise often enough to establish both auditory and kinesthetic memory of loudness levels. When you talk to an individual or a group, watch their expressions for signs of your being inaudible or overly loud.

2. *The basketball projection exercise* is another way of developing a kinesthetic awareness of antagonistic muscle tensions when controlling breath for increased loudness. Place your wastepaper basket against the wall on one side of the room (on a chair where a listener might sit, if that helps). Stand on the opposite side and speak to the basket. Think of each phrase as being tossed through the air like a basketball to arch up and over and plop precisely in the basket. To help visualize this concept and maintain appropriate muscle tensions, you might hold an imaginary basketball in your hands and "throw" it into the basket with every phrase. Be aware of your posture and general

muscle tone. You should feel vigor, without excess tension, in propelling your voice to its target. Specifically, you should be conscious of the degree of tension in respiratory muscles.

Prevent fading of vocal intensity. If the last few words of many of your sentences become inaudible, though they begin loudly enough, your problem is one of fading. Listening to fading speech is annoying, because just enough information is lost to make all that is said confusing. It is likely to leave the impression that the speaker does not really care enough about what he is saying to project all of it to his listeners. He seems to start a sentence with communicative purpose and then to end it as if it were not worth saying anyway. Perhaps you do care about communicating all the way to the end of your sentences. Then why do you fade? The reason is probably undependable monitoring for vocal intensity.

Sustaining vocalization at an adequate level of loudness is a skill which must be learned. Young children commonly fade because they have not learned delicate control of their respiratory muscles. To prevent fading, exhalation must be controlled to the very end of the sentence. It must also be controlled at the beginnings of sentences to prevent breath wastage, because breath wasted early cannot sustain tone later. In the following exercises, use auditory and kinesthetic self-monitoring. Listen to the intensity of the tone. Keep it strong to the very end. Avoid wasting breath. Feel the tension of antagonistic muscles of breathing as they control the rate and force of exhalation.

1. *At pulse rate*, count through each sequence on a single exhalation. Remember to suspend exhalation, without loss of breath, at each pause (marked /). Keep the tone strong to the end of each sequence.

   (a) 1–2–3–4–5–6–7–8–9–10.
   (b) 1–2–3–4 / 5–6–7–8–9–10.
   (c) 1–2 / 3–4–5–6 / 7–8–9–10.
   (d) 1–2–3–4–5 / 6–7–8–9–10–11–12.

2. Read the following paragraph at a loudness level adequate for a classroom of thirty listeners. If possible, record your reading on tape. At the suggested pauses, marked with a /, suspend phonation without wasting breath. Inhale at the spots marked **B**. If you have not wasted breath early in a sentence, you should be able to complete it with adequate strength on one exhalation. Monitor your voice as you read. While you are reading, mark with a √ each place you hear your voice fade, and an ✕ each place you feel a loss of exhalation control. This is simultaneous self-criticism based on feedback. Be as honest in your criticism as possible. (You might prefer marking in pencil, to be erased in the event you wish to repeat this exercise later.)

It is difficult / to monitor my speech / consciously / when I am composing sentences.**B** I become so engrossed / with the ideas / I want to express,**B** the choice of words / to express those ideas, / the grammar and syntax,**B** that I don't seem to find time / to monitor my speech.**B** Reading something / that someone else has written / is easier / than composing speech / as I talk,**B** because all I must do in reading / is to convey the author's ideas.**B** Even reading, however, / requires considerable thought / by the reader.**B** The ideas / inherent in the author's words **B** must be internalized by the reader / before he can project them / to an audience.

Now that you have made a simultaneous judgment, you are ready to double-check your performance. The same selection is reprinted below. Cover up the selection above so that you will not see your first markings. Replay your tape recording and re-criticize what you hear. Mark with a √ on the selection below each spot where you faded. After you finish, compare your second judgment with your simultaneous criticism. Did you hear all of the fades as you were reading? Were your kinesthetic symptoms of loss of exhalation control also spots where you faded? When you can train your auditory and kinesthetic monitoring to inform you reliably of your vocal intensity, your fading will be conquered.

It is difficult to monitor my speech consciously when I am composing sentences. I become so engrossed with the ideas I want to express, the choice of words to express those ideas, the grammar and syntax, that I don't seem to find time to monitor my speech. Reading something that someone else has written is easier than composing speech as I talk, because all I must do in reading is to convey the author's ideas. Even reading, however, requires considerable thought by the reader. The ideas inherent in the author's words must be internalized by the reader before he can project them to an audience.

PART TWO • Laryngeal Control for Vocalization

THE MECHANISM OF VOCAL FOLD VIBRATION

The source of the vocal tone is the *larynx*. We cannot say that *voice as we hear it* comes from the larynx, because the basic tone is modified and amplified by resonance after it leaves the larynx, and is shaped into meaningful sound symbols of language by the articulators before we hear it.

The larynx, part of the respiratory mechanism, is a valve between the air passages of the mouth, nose, and pharynx above, and the trachea and lungs below. In structure, it is a modification of the top two cartilage rings of the trachea, which serve as the housing for the muscular valve within and the point of attachment for certain other muscles and cartilages which operate the laryngeal valve. You may locate your own larynx (also popularly called the "voice box") by your "Adam's apple," the front prominence of the largest laryngeal cartilage. If your "Adam's apple" does not show prominently, you can feel it if you run your finger tip down the front midline of your neck just beneath the point of your chin (Figure 2). You should find a hard structure with a sharp upper border having a tiny V-notch exactly in front (Figure 14). If you hold your finger on this cartilage while you say "ah," you can feel the vibration transmitted from inside the larynx.

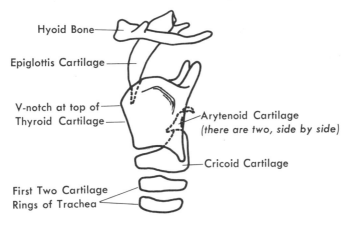

Hyoid Bone

Epiglottis Cartilage

V-notch at top of Thyroid Cartilage

Arytenoid Cartilage *(there are two, side by side)*

Cricoid Cartilage

First Two Cartilage Rings of Trachea

Fig. 14 Cartilages of the Larynx

(viewed from left side)

The larynx is a midline structure. Its right and left halves are identical, like the two sides of the face. The opening of the valve within the larynx, called the *glottis*, is a slit running from front to back at the midline (Figure 3-A). When you inhale, this slit widens at the back, making the glottis triangular (Figure 3-B). Before you can hold your breath, cough, clear your throat, or phonate, the glottis must be closed in the slit shape.

To visualize the laryngeal structure, let us suppose we cut the larynx open, making a vertical slice from right side to left, so that we could remove the front half and look into the back half (Figure 15). We would see the air

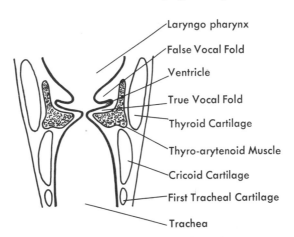

Laryngo pharynx

False Vocal Fold

Ventricle

True Vocal Fold

Thyroid Cartilage

Thyro-arytenoid Muscle

Cricoid Cartilage

First Tracheal Cartilage

Trachea

Fig. 15. Coronal Section of the Larynx

(a vertical cut from side to side)

passage of the trachea narrow upward like a cone. At the top of this cone are the *vocal folds*, the two shelves or folds of tissue extending toward the midline from the sides of the larynx. The medial edges of the vocal folds, which are covered with a glistening whitish elastic tissue, are called the *vocal bands*. The space between the vocal folds is the *glottis*. Above the vocal folds, left and right, are small caverns or pockets in the tissue called *ventricles*. Above them is a second pair of tissue folds, extending from the sides toward the midline, called *false vocal folds*. Above the false vocal folds, the air passage gradually widens, like an inverted cone. The upper laryngeal valve, composed of the false vocal folds, works efficiently to keep air, liquid, or food out of the larynx. It prevents food and drink from entering the lungs when you swallow and keeps air out of your lungs when you enter a room filled with noxious gases or smoke. We are more concerned with the lower laryngeal valve, formed by the true vocal folds, which functions best as a regulator of outgoing air, or exhalation. Let us now see how the vocal folds function to initiate a sound wave.

THE NATURE OF VOCAL FOLD VIBRATION

As we noted in Chapter 1, an airborne sound wave is a progression of alternating areas of condensation and rarefaction of air molecules. A source of sound creates a sound wave by movement which displaces molecules of air. At one time it was thought that two bands of tissue (or "cords" as they were often called) in the larynx vibrated as exhaled air passed across them, much as a string on a violin vibrates when a bow rubs across it. High-speed motion pictures of the actual vocal fold vibration [5] reveal that the sound source behaves more like a siren (a disc perforated by small holes through which an air jet blows in rapid succession). As each pressurized puff of air is emitted through a hole in the siren's disc, it moves out as the condensation phase of a single wave cycle, to be followed by a rarefaction phase. The number of cycles produced per second is the frequency of vibration, which, in turn, determines the pitch we hear. Essentially this is the nature of sound production in the larynx.

Let us consider the laryngeal mechanics of producing a single cycle of the sound wave — a band of condensed air molecules followed by a band of rarefied molecules as they are emitted from the glottis. When we hear a vocal tone with a pitch of middle C, the frequency of vibration at the glottis is 256 cycles per second. A single cycle at that pitch would take only $\frac{1}{256}$ second to complete. Clearly, the process which follows happens very fast.

Before vibration from the glottis can occur, the glottis must close. The vocal folds are pulled together at the midline and adjusted for proper elasticity (the ability to spring back into position after being displaced by air

---

[5] Bell Telephone Laboratories released pictures of vocal fold vibration at 4000 frames per second in 1940. The most recent and revealing high speed laryngeal films were released by Paul Moore and Hans vonLeden. Studies of vocal fold vibration by high-speed photography continue in a number of locations.

pressure). Thus the vocal folds are *adducted* (pulled together) and ready to react to the force of exhaled air. Simultaneously, the exhaled breath moves upward through the trachea, beneath the glottis. As molecules enter the sub-glottal arched cone, those moving along the walls have farther to travel than those in the center of the tube (Figure 16) and therefore move faster and exert less pressure.[6] This negative pressure "sucks" the vocal bands together tightly. Then the upward pressure of air molecules in the center of the cone bursts through the glottis, causing *abduction* (opening of the vocal bands) and ejection of a puff of condensed air molecules. The next cycle begins when the vocal bands spring back together because of their elasticity and the sucking inward from the negative pressure beneath them. Since the air flow is momentarily interrupted when the glottis is closed, a band of rarefied air molecules moves after the band of condensed molecules.

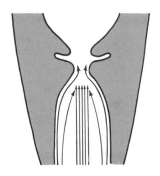

Fig. 16 Air Movement in the Larynx to Produce Vocal Fold Vibration

(Bernoulli effect)

The force which produces the vibration is the exhaled air stream. The actual source of the tone is the pair of vocal folds, vibrating much like the lips of a trumpet player. Neither the vocal folds nor the breath stream alone can produce voice. A delicate synchronization of the two mechanisms is necessary — particularly to regulate the loudness, pitch, and quality of the vocal tone. Misuse of the laryngeal mechanism can result not only in inefficient performance but also in actual damage. Therefore, it is advisable that you learn how the larynx operates and what controls you can exercise in making your own voice more effective and dependable.

PHYSIOLOGY OF THE LARYNX

Five principal cartilages and one small bone comprise the laryngeal framework (Figure 14). They are literally suspended in the neck, between the jaw bone and skull above, and the breast bone below. *Extrinsic muscles* position the larynx in the neck. They are capable of pulling it high under the chin or depressing it toward the breast bone. *Intrinsic muscles* attach solely to points within the laryngeal structure. They regulate the characteristics of the glottis

---

[6] This characteristic of the movement of gases is called the Bernoulli effect, after the physicist who formulated the principle.

which affect the nature of phonation and other functions such as breathing, coughing, etc.

The five principal cartilages of the larynx are shown in Figure 14. The large double shield-shaped cartilage, the *thyroid* cartilage, is the one you felt in your neck as your Adam's apple. It has downward-pointing legs on each side which articulate with the *cricoid* cartilage below it. The cricoid cartilage is shaped like a signet ring, with the signet facing to the back. Perched on top of the signet of the cricoid cartilage is the pair of small, pyramid-shaped *arytenoid* cartilages, which are extremely important to voice inasmuch as all but one pair of the intrinsic muscles of the larynx attach to them. The pull of muscles against these cartilages determines the nature of the sound produced in the larynx.

With one exception (the transverse-arytenoid), all the intrinsic muscles of the larynx are paired — that is, duplicated on the left and the right. In fact, the left half of the larynx is the mirror image of the right half. Symmetry in the two halves of our bodies is well recognized. For instance, the same muscles are duplicated in both arms. A muscle in one can contract independently of the identical muscle in the other. However, in the normal larynx, a muscle on one side always contracts when the same muscle on the opposite side contracts.

The vocal folds themselves have muscular tissue within them (Figures 3, 15, and 17-B). These muscles (the *thyro-arytenoid* muscles) attach side by side within the forward angle of the thyroid cartilage and run back to the arytenoid cartilages. When they contract, they grow shorter and thicker.

Adduction (closing the glottis by moving the vocal folds together at the midline) is effected by three sets of muscles. Working together, the *arytenoid* muscles, which consist of a pair of oblique muscles and a single transverse muscle (Figure 17-A), and the pair of *lateral crico-arytenoid* muscles (Figure 17-B) slide and tilt the arytenoid cartilages together so that the points where the vocal bands attach to them are brought face to face. Also, the pair of *thyro-arytenoid* muscles within the vocal folds (Figure 17-B) pulls the arytenoid cartilages closer together. These concerted muscular contractions bring the vocal bands together by bringing the arytenoid cartilages to which they attach together.

Of course, this process of muscular adduction does not have to be repeated for each vibratory cycle of the vocal folds.[7] At the beginning of phonation, the vocal folds are adducted. They remain adducted until the end of that sequence of spoken syllables which requires voice. Obviously, there are varying degrees of adduction. For holding the breath, tight adduction is necessary. For speech, the vocal folds must be held at the closed position, with just enough tension to allow them to be forced apart by sub-glottic

[7] The neuro-chronaxic theory of vocal fold vibration, which proposed that a separate nerve impulse causes muscular contraction for adduction of the vocal folds for each closing phase of the vibratory cycle, has been effectively refuted by Hollien and Moore. The description presented here is based on the myoelastic-aerodynamic theory of vocal fold vibration.

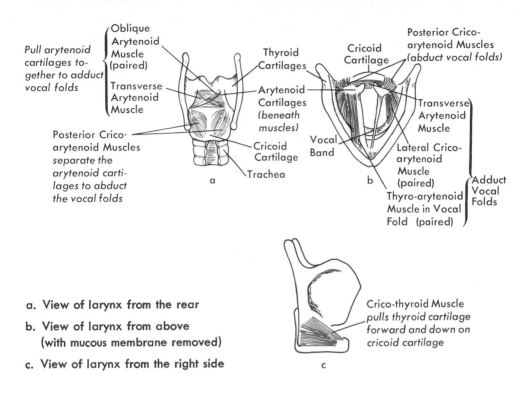

Pull arytenoid cartilages together to adduct vocal folds

Oblique Arytenoid Muscle (paired)

Transverse Arytenoid Muscle

Posterior Crico-arytenoid Muscles separate the arytenoid cartilages to abduct the vocal folds

Thyroid Cartilages

Arytenoid Cartilages (beneath muscles)

Cricoid Cartilage

Trachea

a

Cricoid Cartilage

Posterior Crico-arytenoid Muscles (abduct vocal folds)

Transverse Arytenoid Muscle

Vocal Band

Lateral Crico-arytenoid Muscle (paired)

Thyro-arytenoid Muscle in Vocal Fold (paired)

Adduct Vocal Folds

b

a. View of larynx from the rear

b. View of larynx from above (with mucous membrane removed)

c. View of larynx from the right side

Crico-thyroid Muscle pulls thyroid cartilage forward and down on cricoid cartilage

c

Fig. 17 Intrinsic Muscles of the Larynx

breath pressure, and enough elasticity to spring back together when the puff of compressed breath is released.

Abduction (separating the vocal folds) occurs in several ways. The abduction phase of vocal fold vibration is that part of the cycle when the folds are forced apart by pressure of sub-glottic air. This involves no muscular activity. Abduction during quiet breathing requires only the relaxation of adductor muscles, since the rest position for the glottis is open. When phonation stops at the end of an utterance or briefly for the production of a voiceless consonant,[8] abduction is also accomplished simply by relaxing the adductor muscles. When a wide glottal opening is needed, as in forced inhalation, abduction is accomplished by contraction of the pair of *posterior crico-arytenoid* muscles (Figure 17-A), causing the arytenoid cartilages to slide outward to further separate the vocal folds.

Length and *thickness* of the vocal folds are two variables of phonation[9]

[8] Consonants such as /t/, /s/, /f/ are called voiceless because they are produced with unphonated breath. Thus for a word like **sit** the vocal folds would be abducted for /s/, adducted for the vowel /ɪ/, and then abducted again for the /t/. These phonetic characteristics will be discussed in Chapter 6.

[9] Paul Moore and Hans vonLeden, films: "The Larynx and Voice: The Function of the Normal Larynx," January, 1957; "The Larynx and Voice: Physiology of the Larynx Under Daily Stress," Laryngeal Research Laboratory, William and Harriet Gould Foundation, Northwestern University, Chicago.

which appear to be inversely related. That is to say, the shorter the vibrating length of the vocal folds, the thicker they are; and conversely, the longer the vibrating length, the thinner they are. When the length is shortest, each vibrating vocal band looks like a squared-off ledge, with an upper and lower edge which meet and recede with each vibration. The lower edge *adducts* first, followed quickly by the upper edge. Then the lower edge *abducts* first, and the upper edge follows. As the vibrating length of the glottis is increased for higher pitch, each vocal band gradually thins out so that its cross-section mass diminishes. Each vibrating vocal band then appears to be a keen edge.

The antagonistic contraction of two sets of intrinsic muscles controls the length and thickness of the vocal folds. We have said that the vocal folds are, beneath a thin mucous membrane, a pair of muscles (the *thyro-arytenoids*) which attach inside the notch of the thyroid cartilage in front, and to each arytenoid cartilage in the back. When these muscles contract, they grow shorter and thicker unless stretched by some other force pulling against them. You know how a slingshot operates (Figure 18). When you want to stretch its rubber bands, you hold the sling steady with one hand and pull back on the handle with the other. You apply force in opposite directions by pulling against the two ends of the apparatus.

The contracted *thyro-arytenoid* muscles are lengthened in much the same way. One force pulls back on them, and another pulls forward against them. The *posterior crico-arytenoid* muscles (Figure 17-A, 17-B) pull backward on the arytenoid cartilages to which they attach. The forward pull is exerted on the thyroid cartilage, to which they attach in front. The thyroid cartilage is pulled forward and downward toward the cricoid cartilage by the *crico-thyroid* muscle on each side of the larynx (Figure 17-C). Unlike the rubber bands on the slingshot, the vocal folds are never stretched to a length greater than their relaxed length. This is because tension within them has a shortening effect, even though tension against them has a lengthening effect.

Elasticity of the vocal folds is their capacity for quick return to the adducted position after displacement by breath force. So far as we know, their elas-

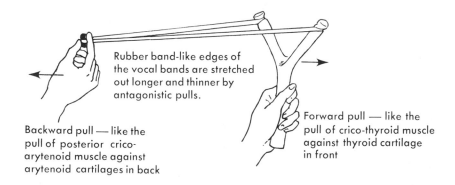

Rubber band-like edges of the vocal bands are stretched out longer and thinner by antagonistic pulls.

Backward pull — like the pull of posterior crico-arytenoid muscle against arytenoid cartilages in back

Forward pull — like the pull of crico-thyroid muscle against thyroid cartilage in front

Fig. 18   Slingshot Principle of Length-Mass Control of the Vocal Bands

ticity is determined by the tension within the *thyro-arytenoid* muscle (Figure 17-B), particularly those fibers nearest the midline (often called the *vocalis* muscle).

Intensity Control

How do these variables of laryngeal adjustment affect the vocal tone? *Increased intensity* of the vocal tone results from two factors: (1) the force of sub-glottic breath, and (2) the elasticity of the vocal bands. The *amplitude* of the vibration, or the amount of vocal fold opening with each breath explosion, increases as loudness increases. Also, there is a change in the time relationship between the successive glottal adjustments during a vibratory cycle as the loudness increases. The *timing* of a cycle, with phase relationships within it, has been measured from high-speed motion picture film of various speakers' phonation and plotted on graphs.[10] Figure 19 shows two typical graphs, one at low intensity, the other at high intensity. Comparison of such

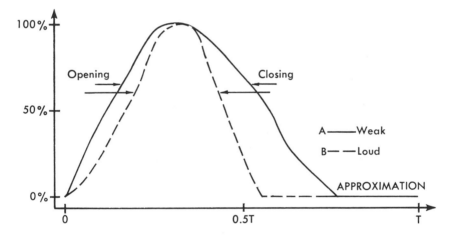

Fig. 19 Laryngeal Vibratory Cycles at Weak and Loud Intensities *

* From R. Timke, H. vonLeden, P. Moore, "Laryngeal Vibrations: Measurement of the Glottic Wave." (See footnote 10 below.)

graphs for numbers of speakers (at various pitch and intensity levels) produces the following conclusions: (1) the glottis opens more slowly for a loud tone than for a soft tone; (2) the glottis closes more quickly for a loud tone than for a soft tone; (3) the glottis remains closed longer for a loud tone than for a soft tone. (It was found that phase relationships did not change with change of pitch, only with changes of intensity.) This information has interesting implications. The increased portion of the cycle used for opening the vocal

[10] R. Timke, H. vonLeden, and P. Moore, "Laryngeal Vibrations: Measurement of the Glottic Wave," Part II, *American Medical Association Archives of Otolaryngology*, LXVIII (July, 1948), 11–19.

folds at loud intensity is related to the greater quantity of breath expelled at a single puff. The briefer time consumed in closing the glottis for loud voice relates to the greater elasticity of the vocal folds; also, this more abrupt closure propels the breath puff upward more forcefully. The longer period of the closure phase for loud voice is further evidence of the increased tension in the vocal bands; it allows time for a build-up of greater sub-glottic breath pressure for the explosion of the next cycle.

Pitch Regulation

Pitch changes in the vocal tone are regulated by varying the length and thickness of the vibrating vocal bands. Actual measurements from high-speed motion picture films showed progressive increase in the vibrating length of each subject's vocal bands as the pitch of the phonated tone rose.[11]

Though accurate measurement of the thickness (and mass) of the vibrating edge of a vocal fold has not been possible, observation of these films leads to the conclusion that as the vocal folds lengthen, their mass or thickness decreases. It is entirely possible that the specific mass or thickness of the vibrating band is the real determiner of pitch, rather than the actual length. For producing a particular pitch, the *actual* length of the vibrating vocal band is a bit shorter for a high male voice than for a low male voice, a bit shorter still for a low female voice, and even shorter for a high female voice.[12] Within the limits of pitches phonated by a single subject, the *relative* length was progressively greater with rise in pitch.[13]

The possibility of vocal strain when producing a loud voice at high pitch should be apparent. The combination of increased tension within the vocal fold for greater intensity and the thinning out of the edge of the vocal band when stretched for pitch rise creates an ideal situation for tissues to be irritated by friction in the adducted phase of the vibratory cycle. Continual abuse of this kind can be as injurious to the vocal bands as continual dancing in too-tight shoes is to the feet. This is one of the dangers in professional singing for a young teenager whose muscular adjustments have not been adequately trained. It also explains why screaming (cheering at a sports event, for example) can be injurious to the vocal folds.

PROBLEMS PRODUCED BY LARYNGEAL HYPERTENSION

Four quality problems relate to hypertension of laryngeal muscles. They are *harshness, hoarseness, glottal fry,* and *glottal shock.*

---

[11] H. Hollien, "Some Laryngeal Correlates of Vocal Pitch," *Journal of Speech and Hearing Research*, III (1960), 52–58.

[12] H. Hollien and G. P. Moore, "Measurements of the Vocal Folds During Changes in Pitch," *Journal of Speech and Hearing Research*, III (1960), 157–165.

[13] Falsetto, which extends to higher pitch levels than the normal range, does not require a further lengthening of the vocal folds. It involves a thinning out and relaxation of the vocal folds so that only the membrane covering the folds vibrates, with less amplitude of vibration and less adduction of the folds than in normal range.

Harshness

A *harsh* voice sounds hard, grating, strained, and tense. It has an unmusical sound, with dissonant noise elements in the tone. It is likely to be interpreted by the listener as cold and unsympathetic, or even overbearing and aggressive.

Harshness is produced by laryngeal hypertension, which involves both the tensor and the adductor mechanisms. Hypertension of the tensors (the *thyro-arytenoid* muscles) causes the vocal folds to "bang" together with excessive force and to stay closed too long within each vibratory cycle. This enables the speaker to use even a small breath pressure to the fullest; in fact, it may make him overloud. If the adductors (which draw the vocal folds together) are too tense, each vocal band tends to inhibit the vibration of the opposite one. Constriction of the larynx hampers the free vibration of the vocal folds. One pair of adductors, the *oblique* arytenoid muscles, runs above the arytenoid cartilages (as the *ary-epiglottic* muscles) and connects to the epiglottis. Hypertension there curls the epiglottis back and down against the larynx, compressing the false vocal folds against the vocal folds.[14] Either of these types of hypertension is likely to distort or inhibit the vibratory pattern of the vocal folds.

Corrective exercises for harshness are aimed at reducing hypertension in the tensor and adductor muscles of the larynx. If your voice is harsh, you should try all the exercises below and then practice those which work best for you until you establish new habits of phonation.

Relaxation is a word often carelessly and naively used. It is very easy to tell a person to relax, as though all he needs to do is to press a magic button and achieve instant results. It is not that simple, and you will accomplish more if you face this fact realistically.

In the first place, you have to learn how progressive stages of relaxation *feel* in order to recapture them. Whatever your present habitual state of tension in the muscles under discussion, that state seems normal and natural to *you*. If you protest, "But I couldn't feel more relaxed than I am!" you are reacting quite normally. You know only what you have experienced, not what you have *not* experienced.

Second, you do not control the amount of tension in a muscle by an act of will, as you might turn down the thermostat a few degrees. You must content yourself with what seems like roundabout methods. You control muscles not by thinking muscle tension or relaxation, but by thinking of performing certain activities which involve the muscles in question.

RELAXATION OF NECK AND LARYNGEAL MUSCLES. The following exercises do not change your voice quality instantaneously, like shifting gears in a car. As you perform them, keep in mind your true purpose: to learn how your

---

[14] Such an observation was first made in examinations of the larynx during speech by means of a laryngoperiscope, reported in: G. Oscar Russell, *Speech and Voice* (New York: Macmillan Company, 1931).

throat feels when your laryngeal muscles are more relaxed so that the memory of this kinesthetic sensation can help you control the degree of muscle tension in the future. While you are performing the exercises, you should also listen attentively, because any improvement in quality is evidence of achievement. However, you may become conscious of kinesthetic differences which point toward improvement even before your voice sounds noticeably better.

Relaxation of neck muscles, including the extrinsic laryngeal muscles, can help reduce excess tension in the intrinsic laryngeal muscles. Try the following exercises for developing an awareness of reduced neck tension.

1. *Head Rotation.* Sit comfortably erect in a chair without a headrest. Let your head drop forward toward your chest. Now let it flop over toward your right shoulder, then backward, to your left shoulder, and down toward your chest. Move it slowly, nudging it from one position to another, not just twisting it around and around. Think of your neck as limber and your head as heavy. You will feel the neck muscles stretch on the side opposite the inclination of your head; this is not tension but the extension of relaxed muscles. When your neck feels relaxed, phonate a prolonged "ah" softly, then louder. Does your throat feel more relaxed? Does your tone sound less harsh? Can you keep the same relaxed feeling on the loud and the soft tone?

2. *General to Selective Relaxation.* Since correcting harshness requires the reduction of excessive tension in particular muscles, it would be unrealistic to try to be totally relaxed when talking. Even to hold up your head there must be antagonistic tension in muscles on opposite sides of your neck. Your aim in this exercise is to relax selectively the specific laryngeal muscles which adduct and tense the vocal folds. Even in these particular muscles, reduction of *excessive* tension is the goal, not the elimination of all tension. After all, some tension is necessary for their normal function. Good voice quality does not require flaccid muscles all over the body, or even within the larynx. Yet in learning to perceive the kinesthesia of reduced tension in the larynx, it is helpful to experience first general relaxation and then selective relaxation.

Lie on your back comfortably, but preferably not elevating your head too sharply. Think of untying knots in the muscles of your spine, your legs, your arms, your neck. Think of being passively supported by the bed, letting yourself sink heavily into its firm support. If convenient, have someone else test your relaxation by lifting a foot, then an arm, to see if you have eliminated your muscle resistance.

Inhale deeply and then let the breath release immediately like the flow of the tide. Inhale again, deeply, and phonate an easy, prolonged "ah." Try to remember the relaxed sensation of your neck as you sit up and then stand up. Try to avoid tension in the neck by thinking of your head as a fragile object lightly balanced on the stem of your neck. Again, inhale deeply without increasing neck tension, and exhale on a gentle, prolonged "ah." Did you experience selective reduction of tension in your throat?

3. *Rag Doll Exercise.* This is a variation of Exercise 2 which is more convenient to practice when you are not in your bedroom. Instead of lying on a

bed to achieve the sensation of total bodily relaxation, sit in a chair with your knees together. Drop your body forward so that your shoulders rest on your knees and your head and arms hang limply like a rag doll. Notice the release of tension in your shoulders and neck. Sit up, keeping the relaxed feeling in shoulders and neck as much as possible. Inhale deeply but with minimum throat tensions, and phonate a prolonged, soft "ah." Did you carry over the general relaxation to the more selective relaxation of the larynx? Did your throat feel different on phonation? Did the tone sound less harsh?

4. *Contrast Tension and Relaxation.* In a chair with a headrest or with your chair backed against the wall, sit stiffly erect. Raise your shoulders. Pull in your chin firmly. Tighten the neck muscles as much as you can. Relax. Let your head drop back lazily against the headrest of your chair or the wall. Let your shoulders slump. Phonate a prolonged, soft "ah" on several successive breaths, noting the sound of your voice and the decrease of tension in your throat. Say softly, "How lazy I feel," and "This is easy," monitoring your voice production with audition and kinesthesia.

5. *Open Throat.* With your neck as relaxed as you can make it, yawn, letting your mouth open easily, without inhibition. Feel the openness of the passageway through your mouth and throat. Now pretend that you are going to yawn, imitating the muscular adjustment of the open throat. Inhale with the throat open, feeling the free passage of air through your pharynx and larynx. Now phonate an easy "ah" and prolong it, noting the sound of your voice quality and trying to sense the decrease in throat tension.

6. *Lax-vowels Reading.* Vowel phonemes which require less tongue tension in articulation tend to be produced with less harshness than tense vowels. Apparently, the reduction in tension of the tongue relates to reduction of tension in the throat and larynx as well. Reading exercises which are full of lax-vowel phonemes will give you a good opportunity for auditory and kinesthetic feedback of reduced tension. Read the following paragraph, preferably recording it for re-play. The lax vowels should encourage a reduction of hypertension, as should the ideas expressed in the passage.

> I am sitting in a comfortable chair. I will let my head lie back against the soft headrest. My head is gently resting. My neck muscles are relaxed. My arms are hanging limply at my sides. My hands are resting on the arms of the chair. My fingers are relaxed. My wrists are relaxed. My arms are relaxed. I will untie the tension in the muscles of my spine. My back is relaxed. My body is relaxed. I am as limp and relaxed as a rag doll. I will fill my lungs with breath. I will pull breath in gently. I will let my breath out in a gentle sigh.

You will find additional exercises suited to this purpose in Chapter 5, in the sections dealing with the lax vowels /ɪ/, /ɛ/, /æ/, /ɑ/, /ɔ/, /ʊ/, /aɪ/, and /aʊ/.

7. *Stretch Head Backward.* Place your chair just far enough from the wall that when you lean your head back it will barely touch with your neck

stretched. Sit erect and rest the back of your head against the wall. Phonate "ah," gently prolonged. Stretching the front neck muscles in this manner tends to reduce tension in them and to alleviate any crowding of the larynx. Listen well to your vocal tone as you phonate "ah" repeatedly. You should note a reduction in harshness.

INCREASE OF BREATH FLOW ON PHONATION. The following exercises are based on the premise that harsh quality and breathy quality are at opposite ends of a continuum of glottal adjustment. Harshness involves *hyper*tension, breathiness *hypo*tension. If your voice is harsh, you can reduce the excess tension by deliberately changing toward breathiness. Obviously, it is a poor exchange if you merely swap one vocal problem for another. In exercises you will try to be breathy, to learn a different type of muscular control than you use when harsh. You should continue to practice, using your auditory and kinesthetic monitoring attentively, until you achieve a quality half way between harsh and breathy.

1. *Sigh phonation.* With your neck as relaxed as possible (precede this with exercises above if you need to), inhale deeply, keeping your throat as open as you can. Exhale on a prolonged vocalized sigh. A sigh is mostly breath. Listen for the breathy quality. Did your throat feel relaxed?

2. *Glide-down sigh.* Repeat Exercise 1 above, but begin phonation on a fairly high note and glide down fairly low in pitch during the sigh. Remember that your vocal folds become more relaxed as you lower the pitch. If your sigh was well supported with breath, your tone should have grown less harsh as you lowered the pitch.

3. *Sip breath and sigh.* Sip a deep breath (as you would sip a drink through a straw), feeling how your throat opens up with the inhalation. Now sigh a gentle, prolonged "ah," trying to keep the same open feeling in your throat which you felt on inhalation. Does your voice sound less harsh?

4. *The H-attack.* When you say a word beginning with the phoneme /h/, such as **high**, your vocal folds are abducted (separated) for the /h/. If you deliberately continue the breathy quality of /h/ through the vowel sound which follows, you will reduce the laryngeal tension on phonation. Since the glottal adjustments for harshness and breathiness are at opposite ends of a continuum, when you become more breathy, you automatically become less harsh. Pronounce each of the following words, concentrating on achieving a breathier quality on the vowel following /h/:

high   help   hello   how   horse   hold   head   happy

Read each of the following sentences, attempting to carry over the breathy quality of /h/ throughout all the words:

1. Hello, Helen.
2. Help Harry hoe.
3. Hold Henry's horse.

4. Harold has hiccoughs.
5. High heels hurt her feet.
6. How heavy is a hay fork?

Make a recording of the following reading. Before beginning to read, go through any of the exercises above which helped you achieve a greater feeling of throat relaxation. Suggested pauses are marked with **/** and appropriate places for inhalation with **B**. Be sure you have enough breath to support phonation at all times. Do not try to conserve your breath as you read, but deliberately try to sound breathy. *As you read*, make a spontaneous judgment of your control of harshness. Write a √ at any point where the tone sounded harsh to you, and an X at any point where you felt that your larynx was too tense.

Husbandless Hannah Hughes/ hounded Hazel Humphrey/ for helpful hints **B** on how Hazel/ had harnessed Harold Humphrey/ wholly for herself.**B** Here is a handful/ of the hundred hints/ Hazel handed Hannah.**B** Habitually herald his homecoming/ as a heaven-sent harvest.**B** Have a hot hash handy/ as he hails "Hello." **B** Highest on her list, however,/ was: "Have not a harsh voice,**B** for he who hears/ Hannah's harsh voice **B** hesitates/ to hold Hannah's hand." **B**

Hannah said,/ "I ought to take voice lessons," **B** and she did.**B** After that,/ every man she met **B** acted eager/ to become engaged to her **B** because she was absolutely/ irresistible.**B** But she accepted an offer/ to appear on television instead,**B** and accumulated/ an enormous/ fortune.**B**

Now re-play your recording and make a second evaluation. Without reference to the marks you made above, mark the following reprint of the reading, putting a √ at every point where you sounded harsh.

Husbandless Hannah Hughes hounded Hazel Humphrey for helpful hints on how Hazel had harnessed Harold Humphrey wholly for herself. Here is a handful of the hundred hints Hazel handed Hannah. Habitually herald his homecoming as a heaven-sent harvest. Have a hot hash handy as he hails "Hello." Highest on her list, however, was: "Have not a harsh voice, for he who hears Hannah's harsh voice hesitates to hold Hannah's hand."

Hannah said, "I ought to take voice lessons," and she did. After that, every man she met acted eager to become engaged to her because she was absolutely irresistible. But she accepted an offer to appear on television instead, and accumulated an enormous fortune.

Now compare your spontaneous judgment with your second judgment. Was your perception of harshness as good while you were reading as it was when you re-played the recording? Were your kinesthetic sensations of laryngeal tension reliable indications of harsh quality?

In which part of the selection did you make the most √ marks? Were your controls for reducing laryngeal tension more difficult to maintain during the second paragraph? Why? Did you notice that only the first word in that paragraph began with an /h/? The most troublesome words for you were probably those which began with vowel sounds. The second paragraph was designed as a test of the carry-over of your control. When you can read it without any harshness, you will have made real progress in reducing your laryngeal hypertension.

5. *Shorten breath spans.* Sometimes harshness occurs only toward the end of what is said on one exhalation when the speaker tries to force out expiratory reserve for phonation. If this is your problem, it may be that you are wasting breath near the beginning of the breath span. More commonly, though, the speaker tries to speak too many words on a single exhalation. Harsh voice quality, like the fading of vocal intensity at the ends of breath spans, results from the attempt to produce adequate loudness with inadequate breath support. The solution is to cut breath spans shorter, saying fewer words on each breath and inhaling more often. Review the discussions "Inhale at Sense Pause," (pp. 54–55) and "Prevent Fading of Vocal Intensity," (p. 57). Phrasing exercises may be found on pp. 154–156 in Chapter 4.

Hoarseness

Hoarseness sounds like strained or gargling breathiness. Escaping breath mixes with the tone, and sometimes there is no tone at all. There is evidence of considerable effort, or even discomfort, in the speaker's attempt to force a clear tone.

Temporary hoarseness is most frequently caused by acute laryngitis. Your physician will prescribe medication if you have an infection in the tissues of the larynx. Vocal abuse can also produce temporary hoarseness. Prolonged over-loud talking or yelling, particularly in the hypertense manner described under Harshness, constitutes vocal abuse. Loss of voice or hoarseness after a football game should be treated as a severe warning of injurious use of your voice. Frequently recurring attacks of laryngitis should not be accepted casually. If hoarseness persists for more than two weeks, consult your physician.

Hoarseness is produced by a combination of incomplete closure of the vocal folds and excessive strain of laryngeal muscles. When you have laryngitis, the mucous membrane covering the vocal folds is red and swollen from some localized infection or injury. The vocal fold edges are no longer straight; each of them bulges toward the midline. When the front part of the glottis closes, the back part stays open. When you strain to adduct the back part, you over-adduct the front part. The more you strain to eliminate the breathy sound, the tighter you press the swollen tissue together and the more you aggravate the irritation. Other physical problems in the larynx may also relate to hoarseness, and in some cases hoarseness exists as a functional problem (poor use of the laryngeal musculature). In any case, continual hoarseness signals poor vocal habits which demand retraining. If your voice is hoarse, whether you are assigned to a speech therapist for voice training or work solely in this class, you must follow a strict routine if you are to improve.

VOCAL REST. Vocal rest is commonly prescribed for hoarseness, sometimes in addition to and sometimes in place of medication. Your physician should decide. Your larynx is too valuable for you to take chances with home remedies and self-prescriptions.

Suppose you had been on a long hike and had developed blisters. Resting your feet would help the blisters to heal. If you had to walk, you would walk as little as possible and go barefoot. The best shoes to wear would be loose-fitting or sandals with open places where your blisters are. Now apply this analogy to vocal rest.

Complete silence is obviously the truest application of vocal rest. In certain problems with the vocal folds, complete silence is often prescribed. This means no talking at all for a period of weeks. During that time you would use sign language, write messages on a pad, or shun people, but you would not talk under any circumstances.

REDUCTION OF VOCAL ABUSE. In some fortunate cases, a less severe regimen than absolute silence will enable irritated or swollen vocal folds to heal. Obeying these rules will reduce the continuing injury to the vocal folds:

(1) Drastically reduce the quantity of speech. Talk only when absolutely essential. Cut out all the useless chatter which enriches living but abuses your vocal folds. When you have to talk, say as few words as you can to accomplish your purpose. If your friends are likely to think you have suddenly turned anti-social, print a sign which explains your problem and show it to everybody.

(2) Reduce the loudness of speech. As we have seen, loud phonation involves more forceful and faster closing together of the vocal folds, with a longer period of complete closure. This means that for loud voice there is more opportunity for the irritated tissues of the vocal folds to be slapped, rubbed, and squeezed together. The softer you talk, the more gently the vocal folds close together and the shorter their adduction time.

(3) Reduce laryngeal tension. All of the exercises on Harshness are applicable (except that you do not increase loudness of the tone, until your throat has healed.) Deliberately try to make your voice as breathy as possible to reduce tension. This is difficult because the person who is hoarse usually dislikes a breathy quality and in fighting it merely increases his hoarseness. Keep in mind that the breathier the tone, the less laryngeal abuse and the faster the recovery.

(4) Often it is necessary to change the modal pitch. (For a discussion of modal pitch, with exercises, see Chapter 4.) The specific cause of the hoarseness determines whether the pitch should be raised or lowered if it is changed.

GENTLE ADDUCTION OF THE VOCAL FOLDS. Chronic hoarseness sometimes results from difficulty in bringing the vocal folds closely enough together, no matter how much the person may strain. Rather than being held apart by swollen or excess tissue, in these cases there may be a space between the vocal folds at some point. If your physician has described your problem in this way, he will also indicate the line of treatment. Vigorous efforts toward adduction would follow the types of exercises given for Breathiness beginning on page 78. A gentler regimen for inducing the vocal folds to adduct follows.

Humming. *Hum* lightly a short tone on each note you can sing up the scale; then hum down the scale. Be sure to have ample breath to support the tone. Inhale frequently. Find a pitch level where the tone is clearest with least effort.

Next, practice prolonging a hummed tone (still not a loud tone) on the note you can produce most clearly and easily. Try to produce a slight increase of loudness on that note without becoming hypertense.

M and N Words. After you have learned to prolong a fairly clear, weak humming tone, practice words beginning with /m/, then words beginning with /n/, using the initial nasal consonant as a springboard to help you produce a clearer tone throughout the word. Read the list gently, inhaling before each word:

mop	met	mittens	mirth	moon	mice	mouth	maybe
mob	medicine	mix	murmur	move	my	mouse	maple
mad	medical	myth	moth	moose	mine	mountain	me
matter	metal	mud	mall	music	mile	mound	mean
map	merry	mother	mood	municipal	mind	make	meal

need	nil	neck	knack	nautical	noon	night
niece	nip	net	knock	nobody	knew	knife
neat	name	nest	nod	nose	news	now
knee	nail	gnat	not	note	nine	noun
knit	naked	nap	naughty	nook	nice	noise

M and N Sentences. After achieving reliable adduction on single words, try to extend your control to whole sentences, such as the following:

1. Mother knits many mittens.
2. Martin makes much money.
3. Nobody knows Nancy Noodle.
4. Mary's measles made Mary miserable.
5. Milking machines make much noise.
6. Mild-mannered Mabel married meek miserly Marvin.
7. Mark Mabley marched many many miles.
8. Millions made money in the market in March.

Obviously, the control you learn from /m/ and /n/ words must be applied in your general speech. Auditory and kinesthetic monitoring will help you establish better laryngeal control.

Glottal Fry

Glottal fry derives its name from the fact that the sound produced at the glottis resembles the noise of frying in a skillet. Variously described as rattling, gravelly, gargling, cracking, ticker-like, and the sound of rapidly popping corn, glottal fry sounds strained, extremely low-pitched, and more noisy than tonal. It usually occurs toward the end of a breath span.

During glottal fry, the vocal folds become extremely tense and compressed, with thin, taut edges, although the pitch drops as much as a full octave where glottal fry sets in. The arytenoid cartilages remain tightly pressed together. The glottal fry vibration of the vocal folds has been observed as syncopated, with greatly reduced amplitude.[15] The predominant characteristics of glottal fry are the extreme tension and stiffness of vocal folds in comparison to an apparent drop in sub-glottic breath pressure. Continual glottal fry, like hypertense phonation, can be injurious to the vocal folds.

If you have glottal fry at the ends of breath spans, you are probably trying to force phonation beyond the point of adequate breath support. Glottal fry is a type of harshness which appears particularly when phonation is continued after breath has been depleted.

Since glottal fry most often coincides with a drop in pitch at the end of a sentence, the pitch drop is thought to be a contributing cause. If your modal pitch is too low,[16] when you need to drop pitch several notes at the end of a sentence, you may attempt to force pitch lower than you can normally produce it.

The following exercise can help you prevent glottal fry:

1. Using one of the methods presented in Chapter 4, pp. 167–168, find your optimum pitch.
2. Sing a glide down from optimum pitch to a tone four notes lower on the musical scale; level off on the lowest note and hold it. Repeat over and over, making sure each time that you have good breath support to the very end. Check for any signs of increasing tension in the throat. Do not *push* the tone lower. Let it glide down easily, gently. Give attention to auditory and kinesthetic feedback.
3. Practice the Slide-Down Exercise in Chapter 4, pp. 186–187.
4. Read aloud any material you choose. In advance, mark each place where you will need to drop your pitch to end a statement. Anticipate your breath needs. Inhale before you exhaust your breath supply. At

[15] G. P. Moore and H. vonLeden, "Dynamic Variations of the Vibratory Pattern in the Normal Larynx," *Folia Phoniatrica*, X, No. 4 (1958), 224–233.
[16] For a discussion of modal pitch, see Chapter 4, pp. 164–168 and p. 170.

the end of each sentence, depend on breath for the strength of your voice. Instead of straining to force the tone, relax your throat and let your tone glide down on a firm cushion of breath.

Glottal Shock

Glottal shock, an intermittent quality disturbance rather than an overall problem, sounds like an explosive, hard, abrupt onset of phonation for an initial vowel sound.

To produce glottal shock, the vocal folds adduct quite firmly until sufficient sub-glottal breath pressure builds up to burst them apart. The firm closure and abrupt opening of the folds present an opportunity for momentary friction of opposing tissues, and could cause damage if repeated continually. At the release of a glottal shock there is general disorganization of vocal fold vibration, rather similar to the disturbance of the glottis caused by a cough. Excessive use of glottal shock tends to cause laryngeal hypertension (and harshness) throughout speech.

Though too much glottal shock is injurious to the speaker's larynx and unpleasant to the listener's ears, used judiciously it is an effective device. A glottal shock is extremely valuable as a marker for strong emphasis. Suppose your roommate is irritated because something is lost and begins to intimate that someone else has mislaid it. Now if you say, "You don't think *I* had it, do you?" with really strong emphasis, you will — and you should — begin the word **I** with a glottal shock. Without glottal shock, the word lacks force.

Glottal shock is frequently used to separate vowels for greater clarity. Words like **reemphasized** and **coexist** are clearer, particularly in public speaking, if a glottal shock is used between the prefix and the root.

The principal problem with glottal shocks is over-use. If you use them to begin almost every initial vowel, whether emphasized or not, you are over-using them. Read the following sentences, preferably recording them on tape to play back:

1. Alice always eats oranges every afternoon.
2. If Edward acts envious, it is obviously affected.
3. Everybody admires Irene's elegant artificial eyelashes.
4. Ask Edna if Edith ever arrived at Atlanta.

If you used more than two glottal shocks in any one of those sentences, you were overdoing it. Since every word in these sentences begins with a vowel, this is a good test of your use of glottal shocks.

Two techniques help to reduce the indiscriminate use of glottal shocks: (1) Learn to begin phonation more gradually. Producing a glottal shock requires a tight closing of the glottis and an abrupt explosion of breath in the first cycle of vibration. The opposite way of beginning phonation is to start with the vocal folds separated, as for /h/. When you practice the following pairs of words, feel the ease of beginning phonation on the vowel following an /h/, and then try to imitate this easy, gradual beginning of phonation on the second word of each pair, which does not begin with an /h/.

heat — eat	head — Ed	hoe — owe
heel — eel	hat — at	hold — old
hit — it	hacked — act	whose — ooze
his — is	hotter — otter	high — I
hate — ate	hod — odd	hide — I'd
hail — ale	haul — all	howl — owl

(2) Practice linking the end of one word to the beginning of the next. Only the words which begin with vowels are problem spots, remember. Try the following reading, which is marked with ‿ for linking. For additional practice, mark reading material for yourself, remembering to carry over a final consonant to begin the next vowel.

> If‿I studied‿as much‿as you said‿I should,/ then‿I would not
> get‿enough sleep‿and‿I would‿often doze‿in‿all my classes/
> and‿incur the wrath‿of‿every professor‿I have.

PROBLEM OF LARYNGEAL HYPOTENSION

Breathy Quality

Hypotension (inadequate tension) of laryngeal muscles frequently produces a quality distortion called *breathiness*. A breathy quality, which sounds like escaping breath in addition to or instead of the vocal tone, may range from a whisper to an over-relaxed, husky tone which is not quite clear. Some actresses have cultivated breathiness to sound overly-feminine, submissive, or coquettish. And certain actors have used a breathy voice to sound sinister and villainous.

In both breathiness and hoarseness, the vocal folds are not adequately adducted, resulting in an escape of unphonated breath. In hoarseness, there is strain to prevent the escape of breath; in breathiness, strain is not present.

Low loudness level is common in the breathy voice. A deliberate increase in loudness is often effective in decreasing general breathiness of the vocal tone. In order to produce a louder tone, the vocal folds must adduct faster and remain adducted longer during each vibratory cycle. If you have a breathy tone and can increase your loudness at will, note the effect of increased loudness on the breathiness.

Use of excessively low pitch produces breathiness in some voices. When you attempt to speak at the lowest pitch level you can phonate, you shorten your vocal bands as much as possible. The result may be overrelaxation and breathiness. Try speaking at various pitch levels and compare the clarity of the vocal tone. Do you sound as breathy when your pitch is higher? If you need to establish a new pitch level for speaking, refer to the section on Optimum Pitch in Chapter 4.

Exercises for increasing tension in the larynx produce better adduction of the vocal folds and prevent leakage of breath. The following exercises create situations in which you are most likely to achieve the desired degree of laryngeal tension so that you can learn the kinesthesia of muscle adjustment and remember the sound of your voice when less breathy. Exercises in themselves do not change your voice. If properly performed, they train you to monitor your voice more reliably. Also, they give you patterns of good performance to aim at the next time you practice, eventually to be habituated for all your speech.

1. *Vertical push-ups.* Stand facing the wall an arm's length away from it. Place your palms against the wall at shoulder height. Let your body incline forward until your weight rests against your hands. Now push yourself back to an erect posture by strength of your arms. While you are pushing, say, "All right," or "Arms extended," or some other sentence which starts with a vowel sound. Feel the increased tension in your shoulders and neck muscles. Listen to your voice for the firmness and clarity of tone.

2. *Spring up from sitting.* Sit in a straight chair. Lift your arms free of contact with the chair or your own knees. Pull your feet back underneath your knees so that your weight will be balanced, and spring up from the chair without help from your hands and arms. As you rise from the chair, say, "All right" or some other sentence beginning with a vowel sound. This activity requires concerted action of many muscles of the legs and torso. The general increase in muscle tension is likely to carry over to your larynx to cause better adduction. Concentrate on the kinesthesia of increased tension in the muscles of your neck and the greater clarity in the vocal tone.

3. *Hold a book shoulder high.* Stand tall, with your weight balanced on both feet, preferably on the balls of your feet. Hold a book suited to your strength with both hands, keeping your elbows shoulder high. Maintaining this position, count firmly: 81–82–83–84–85. Repeat several times, noting the kinesthesia of increased neck tension and the sound of firmer tone quality.

4. *Grip your chair.* Sit erect in a straight chair. Close your hands over the sides of the chair on each side of your lap. Grip hard, until you feel your arms and shoulders tense, and count firmly: 81–82–83–84–85. Note the neck tension and the reduced breathiness of your tone.

5. *Push the table.* Sit with your knees under a table. Place your hands, palm down on the table, on each side of you. Raise yourself off the chair, supported on your arms. As you push up, count 81–82–83–84–85. Note the kinesthesia of neck tension and the sound of your voice quality.

6. *Tighten the neck muscles.* While observing yourself in a mirror, tense your neck muscles until you can see them bulge. Hold this degree of tension while you say, "I am increasing adduction." Repeat several times, using the

appearance of your neck muscles to reinforce your kinesthetic and auditory monitoring.

7. *Glottal Shock Attack*. Earlier, glottal shock was explained as a bursting of compressed breath from a firmly closed glottis. To increase the tension of your adductor muscles, count 81–82–83–84–85, beginning each number with a definite glottal shock. Listen carefully to be sure you used firm glottal closure before each phonation. Remember the kinesthesia of this firm closure.

Breathiness on consonants is a problem which needs different treatment than general breathiness. Consonantal breathiness consists of the excessive release of breath on consonants which, because they are voiceless, are produced only with articulated breath. The consonant /s/ is one of the worst offenders, but any voiceless consonant might waste breath. Say the following list of words, preferably recording them, and listen to the amount of breath you release on the first consonant of each:

sing	shine	fine	thing	hold
toys	pie	cool	cheese	when

Pronounce the following words, listening to the amount of breath released at the end:

miss	mash	laugh	bath	not
up	back	match	ax	wished
laughed	missed	risk	act	patched

If you heard a considerable air wastage on the voiceless consonants in these words, the cure lies in a re-evaluation of time values. What you need to do is to cut the voiceless consonants shorter. Say the first group again, this time minimizing the voiceless consonants and strengthening the vowels, as suggested by the printing.

s**ing**	sh**ine**	f**ine**	th**ing**	h**old**
t**oys**	p**ie**	c**ool**	ch**eese**	wh**en**

Does this technique help you reduce air wastage on voiceless consonants?

Intermittent breathiness is so called because it occurs off and on rather than continuously. However, it is usually quite predictable in a pattern of speech behavior. It needs special mention because it nearly always has a different cause than general breathiness and therefore needs different treatment. General breathiness normally results from inadequate tension in the larynx. Intermittent breathiness more frequently results from poor control of the breathing muscles.

If you tend to be breathy at the beginnings of sentences and strained toward the ends of them, you are probably not using breathing muscles to control the rate of exhalation, with the result that the major part of an exhalation rushes out too quickly. When you begin to run out of breath toward the end of a sentence and try to conserve it for phonation by increasing laryngeal tension, your voice may become strained.

On the other hand, your breathiness may occur chiefly at the ends of sentences. This often combines with hypertension at the beginnings of sentences. If you try to control the rate of exhalation solely with the laryngeal muscles, you can do it only if you use a great deal of tension. You will sound strained in the process. However, because it is a difficult control to maintain, it is likely to break down and release excessive breath toward the ends of sentences.

The solution in both types of intermittent breathiness is to develop adequate control of exhalation in the breathing musculature. For specific suggestions, refer to the exercises on pp. 55–58.

READING SELECTIONS FOR PRACTICE

You should prepare a reading selection carefully if you hope to profit from the exercise. First, read the material through for meaning, underlining words which should be emphasized to convey that meaning best. Decide where pauses are needed to separate idea-units and mark / at each intended pause. To discover how frequently you need to inhale, experiment with reading the selection aloud. Be sure to inhale only at meaningful pauses, though, of course, you need not breathe at every pause. Mark **B** at each place you plan to inhale.

Analyze the reading for its danger spots for you. If your voice tends to fade or develop glottal fry, you will find it difficult to complete a long sentence on a single breath. Perhaps you should inhale at a pause somewhere within a sentence; or perhaps you should use breath more sparingly early in the sentence to avoid breathlessness at the end.

Analyze the phonemic content of the selection and use it to your advantage. Remember that reading a passage in which many words begin with /h/ or nasal consonants helps to relax the larynx. But if your voice is breathy, be careful to avoid wasting breath on voiceless consonants.

First, practice reading at a loudness level at which you achieve best vocal quality; then adapt loudness to audience needs after you gain control of quality. Breathiness normally diminishes as loudness increases. But control of harshness (or other hypertension problems) is easier at reduced loudness. Be sure to avoid laryngeal strain when you increase loudness; depend instead on breath support for projection.

Record the same reading a number of times, replaying and criticizing each recording. Do not attempt to criticize all aspects of your performance at once. For example, though you may note errors in articulation, give your major attention to voice quality and projection. Try to perceive your problems in quality and projection and locate the specific places where they were most evident. Above all, try to understand *why* your control failed at those precise times, so that you will be able to exercise conscious controls to improve successive performances.

A.   from *The Hills Beyond* [17]

The street itself was one of those shabby and nondescript streets whereon the passage of swift change and departed grandeur is strikingly apparent. Even at this dreary season and hour it was possible to see that the street had known a time of greater prosperity than it now enjoyed and that it had once been a pleasant place in which to live. The houses were for the most part frame structures in the style of that ugly, confused, and rather pretentious architecture which flourished forty or fifty years ago, and, so late at night, they were darkened and deserted looking. Many of them were set back in yards spacious enough to give an illusion of moderate opulence and security, and they stood beneath ancient trees, through the bare branches of which the wind howled mournfully. But even in the darkness one could see on what hard times the houses and the street had fallen. The gaunt and many-gabled structures, beaten and swept by the cold rain, seemed to sag and to be warped by age and disrepair, and to confer there dismally like a congress of old crones in the bleak nakedness of night and storm that surrounded them. In the dreary concealments of the dark, one knew by certain instinct that the old houses had fallen upon grievous times and had been unpainted for many years, and even if one's intuition had not conveyed this, the strangely mixed and broken character of the street would have afforded telling evidence of the fate which had befallen it. Here and there the old design of pleasant lawns had been brutally deformed by the intrusion of small, cheap, raw, and ugly structures of brick and cement blocks. These represented a variety of enterprises: one or two were grocery stores, one was a garage, some were small shops which dealt in automobile accessories, and one, the most pretentious of the lot, was a salesroom for a motor car agency. In the harsh light of a corner lamp, broken by the stiff shadows of bare, tangled boughs, the powerful and perfect shapes of the new automobiles glittered splendidly, but in this splendor there was, curiously, a kind of terrible, cold, and desolate bleakness which was even more cruel, lonely, and forbidding than all the other dismal bleakness of the dark old street.

THOMAS WOLFE

B.   These fashionable parties were generally confined to the higher classes, or noblesse, that is to say, such as kept their own cows and drove their own wagons. The company commonly assembled at three o'clock, and went away about six, unless it was in wintertime, when the fashionable hours were a little earlier, that the ladies might get home before dark. The tea table was crowned with a huge earthen dish, well

[17] Pp. 109–110 in *The Hills Beyond* by Thomas Wolfe. Copyright 1937, 1941 by Maxwell Perkins as Executor. Reprinted by permission of Harper & Row, Publishers.

stored with slices of fat pork, fried brown, cut up into morsels, and swimming in gravy. The company being seated around the genial board, and each furnished with a fork, evinced their dexterity in launching at the fattest pieces in this mighty dish — in much the same manner as sailors harpoon porpoises at sea, or our Indians spear salmon in the lakes. Sometimes the table was graced with immense apple pies, or saucers full of preserved peaches and pears; but it was always sure to boast an enormous dish of balls of sweetened dough, fried in hog's fat, and called doughnuts, or olykoeks — a delicious kind of cake, at present scarce known in this city, except in genuine Dutch families.

The tea was served out of a majestic delft teapot, ornamented with paintings of fat little Dutch shepherds and shepherdesses tending pigs, with boats sailing in the air, and the houses built in the clouds, and sundry other ingenious Dutch fantasies. . . . To sweeten the beverage, a lump of sugar was laid beside each cup, and the company alternately nibbled and sipped with great decorum, until an improvement was introduced by a shrewd and economic old lady, which was to suspend a large lump directly over the tea table, by a string from the ceiling, so that it could be swung from mouth to mouth — an ingenious expedient, which is still kept up by some families in Albany . . . .

WASHINGTON IRVING

C.   from *Introduction to Psychology* [18]

The concept of level of aspiration is a convenient and important one in understanding human motivation in a variety of situations. It will determine whether a person works hard, not so hard, or not at all at any given task. It may determine whether he aspires to a high school, college, or professional education, whether he prepares to be a plumber or doctor, and so on. Consequently, we are all familiar with differences in level of aspiration among the people we know, even if we have not consciously used the term or concept.

Level of aspiration has also been the subject of experimental work. In this work, a variety of situations has been employed. People may be presented with some problem to solve, for example, a puzzle, and asked to indicate how successful they think they will be in solving it. Students may be asked to state the grade they expect in an examination or intelligence test. Thus levels of aspiration may be measured. Then, with such measures, it is possible to determine how previous experience with a task, or performance in successive attempts at the task, can affect level of aspiration.

[18] From *Introduction to Psychology* by Clifford T. Morgan. Copyright © 1956 by Clifford T. Morgan. Used by permission of McGraw-Hill Book Company.

From studies of this sort we have learned that level of aspiration depends upon many factors. One is the individual characteristics of a person; some people have consistently low levels of aspiration, others quite high levels, and still others intermediate levels. Another factor is ego involvement, or self-esteem; a person's level is usually higher when he compares himself with a group of comparable ability than when his performance has nothing to do with anyone else. Students, for example, often seem as concerned with how many other students in a class received *A*'s as with whether they received them. Finally, of course, there is the factor of one's own performance. A person usually does not aspire to a performance far above that which he has been able to reach. If he fails to reach his aspiration, he usually lowers his level. On the other hand, if he achieves one level, he is likely to raise it a little. In general, people keep a level of aspiration that is slightly above their level of performance — at least most normal people do.

Clifford T. Morgan

D.　　　　*Stopping by Woods on a Snowy Evening* [19]

Whose woods these are I think I know.
His house is in the village though;
He will not see me stopping here
To watch his woods fill up with snow.

My little horse must think it queer
To stop without a farmhouse near
Between the woods and frozen lake
The darkest evening of the year.

He gives his harness bells a shake
To ask if there is some mistake.
The only other sound's the sweep
Of easy wind and downy flake.

The woods are lovely, dark and deep,
But I have promises to keep,
And miles to go before I sleep,
And miles to go before I sleep.

Robert Frost

[19] From *Complete Poems of Robert Frost.* Copyright 1923, 1930, 1939 by Holt, Rinehart and Winston, Inc. Copyright 1951, © 1958 by Robert Frost. Reprinted by permission of Holt, Rinehart and Winston, Inc.

E.   from *Please Don't Eat the Daisies* [20]

In the beginning we made the usual mistake of looking at houses we could afford. I am working on a proposition, hereafter to be known as Kerr's law, which states in essence: all the houses you can afford to buy are depressing. For months and months we followed happy, burbling real estate agents through a succession of ruins which, as the agents modestly conceded, "needed a little paint and paper to make them happy." These houses invariably had two small dark living rooms and one large turn-of-the-century kitchen — and I don't mean the nineteenth century. At my various feeble protests that I would like to get away from a pump in the kitchen, the agent was usually very stern. "If you want six bedrooms in your price range," he'd say, "you must expect an older house." Well, I did expect an older house, but not any older, say, than the battle at Harper's Ferry. I remember one house in Larchmont. No one knew when it had been built, but it had two cells in the basement and a tunnel going down to the Sound for the protection of runaway slaves. Looking back, it seems to me that we should have snapped up that place. With four boys, you never know when you're going to need an escape hatch.

JEAN KERR

F.   *Sonnet XXIX*

When, in disgrace with Fortune and men's eyes
I all alone beweep my outcast state,
And trouble deaf Heaven with my bootless cries,
And look upon myself and curse my fate,
Wishing me like to one more rich in hope,
Featured like him, like him with friends possessed,
Desiring this man's art, and that man's scope,
With what I most enjoy contented least;
Yet in these thoughts myself almost despising,
Haply I think on thee; and then my state,
Like to the lark at break of day arising
From sullen earth, sings hymns at heaven's gate;
    For thy sweet love remembered such wealth brings
    That then I scorn to change my state with kings.

WILLIAM SHAKESPEARE

G.   from *Ode on a Grecian Urn*

II

Heard melodies are sweet, but those unheard
　Are sweeter; therefore, ye soft pipes, play on;
Not to the sensual ear, but, more endeared,
　Pipe to the spirit ditties of no tone:
Fair youth, beneath the trees, thou canst not leave
　Thy song, nor ever can those trees be bare;
　　Bold Lover, never, never canst thou kiss,
Though winning near the goal — yet, do not grieve;
　　She cannot fade, though thou hast not thy bliss,
　For ever wilt thou love, and she be fair!

III

Ah, happy, happy boughs! that cannot shed
　Your leaves, nor ever bid the Spring adieu;
And, happy melodist, unwearied,
　For ever piping songs for ever new;
More happy love! more happy, happy love!
　For ever warm and still to be enjoyed,
　　For ever panting, and for ever young;
All breathing human passion far above,
　That leaves a heart high-sorrowful and cloyed,
　A burning forehead, and a parching tongue.

JOHN KEATS

H.   from *The Edge of Tomorrow* [21]

Finally the witch doctors put a "hex" on our hospital. They surrounded the compound with little mats of woven bamboo mounted on short posts stuck in the ground. That may sound silly. But, for all practical purposes, that hex worked like the proverbial charm. No one, no matter how desperately ill, would come near our hospital for help.

These witch doctors were all respected village elders. But our two most formidable adversaries were Old Joe and a crone we called Maggie.

So we decided to adopt an old American stratagem — "if you can't lick 'em, join 'em." Instead of antagonizing the witch doctors (and

[21] Reprinted from *The Edge of Tomorrow* by Thomas A. Dooley, by permission of Farrar, Straus & Giroux, Inc. Copyright © 1958 by Thomas A. Dooley.

this may raise the hackles of the American Medical Association), we began to treat them as "colleagues in the healing arts" who practiced a somewhat different discipline of medicine with which we disagreed and yet respected.

One afternoon I returned from an emergency call in the jungle to find Pete holding an earnest professional conference with Old Joe. Pete gave me the eye, and I squatted down and listened respectfully.

Old Joe had spread out before him a weird assortment of sticks, bamboo slivers, betel nuts, boiled leaves, pig grease, cow dung, and was explaining the theory behind his *materia medica*. Most of it was fantastic. But here and there I recognized fragments of the universal folk remedies (like the use of spider webs in open wounds), the effectiveness of which are acknowledged by modern medicine.

"Well," said Pete, "we just belong to different schools of medicine. We use different drugs, different methods, but we are both working for the same thing — to free the people from the evils of disease and suffering. The important thing is for us to work together. We'll teach you what we know, and you will teach us." That sounded fair enough to Old Joe.

From that time on Old Joe rarely missed a sick-call. We would administer a shot of penicillin, Joe would invoke the proper spirits. We would splint a fracture, then permit Old Joe to tie the indispensable red, white and black strings around the splints. If we were paid two coconuts for fee, Old Joe received one. (In America this practice is held in a bad light; they call it "fee splitting.")

THOMAS A. DOOLEY

I.   from *To A Skylark*

Hail to thee, blithe Spirit!
Bird thou never wert,
That from Heaven, or near it,
Pourest thy full heart
In profuse strains of unpremeditated art.

Higher still and higher
From the earth thou springest
Like a cloud of fire;
The blue deep thou wingest,
And singing still dost soar, and soaring ever singest.

PERCY BYSSHE SHELLEY

J. ### from *The Red Pony* [22]

The horse plodded stumble-footedly up the hill and the old man walked beside it. In the lowering sun their giant shadows flickered darkly behind them. The grandfather was dressed in a black broadcloth suit and he wore kid congress gaiters and a black tie on a short, hard collar. He carried his black slouch hat in his hand. His white beard was cropped close and his white eyebrows overhung his eyes like mustaches. The blue eyes were sternly merry. About the whole face and figure there was a granite dignity, so that every motion seemed an impossible thing. Once at rest, it seemed the old man would be stone, would never move again. His steps were slow and certain. Once made, no step could ever be retraced; once headed in a direction, the path would never bend nor the pace increase nor slow.

JOHN STEINBECK

K. ### from *Psalm* 8

When I consider thy heavens, the work of thy fingers, the moon and
  the stars, which thou hast ordained;
What is man, that thou art mindful of him? and the son of man, that
  thou visitest him?
For thou hast made him a little lower than the angels, and hast crowned
  him with glory and honour. . . .

L.   These are the times that try men's souls. The summer soldier and the sunshine patriot will, in this crisis, shrink from the service of his country; but he that stands it *now*, deserves the love and thanks of man and woman. Tyranny, like hell, is not easily conquered; yet we have this consolation with us, that the harder the conflict, the more glorious the triumph. What we obtain too cheap, we esteem too lightly; it is dearness only that gives everything its value. Heaven knows how to put a proper price upon its goods; and it would be strange indeed if so celestial an article as FREEDOM should not be highly rated.

THOMAS PAINE

[22] From *The Red Pony* by John Steinbeck. Viking Portable Edition, copyright 1946. Reprinted by permission of The Viking Press.

M.   from *Language: An Introduction to the Study of Speech* [23]

... It is ... true that in a certain sense the individual is predestined
to talk, but that is due entirely to the circumstance that he is born not
merely in nature, but in the lap of a society that is certain, reasonably
certain, to lead him to its traditions. Eliminate society and there is
every reason to believe that he will learn to walk, if, indeed, he survives
at all. But it is just as certain that he will never learn to talk, that is,
to communicate ideas according to the traditional system of a particular society. Or, again, remove the newborn individual from the
social environment into which he has come and transplant him to an
utterly alien one. He will develop the art of walking in his new environment very much as he would have developed it in the old. But his
speech will be completely at variance with the speech of his native
environment. Walking, then, is a general human activity that varies
only within circumscribed limits as we pass from individual to individual. Its variability is involuntary and purposeless. Speech is a human
activity that varies without assignable limit as we pass from social group to social group, because it is a purely historical heritage of
the group, the product of long-continued social usage. It varies as all
creative effort varies — not as consciously, perhaps, but none the less
as truly as do the religions, the beliefs, the customs, and the arts of
different peoples. Walking is an organic, an instinctive, function (not,
of course, itself an instinct); speech is a non-instinctive, acquired,
"cultural" function.

EDWARD SAPIR

3

Vocal Resonance: Its Relationship to Loudness and Quality

Resonance as an Acoustic Phenomenon

In the preceding chapter we discussed the creation of sound waves by the vibration of the vocal folds, activated by the force of exhaled breath. We also discussed frequency of vibration in relation to pitch of the vocal tone, and amplitude in relation to intensity. We noted that the vibration at the glottis forces molecules of the outgoing air into a pattern of condensation and rarefaction, which constitutes a sound wave. Our present concern is with that airborne sound wave, a forced vibration within a gaseous medium (exhaled air, largely CO_2), as it passes through the vocal tract above the glottis and out of the mouth or nose. Channelling and reflecting these airborne sound waves through the supra-glottal vocal tract produces resonance.

RESONANCE AMPLIFIES SOUND

The tone produced at the glottis is probably not loud enough to be heard very far away. This must be expressed as a probability, because no one has been able to listen to vocal tones immediately on their release from the glottis, since no subject has been found who could phonate with his head cut off at that point. We assume that the vocal tone needs amplifying because most sounds of musical instruments (e.g., the reed tone of a clarinet when

outside the clarinet, or the string tone of a violin when strung between ordinary pegs) are quite weak without amplification. The process which ampli-
fies and augments the intensity of the tone is called *resonance*.

Because it is a complex phenomenon, resonance is an often misunderstood
attribute of voice. The operation of resonance can be clarified by examples
from sound systems simpler than the human voice.

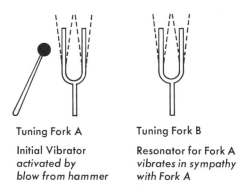

Tuning Fork A   Tuning Fork B

Initial Vibrator   Resonator for Fork A
activated by   *vibrates in sympathy*
blow from hammer   *with Fork A*

Fig. 1   Sympathetic Vibration

A tuning fork (Figure 1) is a bar of steel bent into a U shape, with a shank
attached. Constructed for musicians, each tuning fork is made in such pro-
portions that when struck, it will produce an exact frequency of vibration and
hence a precise pitch. Now suppose you have two tuning forks, A and B,
both with a frequency of 256 cycles per second. Hold them close together,
but not touching. Strike A with a small rubber hammer and it will begin to
vibrate, but its sound is not very loud. However, because it is tuned to the
same frequency, B, if held near A, will begin to vibrate in phase with A.
Tuning fork B acts as a resonator for fork A, and their combined vibration
produces a greater intensity than the vibration of fork A alone. This is *sympathetic vibration*, because the natural frequency of the second vibrating body
is the same as that of the body which set it into vibration.

Does resonance add energy to the initial sound? In the case of the tuning
forks just discussed, we can consider the oscillation or vibration of fork A as
representing an expenditure of energy. In movement it encounters friction,
which tends to reduce its efficiency. A single blow of the hammer gives fork
A only so much energy to expend. When part of that energy is transferred to
fork B, the total energy output per unit of time is greater, and the sound is
more intense. Fork B does not supply any energy; instead, it uses energy
from fork A. Thus the energy is dissipated faster, and the sound, though
louder, does not continue as long. Keep this principle in mind: *Resonance
does not add energy; it increases the rate of energy output in reduced time.*

Misunderstanding of this principle can confuse the procedure in vocal practice. If resonance actually added to the energy of voice, the need for control

of exhalation in synchrony with laryngeal adjustments would be reduced. The truth is that resonance increases the rate of energy output so that energy initiated in the glottis is dissipated faster. Therefore, efficient use of resonance in the vocal tract places a greater demand on the continuous production of adequate vibration at the glottis.

TYPES OF RESONANCE

In our illustration above, tuning forks A and B were tuned to the same frequency. Sympathetic vibration of fork B was activated by vibration of fork A because they had the same natural frequency. A second body may also be set into vibration by action of the first when the two do not have the same natural frequency. Suppose you strike tuning fork A to initiate its vibration and then touch its shank to a large table top (Figure 2). The wood of the table top is set into vibration and becomes a resonator for the tuning fork. Since the table top does not have the same natural frequency as the tuning fork, its vibration is *forced vibration*. Because it could resonate a great many different frequencies by forced vibration, this resonator may be said to have a *broad response*, or *broad resonance*. The sympathetic vibration of tuning fork B (Figure 1), on the other hand, was a *sharp response* (selective or narrow), or *sharp resonance*, because it had the same natural frequency as the initial vibration.

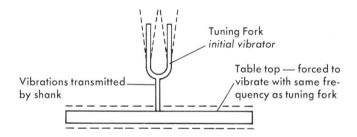

Fig. 2 Forced Vibration

A piano uses broad resonance. The sounding board to which the strings attach, the wooden case, and the volume of air within the case all resonate the vibration of any string which is struck. This is forced vibration with a broad response. Stringed instruments of the violin family also use broad resonance. Vibration of a string at any frequency is transmitted by way of the wooden bridge to the wooden body of the instrument and the air volume enclosed by the body, all of which resonate the tone by forced vibration.

Certain other musical instruments use sympathetic vibration. Each metal tube of a xylophone is a tuned resonator for the bar above it. When the bar is struck, the air within the metal tube vibrates as a sharp resonator.

Some musical instruments have both broad and sharp resonance. Most wind instruments are in this category. Their straight or coiled tubes act totally as broad resonators, while portions of those cavities (created usually by depressing keys) act as sharp resonators. These instruments bear a strong resemblance to the vocal tract, which *in toto* acts as a broad resonator but at the same time is adaptable to the creation of smaller cavities (by movements of articulators) for sharp resonance at particular frequencies. A broad resonator has the advantage of responding to a wide range of frequencies. However, a sharp resonator produces a greater increase in intensity at its natural frequency than a broad resonator at any frequency.

CAVITY RESONANCE

Any body is capable of vibration, and therefore can serve as a resonator, if it is elastic. Perhaps you have thought of elasticity as exclusively the property of rubber. Actually, elasticity is a characteristic of any body of matter which resists displacement and is capable of recovering its size and shape after displacement. Solids such as steel or wood are elastic. Gas, such as air, is also elastic. At a given pressure level, molecules of air are dispersed at specific intervals in space. They move about, but in an orderly relationship to other molecules. Force is required to move molecules into condensed areas. When displaced, molecules spring back, because air is an elastic medium. When a volume of air enclosed in a cavity is subjected to waves of compression, it behaves like a coiled spring, pushing against the sides of the cavity and bouncing back. Such a cavity of air makes an excellent resonator. Its properties are important to us here because to some extent cavities of air make up the vocal resonators.

The following principles of cavity resonance have been postulated (see Figure 3):

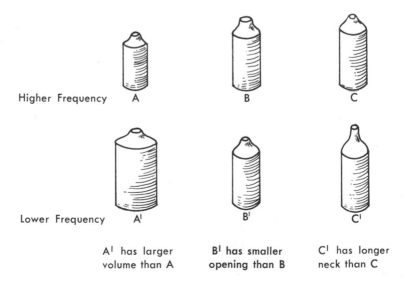

Higher Frequency   A   B   C

Lower Frequency   A¹   B¹   C¹

A¹ has larger   B¹ has smaller   C¹ has longer
volume than A   opening than B   neck than C

Fig. 3 Determinants of Cavity Resonance

(1) *The greater the cavity volume, the lower the frequency it will resonate.* This is true because a low frequency has a longer wave length.[1] A longer wave requires larger space to travel and reflect within the cavity.

(2) *The smaller the opening into the cavity, the lower the frequency it will resonate.* The air in the opening acts like a plug, offering impedance or resistance to the exit of sound waves. The shorter waves are "killed off" or damped by friction of this resistance. The longer waves go past it.

(3) *The longer the neck of the opening into the cavity, the lower the frequency it will resonate.* A long cavity-neck furnishes resistance just as a small opening does. The effect is friction and the damping of high frequencies.

(4) *The more elastic and dense the cavity walls, the higher the frequency it will resonate.* Again, this involves friction and damping. If the walls of the cavity are irregular in contour and spongy in texture, short waves become trapped or absorbed in the "pockets" and irregularities and are not reflected.

We shall soon examine these principles of resonance in relation to voice. Before proceeding further, however, we need to discuss characteristics of the vocal tone which is resonated.

COMPLEX CHARACTER OF VOCAL TONE

In Chapter 2, the production of sound waves at the glottis was described as if it were a *pure tone*. This is not true, though this inference seemed expedient in view of our purpose in that discussion. Actually, the vocal tone which leaves the glottis is a *complex tone*. Simultaneously, the glottis emits a wave form of a frequency we identify as *the pitch* of the tone, and numerous other frequencies which are integral multiples of the basic frequency. Thus if the pitch we identify is C_4, its *fundamental frequency* is 250 c.p.s.[2] At the time this frequency is produced, other frequencies of 500 c.p.s. (2×250), 750 c.p.s. (3×250), 1000 c.p.s. (4×250), 1250 c.p.s. (5×250), etc., are also produced. The basic frequency is called the *fundamental*, and the frequencies of the tone complex above the fundamental are called *overtones*. Or we could call all of the frequencies of the tone-complex *partials*. The fundamental would be the first partial, the first overtone the second partial, and so on.

TUBE RESONANCE

Tube resonance is somewhat applicable to voice. As we shall see presently, the vocal tract above the glottis is a sort of tube, open at the top (at the lips) and closed at the bottom (at the glottis). A tube which is open at one end is a sharp resonator for a fundamental frequency whose wave length is four times the length of the tube. Further, it will resonate all of the odd-numbered partials of that frequency, e.g., 3rd, 5th, 7th, 9th, etc.

[1] Wave length is the actual distance between the crest of one period of condensation through the following period of rarefaction to the crest of the next period of condensation, or one wave cycle. Sound travels at approximately 1100 feet per second. To compute wave length, divide 1100 feet by the frequency of the tone. Thus if the frequency is 250 c.p.s., the wave length is 1100/250, or 4.4 feet.

[2] C_4, which is the most common modal pitch for female adults, has an actual frequency of 256 c.p.s. but has been "rounded off" here to 250 c.p.s. to facilitate computation.

The Functions of Vocal Resonance

Vocal resonance serves two functions. First, it increases the general loudness of the voice. For the frequencies occurring in a particular voice, this would be a broad-response type of resonance. Second, it affects the quality of the vocal tone. This process involves selective intensification of particular groups of overtones in the tone-complex and is to some degree a sharp-response resonance. The production of the sound segments which comprise spoken language depends on the prominence of particular partials in the vocal tone (see Figure 4). Articulation of vowel and consonant phonemes determines the relative prominence of various overtones, and the clarity of speech depends on this phenomenon. Whether the quality of a voice is generally pleasing or offensive is also determined by the relative prominence of the partials in the vocal tone.

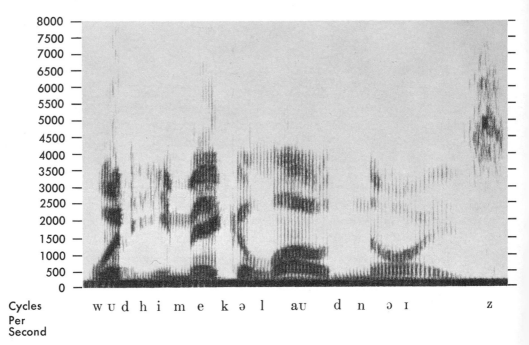

Cycles
Per
Second

Fig. 4 Sound Spectrogram of the Sentence, "Would he make a loud noise?"

Tracings on the spectrogram show the relative strength of partials in the vocal tone at each successive point in time. Note that the resonant frequencies of vowels (called formants) comprise identifiable patterns, each different from the other. The semi-vowels /w/, /m/, /l/, and /n/ look somewhat like vowels, but the stop-consonants /d/ and /k/ show as "dead spots" (stop-gaps), and the fricative /z/ shows as very high-frequency random noise (spike-fill). (Wide band spectrogram of an adult male's voice, produced on the Sona-Graf 6061A Sound Spectrograph [85–8000 c.p.s. spectrum analyzer]. Kay Electric Co., Pine Brook, N. J.)

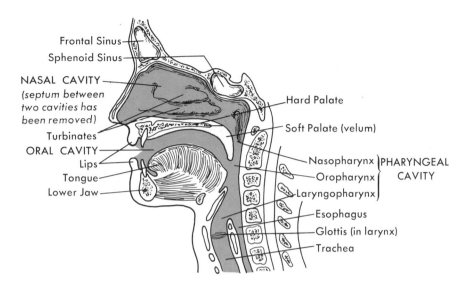

Fig. 5 Resonance Tract for Voice

(Midsagittal section of head and neck, looking into right side from central plane)

The Physiology of Vocal Resonance

The resonance apparatus for the human voice is made up of a series of connected passageways in the neck and head (Figure 5). For most English speech, the resonance system is like a bent tube. The lower end of the tube is the *glottis*, at which point the sound pulses enter the resonance system. The vertical part of the tube, the *pharynx*, is mostly hidden from view in the throat. It "bends" forward into the *oral cavity* at the point where you could see your throat if you looked into a mirror and said "ah." The opening out of the tube is formed by the *lips*.   At the bend in the tube, there is a muscular valve called the *velum* (soft palate). When the velum is lifted, it closes off the *nasal cavity* so that sound waves are prevented from entering that cavity. When the velum is lowered, the nasal cavity becomes a *side cavity* in the resonance system.[3]

Precisely how the vocal resonating system operates (as an acoustical apparatus) has been the subject of considerable discussion and some disagreement. Present thinking is that different sections of the vocal tract may behave as tube resonators or cavity resonators under varying circumstances. The vocal tract does not conform precisely to principles of tube resonance because it is not of uniform diameter throughout its length. In an irregular tube of this sort, resonances at any particular moment are influenced by: (1) the length

---

[3] Certain other characteristics of the nasal passages which might affect voice quality will be discussed in the sections on *nasality* and *denasality*.

of the tube, (2) the cross-sectional area of the lip opening, (3) the cross-sectional area and locations of constrictions along the length of the tube, and (4) the elasticity of the tube walls.

Where constrictions in the passageway occur, the tube is divided into cavities which are coupled together. These cavities can act as separate sharp resonators if the constriction is great and extensive. When the coupling is close, with a large passageway between the cavities, however, the coupled cavities interact in resonance effect, producing resonance characteristics of the coupling as an influence on their separate resonances. The result is strong intensification of certain bands of overtone frequencies, with damping out of certain others.

Though each person's resonance system has, to some extent, a fixed size and shape (the length and diameter of the pharynx, the length of the jaw, the height and width of the palatal arch, the size of the tongue and the velum), the dimensions of the resonance cavities can be changed noticeably by muscular action. Whether you intend to or not, and whether you are conscious of it or not, you change the size and shape of your resonance cavities in myriad details whenever you talk. Other activities, such as yawning, chewing, and swallowing, also involve considerable alteration of the size and shape of these cavities. In most cases, resonance can be improved by consciously changing unsatisfactory muscular controls.

THE ORAL CAVITY AS A RESONATOR

The *oral cavity* is the most variable in size and shape of all the resonance cavities. If you open your mouth widely and look into a mirror, you will see the structures pictured in Figure 6. Notice the constant factors of the cavity dimensions: the shape of your dental arch, the width and height of your hard

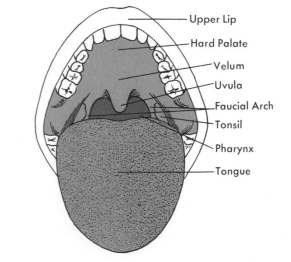

Fig. 6 The Oral Cavity

Upper Lip
Hard Palate
Velum
Uvula
Faucial Arch
Tonsil
Pharynx
Tongue

palate, the size of your velum, the shape of your faucial arch, and the size of your tongue. Now let us examine some of the ways the shape of your oral cavity may be changed.

The *tongue*, the most mobile of the articulators, is the structure in the vocal tract which can effect the greatest number of changes in the shape and size of the resonance tube. There is more of the tongue than you can see, for it extends all the way down behind the tip of the epiglottis in the pharynx (Figure 5). To understand its remarkable capacity for motion, remember that, together with its extrinsic muscles, it occupies the entire floor of the mouth and the space within the circle of the lower jaw. You can feel extrinsic tongue muscles contracting if you press your fingers up underneath your chin while you move your tongue back and forth in your mouth.

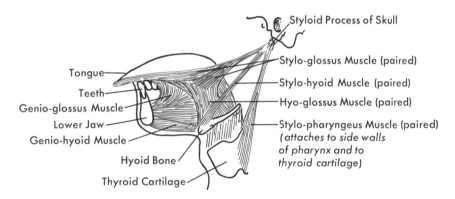

Fig. 7 Extrinsic Muscles of the Tongue

(left side)

Extrinsic muscles, which control the positioning of the tongue, connect the tongue to the lower jaw, to the hyoid bone (above the larynx), and to a process of the skull beneath the ear. Figure 7 shows the four principal extrinsic muscles. *Stylo-glossus* both retracts (pulls the tongue backward into the pharynx) and lifts (raises the whole tongue higher in the oral cavity). To pull the tongue forward in the mouth, *genio-glossus* contracts; also *genio-hyoid* pulls the back of the tongue forward by pulling forward the hyoid bone to which the tongue attaches. To lower the back part of the tongue, the *hyo-glossus* tenses; to lower the front part, the *genio-glossus* tenses.

Intrinsic muscles control the shape of the tongue. (These are not shown on Figure 7.) Muscle fibers run through the body of the tongue in three directions: (1) The *transverse* fibers run from side to side. When tensed, they make the tongue narrower and rounder. (2) The *vertical* fibers run up and down. When tensed, they flatten the tongue. (3) The *longitudinal* fibers (two sets of them, superior and inferior on both sides) run lengthwise, from front to back. When tensed, they shorten the tongue.

The various combinations of intrinsic and extrinsic muscles can produce almost limitless shapes and positions of the tongue. For example, in Figure 8 note the changing shape and positioning of the tongue for three different vowel articulations.

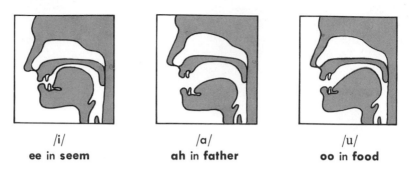

/i/
ee in **seem**

/a/
ah in **father**

/u/
oo in **food**

Fig. 8 Tongue Positions for Three English Vowel Sounds

Compare the size and shape of the oral cavity and of the pharynx in the three drawings. Notice that for both /i/ and /u/ the tongue is bunched and lifted toward the palate to form a narrow constriction, but that for /a/ the lack of such a constriction by the tongue leaves the oral cavity a continuous tube. Look at the place in the oral cavity where the tongue forms a constriction (a coupling between resonance cavities). For /i/ the coupling is far forward in the mouth, forming a large cavity behind, which connects to a large pharyngeal cavity, but leaving only a short, small cavity in the front of the mouth. Compare this with /u/, which is formed by a constriction or cavity-coupling far back in the mouth, producing a long resonance cavity in front of the coupling; practically no oral cavity remains behind the constriction, and the backward movement of the tongue also makes the pharynx a smaller tube for /u/.[4]

The *lower jaw* changes position to affect the size of the oral cavity, and therefore to affect resonance. In Figure 8, you will note that the jaw is lowered to open the mouth rather wide for /a/ but that it is almost closed for /i/ and /u/. Flexible jaw movement is necessary for good resonance. The strongest muscles attaching to the lower jaw are elevating or closing muscles (Figure 9). These elevating muscles are some of the most powerful in the body, because tremendous force is needed for mastication. To open the mouth wide, jaw-lowering muscles must be used, but the position of the lower jaw in relation to the skull allows gravity to assist in jaw-lowering when the head is upright, and

[4] Articulations described here, as for all articulations of vowels, represent adjustments of *relative* cavity size and shape for the production of resonance characteristics which produce meaningful segments of language. Any idea that precise measurements are indicated cannot be supported. Individual differences in structures involved produce some differences in positioning of articulators. Considerable latitude in an individual's articulation is allowable before distortion of meaning results.

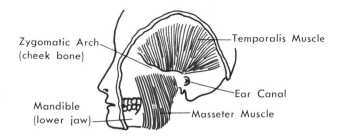

Fig. 9 Muscles Which Close the Jaw

(Muscles of mastication, viewed from left side)

gravity alone can drop the jaw slightly if the elevating muscles are relaxed. Habitual jaw posture affects jaw movements in speech. The individual who clenches his jaw and grinds his teeth when he is not eating will also talk with clenched teeth, and thus seriously limit the effectiveness of the oral cavity as a vocal resonator.

The *cheeks* comprise the side walls of the oral cavity, the only walls of that cavity whose elasticity and density can be controlled. Think of the oral cavity as having four walls. The upper wall, formed by the hard palate (bone covered by a thin mucous membrane) and teeth, is an efficient but unchangeable reflector of sound waves. The lower wall, the tongue surface, is quite mobile but is not adjustable for surface texture as a sound-wave reflector. The side walls, the cheeks, are adjustable in elasticity and density through control of muscle tension within them, and thus contribute to oral resonance.

Obviously, the cheeks are covered with skin outside and with mucous membrane inside. The amount of fat deposit varies with individuals. Essentially, the wall of the cheek consists of layers of muscle tissue. Muscles of mastication which you saw in Figure 9 are far enough back on the jaw that they have little effect on the cheek wall. In Figure 10 you will see muscles which are used for drawing the corners of the mouth outward and upward — the smiling muscles. When they are relaxed, the cheeks are relaxed and flabby, and their

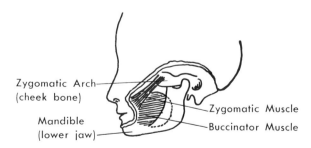

Fig. 10 Cheek Muscles (viewed from left side)

Increased tension makes cheeks firmer and more elastic.

inner surface has a damping effect on sound waves, particularly the higher partials. The firmer the cheeks, the more elastic and dense their inner surface becomes, and the better reflectors of sound waves they are.

The *lips* form the opening out of the oral resonance cavity. Three actions increase the size of the lip orifice: pulling the corners outward and upward, with muscles shown on Figure 10; lifting the upper lip; and lowering the lower lip (Figure 11). A ring-shaped band of muscle tissue circling the lips rounds or puckers them to make the opening smaller (Figure 11). Rounding the lips may also involve protrusion, which lengthens the "neck" of the resonance cavity. The larger the opening at the lips, the higher the frequencies which will be resonated. The smaller the opening and the greater the protrusion, the lower the resonant frequencies.

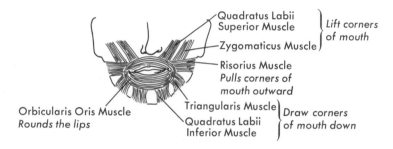

Fig. 11 Muscles Which Control Lip Shape

The *faucial arch* is the passageway between the oral and the pharyngeal cavity (Figure 6). The top of the arch is the velum, which we shall discuss presently. The pillars of the arch, two on each side, are formed by muscle fibers. The pair of pillars you see first is the *palato-glossus* muscles, which run from the velum into either side of the back part of the tongue. The pair of pillars behind them is the *palato-pharyngeus* muscles, which run from the velum into the lower pharyngeal walls. When the *palato-glossus* muscles contract, they pull the velum downward and also narrow the faucial arch. If the tongue rises in the back simultaneously, this closes the passageway between the mouth and the pharynx. The broad-resonance response of the vocal tract is best facilitated by keeping the faucial arch open.

THE PHARYNGEAL CAVITY AS A RESONATOR

The *pharynx* is a muscular tube which may be divided into three separate cavities by means of muscular constrictions. The tongue forms the front wall of the pharynx. The sides and back wall are encircled by three sets of overlapping muscle sheets called *pharyngeal constrictors* (Figure 12).

Narrowing of the entire pharynx, from the velum down to the larynx, is accomplished by contraction of the encircling *pharyngeal constrictor* muscles. The front-to-back dimension is decreased by retraction of the tongue (pulling

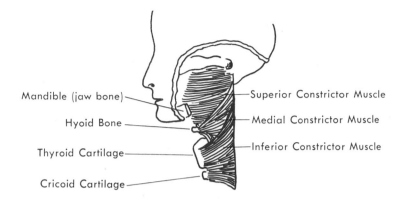

Mandible (jaw bone)

Hyoid Bone

Thyroid Cartilage

Cricoid Cartilage

Superior Constrictor Muscle

Medial Constrictor Muscle

Inferior Constrictor Muscle

Fig. 12 Constrictor Muscles of the Pharynx

(viewed from left side)

the tongue backward toward the back wall of the pharynx). The pharynx can be widened (thus made larger in diameter) by contraction of the *stylo-pharyngeus* muscle (Figure 7), which runs from the side wall of the pharynx to a process of the skull beneath the ear. The larger the cavity, the lower the frequencies it will resonate.

The pharynx can be shortened by tension of the *palato-pharyngeus* and the *thyro-hyoid* muscles, which pull the larynx and the lower pharynx upward (Figure 13). It can be lengthened by the downward pull of the *sterno-thyroid* muscles (Figure 13). The longer the pharyngeal cavity, the lower the frequencies it will resonate.

If the lower constrictor muscles are tensed and the tongue is pulled backward into the pharynx, the laryngo-pharynx (just above the larynx) and the

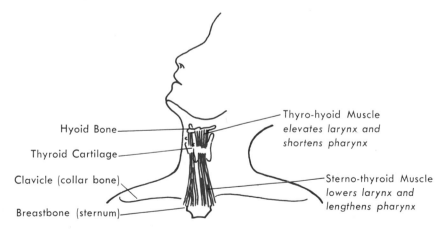

Hyoid Bone

Thyroid Cartilage

Clavicle (collar bone)

Breastbone (sternum)

Thyro-hyoid Muscle
*elevates larynx and
shortens pharynx*

Sterno-thyroid Muscle
*lowers larynx and
lengthens pharynx*

Fig. 13 Extrinsic Muscles of the Larynx

(half-front view)

oro-pharynx can be separated into two coupled resonating cavities. Lifting and retracting the velum can completely close off the naso-pharynx from the oro-pharynx.

The surface texture of the pharyngeal walls, as in the oral cavity, is regulated by the degree of muscle tension within the walls. Increased tension in the pharyngeal muscles (Figure 12) not only makes the cavity smaller but also makes the walls more taut and dense. Increased elasticity and density of cavity walls results in better reflection of high-frequency (short wave) partials of the vocal tone. On the other hand, when the pharyngeal muscles are relaxed, the cavity walls are soft, spongy, and inelastic. This has a damping effect, particularly on high-frequency partials, which become entrapped in the many crevices and pockets of the spongy tissue (rather like acoustic tile), and lose energy because they are not bounced off the walls.

THE NASAL CAVITY AS A RESONATOR

The *nasal cavity* is the least used of the vocal resonance cavities. This is fortunate, since its size and shape are the least subject to volitional control of the entire vocal tract. The nasal cavity is actually a pair of cavities. The dividing wall, or *septum*, between the nostrils extends back as far as the point where the velum joins to the hard palate. As you can see in Figure 14, this septum is composed of bone covered with mucous membrane, extending from the roof of the hard palate to the floor of the brain cavity. (The septum is cartilage in the front part of the nose.) Extending into each of the nasal cavities from the sides are curled-over shelves of bone, called *turbinates* (Figures 5 and 14). The passages are tortuous and crowded. At the rear, this pair of convoluted passages converges into the single cavity called the naso-pharynx.

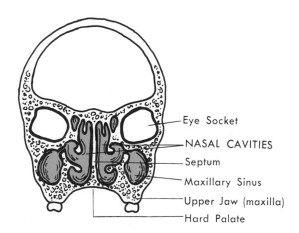

Eye Socket
NASAL CAVITIES
Septum
Maxillary Sinus
Upper Jaw (maxilla)
Hard Palate

Fig. 14 Nasal Cavities Shown in Coronal Section of the Head

(a vertical cut from side to side)

The nasal cavity is ideally constructed for its primary function as an air filter in inhalation. The great expanse of mucous membrane in closely convoluted passages warms the incoming air before it reaches the lungs, while the innumerable small hair cells on this membrane trap dust particles to prevent their entry into the lungs. As a resonator, however, the nasal cavity is not well constructed, and its shape and size cannot be varied by volitional control.

The only muscular controls for passage of the breath or voice out of the nasal cavity must be exercised at the exit (the nostrils) or the entrance (the velum). The size of the nostrils can be regulated, but some individuals find it as strange as wiggling the ears. The nostrils can be constricted (narrowed) by a muscle which runs across the nose. They can be spread wide open by tensing a short muscle which runs from each side of the nose to the cheek. Some of the popular teen-age singers have adopted nostril flaring, possibly to affect their resonance but more probably to elicit ecstatic responses from their admirers. The resonance value of either constricting or enlarging the nostrils has not been established.

The *velum* is critically important in the control of nasal resonance. It functions as an inlet valve between the oro-pharynx and the naso-pharynx. When the velum is drawn back and upward until its borders make a tight seal with the side and back walls of the pharynx, no breath or sound waves can pass from the pharynx into the nasal cavity.

You might compare velar action with that of a trap door in the ceiling (of the pharynx), hinged on one side (where it connects to the hard palate). When the door drops down, the hole in the ceiling is open; when it is lifted up, the hole is closed. Closing the velum is slightly more complicated than merely pulling it upward by a handle on its back edge. Figure 15 is a diagram of the

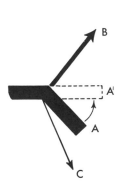

A   Relaxed (lowered, open) position of velum, hinged to hard palate

A'   Elevated (closed) position of velum

B   Direction of pull by Levator Veli Palatini Muscles, which run through velum like a sling

C   Direction of pull by Palatopharyngeus Muscles

B   Pulls upward

C   Pulls backward

Fig. 15   Vector Action in Elevating the Velum

(schematic representation)

vector action by which the combined activity of two pairs of muscles moves the velum back and upward for closure. Tight velar closure is necessary whenever pressure must build up in the oral cavity (e.g., for stop consonants such as /p/ or /k/, or for fricative consonants such as /s/ or /f/).

For the three nasal consonants /m/, /n/, and /ŋ/ (ng), voice is emitted from the nasal cavity instead of the oral cavity. For these consonants, the velum must be pulled downward to allow free passage of the voice through the nasal cavity, while the oral cavity is blocked off by closure of the lips or a firm seal of the tongue raised in the mouth.

For some vowels the velum is completely closed (raised and retracted). For others it is very slightly opened (usually raised but not as tightly retracted). It is generally thought that some nasal resonance enhances the vocal quality. The fine line between desirable nasal resonance and undesirable nasality is primarily a matter of esthetics. The physiological difference between nasal resonance and nasality depends on the amount of velar opening. A definitely lowered velum is normally equated with nasality.

The acoustic effect of lowering the velum during the phonation of vowel sounds is to open a side-cavity resonator which is coupled to the main resonating tube. The nasal cavity from the naso-pharynx forward becomes progressively smaller in volume (or average cross-section diameter). Essentially, it is a cul-de-sac resonator — a "blind alley" or "dead-end street" sort of cavity. Entering sound waves cannot progress through it because they meet impediments and barriers. They must reflect back on their own path and rejoin the main stream of sound waves in the pharyngeal and oral cavities. Partials at certain frequencies will be damped because their wave lengths are not appropriate for reflection, or because they become trapped in the tortuous passageways where they cannot be reflected. Partials at some other frequencies will be resonated and reflected back through the velar opening. Some of them, which coincide with partials of the sound wave in the pharynx, will add to the strength of those frequencies. Others, which do not coincide with partials in the pharyngeal sound wave, will act as antiresonances to cancel out certain frequencies in the wave complex.

THE SINUSES AND CHEST AS RESONATORS

Because some teachers of voice have attributed considerable importance to sinus resonance and chest resonance, the possible contributions of the sinus and chest cavities to the strength or quality of voice should be examined. Five sinus cavities lie next to or near the nasal passages. The *sphenoid sinus* is located above the naso-pharynx (Figure 5); the two *frontal sinuses* lie roughly beneath the eyebrows, above the eye sockets (Figure 5); each *maxillary sinus* (also called an antrum sinus) is situated to the side of the nasal cavity (Figure 14). Each of the sinus cavities connects to the nasal passage by a tiny drainage duct. A sinus is a small cavity or pocket within the bony structure of the skull, lined with mucous membrane and often rather damp with mucous. Sound waves in the nasal passage cannot enter a sinus directly, and whatever vibration is transmitted to a sinus by conduction of the bone surrounding it probably decays quickly within the closed, soggy pocket. No significant contribution of the sinuses to vocal resonance has been supported by research in voice science.

Chest resonance has appeared plausible because vibrations from the speaker's chest can be felt with the hand or heard with a stethoscope, or even with the ear pressed against the chest. Cavity resonance in the chest is possible only in the trachea and bronchi (the semi-rigid tubes through which breath flows to the lungs), since the masses of air sacs which make up the lobes of the lungs are much too spongy to reflect sound waves. Even so, whatever reflection of sound waves exists in these tubes would reach the external air only by conduction through the bones surrounding the chest. Sound vibrations in the breast bone or ribs are too weak to be heard even a few inches away. In short, any attempt to cultivate either sinus resonance or chest resonance has little prospect of success.

Practical Resonance Controls

QUALITY PROBLEMS OF RESONANCE

Ineffective use of resonance may result in various distortions of voice quality. The descriptive terms we shall use to categorize undesirable vocal quality in relation to resonance are: *nasal, denasal, strident, throaty, thin,* and *muffled.*

Nasality

Nasality, as we commonly use the term, refers to a whining, honking type of voice which has the sound of humming running through it. Though it is a quality problem which affects the vowel sounds most noticeably, it may also be heard in some of the voiced consonants, like /l/ and /r/. If you have been criticized as being nasal, listen to a tape recording of your speech, attempting to discover whether yours is *general nasality*, which runs through most of your syllables.

Perhaps you can isolate particular vowels in your speech which are much more nasal than others. If so, your problem is *phonemic nasality*. In that event, you would do well to concentrate on good production of the specific nasalized vowels when you practice.

On the other hand, you may discover that all of your vowels are noticeably nasal when they occur next to a nasal consonant (/m/, /n/ or /ŋ/) but not in other occurrences. This is *assimilation nasality*, because the vowel borrows or absorbs the nasal characteristic from the adjoining nasal consonant. Practice for this problem is aimed at timing velar movements properly between a nasal consonant (velum lowered) and the adjoining vowel phoneme (velum raised).

Finally, you should give attention to the amount of *nasal emission* on consonants. If you hear something like a snort at the beginning of a word like

take or **sat**, you are allowing breath which should be pressurized in the oral cavity to leak past an incompletely sealed velum to be emitted from the nose. Nasal emission is not only distracting; it also interferes with the clarity of speech because it robs consonants of the breath needed for their oral articulation. If you have nasal emissions, you need to concentrate on good velar closure during the production of consonants, particularly the voiceless ones.

EXERCISES FOR GENERAL NASALITY. Several types of procedures are effective in reducing general nasality. You must discover which line of attack is most effective for you, or which ones you should combine in your practice to get the best results.

Lowering the pitch of your voice may reduce nasality if your optimum pitch is lower than your modal pitch. Procedures for discovering your modal pitch and optimum pitch, and for making your optimum pitch a habit, are given in Chapter 4, pp. 167–174. For many speakers, the adoption of optimum pitch (which, after all, is ideally suited to the individual's particular resonance tract) produces an automatic shift in resonance characteristics which results in the reduction or elimination of nasality.

Increasing vocal intensity may help you reduce nasality, especially if you habitually talk at a low level of loudness. First, you have to increase the efficiency of your resonance in order to be louder. Better resonance in the pharyngeal and oral cavities tends to offset a small amount of cul-de-sac resonance from the nasal cavity. Second, the general increase in muscle tone incidental to an increase in loudness tends to increase activity of the velar-lifting muscles. Even if your voice is adequately loud, you may profit from increasing the loudness experimentally. Perhaps you will hear a decrease in nasality at the louder level which you can use as an auditory reference for quality when you reduce the loudness to normal limits.

Improving pharyngeal and oral resonance often decreases nasality. The exercises for relaxing the pharyngeal muscles given for strident quality later in this chapter are good for improving pharyngeal resonance. The exercises for jaw relaxation and tongue positioning given for thin quality later in this chapter will help you improve oral resonance. If resonance in the main vocal tract is good, it can normally offset some cul-de-sac effect of the nasal side tract.

Developing conscious control of the velum is indicated in many cases of general nasality. Continual practice of the exercises which follow should help you develop a good auditory reference for voice quality and a reliable kinesthetic reference for velar movements. As your velar control becomes automatic, you will maintain adequate velar closure when needed without giving conscious attention to it.

1. Nasal Inhalation–Oral Exhalation. With your mouth open fairly wide but not strained, take a deep breath through your nose, then exhale through your mouth. Repeat over and over, giving your attention to the kinesthesia of your velar movements. Look at Figure 16 while you do the exercise: (1) Velum lowered — inhale through the nose; (2) Velum raised — exhale through the mouth.

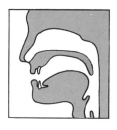
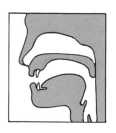

a. Lowered Velum
(nasal passage open)

b. Raised Velum
(nasal passage closed)

Fig. 16   Velar Positions

2. The Mirror Test. To discover whether you can consciously make a tight velar seal, perform this test of air leakage through the nasal cavity. Hold a small mirror facing upward underneath your nostrils, with its edge pressed against your upper lip. With your mouth open, inhale and exhale *through your mouth.* This requires your velum to be *raised,* to close off the nasal side-tract. If any breath leaks past the velum, it will cloud the mirror beneath your nostrils. Repeat several times in each practice period to learn the kinesthesia of a lifted velum. Remember, when the velum is lifted and closes off the nasal cavity, no clouding of the mirror will occur.

One word of caution: Nasal emission of breath does not *necessarily* accompany nasal quality. Therefore, this is not an infallible test of nasality. It is, however, a good training device which permits you to feel the muscular activity involved in closing the velum.

3. The /ŋ/-/ɑ/ Drill. The phoneme /ŋ/ is the nasal consonant which ends a word like **sing.** In order to produce the nasal /ŋ/, you must *lower* the velum. /ɑ/ is the vowel sound in the first syllable of **father.** To produce /ɑ/ you should *lift* the velum. Say /ŋ/, feeling the velum lie relaxed against the humped-up back of the tongue. Then say /ɑ/, concentrating on the feeling of muscle pull to lift and retract the velum, and listening for any trace of nasality in the vowel. Keep alternating /ŋ/ and /ɑ/, at first slowly and deliberately, then faster as you gain increased awareness of your auditory and kinesthetic controls.

4. Negative Practice. This, too, involves contrast, but on a more refined level. Deliberately produce /ɑ/ with as nasal a quality as you can. (We mark /~/ over a vowel to indicate nasalization, so let us indicate this deliberately nasal /ɑ/ as /ɑ̃/.) Then produce /ɑ/ as free of nasality as you can. Use audition to guide your production of both the incorrect and the correct forms of the vowel. During their production be very aware of the different kinesthesia of the lowered velum for /ɑ̃/ and the raised velum for /ɑ/. Negative practice entails contrasting the wrong way with the right way, to increase discrimination. Repeatedly contrast /ɑ̃/–/ɑ/, increasing the rate of alternation as your control becomes more reliable.

Repeat this exercise for other vowels: /e/ as in **late**: /ẽ/–/e/; /u/ as in **food**: /ũ/–/u/; /i/ as in **see**: /ĩ/–/i/;/o/ as in **go**: /õ/–/o/; /aɪ/ as in **high**: /ãɪ/–/aɪ/; /aʊ/ as in **how**: /ãʊ̃/–/aʊ/.

5. Pull-out Exercise.[5] Repeat the word **house** ten times, beginning as nasally as you can and then achieving nasal-free repetitions as fast as possible. Make a recording of the exercise. As you repeat, keep a record of how soon you "pulled out" of nasality and whether you kept the remaining repetitions free of nasality. Replay your recording and make a second judgment. Was your simultaneous judgment accurate? How many times did you have to repeat the word before it was free of nasality? Try to better your pull-out time when you repeat the exercise. Did you become less attentive and slip into nasality again toward the ninth or tenth repetition? Complacency can creep up on you insidiously; it is very easy to let your concentration lag. Beware of becoming automatic in this exercise. The point is not simply to say a *word* ten times, but to use those ten repetitions as material for sampling and examining your voice.

Use other words for this exercise. At first, until your velar control becomes reliably established, keep to the words which do not contain nasal consonants. An excellent plan is to use this for intensive drill on words you produce nasally in Exercise 7.

6. Pneumatic Drill. When you articulate a voiceless stop consonant, such as /p/ or /t/, particularly when the consonant begins a word, air pressure must increase in the oral cavity. This requires a tight velar closure, so that air will not leak out through the nasal tract and thus lower the oral pressure level. Normally the production of a voiceless stop exerts pneumatic pressure against the velum to force it upward even tighter than the lifting muscles position it. This affords an ideal opportunity for you to feel the velar closure. For contrast of tight velar closure with velar opening, practice the following pairs of words. All the articulatory movements in each pair are identical except that the first word begins with pressurized velar closure, while the second begins with velar opening. Before completing the word, hold the first consonant until you feel the velar adjustment.

pie — my	tea — knee
Pete — meet	tip — nip
pet — met	tell — Nell

[5] The name of this exercise derives from aviation training. A flyer puts his plane into a nose dive and then has to pull out of the dive with calculated timing to avoid disaster.

pat — mat	tale — nail
pock — mock	tap — nap
pa — ma	taught — naught
pole — mole	toe — no

7. Non-nasal Reading Practice. As soon as you begin to feel that you can consciously control your velar movements, you should test the length of time you can sustain control. Reading material which contains absolutely no nasal consonants requires you to maintain continuous velar lifting. You should record the following sentences periodically, each time making spontaneous and second judgments of your nasality. For your spontaneous judgment, put a √ mark over each syllable where you hear nasality as you are reading; put an X over any syllable where your velum feels lowered though you do not necessarily hear nasality.

a. These pears are delicious.
b. Please keep your dog outside today.
c. Build this house of used brick.
d. Help Peggy do the housework.
e. His lecture was very short yesterday.
f. Red apples usually taste better.
g. Her white dress is spotted with chocolate syrup.
h. Put all this paper with your books.
i. Carry three stacks of wood to the house.
j. Bill took the old tools to the tool shed.
k. Type five copies of this letter by five o'clock.
l. Carrots taste better cooked with butter.
m. Be sure that you keep your soft palate well elevated throughout this whole exercise.

For your second judgment, as you replay your recording cover the sentences which you marked above and mark the reprint of them below. Mark √ on each syllable where you hear nasality.

a. These pears are delicious.
b. Please keep your dog outside today.
c. Build this house of used brick.
d. Help Peggy do the housework.
e. His lecture was very short yesterday.
f. Red apples usually taste better.
g. Her white dress is spotted with chocolate syrup.
h. Put all this paper with your books.
i. Carry three stacks of wood to the house.
j. Bill took the old tools to the tool shed.
k. Type five copies of this letter by five o'clock.
l. Carrots taste better cooked with butter.
m. Be sure that you keep your soft palate well elevated throughout this whole exercise.

Now compare your second judgment with your spontaneous judgment. Did you hear more occurrences of nasality the second time than the first? Were your × marks in spontaneous judgment reliable cues to actual nasality?

For a more demanding test of your sustained velar control, read the following selections. Each of them is completely free of nasal consonants and therefore can be read without ever once lowering your velum. Record each reading and make spontaneous and second judgments as you did with the sentences above. Any word on which you slip into nasality should be practiced with the "pull-out" drill in Exercise 5. Then repeat the sentence in which the troublesome word occurs, preferably recording it for second judgment, repeating it until the nasal word loses its nasality.

A.   *A Space Story*

To explore outer space is a thrill people discuss excitedly. Few people have had the privilege to be propelled outside the earth's gravity field. Leroy G. Cooper was the first space explorer for the U.S. Air Force. He delighted space experts (lay people, too) as his space capsule executed over two-score orbits about the earth. For about thirty hours the flight was flawless. Cooper ate, slept, observed. He chatted with the fellows back at the Cape. He carried out vital tasks. Just as he prepared for the dive back to earth, the autopilot gave out. The world gasped! Cooper would have to guide his craft safely back. Besides the exact skill this required, he had to show a type of courage that few have ever had to display. The world waited with bated breath. At last the sailors of the carrier *Kearsarge* let out a roar of victory which told the hopeful world that he was safe. He was able to do what his autopilot failed to do. Therefore the world has showered "Gordo" Cooper with praise. He is a first hero of the space age.

B.   *Boat Safety*

Ted took a trip last fall to Harry's cottage at Lake Erie. Both the boys love boats. While they were there, they sailed Harry's boat a lot, but always very close to the shore. Harry's father allowed the boys to sail with a set of special rules. They had to keep close to shore where the coast guard patrol could always see their boat. They had to be sure to get the "all clear" weather report every day before they took the boat out. Each boy had to wear a life jacket all the while. Harry's father taught the boys what to do if the waves ever got too rough. "You have to row toward the waves," he said. This is wise advice, because if the big waves hit the side of a boat, they are able to tip it over. The boys had a happy week at the lake, but always observed the safety rules that Harry's father prescribed. Do you have other rules for safety with boats?

C. *The Girls' Visit to Chicago*

Chicago is a happy city to visit. We were there for four days last October. We saw shows, shopped at large stores, visited art exhibits, the public libraries, the city parks. All the people appear to rush about busily. The streets are crowded with cars. We rode the "elevated" or took a bus or a taxi. Several colleges are there, or close by. We visited our two sisters at their sorority house, which is lovely. They like the college. Their classes are history, art, speech, biology. They have to study hard, but they like their schedule. They have a good social life, too. I would like to go to that college also.

D. *The Co-ed's Tale of Woe*

I sat at the breakfast table late today, sadly thoughtful. I thought of all the jobs I should do. I had to walk to the college library to check out two history books. I was supposed to read three whole issues of a weekly periodical for literature class. That essay for art class could hardly wait till later. I really should check Sally's lab syllabus for that biology lecture I skipped last Tuesday. Lots of clothes had to be washed. Two pairs of shoes had to go to the shoe shop to be re-soled. I looked about due for a hair cut, too. Perhaps I should have it bleached. Lots of girls do. Could I get away for coffee with Ted at three? Five hours of classes is really excessive scholarship for a day. What about that group I said I would go with to buy favors for Saturday's party? Should I write a check? Dad's letter is late this week. Bare pockets prove he waits for a letter before he writes. Perhaps I should stay at the house to write Dad, after all. Actually, the weather outside looks positively terrible. Life is really rather hopeless. That is why I decided to go back to bed. Is it really two o'clock already? Ted will be furious if he has to wait at the coffee shop.

EXERCISES FOR PHONEMIC NASALITY. If your nasality occurs regularly on a specific vowel, your problem is in misarticulating that vowel, probably because your auditory reference for it is incorrect. Suppose, for instance, that you say the vowel /æ/ as in **hat** nasally a majority of the time, but have no general problem with nasality. This is comparable to diphthongizing a vowel unacceptably, or substituting another vowel sound for the one you intend to produce. The misarticulation may consist of tensing the tongue too much, or raising the tongue too high in the mouth, as well as relaxing the velum. Correcting the tongue articulation often corrects the nasality on the sound. The chief error, however, is in not having a clear auditory reference for the sound being produced, like shooting at a target you cannot see clearly. Your best exercises are in the section of Chapter 5 devoted to the specific vowel you nasalize.

EXERCISES FOR ASSIMILATION NASALITY. Assimilation is the changing of one speech sound to resemble another close to it. When a vowel sound which follows or precedes a nasal consonant becomes nasal, it is assimilation nasality. If you have assimilation nasality, you will nasalize any vowel when the consonant next to it is a nasal consonant, but you will not nasalize the same vowel sound in other contexts.

The cause of assimilation nasality is poorly timed velar movement. Suppose you say **make** with a nasalized vowel. Your velum has to be lowered (open) for the **m** and should be raised (closed) for the vowel sound. If your velar movement is too slow, the velum stays lowered until after the vowel is articulated, and the vowel comes out nasal. Suppose you say **sing** with a nasalized vowel. The velum should be raised (closed) for the whole word up to the **ng** at the end, where it must lower (open). If you anticipate the velar lowering and thus open the velum too soon, the vowel will be nasalized.

1. Auditory Discrimination Exercise. Auditory training is necessary for correcting assimilation nasality. You need first to become aware that the nasalized vowel you use next to a nasal consonant sounds different from that same vowel when it is not nasalized. This is auditory discrimination. Next, you need to imitate your un-nasalized vowel when saying a word containing a nasal consonant. In the following exercise, both words of each pair contain the same vowel sound, but the first word in the pair has no nasal consonant, while the second does. The oral articulation is identical for both words of the pair, but the velar movement is different. As you pronounce each pair of words, concentrate on the quality of the vowel sound, trying to detect any assimilation nasality in the vowel of the second word. Then repeat that pair, deliberately attempting to imitate the vowel quality used in the first word when you say the second.

be — me	debt — net	dub — dumb	paid — pain
bet — met	deck — neck	hub — hum	owed — own
buy — my	deed — need	cub — come	bird — burn
bite — might	dead — Ned	rib — rim	plaid — plan
bat — mat	dale — nail	cab — cam	sag — sang
bit — mit	doe — no	lube — loom	hag — hang
bait — mate	dice — nice	sub — some	rig — ring
bud — mud	due — new	kid — kin	wig — wing
birth — mirth	dote — note	laid — lain	tug — tongue
bow — mow	dear — near	raid — rain	log — long

2. Reading Exercise. The following sentences are saturated with nasal consonants to give you the best opportunity for (1) auditory monitoring of vowels which are in danger of assimilation nasality, and (2) practice in precise timing of velar movement. Recording your reading on tape for replay and second evaluation is highly recommended.

a. Many men sing in unison who won't sing alone.
b. Abraham Lincoln was one of America's great men.
c. Some things that happen make me angry.
d. Mr. Minnow made many comments about communication.
e. Wrapping on round cartons often comes undone.
f. Mickey Mouse and Minnie Mouse made many Disney movies famous.
g. Move the armchair into the living room.
h. Ten masked bandits came into the bank at closing time.

Read the following nasally-loaded paragraph, as directed for the sentences above.

A.   *Lonely Marvin*

Nearly every night Marvin Nettleman went to the movies. Marvin inevitably lingered near the entrance, hoping to encounter an acquaintance, because Marvin was lonely. Marvin never encountered anyone he knew, so Marvin inevitably sat alone. Miserably lonely, he munched peanuts, popcorn, and candy. Marvin's mother complained that Marvin was growing immense from munching peanuts, popcorn, and candy, and he was ruining his molars. Mama commanded Marvin to stop munching and begin exercising. Then Marvin began going to dances. At a dance he met a marvelous female dentist named Dr. Myrtle Manheim. Now Marvin and Myrtle have married. Marvin has grown slim, and Myrtle is filling Marvin's teeth which he ruined munching peanuts, popcorn, and candy at the movies.

B. I am the very model of a modern Major-General,
I've information vegetable, animal, and mineral,
I know the kings of England, and I quote the fights historical,
From Marathon to Waterloo in order categorical;
I'm very well acquainted too with matters mathematical,
I understand equations, both simple and quadratical,
About binomial theorem I'm teeming with a lot o' news —
With many cheerful facts about the square of the hypotenuse.
In short, on matters vegetable, animal, and mineral,
I am the very model of a modern Major-General.

W. S. GILBERT

C.   from *The Snake Has All the Lines* [6]

I never bring reading material aboard a plane because I am convinced that if I'm not right there, alert every minute, keeping my eye on things, heaven knows what might happen to us. When it comes to selecting a seat I am torn between the wish to sit well back in the tail (surely the safest place to be when we crash) and the feeling that it is my civic duty to take a place next to the window where I can keep a constant watch over the engines. You have no idea how heedless and selfish some passengers are — reading magazines and munching sandwiches the while that I, alone, am keeping that plane aloft by tugging upward on the arms of my chair and concentrating intensely, sometimes for hours. And when it becomes absolutely clear that something is amiss, who has to ask that simple, straightforward question that will clarify things? I do. Honestly, I don't think these people care whether they live or die.

JEAN KERR

You will find additional practice sentences with nasal consonants in exercises for *Hoarseness* in Chapter 2 (p. 74), and in Chapter 6 under /n/ (p. 274 ff.), /m/ (p. 313 ff.), and /ŋ/ (p. 327 ff.).

THE PROBLEM OF NASAL EMISSIONS. Functional nasality (i.e., nasality which is only a habit and not the result of a palatal or velar defect) does not necessarily involve nasal emission of breath on consonant sounds. Nasality is the effect of excessive resonance of the nasal cavity on the vocal tone; therefore, nasality is an unpleasant resonance distortion of vowels and to some extent voiced consonants. Nasal emission is a leakage of breath through the nasal passages, principally during the production of the voiceless consonants which require an increase of breath pressure within the oral cavity. Some, not all, nasal speakers have nasal emissions. But speakers with nasal emissions are usually also nasal.

A nasal emission sounds like a snort occurring simultaneously with a voiceless consonant. The consonant, insofar as its oral production is concerned, sounds weak, and the nasal emission further masks its intelligibility.

Voiceless consonants, on which nasal emission is most likely to occur, are of two sorts: *stops* and *fricatives*. The stop consonants /p/, /t/, /k/ and the affricate (stop-fricative) /tʃ/-**ch** are characterized by a buildup of breath pressure in the oral cavity behind a firm closure by the lips or tongue. The fricative consonants /ʍ/-**wh**, /f/, /θ/-**th**, /s/, /ʃ/-**sh**, and /h/ require strong breath pressure forced through a narrowly constricted passageway. The build-up of air pressure in the oral cavity required for these consonants necessitates an

---

exceptionally tight closure of the velum. If the lifting-retracting movement of the velum is feeble, breath escapes through the nasal passage instead of pressurizing in the mouth, like the loss in air pressure of a leaky automobile tire.

1. Mouth Inflation Exercise. Articulate a /p/ with your lips firmly closed and hold the articulation while you inflate your mouth with air like a balloon; then release. Repeat over and over, concentrating on the feeling of the tight closure of the velum, and listening for any telltale leakage of air through your nose. Repeat the exercise with /t/ and with /k/.

2. Mirror Test. Hold a small mirror beneath your nostrils, with its edge against your upper lip, as you say each of the following words. After each word, remove the mirror and check it for clouding from breath released through your nose. Concentrate on keeping the velum tightly raised so that no breath can escape through your nasal cavity. Make the consonant sounds as crisply and distinctly as you possibly can.

pay	put	chew	she	which	faith	sheath
tea	top	each	he	health	face	sheaf
key	keep	why	oath	half	fish	pass
up	pick	thrill	off	horse	south	cash
at	take	few	race	hash	safe	path
wake	cat	see	rush	thief	sash	catch

3. Reading Exercise. Make a tape recording as you read the following sentences. They are purposely loaded with voiceless stops and fricatives to test your control of nasal emissions. Not one nasal consonant occurs in these sentences. As you read, concentrate on secure velar closure. Apply the mirror test, as in Exercise 2, if you wish. Mark a √ at any point where you think you hear a nasal emission. When you replay your recording, double check for nasal emissions or for nasalized vowel sounds.

a. Patty picks pretty strawberries for stores to sell.
b. She threw her hat through the third hoop at the fair.
c. Katy captured the rat with a tricky trap.
d. Please help pour this sugar out of the pitcher.
e. Take Fred's sweater back to the store Thursday or Friday.
f. Which thief pushed his fist through the glass?
g. Paula stopped at the place where she lost her coat.
h. Keep the package here while I cross the street to cash a check.

Additional practice materials for preventing nasal emissions on voiceless consonants can be found in Chapter 6, in the sections devoted to the voiceless consonants listed here.

Denasality

Denasality is a stuffy, cold-in-the-head kind of vocal tone. Its most obvious characteristic is insufficient nasal resonance on the three nasal consonants, so that /m/ sounds like /b/, /n/ sounds like /d/, and /ŋ/ sounds like /g/, or approximately so.[7] A sentence like "Nothing makes me mad" sounds like "Dothig bakes be bad." Additionally, denasality involves a reduction of the normal nasal resonance of vowel sounds.[8] By American standards, some nasal resonance is considered a pleasing enhancement of the vocal tone. Excessive nasal resonance is hyper-nasality, which we call nasality. Inadequate nasal resonance is hypo-nasality, which we call denasality.

If your voice has been continuously denasal for a long time, you should certainly have a physician examine your nasal passages. Growth of adenoids in the naso-pharynx, or some other enlargement of tissue in the nasal cavity, could produce symptoms of denasality, and could require medical attention. Here is a simple test: close your mouth and breathe through your nose; stop one nostril and then the other by pressure of your finger to see how well you breathe through the unstopped nostril. If breathing through either side of the nasal cavity is difficult, there is probably a blockage somewhere in the nasal tract which a doctor should examine. The best vocal exercises will not cure an organic (physical) problem.

Denasality occurs sometimes as a habit of resonance. If you had some nasal obstruction which has now been removed, or if you have periodic allergic reactions which cause temporary nasal stoppage, you may have established a denasal auditory reference for voice which you now imitate. You may even have imitated someone else who had a nasal blockage, either consciously or unconsciously. The exercises given here are intended for habitual (functional) denasality, though they should be helpful in less severe cases of organic denasality as well.

1. Humming Exercise. Close the lips and hum /m/ gently. Gradually increase the loudness as the tone is prolonged. Concentrate on the sensation of vibration within the nasal cavity. Place your fingers on each side of the bridge of the nose and feel the vibration transmitted from the nasal cavity. Try to learn to perceive the kinesthesia of lowering the velum. Repeat the exercise several times, articulating /n/, and then /ŋ/-**ng**. Be sure to make a tight oral seal with your tongue to prevent breath emission from the mouth.

---

[7] The view that misarticulation of the nasal consonants is the principal problem in denasality is expressed by West, Ansberry and Carr, *The Rehabilitation of Speech*, 3rd ed. (New York: Harper & Brothers, 1957), who add that such a voice "arouses feelings of distaste in the hearer" because it sounds as though the person needs to blow his nose.

[8] Van Riper and Irwin, *Voice and Articulation* (Englewood Cliffs, New Jersey: Prentice-Hall, 1958) qualify the importance of vowel distortion by denasality as "somewhat less than the average amount of normal nasality on the vowels but without sufficient reduction . . . to allow it to be termed a disorder of voice." The decision as to whether denasality is classifiable as a clinical disorder of voice is not of major concern in a course of speech improvement. Our concern is not solely with gross aberrations of voice but also with slight but noticeable deviations from normal tone.

2. Confetti Exercise. Sprinkle a small pile of confetti on a piece of cardboard (the back of a tablet or notebook will do) and hold the edge of the cardboard against your upper lip with the confetti in front of your nostrils. Keep your lips closed and hum /m/ with just enough force to make the confetti move across the cardboard. Do not try to make one tremendous snort, but rather a steady, firm, continuous movement of air.

3. Cotton Ball Exercise. Follow the same directions as in Exercise 2, but use one of the fluffy balls of cotton used for removing makeup or applying medicine. The cotton ball should move *gradually* across the cardboard as you hum.

4. Auditory Discrimination Exercise. Turn back to the pairs of words in Exercise 1 for *Assimilation Nasality*. Your purpose in reading them is to perceive the audible difference between a nasal consonant and the non-nasal consonant articulated precisely like it (except for the velar position), and to perceive the sensation of vibration in the nasal cavity when you produce a nasal consonant. When you say the first word of a pair, there should be no vibration in your nasal cavity; when you say the nasal consonant of the second word, you should feel the nasal vibration. If you prolong the nasal consonant each time (e.g., **mmme** or **hummm**), you will have a better opportunity to hear the nasal resonance and to experience the vibration in your nasal passages.

5. Nasal Resonance Carry-over Exercise. Your purpose is to carry over nasal resonance from nasal consonants to following vowel sounds — not to become nasal, of course, but to increase nasal resonance to a normal level. This exercise is recommended for tape recorder practice so that you can replay it for a second auditory judgment in addition to your spontaneous judgment. The first part of each line is singing for maximum resonance. When you shift into speaking, try to keep good resonance. When you achieve noticeable vibration in the nasal cavity on the consonant, try to carry it over into the vowel sound. Use a good strong vocal tone.

	Singing		*Speaking*
me	mmmeee—mmmeee—mmmeee	me	me me mmmeee
may	mmmay–ay–ay—mmmay–ay–ay mmmay–ay–ay	may	may may mmmay–ay–ay
mah	mmmah–ah–ah—mmmah–ah–ah mmmah–ah–ah	mah	mah mah mmmah–ah–ah
mow	mmmow–ow–ow—mmmow–ow–ow mmmow–ow–ow	mow	mow mow mmmow–ow–ow
moo	mmmoo–oo–oo—mmmoo–oo–oo mmmoo–oo–oo	moo	moo moo mmmoo–oo–oo
	mmee—mmay–ay—mmah–ah—mmow–ow—mmoo–oo	me—may—mah—mow—moo	

	Singing		*Speaking*
knee	knknknee–ee–ee —— knknknee–ee–ee	knee	knee knee knknknee–ee–ee
nay	nnay–ay–ay —— nnay–ay–ay	nay	nay nay nnnay–ay–ay
nah	nnnah–ah–ah —— nnnah–ah–ah	nah	nah nah nnnah–ah–ah
no	nnnooo —— nnnooo —— nnnooo	no	no no nnnooo
noo	nnnoo–oo–oo —— nnnoo–oo–oo	noo	noo noo nnnoo–oo–oo
	knknknee–ee nnay–ay nnah–ah nnoo nnoo–oo	knee nay nah no noo	

6. Nasal-Saturated Reading. Read the selections below, which are saturated with nasal consonants. Record your reading on tape. *As you read*, concentrate on making each /m/, /n/ and /ŋ/ adequately nasal and getting normal nasal resonance in the vowels. *As you read*, make a simultaneous judgment of your resonance. Put a √ over any denasal sound you hear and × over any spot where you felt as if your nasal resonance was inadequate. Replay your tape recording to check the accuracy of your first auditory judgment and to determine whether your perception of inadequate nasal vibration was a reliable evidence of denasality. Repeat this exercise daily until your nasal resonance is adequate.

A.   I am one among the thousands who loved Henry Grady, and I stand
     among the millions who lament his death. I loved him in the promise
     of his glowing youth, when across my boyish vision he walked with
     winning grace from easy effort to success. I loved him in the flush of
     his splendid manhood, when a nation hung upon his words.

                                                        JOHN T. GRAVES

B.   It was many and many a year ago,
             In a kingdom by the sea,
         That a maiden there lived whom you may know
             By the name of Annabel Lee: —
         And this maiden she lived with no other thought
             Than to love and be loved by me.

                         .   .   .   .   .   .

         But our love it was stronger by far than the love
             Of those who were older than we —
             Of many far wiser than we —
         And neither the angels in Heaven above,
             Nor the demons down under the sea
         Can ever dissever my soul from the soul
             Of the beautiful Annabel Lee: —

         For the moon never beams without bringing me dreams
             Of the beautiful Annabel Lee;
         And the stars never rise but I feel the bright eyes
             Of the beautiful Annabel Lee;
         And so, all the night-tide, I lie down by the side
         Of my darling, my darling, my life and my bride,
             In her sepulchre there by the sea —
             In her tomb by the sounding sea.

                                                    EDGAR ALLAN POE

Additional practice material, to be used in this same manner, is in Exercise 2 for *Assimilation Nasality*, in Exercise C on *Hoarseness* in Chapter 2, and in the sections on /m/, /n/ and /ŋ/ in Chapter 6.

Stridency

Stridency sounds metallic, piercing, sharp, shrill, and raucous, with high-frequency prominence. It has sometimes been described as a high-pitched harshness. Though stridency and harshness may occur simultaneously or alternating in the same voice, the two qualities are different in character. The harsh voice, with its noisy dissonance and lack of harmonic, musical tone, sounds hard, flat, and low-pitched. The strident voice has exceptional brilliance of high overtones, to the extent that the fundamental frequency is often obscured, giving the tone a brassy, tinny, blatant sound.

Pharyngeal resonance is inappropriately used in the strident voice. Three characteristics of a resonance tube are involved. All are affected by a single factor: hypertension of muscles. Excessive tension of the muscles which encircle the sides and back of the pharynx (Figure 12) results in a decrease in the diameter of the resonance tube. Since a tube of smaller size resonates high frequencies better, the result is an undue prominence of high-frequency partials of the vocal tone. Excessive tension of these muscles also makes the walls of the pharynx maximally elastic and dense in surface texture, which is the ideal condition for reflection of high-frequency (short wave length) overtones of the voice. The same extrinsic muscles which can lift the larynx (Figure 13) can also pull the lower end of the pharynx upward, helped by vertical muscles in the pharyngeal walls which connect the base of the pharynx to the velum. When these muscles are too tense, the pharynx is shortened. A shorter tube resonates high frequencies best. The decrease in diameter and length of the tube and the increase in elasticity and density of its walls combine to produce highly efficient high-frequency resonance.

Listeners usually evaluate this type of resonance as unpleasantly shrill and earsplitting. The fact that this voice carries well over masking noises probably explains why street vendors, carnival "pitch" men, and auctioneers often adopt it. It is too unrestrained and unmodulated to be used by decorous young people in social gatherings.

Nervousness in a socially demanding situation or in public speaking increases general muscular tonus. General hypertension is very likely to involve pharyngeal hypertension, with resultant stridency. One of the commonly recognized symptoms of the ill-at-ease speaker is the pinched, tense, strident voice. Unfortunately, the speaker's awareness of this change in his voice (perhaps a quite pleasing voice when he is relaxed and self-assured) tends to increase his feeling of inadequacy and nervousness. Obviously, increased social poise helps greatly. But developing more reliable control over vocal resonance will insure good voice production even in trying situations. It will also reflect in the speaker's self-confidence, in his feeling that he can control himself and therefore can control the situation.

Problems with projection sometimes produce stridency in normally good voices. A woman whose voice quality is warm and mellow when she talks to her friends individually may suddenly sound like a shrew when she reads the treasurer's report at her woman's club meeting. Besides nervousness, poor projection technique may be the cause of her stridency. If you have this problem, be sure to learn how to use breath control for projection, along with exercises for better resonance.

Exercises to correct stridency have one goal: to relax the muscles of the pharynx. Relaxing the pharyngeal muscles affects three resonance factors which cause the pharynx to resonate lower frequency partials of the vocal tone: (1) the pharynx increases in diameter; (2) the pharynx increases in length; and (3) the walls of the pharynx become less dense and less elastic.

1. Neck Relaxation Exercise. Review the seven exercises for neck relaxation in the section on *Harshness* in Chapter 2, p. 67 ff. Choose from these exercises the ones which achieve for you the greatest sensation of pharyngeal relaxation. Learn the techniques so well that you can repeat those exercises at frequent intervals without referring to the book. Precede each exercise below with the neck relaxation exercises you find most beneficial, as "warm-up" exercises.

2. Vowel Prolongation Exercise. Pronounce each of the following vowel sounds, prolonging it to a (silent) count of 10. Concentrate on the vocal quality of the vowel as you say it, attempting to reduce any stridency in the tone before you complete phonation. Underline the vowels which you produced most successfully free of stridency. In successive repetitions, use the "best" vowels to begin this exercise, so that they can serve you as a good auditory pattern as you attempt to control stridency throughout the rest of the exercise.

a. /ɑ/ as in **father**	Say the vowel alone.
b. /ɔ/ as in **law**	Say the vowel alone.
c. /o/ as in **go**	Say the vowel alone.
d. /ʊ/ as in **foot**	Say the vowel alone.
e. /u/ as in **food**	Say the vowel alone.

3. Stridency Pull-out Exercise. Repeat each word in the following list ten times. The first time you say a word, make it as strident as possible. Then as quickly as you can, in successive repetitions of that word, pull out of stridency and keep the tone non-strident throughout the remainder of the ten repetitions. For each word, keep a record of which repetition you pulled out on. Each time you practice this list, try to better your previous record. Careful attention to the kinesthesia of tension in pharyngeal muscles and to the sound of your vocal tone is absolutely necessary.

/ɑ/	/ɔ/	/o/	/ʊ/	/u/	/ju/	/aʊ/	/ɔɪ/
father	law	low	put	food	use	now	boy
calm	bought	bow	pull	pool	few	cow	joy
palm	caught	own	look	move	view	town	coil
hot	fought	so	would	do	fuse	out	boil
pond	off	owe	could	you	music	round	toy
pod	saw	tone	book	sue	beauty	how	foil
dock	ball	toll	push	cool	cube	hound	hoist
cod	soft	boat	wool	rule	cue	noun	enjoy
lot	lawn	soul	full	moon	refuse	loud	join

4. Phonemically Loaded Reading. The sentences below are loaded with the vowel phonemes you practiced in Exercise 3. These vowels are especially conducive to the control of stridency because their normal production involves least shortening of the pharynx and least constriction by pharyngeal muscles. Before you read each sentence, achieve your best control of pharyngeal muscles by going through the Open Throat Exercise (p. 69) and the Sip Breath and Sigh Exercise (p. 70). While reading, concentrate on the kinesthesia of relaxed pharyngeal muscles and the sound of your vocal quality. Preferably, record your reading — to replay and make a second judgment for stridency. If any particular word in a sentence gives you trouble, practice that word alone with the Pull-out Exercise, and then reread the whole sentence to test your stridency control.

   a. The old road wound through the marsh.
   b. Would you look at those wooden spoons?
   c. The old woman wore a warm woolen shawl.
   d. Ghouls and voodoo are the foibles of fools.
   e. Solemn music sounded through all the rooms.
   f. Moonlight transforms common stones to blue jewels.
   g. Father always goes home before going to law school.
   h. A group of small boys frolicked through the school.

Additional words and sentences for practice may be found in Chapter 5 under the vowel-headings /ɑ/, /ɔ/, /o/, /ʊ/, /u/, /ju/, /aʊ/, and /ɔɪ/.

5. Weak-to-Loud Exercise. If your stridency runs true to form, you probably have discovered that it gets worse as you get louder. The following sentences are arranged three on a line. The first is to be read quite softly, the second loudly enough to be heard easily in an ordinary room, and the third loudly enough to be heard in a classroom of thirty people. If you are to succeed in keeping stridency out of your vocal tone when the loudness increases, you will need to monitor carefully both the sound of your voice and the kinesthesia of pharyngeal tensions.

To One Person	*To Six People*	*To Thirty People*
a. (1) Hush, baby, don't cry.	(2) Be quiet now, all of you!	(3) Don't anybody make any noise.
b. (1) Do you see my book anywhere?	(2) I think I've lost my book.	(3) Did anybody here see the book I lost?
c. (1) I think I'll do some housework.	(2) Who messed up this room so badly?	(3) Everybody is to clean his room to-day.
d. (1) I'll help you work the problem.	(2) Why don't we all do our math together?	(3) Now, class, this is how you work the problem.
e. (1) I'd like to go swimming.	(2) Does anyone want to go swimming?	(3) Everybody in the pool!
f. (1) Do you want some ice cream?	(2) Is anybody here hungry?	(3) Now, who wants cake and who wants ice cream?
g. (1) Ann, isn't that chest like the one in your hall?	(2) That chest is the prettiest thing they've auctioned.	(3) I bid fifteen dollars!
h. (1) Have you planted any tulip bulbs yet?	(2) I love tulips, don't you?	(3) October is the perfect time to plant tulip bulbs.

6. Reading Exercises. The reading selections which follow should be conducive to pharyngeal relaxation and the reduction of stridency. As you read, try to assume the relaxed, calm mood of the selection. Listen to your voice, paying particular attention to the vowel sounds and attempting to make your quality as rich and full as possible.

A.   *The Twenty-Third Psalm*

The Lord is my shepherd; I shall not want.

He maketh me to lie down in green pastures: he leadeth me beside the still waters.

He restoreth my soul: he leadeth me in the paths of righteousness for his name's sake.

Yea, though I walk through the valley of the shadow of death, I will fear no evil: for thou art with me; thy rod and thy staff they comfort me.

Thou preparest a table before me in the presence of mine enemies: thou anointest my head with oil; my cup runneth over.

Surely goodness and mercy shall follow me all the days of my life; and I will dwell in the house of the Lord for ever.

B.   *Four Little Foxes* [9]

Speak gently, Spring, and make no sudden sound;
For in my windy valley yesterday I found
New-born foxes squirming on the ground —
Speak gently.

Walk softly, March, forbear the bitter blow;
Her feet within a trap, her blood upon the snow,
The four little foxes saw their mother go —
Walk softly.

Go lightly, Spring — oh, give them no alarm;
When I covered them with boughs to shelter them from harm,
The thin blue foxes suckled at my arm —
Go lightly.

Step softly, March, with your rampant hurricane;
Nuzzling one another, and whimpering with pain,
The new little foxes are shivering in the rain —
Step softly.

                                             Lew Sarett

C.   Sweet and low, sweet and low,
                    Wind of the western sea,
              Low, low, breathe and blow,
                    Wind of the western sea!
              Over the rolling waters go,
              Come from the dying moon, and blow,
                    Blow him again to me;
              While my little one, while my pretty one sleeps.

                           Alfred, Lord Tennyson

D.   from *In Another Country*

In the fall the war was always there, but we did not go to it any more. It was cold in the fall in Milan and the dark came very early. Then the electric lights came on, and it was pleasant along the streets looking in the windows. There was much game hanging outside the shops, and the snow powdered in the fur of the foxes and the wind blew their tails. The deer hung stiff and heavy and empty, and small birds blew in the wind and the wind turned their feathers. It was a cold fall and the wind came down from the mountains.

                           Ernest Hemingway

---

[9] From *Covenant with Earth*, by Lew Sarett. Edited and copyrighted, © 1956, by Alma Johnson Sarett. (Gainesville: University of Florida Press, 1956.) Reprinted by permission of Mrs. Sarett.

E.
Who Has Seen the Wind?

Who has seen the wind?
  Neither I nor you;
But when the leaves hang trembling
  The wind is passing through.

Who has seen the wind?
  Neither you nor I;
But when the trees bow down their heads
  The wind is passing by.

CHRISTINA ROSSETTI

F.
from *Gift from the Sea* [10]

I walked far down the beach, soothed by the rhythm of the waves, the sun on my bare back and legs, the wind and mist from the spray on my hair. Into the waves and out like a sandpiper. And then home, drenched, drugged, reeling, full to the brim with my day alone: full like the moon before the night has taken a single nibble of it; full as a cup poured up to the lip. There is a quality to fullness that the Psalmist expressed: "My cup runneth over." Let no one come — I pray in sudden panic — I might spill myself away!

ANNE MORROW LINDBERGH

Throatiness

Throatiness has a hollow, heavy, cavernous quality, with insufficient brightness and sparkle in the tone. It sounds very much as if the person were talking with his hands cupped around his mouth, or through one of those cardboard tubes which paper towels are wound on. Pitch is likely to sound lower than the actual frequency of the fundamental, because the high-frequency partials are exceptionally weak.

The primary problem in a throaty voice is the tongue posture. Extrinsic muscles of the tongue (Figure 7) pull the tongue and hyoid bone backward. (This is often assisted by pulling the chin in tightly.) This retraction (backing up) of the tongue forms a constriction in the laryngo-pharynx (Figure 17). Low-frequency partials (with long wave lengths) can bypass such an impediment, but high-frequency partials (with short wave lengths) are stopped by it. A further effect of the tongue retraction is misarticulation of many of the vowel sounds (Figure 17). Vowels which are normally made with the front or central part of the tongue humped up in the mouth are articulated farther

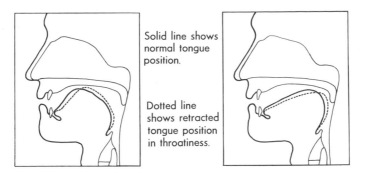

The /i/ vowel, as in **seem**   The /u/ vowel, as in **food**
Fig. 17   Tongue Retraction in Throaty Quality

back in the mouth by a throaty speaker.[11] Since oral resonance determines identification of particular vowel sounds, this compression of vowel articulation toward the back of the mouth reduces the distinctive vowel features. The front and central vowels sound "darker" than they should — too much like back vowels.

CHIN POSITION. If you have a throaty quality, first examine the position of your chin while you are talking. Look at yourself in a mirror. Compare your chin posture with that of other students in your class and with your friends'. Is your chin pulled back against your neck? Does your head appear to tip slightly forward? If you answered "Yes" to both those questions, try this: Lean your head back, and say, "Is this the way?" Then hold your head as you usually do and repeat the question. Did your voice quality change at all? Try this alternation in head position several times, noting the change in your vocal quality. Now, lift your chin, thrust it slightly forward, and again say, "Is this the way?" Perhaps a great deal of your "cure" lies in holding your chin up.

LOW MODAL PITCH. Your modal pitch,[12] and your attitude about it, may be a partial cause of your throatiness. Sometimes a person who thinks his modal pitch is too high adopts a throaty quality (probably unconsciously) as a device for making the pitch sound lower. Since a throaty quality sounds sepulchral and flat, it seems like a poor exchange. If your quality is throaty, first make certain that you are using optimum pitch,[13] at which efficient, pleasing resonance can be best developed.

[11] As you will note in the exercises in this section, the "front" vowels are /i/ as in **be**, /ɪ/ as in **bit**, /e/ as in **pay**, /ɛ/ as in **bet**, /æ/ as in **bat**; the "central" vowels are /ə/ as in **but** and /ɚ/ as in **bird**. You will find more detailed discussions of these vowel phonemes, with additional exercise materials, in Chapter 5.

[12] *Modal pitch* is the pitch at which you say the greatest number of syllables in an utterance.

[13] *Optimum pitch* is the pitch level which best suits your voice for use as your modal pitch. In Chapter 4, you will find sections appropriate to your need titled, *Finding Your Modal Pitch*, pp. 167–168; *Finding Your Optimum Pitch*, pp. 170–172; and *Stabilizing Optimum Pitch as Modal*, pp. 173–174.

TONGUE POSITION. The positioning of your tongue in the oral and pharyngeal cavities can be best controlled through certain vowel articulation exercises which follow. Do not experiment with changing the *shape* of your tongue — to point it, bulge it upward, or protrude it between the teeth. Instead, pull the whole tongue slightly forward in the mouth. The dimensions of the vocal tract are such that a slight change in the place where the tongue constricts the resonance tube can have a considerable effect on the vowel quality.

1. Vowel Fronting Exercise. Repeat each vowel ten times. On successive repetitions, try to pull the tongue nearer the front of the mouth, but do not change the shape of the tongue. Keep your lips pulled back in a smile, so that you can see your tongue articulation in a mirror. Listen carefully for an increase in brightness and liveliness in the tone quality as you repeat each vowel.

/i/ as in **be**
/ɪ/ as in **bit**
/e/ as in **bay**
/ɛ/ as in **bet**

2. Consonant Springboard Exercise. As you say each word, pronounce the beginning consonant vigorously, and keep your tongue *forward* on the vowel which follows, as if you were impelling the word forward. Repeat each word five times, trying to push the tongue farther forward with each repetition. Listen for the brightness and liveliness of the tone.

tea	deal	tick	dish	tail	daze	den
teak	theme	till	dig	tame	name	debt
team	need	tin	thick	tape	nail	dell
teeth	neat	tin	thin	day	nape	deck
deep	kneel	dim	knit	date	tell	death
deed	knee	din	nip	dale	ten	neck
deem	niece	dill	nil	deign	test	net
dean	tip	ditch	take	dame	deaf	nest

3. Fronting Exercise. First, read only the odd-numbered sentences below. They are saturated with front vowels and tongue-tip consonants which help you draw your tongue forward in your mouth. Concentrate on producing your words with maximum clarity and vigor of articulation. Next, read straight through all the sentences, trying to carry over a bright, lively voice quality from an odd-numbered sentence to the following even-numbered one.

(1) Take some tea cakes with this tea to Teddy.
   (2) We use that much butter in a single week.
(3) Little Timmy digs deep pits in the sand every day.

(4) Cut these shirt tails about five inches shorter.

(5) See if these peaches will be ready to eat today.

(6) Burn all that paper in the trash burner.

(7) After six the streets seem completely free of traffic.

(8) Mother loves buttered buns with French onion soup.

(9) Speak with clear distinctness with the tip of the tongue.

(10) The front of the tongue moves closer to the front of the mouth.

4. Reading Exercises. The following reading selections were chosen because they are heavily loaded with front vowels and tongue-tip consonants. As you read, concentrate on positioning your tongue farther front in your mouth than usual and using greater vigor in articulating consonants crisply. Ideally, record your reading on tape for replay. Mark any spot where you detect throatiness as you read, and then relisten to your recording for a second judgment of throatiness.

A.
from *The Mikado*

On a tree by a river a little tom-tit
   Sang "Willow, tit-willow, tit-willow."
And I said to him, "Dicky-bird, why do you sit
   Singing "Willow, tit-willow, tit-willow?"
"Is it weakness of intellect, birdie?" I cried,
   "Or a rather tough worm in your little inside?"
With a shake of his poor little head he replied,
   "Oh, willow, tit-willow, tit-willow!"

W. S. GILBERT

B.
Neat Pete

Pete is a street sweeper. He cleans and sweeps the street with infinite zeal. He greets each day with eagerness and vim. He gathers each bit of waste paper and trash into his neat little trash pail. He whistles gleefully as he sweeps the streets. His street is the cleanest street in the city. His best friend is Mr. Clean. He tells the people to keep the streets neat. Pete says "Every little bit of litter leaves a tell-tale streak. Clean living begins with neatness." Be neat like Pete.

C.
"A planet doesn't explode of itself," said drily
The Martian astronomer, gazing off into the air —
"That they were able to do it is proof that highly
Intelligent beings must have been living there."

JOHN HALL WHEELOCK

D. At teatime, "talking to Daddy" began again, complicated this time by the fact that he had an evening paper, and every few minutes he put it down and told Mother something new out of it. I felt this was foul play. Man for man, I was prepared to compete with him any time for Mother's attention, but when he had it all made up for him by other people it left me no chance. Several times I tried to change the subject without success.

FRANK O'CONNOR

E.   I wish I could remember that first day,
        First hour, first moment of your meeting me,
        If bright or dim the season, it might be
        Summer or Winter for aught I can say;
        So unrecorded did it slip away.

CHRISTINA ROSSETTI

F.   from *Patience*

Now is not this ridiculous — and is not this preposterous?
    A thorough-paced absurdity — explain it if you can.
Instead of rushing eagerly to cherish us and foster us,
    They all prefer this melancholy literary man.
            Instead of slyly peering at us,
            Casting looks endearing at us,
Blushing at us, flushing at us — flirting with a fan;
They're actually sneering at us, fleering at us, jeering at us!
    Pretty sort of treatment for a military man!

W. S. GILBERT

Thin Quality

Thin quality sounds like a small, weak voice even when the loudness is adequate. It suggests childishness or immaturity, or a meek, submissive type of person. It lacks the richness and fullness of tone which we attribute to normal resonance. The pitch sounds higher than the actual frequency of the fundamental. Yet it does not sound strained and metallic like stridency.

This is the type of voice wily young women sometimes affect (with a tinge of baby talk) to cajole their fathers or boy friends. In a "helpless, adorable little me" role, it can be tremendously potent. This is the voice we find so appealing in many young children, and which a few skillful actresses imitate for breakfast cereal commercials supposedly spoken by children. It is a voice quality startlingly inappropriate for an intelligent, mature person, either male or female.

The problem in thinness is chiefly in the positioning of the tongue in the mouth. The tongue crowds too far forward in the oral cavity for all vowel sounds (Figure 18). Back vowels (which are correctly articulated with the greatest humping-up of the tongue in the back part of the mouth) are most noticeably distorted.[14] This compression of vowel articulations toward the front of the oral cavity reduces the distinctive features of the vowels. If the back vowels are articulated too far forward in the mouth, they lose much of their characteristic mellow, rich quality.

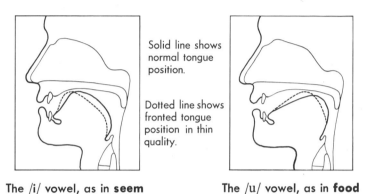

Solid line shows normal tongue position.

Dotted line shows fronted tongue position in thin quality.

The /i/ vowel, as in **seem**   The /u/ vowel, as in **food**

Fig. 18   Tongue Fronting in Thin Quality

Lip shape also contributes to a thin quality. Smiling produces a pleasant expression, but almost constant smiling creates a large mouth opening best suited to high-frequency resonation. Decreasing the size of the opening out of the oral resonance cavity increases the strength of the lower-frequency partials in the vocal tone. Adequate lip rounding on back vowels increases their apparent "depth" of pitch.

If your voice is thin, it *may* also be weak in intensity. The thin voice sounds weak even at normal intensity. If your voice is both thin and weak, you should practice the exercises for increasing the strength of the tone in Chapter 2, as well as the exercises in this section.

Are you using optimum pitch? [15] Good resonance is most easily developed at optimum pitch. If your modal pitch is too high, it may contribute to your thin quality. Obviously, high pitch intensifies the effect of immaturity which a thin quality suggests.

Correct positioning of your tongue can best be learned through certain vowel articulation exercises which follow. Remember that you are practicing

[14] As you will note in the exercises in this section, the "back" vowels are /u/ as in **food,** /ʊ/ as in **foot,** /o/ as in **foe,** /ɔ/ as in **fought** and /ɑ/ as in **father.** You will find more detailed discussions of these vowel phonemes, with additional exercises, in Chapter 5.

[15] At optimum pitch the voice is stronger and has best quality. Modal pitch, at which the greatest number of syllables are said, should be optimum pitch. For exercises refer to Chapter 4: *Finding Your Modal Pitch*, pp. 167–168; *Finding Your Optimum Pitch*, pp. 170–172; and *Stabilizing Optimum Pitch as Modal*, pp. 173–174.

drawing your whole tongue farther back in the oral and pharyngeal cavities. Do not try to change the *shape* of your tongue, or to turn the tongue tip backward. Your tongue position will shift only slightly, but a very little change in the relative size of your resonance cavities will affect the tone quality considerably.

1. Vowel Backing Exercise. Repeat each vowel ten times. On successive repetitions, try to pull the tongue farther back into the throat. Watch your mouth in a mirror. Keep your lips in a position to hide your teeth throughout this exercise. The lips should be slightly rounded for the second vowel and should become progressively more rounded for successive vowels after that. Think of a long tube from the lips back to the point where your tongue humps up in your mouth. As you repeat a vowel, listen carefully for the increasing mellowness and fullness of the vocal tone.

/ɑ/ as in **father**
/ɔ/ as in **fought**
/o/ as in **foe**
/ʊ/ as in **foot**
/u/ as in **food**

2. Consonant Springboard Exercise. As you pronounce each word in the following list, be aware of the articulation of the initial consonant, using it as a springboard to impel the vowel articulation backward toward the back of your mouth. Keep your lips rounded. Repeat each word five times, trying to pull the tongue farther back in your mouth with each repetition. Listen for the mellowness and depth of resonance.

walk	wove	go	goose	coat	cause	coop
woe	won't	gone	good	coal	cough	cone
wool	woke	goat	gauze	cold	could	code
would	wood	goal	golf	comb	cooed	coach
woo	wound	gold	goad	caught	cool	coo

3. Backing Exercise. First read only the odd-numbered sentences below. They are saturated with back vowels and consonants which help you position your lips and tongue for maximum low-frequency resonance. Concentrate on making your tone mellow and full. Next, read straight through all the sentences, trying to carry over the mellow quality of voice from an odd-numbered sentence to the even-numbered one which follows.

(1) Claude wore a warm wool coat.
   (2) Who goes there, friend or foe?
(3) Maude won't go home alone. Would you?
   (4) Miss Tombs taught me in fourth grade.
(5) The moon looks blue on a frosty cold night.

(6) Wicker furniture would look good on the porch.
(7) Bob woke up coughing because he caught a cold.
(8) Put all those purple grapes in a bowl.
(9) Roast goose is good when cooked with wine sauce.
(10) Grass on the other side of the wall looks greener.

4. Reading Exercises. The reading exercises below have been chosen because they are heavily loaded with back vowels and consonants which encourage tongue retraction and lip-rounding. As you read, concentrate on making your oral cavity a long resonance tube, with your tongue pulled back and your lips rounding where necessary. Ideally, record your reading and replay the recording for a second judgment of thinness.

A. The splendor falls on castle walls
    And snowy summits old in story;
The long light shakes across the lakes,
    And the wild cataract leaps in glory.
Blow, bugle, blow, set the wild echoes flying,
Blow, bugle; answer, echoes, dying, dying, dying.

ALFRED, LORD TENNYSON

B. During the whole of a dull, dark, and soundless day in the autumn of the year, when the clouds hung oppressively low in the heavens, I had been passing alone, on horseback, through a singularly dreary tract of country; and at length found myself, as the shades of the evening drew on, within view of the melancholy House of Usher. I know not how it was — but, with the first glimpse of the building, a sense of insufferable gloom pervaded my spirit. I say insufferable; for the feeling was unrelieved by any of that half-pleasurable, because poetic, sentiment with which the mind usually receives even the sternest natural images of the desolate or terrible. . . .

EDGAR ALLAN POE

C. I can see the breezy dome of groves,
    The shadows of Deering's Woods;
And the friendships old and the early loves
Come back with a Sabbath sound, as of doves
    In quiet neighborhoods.
        And the verse of that sweet old song,
        It flutters and murmurs still:
        "A boy's will is the wind's will,
And the thoughts of youth are long, long thoughts."

HENRY WADSWORTH LONGFELLOW

D.
        The west winds blow, and, singing low,
          I hear the glad streams run;
        The windows of my soul I throw
          Wide open to the sun.

        .   .   .   .   .

        The woods shall wear their robes of praise,
          The south-wind softly sigh,
        And sweet, calm days in golden haze
          Melt down the amber sky.

                    JOHN GREENLEAF WHITTIER

E.
                    from *For Whom the Bell Tolls*

It was dark now and he looked at the light across the road and shook his arms against his chest to warm them. Now, he thought, he would certainly leave for the camp; but something kept him there beside the tree above the road. It was snowing harder and Anselmo thought: if only we could blow the bridge tonight. On a night like this it would be nothing to take the posts and blow the bridge and it would be all over and done with. On a night like this you could do anything.

Then he stood there against the tree stamping his feet softly and he did not think any more about the bridge. The coming of the dark always made him feel lonely and tonight he felt so lonely that there was a hollowness in him as of hunger. In the old days he could help this loneliness by saying of prayers and often coming home from hunting he would repeat a great number of the same prayer and it made him feel better. But he had not prayed once since the movement. He missed the prayers but he thought it would be unfair and hypocritical to say them and he did not wish to ask any favors or for any different treatment than all the men were receiving.

No, he thought, I am lonely. But so are all the soldiers and the wives of all the soldiers and all those who have lost families or parents. I have no wife, but I am glad that she died before the movement. She would not have understood it. I have no children and I never will have any children. I am lonely in the day when I am not working but when the dark comes it is a time of great loneliness. But one thing I have that no man nor any God can take from me and that is that I have worked well for the Republic. I have worked hard for the good that we will all share later. I have worked my best from the first of the movement and I have done nothing that I am ashamed of.

                    ERNEST HEMINGWAY

F.   Roll on, thou deep and dark blue Ocean, roll!
           Ten thousand fleets sweep over thee in vain;
           Man marks the earth with ruin, his control
           Stops with the shore; upon the watery plain
           The wrecks are all thy deed, nor doth remain
           A shadow of man's ravage, save his own,
           When, for a moment, like a drop of rain,
           He sinks into thy depths with bubbling groan,
           Without a grave, unknell'd, uncoffin'd, and unknown.

LORD BYRON

G.   from *The Foghorn* [16]

... Her roving eyes moved to the Golden Gate, narrow entrance between two crouching forts, separating that harbor of arrogant beauty from the gray waste of the Pacific — preponderous, rather stupid old ocean ...

For the first time he spoke: "The fog! Chief of San Francisco's many beauties."

She had nodded, making no other reply, watching that dense yet imponderable white mass push its way through the Golden Gate like a laboring ship ... then riding the waters more lightly, rolling a little, writhing, whiffs breaking from the bulk of that ghostly ship to explore the hollows of the hills, resting there like puffs of white smoke. Then, over the cliffs and heights on the northern side of the Bay, a swifter, more formless, but still lovely white visitant that swirled down and over the inland waters, enshrouding the islands, Sausalito, where so many Englishmen lived, the fulgent zone in the east; but a low fog — the moon and stars still visible ... the foghorns, one after another, sending forth their long-drawn-out moans of utter desolation ...

GERTRUDE ATHERTON

Muffled Quality

A *muffled quality* has a thick, mushy, dull sound. It lacks clarity and distinctness. Approximately the same effect can be achieved by holding a folded wool sweater against your mouth while talking. This quality has been described as a "hot potato" voice and "mush-mouthed," both of which suggest talking with food in the mouth. Muffled quality consists of a reduction in intensity of high-frequency overtones and inadequate stopgaps for consonants.

The causes of muffled quality all relate to articulation. The lower jaw may be held too tensely closed (Figure 9), limiting tongue movements necessary for articulation; this would affect the quality of "open" vowels [17] and of all consonants articulated with the tongue. The cheeks may be over-relaxed, furnishing inadequate elasticity to reflect high-frequency partials of the tone (Figure 10). The lips may be too relaxed, acting as a baffle at the mouth opening to reduce the frequency of resonance (Figure 11). The tongue may move sluggishly to articulate consonants, so that they are not quite crisp and distinct enough to be clearly heard.

Mirror practice is invaluable for the speaker with a muffled voice. No other method is as effective in revealing his own habits of articulation. Use your vision for much of your monitoring, while you develop the kinesthesia of more purposeful movements of articulators. A helpful device, too, is to speak as if your listeners were slightly hard of hearing and had to read your lips for your meanings. During practice, exaggerate your articulation.

1. Jaw-opening Exercise. Let your lower jaw drop open of its own weight. Can you get a finger between your upper and lower teeth in front? This is about the minimal jaw opening for the open vowels.

A. While practicing the following nonsense syllables and words, exaggerate your jaw opening. Try to keep the jaw lowered enough for two fingers between your teeth. Say the following, *keeping* your jaw open. Make your tongue move without the jaw for the consonants, and make the consonants very vigorously and clearly.

hah	hot	yacht	dot	not	lark	cot
yah	hat	yard	dart	nod	rot	cart
tah	had	yarn	dark	knock	rat	car
dah	hack	tot	darn	lot	rack	caught
nah	hag	tat	doll	lad	rock	got
lah	hog	tar	dock	lock	cat	god

B. The next practice words have diphthongs for which the jaw is widely open at the beginning and then shifts to a relatively closed position. You must watch yourself carefully, for the jaw closing at the end of one word will tempt you to keep the jaw closed to begin the next. Articulate the consonants with special precision and energy.

high	tie	die	nigh	lie	rye	kite
hide	tight	died	night	light	right	kind
hike	tile	dine	nice	like	rise	cow
how	town	dike	now	lies	round	cowl
howl	towel	dowel	noun	loud	rouse	coin
out	toil	down	noise	loyal	royal	coil

---

[17] Open or low vowels are those which require the lower jaw to drop: /æ/ as in **cat**, /ɑ/ as in **cot**, /ɔ/ as in **caught**, /aɪ/ as in **kite**, /aʊ/ as in **cow**, and /ɔɪ/ as in **coy**. You will find more detailed discussions of these vowel phonemes in Chapter 5.

C. Read the following sentences, paying special attention to opening the jaw adequately and articulating consonants clearly and energetically.

(1) Tie the cows outside by the barn.
(2) Father asked why I buy towels at Thompson's.
(3) The side of my car was smashed while it was parked.
(4) Our house is outside the boundary line of Whiteside County.

2. Lip and Cheek Exercises

A. Grin as widely as you can, stretching your lips far back and up at the sides. Hold. Feel the tension in muscles of the cheeks. Look in your mirror to see how many teeth are bared. Now pucker your lips as tightly as you can, drawing them up into a close, tense "O." Feel the tension in the muscles which encircle your lips. Observe in your mirror the tight puckering and the protrusion of your lips. Alternate these two extreme positions five times.

B. Draw the corners of your mouth back and up in a slight smile, just enough to feel the cheeks become firm and solid. Hold this position while you pronounce the following words. Notice the feeling of antagonistic muscles working when you say /b/, /p/, /m/, /ʍ/ or one of the lip-rounded vowels. Observe that when your lips are held in this position they are finer, more precise articulators.

pea	be	we	paper	speak	bewail	primary
pay	bay	way	weapon	spoke	bewitch	primping
pie	buy	wide	wiping	spend	beware	premium
pole	bow	woe	baby	spoon	prepare	booming
pool	boot	wool	webbing	spite	prepay	blaming

C. Again for this exercise, keep the corners of your mouth pulled back and upward just enough to create a feeling of firmness in the cheeks and an antagonistic pull against the lip-rounding muscles. Say the word **beaver** five times, making sure you touch the lips together firmly for /b/ but touch the lower lip to the upper teeth (and show your upper teeth) for /v/. Now pronounce the following words, exaggerating the contrast between these lip articulations: lips together for /p/, /b/, and /m/, lips rounded for /w/, lip against teeth for /f/ and /v/.

before	proving	ferment	private	deprivation
previous	bovine	preview	verbal	vestment
weaving	waving	verbose	moving	provocative
viper	prevail	weevil	frequent	privateer

D. Read the following sentences, paying special attention to lip articulations and keeping adequate tension in the "smiling" muscles of the cheeks.

(1) Mr. Westley very often leaves before his wife.
(2) We haven't woven very many wool scarves before.
(3) Driving on Western Avenue offers many advantages.
(4) We are frequently more verbal after a fine supper.

3. Tongue Articulation Exercises. For greater precision in tongue articulation of consonants, practice Exercises 2 and 3 under *Throaty Quality*, making your tongue contact firm and vigorous. Additional consonant exercises may be found in Chapter 6.

4. Reading Exercises for Muffled Quality. The following passages have been specially selected because they require crisp articulation, with rapid shifts in position of tongue, jaw, and lips. Read first for precision, watching your control of articulation. When your articulatory precision is good, then, and only then, increase the rate of reading to normal.

A.   *The Bear Who Let It Alone* [18]

In the woods of the Far West there once lived a brown bear who could take it or let it alone. He would go into a bar where they sold mead, a fermented drink made of honey, and he would have just two drinks. Then he would put some money on the bar and say, "See what the bears in the back room will have," and he would go home. But finally he took to drinking by himself most of the day. He would reel home at night, kick over the umbrella stand, knock down the bridge lamps, and ram his elbows through the windows. Then he would collapse on the floor and lie there until he went to sleep. His wife was greatly distressed and his children were very frightened.

At length the bear saw the error of his ways and began to reform. In the end he became a famous teetotaller and a persistent temperance lecturer. He would tell everybody that came to his house about the awful effects of drink, and he would boast about how strong and well he had become since he gave up touching the stuff. To demonstrate this, he would stand on his head and on his hands and he would turn cartwheels in the house, kicking over the umbrella stand, knocking down the bridge lamps, and ramming his elbows through the windows. Then he would lie down on the floor, tired by his healthful exercise, and go to sleep. His wife was greatly distressed and his children were very frightened.

Moral: You might as well fall flat on your face as lean over too far backward.

JAMES THURBER

[18] Copr. © 1940 James Thurber. From *Fables for Our Time*, published by Harper and Row.

B.   from *H.M.S. Pinafore*

When I was a lad I served a term
As office boy to an attorney's firm.
I cleaned the windows and I swept the floor,
And I polished up the handle of the big front door.
I polished up that handle so carefullee
That now I am the ruler of the Queen's Navee!

Of legal knowledge I acquired such a grip
That they took me into the partnership
And that junior partnership, I ween,
Was the only ship that I ever had seen.
But that kind of ship so suited me
That now I am the ruler of the Queen's Navee!

W. S. GILBERT

C.   *The Rabbits Who Caused All the Trouble* [19]

Within the memory of the youngest child there was a family of
rabbits who lived near a pack of wolves. The wolves announced that
they did not like the way the rabbits were living. (The wolves were
crazy about the way they themselves were living, because it was the
only way to live.) One night several wolves were killed in an earth-
quake and this was blamed on the rabbits, for it is well known that
rabbits pound on the ground with their hind legs and cause earth-
quakes. The wolves threatened to civilize the rabbits if they didn't
behave, and the rabbits decided to run away to a desert island. But
the other animals, who lived at a great distance, shamed them, saying,
"You must stay where you are and be brave. This is no world for
escapists. If the wolves attack you, we will come to your aid, in all
probability." So the rabbits continued to live near the wolves and
one day there was a terrible flood which drowned a great many wolves.
This was also blamed on the rabbits, for it is well known that carrot-
nibblers with long ears cause floods. The wolves descended on the
rabbits, for their own good, and imprisoned them in a dark cave, for
their own protection.

When nothing was heard about the rabbits for some weeks, the other
animals demanded to know what had happened to them. The wolves
replied that the rabbits had been eaten and since they had been eaten
the affair was a purely internal matter. But the other animals warned
that they might unite against the wolves unless some reason was given

[19] Copr. © 1940 James Thurber. From *Fables for Our Time*, published by Harper and Row.

for the destruction of the rabbits. So the wolves gave them one. "They were trying to escape, and, as you know, this is no world for escapists."

Moral: Run, don't walk to the nearest desert island.

JAMES THURBER

D.   *The Dinosaur*

Behold the mighty Dinosaur,
Famous in prehistoric lore,
Not only for his weight and strength,
But for his intellectual length.
You will observe by these remains
The creature had two sets of brains —
One in his head (the usual place),
The other at his spinal base.
Thus he could reason *a priori*
As well as *a posteriori.*
No problem bothered him a bit;
He made both head and tail of it.
So wise he was, so wise and solemn,
Each thought filled just a spinal column.
If one brain found the pressure strong,
It passed a few ideas along;
If something slipt his forward mind,
'Twas rescued by the one behind;
And if in error he was caught,
He had a saving afterthought.
As he thought twice before he spoke,
He had no judgments to revoke;
For he could think, without congestion,
Upon both sides of every question.
Oh, gaze upon this model beast,
Defunct ten million years at least!

BERT L. TAYLOR

E.   *The Little Girl and the Wolf* [20]

One afternoon a big wolf waited in a dark forest for a little girl to come along carrying a basket of food to her grandmother. Finally a little girl did come along and she was carrying a basket of food. "Are you carrying that basket to your grandmother?" asked the wolf. The little girl said yes, she was. So the wolf asked her where her

[20] Copr. © 1940 James Thurber. From *Fables for Our Time*, published by Harper and Row.

grandmother lived and the little girl told him and he disappeared into the wood.

When the little girl opened the door of her grandmother's house she saw that there was somebody in bed with a nightcap and night-gown on. She had approached no nearer than twenty-five feet from the bed when she saw that it was not her grandmother but the wolf, for even in a nightcap a wolf does not look any more like your grand-mother than the Metro-Goldwyn lion looks like Calvin Coolidge. So the little girl took an automatic out of her basket and shot the wolf dead.

Moral: It is not so easy to fool little girls nowadays as it used to be.

JAMES THURBER

F.   *On Clothes* [21]

And the weaver said, Speak to us of Clothes.
And he answered:
Your clothes conceal much of your beauty,
yet they hide not the unbeautiful.
And though you seek in garments the free-
dom of privacy you may find in them a harness
and a chain.
Would that you could meet the sun and the
wind with more of your skin and less of your
raiment.
For the breath of life is in the sunlight and
the hand of life is in the wind.
Some of you say, "It is the north wind who
has woven the clothes we wear."
And I say, Ay, it was the north wind,
But shame was his loom, and the softening of
the sinews was his thread.
And when his work was done he laughed in
the forest.
Forget not that modesty is for a shield against
the eye of the unclean.
And when the unclean shall be no more, what
were modesty but a fetter and a fouling of the mind?
And forget not that the earth delights to feel
your bare feet and the winds long to play with
your hair.

KAHLIL GIBRAN

[21] Reprinted from *The Prophet* by Kahlil Gibran with permission of the publisher, Alfred A. Knopf, Inc., copyright 1923 by Kahlil Gibran; renewal copyright 1951 by Administrators C.T.A. of Kahlil Gibran estate and Mary G. Gibran.

CHAPTER 4

Variations in Rate, Loudness, and Pitch for Reinforcement of Meanings and Attitudes

PART ONE • The Functions of Vocal Variations

Skillful use of variations in rate, loudness, and pitch reinforces meanings and clarifies the speaker's attitudes and emotions. Inept use of variations can offend the ears of his listeners, obscure meanings, and produce misunderstandings or misevaluations.

At some time in your life you may have had the misfortune of hearing an actor or public speaker who shrieked and ranted with the misguided intent of swaying your emotions. Or it may have been a minister, a political figure, or a professor who droned along so monotonously that you were moved more to drowsiness than to persuasion. Or was it a friend, relating an exciting experience or a funny story, who obscured the ideas and emotions by poor emphasis, harum-scarum phrasing, and inexpressive intonations? Any such experience is disappointing, sometimes even frustrating.

To Clarify and Vivify Meanings

Students say that much of their anxiety about university courses relates to their difficulty in taking good lecture notes. Often they blame the lecturer for not simplifying their task. You yourself may have thought on occasion, "How much easier it would be if the professor used his voice to *clarify* the structure of his lectures." Why should note-taking be such a frantic scramble?

What if the speaker could somehow italicize the important words? Would it help if he delivered information to you in neat "idea-packages" which you could assimilate and record coherently in your notebooks? Should he somehow indicate with his voice the topic sentence of a paragraph, and the sentences which merely develop it? Dare we hope that a man who lectures on a subject to which he has devoted a lifetime of research (and, we would think, devotion) might transmit to his listeners some of his own enthusiasm about that subject?

Professors and teachers are not the only offenders, however. Think of other public speakers you have heard. Evaluate their speech in terms of the impact, both mental and emotional, which their words had on you.

As you sat in a house of worship, were you held in the grip of strong ideas and feelings? Did you leave that gathering forcefully impressed by the speaker's words? Were you convinced of his genuine concern for your behavior and attitudes, and drawn closer to a deep religious devotion? If your thoughts wandered during the sermon and you were bored, or you would have found it difficult to outline the sermon later, one reason might have been that the speaker's voice did not adequately organize and underscore his ideas.

Perhaps you have been in a committee meeting or executive conference when someone made an excellent recommendation or proposal, only to have it completely disregarded. Later in the meeting another member of the group repeated the same idea, and he not only won agreement on the proposal but was acclaimed for his wisdom and ingenuity. The man whose idea was "borrowed" doubtless felt cheated of recognition and resentful. On a purely practical level he might remember that it is not enough to *have* ideas. If ideas are to be put into action, they must be presented in such a way that they influence the thinking of an audience. Often the difference between an effective and ineffective presentation lies in the vocal coloration and reinforcement of the words spoken.

Though the speaker may be intellectually competent and have good intentions, there is no guarantee that he will convey to his listeners the meanings he intends. The actual logical content of his speech may be obscured by poor use of variations in loudness, rate, and pitch. Also, the emotional content — his attitude toward his subject, the audience, and himself — may be misevaluated if he presents misleading vocal cues to his feelings and state of mind.

To Convey the Speaker's Attitudes

We joke about politicians all too often. You may have heard that a political speech is a list of campaign promises which won't be kept, or that a good campaigner is the one who can talk the most without saying anything. It would seem that in these latter years when television brings a politician literally into your home, he bears a heavier responsibility. Not only are his ideas weighed, but his sincerity is tested. It is the *way* he speaks — the vocal reinforcement — which gives us many of the cues by which we judge him. Does he sound as though he is reading the speech of a ghost writer, or are these *his* ideas, about which he feels strongly? Does he talk like an intelligent man who really understands the problems and issues he discusses? Does he show real concern about the public welfare (*our* welfare)? Many voters evaluate the candidate, or the office holder, more on the *way* he talks than on what he actually says. It is possible for the better candidate to lose the election because he is not as adept as his opponent in projecting his image to the public. Voters act on their convictions. A political candidate must not only *have* a good platform; he must "sell" it to the public.

To Convey Unconscious Attitudes

This vocal reinforcement of the speaker's words has personal as well as public application. Friends or relatives are affected by speech expressiveness as much as an audience listening to a public address. The fact that we affect fewer people in conversation makes the repercussions of our speech no less important. It is, after all, our private life which is affected.

Inherent in many unrewarding conversations, misunderstandings, and hurt feelings is someone's ineptness at conveying his ideas and emotions. When we say, "I know you said thus and so, but you *really* meant such and so," we are interpreting the *way* the speaker spoke in addition to — or perhaps instead of — the words he actually spoke. All of us occasionally *intend* to convey a double meaning; the pity is that we sometimes do it *unintentionally*.

Let us examine the case of John and Mary, who are newlyweds. John is reading the paper after dinner when Mary enters the room modelling a new hat. John says, "Oh, you have a new hat." Mary says, "You're angry with me for buying it!" He spends ten minutes reassuring her that he is not. Then she looks beseechingly at him and says, "Do you *like* it?" John says, "I like it." Mary rushes from the room sobbing, "You think I have no taste. You're a beast. I hate you!" For hours she is inconsolable. What is wrong, short of Mary's being a self-pitying neurotic? You would agree with John that not one word he said was offensive. But *how* did he say it? It is possible that John's budget is strained and he guesses the hat was too expensive. Or that he does think it is a hideous hat. He may have revealed his attitudes quite accurately. On second thought, he may decide that Mary's feelings outweigh the budget or his own taste. In any event, it is important that he use his voice to convey the attitude he intends and to elicit the desired reaction from his "audience."

To Form a "Language" More Basic Than Words

If you have ever observed the reactions of your pets, you have noticed that they react to the way words are spoken more than to the words themselves. Say to your dog in a loving voice, "You're a worthless, ugly little cur, and I'm going to give you away," and he will wag his tail in happy acknowledgment of your devotion.

Babies infer the attitudes of their mothers (and others) by the way words are spoken. They sense her mood and her approval or disapproval by the way she speaks to them. The mother of an insecure child may deny stoutly any overt act of rejection or hostility toward the child. She is completely unaware that he is reacting to her vocal cues — not *what* she says, but *how* she says it. Whether she does feel hostile toward the child or not, the effect is essentially the same. He suffers emotionally because he infers from vocal cues that he is unworthy and unwanted.

THE NEED FOR PERSONAL EVALUATION

It is understandable if you are somewhat defensive about the way you talk. Your personal characteristics, of which speech is one, are familiar and comfortable. The prospect of changing variables of your speech rate, loudness, and pitch threatens to undermine your personality structure. It is easier to convince yourself that you do not need to change — that any change would be questionable and dangerous.

Is your vocal expressiveness good enough? As you study this chapter, try to evaluate your speech as candidly as if you were a stranger. That is an extremely difficult assignment. It is much safer to protect your self-image by remembering that you *intend* to speak meaningfully, that your intellectual grasp of ideas is good, and that your emotional responses are quite normal. Remember, though, that your intellect and emotions are not in question. We are examining, and attempting to change where necessary, the acquired vocal techniques you use to express those thoughts and emotions. Where change in *technique* of vocal expressiveness is needed, the change cannot involve a threat to personality. In fact, improving your skill in using vocal changes to better project your ideas and attitudes can enhance your personality.

Vocal Expressiveness Represents Learned Behavior

A conscious resolve to be more expressive is not adequate. Remember that when you are talking meaningfully, to one person or a large audience, your attention must be directed toward many details — the content of your speech, your choice of words, the organization of sentences and paragraphs, audience reaction, etc. It is practically impossible, at the same time, to concentrate actively on the complex variations in rate, loudness, and pitch. The variations you now use have become a habit. Variations occur automatically in response to the ideas or attitudes you wish to express. If improved variations in pitch, rate, and loudness are to be meaningful in your speech, they must be practiced *in exercises* with conscious control until they become automatic. You must learn new habits to replace the old ones.

Vocal expressiveness is not the natural product of thought and emotion. In the past, adherents of the "think the thought" school of voice training taught us that if we really are sincere we will be convincing, if we visualize the meanings of descriptive words we will "color" those words expressively, and if we actually feel an emotion we will successfully project it in our words. This is all true for the person *who has developed skill in using his voice effectively.* It is patently false for the person who has not developed the necessary vocal skills. Furthermore, it is an insult to the intelligence and emotional responsiveness of a speaker to say that he does not communicate adequately because he is deficient in sense or feeling. Though I were to feel a musical theme surging through my brain, there is no guarantee that I could play that theme on the piano — *unless* I had mastered the skill of playing the piano. Though I could visualize a painting of infinite beauty, I could not render it in oils if I had not learned how to paint. If a speaker has not learned how to vary his rate, loudness, and pitch for effective vocal reinforcement, no matter what comprehension or emotional responsiveness he may have, his voice will not reflect his thought and feeling adequately.

Learned expressiveness need not be ostentatious. Fear that you will sound artificial and "arty" is a real threat. None of us wants to be thought of as a "show-off." If you confuse expressiveness with exhibitionism, it is obvious that you would be wary of it. Wholesome motives do not prompt speakers to make spectacles of themselves. But if you accept expressiveness as a means of revealing (vocally) the true *you* and facilitating your communication with other people, you will be willing to work to improve your expressiveness.

Learned expressiveness need not be insincere. You may fear that consciously acquired vocal expressiveness produces insincerity, that base motives masquerade as high ideals in the speech of a crafty speaker. If meanings can be affected by vocal variations — at a conscious level — an unscrupulous speaker might deceive people and lead them to accept unworthy projects and ideas. It is true that effective speech can serve unworthy ends; Adolf Hitler was a notable example of such a speaker who was monstrously effective. But remember, too, that the effective vocal expression of Winston Churchill and Franklin Roosevelt served well to marshal the forces which successfully defeated Hitler's dictatorship. Developing vocal expressiveness will neither elevate nor debase your moral principles; it will facilitate your communication of ideas and emotions — whatever they are — to your audience.

Vocal expressiveness is not decorative but meaningful. One of the most fallacious attitudes toward vocal variations is that these factors are artful decorations of speech, like pretty frosting on a cake. The person who "embroiders" his speech with improvised, meaningless fluctuations in pitch, rate, or loudness actually deletes meaning from his words; he interferes with the flow of ideas. The true purpose of these variations is to reinforce meanings. They must conform to patterns which are recognizable to your listeners. The person who hears you will interpret what you say within the framework of his experience with heard language. Particular variations in pitch, rate, and loudness are as specifically meaningful as specific sound-elements of a word. Just as you cannot expect to communicate the idea of **dog** to your hearer if you call it a **bog**, neither can you communicate a meaning by lowering your pitch where it would usually be raised to express your meaning.

PART TWO • Rate of Speech

In general terms, rate of speech is a measurement of the quantity of speech within a stated time interval. A speaker with fast rate speaks the same words in less time than a speaker we judge excellent, and a slow speaker takes longer to say the same words. These measurements are of some value in appraising a speaker, but they do not furnish us with adequate information for correcting inappropriate rate.

COMPONENTS OF RATE

The effectiveness of a speaker depends more on the time relationships between the parts of an utterance than on the overall rate of speaking.

1. *The relative duration of syllables* is highly significant. If all syllables are spoken at the same rate, speech sounds mechanical and staccato, and communication of meaning is hampered. Emphasized syllables are normally held longer, and the little words like connectives or articles are spoken more quickly. If the duration of syllables is levelled — either all slow or all fast — we judge rate to be amiss.

2. The *number of pauses* affects rate. It is not simply the time a speaker is *vocalizing* which we perceive as his speaking time. The silent spots must also be reckoned with. If two speakers say the same words, with the same duration of actual syllables spoken, the one who pauses on an average of every three words will take longer than one who averages a pause only every ten words. Incidentally, our subjective judgment of rate is affected also by *where* the pauses occur. If pauses occur at breaks between idea-units, they are appropriate. Either a failure to separate idea-units (phrases) with pauses, or breaking into an idea-unit with a pause, strikes the listener as a disruption of rate, because it interferes with comprehension.

3. *Length of pauses* affects the rate of speaking. A pause may vary in length from a barely perceptible break in the continuity of vocalization to a long hiatus. A long pause may be occasioned by the speaker's intention to allow what he has just said to "soak in" forcefully, by his difficulty in remembering or composing what he ought to say next, or by his inability to inhale breath quickly. Ideally, the length of a pause should be appropriate to the listener's comprehension and assimilation of ideas, and not simply a matter of convenience for the speaker.

DETERMINANTS OF SPEECH RATE

As you have listened to acquaintances and observed the differences among them, perhaps you have formulated some opinions as to the reasons for their characteristic speaking rates. Often a student will protest that he would *like* to talk faster or slower, but that he simply *can't*. What produced his typical rate, and how much is it subject to change?

Emotional factors relate to speaking rate. Consider, for instance, a person who is not sure of himself, who tends to be self-critical and apologetic. He may speak hesitantly, attempting to weigh each word for fear he will say something ill-advised or incoherent. On the other hand, he may begin a sentence with some confidence and then, losing self-assurance and a conviction that what he is saying is worthwhile, rush through the remainder of the sentence as if he were "throwing it away."

Suppose a person has been reared in a highly competitive environment, like a very talkative large family, where he had to "fight" for a chance to say something at the dinner table or in the play room. He may have become convinced that he has to say what he's going to say fast or not get it said, or that if he even pauses for breath he will surely be interrupted. He talks under pressure, as if talking were more of an emotional catharsis than communicating with his listeners.

What of the timid speaker who is afraid of his audience? Though his speaking rate may usually be acceptable in conversation, he may be so nervous when speaking to a group that he loses control of his speech. Perhaps he becomes primarily concerned with getting through with the speech and escaping the odious experience of speaking in public. He loses sight of the communicative aspect of speaking. His words are likely to pour out in a torrent, with little attention to phrasing and emphasis. These emotional aspects of rate, as well as more severe disturbances related to actual neuroses, are obviously not rectified entirely by exercises in speech rate. Yet exercises in phrasing and emphasis can be of benefit after a person has reevaluated his attitudes and emotional responses.

Physiological factors in the speaker's breathing pattern may affect his rate of speech. If you talk to a man who has just emerged from swimming the length of a pool underwater, or who has just run around the track, you will observe the disruption of his speech timing. His words will likely be ejected in quick spurts, and he will probably pause frequently for long intakes of breath. His body's need for oxygen after strenuous physical effort takes precedence over his speech.

A person who has had frequent asthmatic seizures or other respiratory ailments is likely to show modified habits of breathing which affect his phrasing and emphasis in speech. An individual may have acquired poor posture, which affects his breathing habits. Or perhaps he has modified his control of breathing deliberately, in a misguided attempt to improve his speaking or singing. Specific exercises in breath control should be practiced (Chapter 2) if your problems in rate relate to this function.

Training is responsible for the largest proportion of speech rate problems. By training we mean the habits which you have acquired, mostly on the unconscious level, from imitating speech models in your environment. Interestingly enough, we often choose our speech models on some other basis than speech. A little boy copies the speech of a big boy he admires, a parent, a teacher, a movie actor, or a scout leader, any of which may be quite admirable but not necessarily a good model for rate of speech. Later, when the little boy is a man, he remembers nothing of the copying and thinks his rate of speech is "natural."

In many cases the problem is more a lack of training. Perhaps you have not paid much attention to your own rate of speech, or even to other people's. You have not learned to perceive the effects which can be created by good phrasing and emphasis. You may have a poor sense of rhythm generally, or perhaps only in regard to spoken language. Habit is the one cause of poor rate most amenable to change. Exercises in this section are directed primarily at improving habits. With increased awareness of the ingredients of rate, and continued practice in modifying your own rate, you can expect to improve.

Appropriate Reading Rate

In research studies, speech and reading rates have been measured in words per minute (w.p.m.). For factual, unemotional material, college students have demonstrated an average oral reading rate of from 166 w.p.m.[1] to 170 w.p.m.[2] Reading rates ranging from 151 w.p.m. to 181 w.p.m. have been judged satisfactory, with rates ranging from 160 w.p.m. to 170 w.p.m. judged excellent.[3]

If you would like to compare your own reading rate with these norms, here is how to do it. Choose several paragraphs of factual, unemotional material. Avoid a selection containing extremely complicated sentence structure and words you have difficulty pronouncing. Count the number of words in the selection. Two or three hundred words is long enough for the test. Preferably get someone else to time your reading in seconds. Read as if you were attempting to impart the information to an audience of thirty people. When you have timed your reading (in seconds), multiply the number of words read by sixty, and then divide by the number of seconds reading time. The result will be your reading time in w.p.m. Is your rate in the 151–181 w.p.m. range? If not, perhaps you would improve your reading effectiveness by training yourself to read at a more acceptable rate.

Appropriate Speaking Rate

Appropriate speaking rate is normally somewhat slower than reading rate for the same type of material. In extemporaneous speaking, on unemotional subjects, the average rate of college students tested was 159 w.p.m.[4] This difference in rate is explained by the longer pauses and longer duration of stressed syllables. To test your speech rate, make a tape recording of an extemporaneous speech (not read or memorized!) about one minute long. Speak as though you were addressing an audience of thirty. Replay the tape

[1] F. L. Darley, *A Normative Study of Oral Reading Rate*, Master's Thesis, State University of Iowa, 1940.

[2] Grant Fairbanks, *Voice and Articulation Drillbook*, Second Edition, Harper and Brothers, 1960, p. 115.

[3] *Ibid.*

[4] J. C. Kelly and M. D. Steer, "Revised Concept of Rate," *Journal of Speech and Hearing Disorders*, Vol. 14 (1949), pp. 222–226.

and count the words. Replay it again and time it in seconds. Apply the same formula as above: sixty times the number of words; divide by the number of seconds. The answer will be your w.p.m. for unemotional speaking. How does your rate compare with the 159 w.p.m. average?

Other Criteria of Rate

Measurement of reading and speaking rate in words per minute is valuable, but it cannot be considered absolutely definitive. Perhaps the thought has already occurred to you that all words are not of equal length, and therefore a rate measurement in w.p.m. is somewhat inexact. The actual time required to articulate a word like **inconceivable** is obviously greater than the time needed for a small word like **and** or **the**. If you tested your rate with material containing mostly short words, your rate was probably nearer the upper range of acceptability (or above it), while if your reading or speaking was heavily loaded with long words, your rate might have been pulled down to (or below) the lower limits of acceptability. These considerations should enter into your appraisal of your own rate. Actually, a more accurate rate index than words-per-minute would be syllables-per-minute, if norms had been established on that basis.

Remember, too, that a rate measurement in w.p.m. is not always a true measure of the effect your speech will have on listeners. One student's speech may sound faster than another's because he reduces the duration of syllables within his phrases while he increases the length of his pauses. This type of reading or speech is like "jackrabbit" driving. The driver who presses his accelerator to the floor for a quick get-away when the traffic light turns green and then jams on his brakes at the next red light may not reach his destination any faster than the driver who paces his speed to the timing of the traffic lights. The jackrabbit travels faster between lights but stops longer at each light. Are you a jackrabbit speaker? Do you give your syllables maximum acceleration, and then stop for long pauses between phrases? If so, your speech will sound as jerky as the car feels when it races between traffic lights.

The listener needs time to assimilate what you are saying. One long pause does not serve the same purpose as several short pauses, though if you added the time used in the short pauses, they might be mathematically equal to one long pause. If your listeners are still grappling with an idea you have just thrown at them, while you rush on to another idea without a pause, the chances are that they will feel rushed, and possibly miss some of what you are saying. In mathematics, the whole is equal to the sum of its parts. The "parts" we add to produce speech timing are duration of syllables, number of pauses, and length of individual pauses. In speech, the interrelationship of the parts is more important than the pure mathematical sum of those parts.

STRESS

Within any spoken sentence, some words strike the ear of the listener more emphatically than others. Those words which sound more prominent and forceful are said to be stressed. Words which convey the core idea of the sentence receive stress. If you said a sentence and then reduced it to a tele-graph message, the words you would keep would be the ones you normally stress. Or if you were talking to a hard-of-hearing person, the words he would hear most clearly would be your stressed words. In each case, the words stressed are those which are most important for conveying meaning.

Whenever a syllable is stressed, it is said more loudly and more slowly. One of the easiest ways to perceive stress is in the pronounced rhythm of nursery rhymes. Read this one in the same rhythmical fashion a child would. Every stressed syllable is marked with ′ above the vowel.

> Síng a sóng of síxpence,
>
> A pócket fúll of rýe.
>
> Fóur and twénty bláckbirds
>
> Báked in a píe.
>
> Whén the píe was ópened,
>
> The bírds begán to síng.
>
> Now wásn't thát a dáinty dísh
>
> To sét befóre a kíng?

Heavy Stress

When you speak a sentence, you may stress several words. Within any phrase there will be one syllable which has more stress than the other stressed syllables. In our exercises we will designate *stress* with ′ and *heavy stress* with ′ above the vowel of the syllable. To perceive the difference between stress and heavy stress, read the following commonplace phrases, which are similar to those we say every day. They are marked in the pattern of stress which would normally be used.

clímb úp	réad a bóok	brúsh your téeth	táke a náp
júmp óff	táke it hóme	clóse the dóor	sít on the flóor
gét óut	sáw a shów	ópen the wíndow	féed the báby
pút it ón	wént shópping	túrn on the líght	clímb a trée
bring it ín	léave it thére	háng up your cóat	wálk the dóg
páss the tést	táke a báth	dríve a cár	cómb your háir

Stress Patterns

At this point there is danger that you might confuse *stress patterns* with *stereotyped stress*, which was listed in Chapter 1 as a fault of rate. Let us clarify the two terms.

Every language has certain patterns of stress which are familiar and meaningful. English is no exception. Unless you observe normal conventions in the use of stress, you violate the code of communication which has meaning for your listeners. Use of variations in loudness and rate does not mean improvising a unique mode of expression. Good use of stress in conventional patterns facilitates communication.

Stereotyped stress is regular, predictably occurring stress which contributes little to the reinforcement of meaning. Here are some extreme (and ridiculous) examples, which you might well have difficulty reading as marked because the stress is so inappropriate:

I thínk that Í shall gó to tówn to búy a hát this áfternóon.

If yóu áre góing tó the líbrary wóuld yóu mínd gétting a bóok fór mé?

At the fóotball gáme which we sáw Saturday níght there were fíve touch-

downs máde during the fírst quarter of pláy.

Whenever stress calls attention to itself because it sounds odd, or confuses the sense of what is said, it is bad. The repetition of a stress pattern is not bad in itself. If you said five sentences in succession with identical stress, it would not be inappropriate so long as the stress served the purpose of reinforcing meaning. The repetition of a pattern is objectionable only when it obscures or violates meaning.

Familiar Stress Patterns

We have said that stress should reinforce meaning. Yet there are certain conventions regarding English stress which are not absolutely logical. These are stress patterns which we customarily use and accept. Furthermore, we object to changing these patterns except in exceptional circumstances, which we will discuss presently.

Many compound nouns have a familiar rhythm of stress. Certain things which we name in pairs have a rhythm which is not always entirely logical but is nonetheless familiar. Read the following for perception of stress and heavy stress:

chérry píe	végetable sóup	bréad and bútter	shírt and tíe
hám sándwich	T-bone stéak	cúp and sáucer	hát and cóat
tówn méeting	créam and súgar	chíle con cárne	shóes and sócks
béef róast	eléctric líght	hám and éggs	sált and pépper

The opposite pattern of stress applies commonly to certain other compound nouns. Pronounce the following, observing the distinction between stress ′ and heavy stress ′.

dóg hóuse	wástepaper básket	stréet cléaner	trénch cóat
bómb síght	depártment stóre	life gúard	háir cút
swimming póol	cóffee táble	cóat hánger	pówder púff
bánk président	dining róom	báby bóttle	lábor únion
gárbage trúck	fámily róom	géar shift	tráffic líght
páper clíp	hóuse kéeper	stéering whéel	bús dríver

People's names and the names of places have an established rhythm, too. Listen to the stress when you read the following names, and note where the stress and the heavy stress occur. Some people make their own names unintelligible because they become so engrossed in the heavy stress on their surnames that they fail to stress their first names.

Jóhn Smíth	Bóston, Massachúsetts	Cóok Cóunty	Gúlf of México
Máry Móore	Náshville, Tennessée	Máine Tównship	Pacific Ócean

Did you ever notice the difference in the way we stress the names of streets and other kinds of thoroughfares? This arrangement of stress, more a matter of custom than of logic, can sometimes lead to confusion in directions. Since we commonly use heavy stress on the word **boulevard, lane, road,** etc., there is danger its *name* will be obscured. Make certain that you stress the name even though your heavy stress is on the type of thoroughfare it is.

Státe Stréet	Párk Ávenue	Tówer Róad	Pennsylvánia Túrnpike
Sécond Stréet	Míchigan Bóulevard	Óuter Dríve	Kénnedy Expréssway
Canál Stréet	Háwthorne Láne	Áirline Híghway	Indiána Tóllroad

Stress and Logical Meaning

The basic function of stress is to reinforce meaning, to clarify the sense of what is said. Emphasizing the intellectual content of words establishes the logical meaning of speech. Which words deserve stress to convey logical meaning? The words which communicate the most basic information are those you would use in the simplest sentence construction: a verb with its subject and its object. You may elaborate on that structure as much as seems appropriate, but you should continue to stress those basic elements. To illustrate this practice, read the following groups of sentences. Observe that successive sentences in each group convey the same basic information with growing embellishments. Logical meaning is maintained by preserving the basic stress.

A. 1. Máry wánts a cát.

2. Máry wánts a bláck cát.

3. My síster Máry wánts a bláck cát.

4. My síster Máry sáid she expécts mé to búy her a black cát.

B. 1. Wé sáw the cár.

2. Téd and Í sáw the cár.

3. Téd and Í sáw that lóvely yéllow convértible.

4. Téd and Í wént óver to lóok at that lóvely yéllow convértible.

Observe in the exercises above that the adjectives which modify a noun are logically not as important as the noun. Americans enjoy adjectives and use them liberally. Notice, however, that the noun which is modified deserves more logical emphasis than its adjectives. Practice the following phrases for perception of this pattern of stress:

my brówn twéed súit	a bíg bláck cát	státely fórmal gárdens
níce frésh végetables	the méan úgly wítch	a pláid Mádras shírt
a táll thín mán	wíde ópen spáces	lémon créam píe
a béautiful yóung lády	a shíny réd trúck	hót fúdge súndae
a póor óld béggar	stáined gláss wíndow	gréen táffeta bédspread

Stress and Emotional Meaning

Many utterances require special stress in order to convey the speaker's frame of thought at the time of speaking them. By a slight change from logical stress, attitudes or emotions of the speaker are implied. For instance, read the following sentences as marked. The comments in parentheses are suggested interpretations.

A. 1. Hé is a smárt bóy. (a straightforward statement)

2. Hé is a smárt bóy. (but he acts stupid)

3. Hé is a smárt bóy. (but his brother is not)

4. Hé is a smárt bóy. (unbelievably smart)

5. Hé ís a smárt bóy. (in spite of what you say to the contrary)

B. 1. She wóre a blúe dréss. (a straightforward statement)

   2. She wóre a blúe dréss. (after she said she would wear white)

   3. Shé wóre a blúe dréss. (but everyone else wore white)

   4. She wóre a blúe dréss. (she didn't carry it)

   5. She wóre a blúe dréss. (such a dress you've never seen!)

PHRASING

As you speak, you present to the mind of your listener *units of thought* like packaged ideas. The listener assimilates these thought units and accumulates them to compose larger concepts. A unit of thought in speech is a *phrase*. The term corresponds somewhat to the grammatical concept of the phrase, but not precisely. A phrase in speaking may be a whole sentence, like "He has finished it," a part of a sentence, or even a single word. Two characteristics identify a phrase: (1) It contains one, but only one, syllable with heavy stress, which is the nucleus word of the phrase. (2) It is followed by a pause, which separates the ending of one phrase from the beginning of the next.

To test your perception of phrases, reread the exercises immediately above. How many phrases are in A.1, A.2, B.1, B.2? Yes, they contain only one phrase each. Why? Because they are simple statements. Now read A.3 and B.3. Do you see a similarity between them? Each has two heavy stresses, and in the same position. Where does the pause which separates the phrases occur? After the first word, because in each case the first word is important to suggest the contrast implied in the sentence. Now reread A.5. Where should the pause occur? Yes, after **is**, because this is the argumentative word. Which B sentence matches A.5 in pattern? It is B.4, which conveys the same attitude. In A.4 and B.5 where should the pause occur? Do you notice that a pause between the last two words (with heavy stresses) elevates each word to *separate* importance?

Turn back to the section on Stress and Logical Meaning and reread the exercises, for the perception of phrases. In each group of sentences, you recall, there was a gradual expansion of the basic sentence in successive repetitions. Mark with / each place you believe a pause belongs, to indicate divisions between phrases. Check the correct answers below *after* you mark your pauses.

Answers: A.1, cat/; A.2, Mary/ . . . cat/; A.3, Mary/ . . . cat/; A.4, Mary/ . . . her/ . . . cat/; B.1, car/; B.2, I/ . . . car/; B.3, I/ . . . convertible/; B.4, I/ . . . at/ . . . convertible/.

If the exercises in Stress and Emotional Meaning persuaded you that the pause always follows immediately after the heavily stressed word, the exercise above should prove your error. The phrase ends when the thought unit ends. In B.4, for instance, **Ted and I** is the whole subject, not simply **Ted**; and **to look at** really acts as a single word roughly equalling **to inspect** or **to admire**. Phrase composition depends on the sense conveyed.

Phrasing and Emphasis

We can state this as a rule of vocal expressiveness: the shorter your phrases, the more emphatic your speech will be. Each phrase, with its one heavy stress, makes a separate impact upon the consciousness of the listener. Suppose you are giving directions to a worker. Which of the following presentations sounds more emphatic?

 1. Thís is the wáy / I wánt you to dó it.

 2. Thís is / the wáy / Í / wánt yóu / to dó it./

The second presentation seems overbearing and aggressive, because it is so very emphatic. Now, suppose you were reading the following statement from history. Which presentation would impress the details on the mind of the listener more clearly? (Only the heavy stress is marked here.)

1. After the capitulation of the Third Reich in August, 1945, / the entire

   fighting forces of the United States, Great Britain, Rússia, and their

   allies / were able to concentrate their power against the Japanése. /

2. After the capitulation of the Third Reích / in August, 1945, / the entíre

   fighting forces / of the United Státes, / Great Brítain, / Rússia, / and their

   allíes / were able to cóncentrate their power / against the Japanése. /

Phrasing and Meaning

Badly placed pauses can actually distort meanings. In a language such as English, which establishes meaning to such a large extent by the relative position of words in a sentence, a slight error in phrasing can sometimes change meanings considerably. Read the following sentences aloud, as marked. Then change each of them to mean something different by relocating the stresses and pauses:

 1. A mán / éating shárk. /   A man eating shark

 2. The blínd mán / pícked up his hámmer / and sáw. /

    The blind man picked up his hammer and saw.

 3. The wáiter / álways sérves our fóod / and drínks in the díning róom. /

    The waiter always serves our food and drinks in the dining room.

 4. He sélls pínk ládies / glóves. /   He sells pink ladies gloves.

5. The árchitect / dráws dríveways / and wálks in círcles. /

The architect draws driveways and walks in circles.

6. The wáiter / álways sérves our cóffee / and rólls dównstáirs. /

The waiter always serves our coffee and rolls downstairs.

7. Lét's éat Móther. /   Let's eat Mother.

Exercises in Stress and Phrasing. The literary excerpts which follow have been chosen for high saturation of meaning. Examine each of them thought-fully before reading it aloud, carefully searching out its meaning. Then ex-periment with reading it aloud, being sure that you convey its meaning as fully as possible. Remember that heavy stress elevates a word to importance. The more ideas in a sentence, the more heavy stresses you need to use. Re-member, too, to use pauses to separate idea-units; do not be guided slavishly by punctuation. Mark ' over each syllable which, in your opinion, needs heavy stress; mark / at each pause you think necessary. Record your reading as you have marked it. Then listen to your recording, evaluating it in terms of how clearly you conveyed the entire meaning of the excerpt. Repeat the pro-cedure, if necessary, until you are convinced that you have delivered its meaning clearly and faithfully.

1. Quotations from Emerson's *Journals:* [5]

   a. Education aims to make the man prevail over the circumstance. (V, 441)

   b. Life consists in what a man is thinking of all day. (VII, 319)

   c. If you have sharp eyes, use them, not brag of them. (VIII, 19)

   d. A man who is always behind time is careworn and painful. (VIII, 208)

   e. Few know how to read. Women read to find a hero whom they can love; men, for amusement; editors, for something to crib; authors, for something that supports their view; and hardly one reads com-prehensively and wisely. (VIII, 277)

   f. The hater of property and of government takes care to have his warranty deed recorded, and the book written against Fame and learning has the author's name on the title page. (IX, 91)

   g. The man who can make hard things easy is the educator. (IX, 342)

   h. It is impossible to extricate oneself from the questions in which your age is involved. You can no more keep out of politics than you can keep out of the frost. (IX, 369)

[5] From *Journals of Ralph Waldo Emerson*, edited by Edward Waldo Emerson and Waldo Emerson Forbes. Boston: Houghton Mifflin Company, 1909. The numbers following each quotation indicate: 1) the volume number of the journal in which that entry appears, and 2) the page number.

i. Time is short, but always long enough for the finest trait of courtesy. (IX, 562)

j. The retrospective value of a new thought is immense. 'T is like a torch applied to a long train of powder. (X, 67)

k. There is no police so effective as a good hill and wide pasture in the neighborhood of a village, where the boys can run and play and dispose of their superfluous strength and spirits, to their own delight and the annoyance of nobody. (X, 95)

l. Extremes meet, and there is no better example than the haughtiness of humility. (X, 231)

m. Culture is one thing, and varnish another. There can be no high culture without pure morals. With the truly cultivated man — the maiden, the orphan, the poor man, and the hunted slave feel safe. (X, 269)

n. In the matter of religion, men eagerly fasten their eyes on the differences between their own creed and yours; whilst the charm of the study is in finding the agreements and identities in all the religions of men. (X, 278)

2. The first and best victory is to conquer self; to be conquered by self is of all things the most shameful and vile.

PLATO

3. Those who live only for the world, and in the world, may be cast down by the frowns of adversity; but a man is not to be overcome by the reverses of fortune.

WASHINGTON IRVING

4. *The Diamond.*[6] The diamond is a pure form of carbon crystallizing in the regular system. It is the hardest substance known and hence scratches all other substances. Faulty specimens are used for the cutting edge of rock drills and in the form of dust to polish good diamonds. Its density, 3.5, is greater than that of graphite and the other forms.

The world production of diamonds (restricted by producers in order to maintain prices) is about 7,000,000 carats annually. The largest diamond ever found, the Cullinan, weighed 3024 carats before it was cut into several smaller but better gems. Since the carat (metric) now equals exactly 0.2 g., this means a crystal of 605 g., or 1.37 pounds. The magnificent Regent diamond, to be seen at the Louvre, weighs 136 carats.

[6] From *Introductory College Chemistry*, 3rd ed., by Harry N. Holmes. Copyright 1939 by Harry N. Holmes. Reprinted by permission of The Macmillan Company.

The cost gives the diamond much of its charm, but it has a real beauty when skillfully cut. This is due largely to its high index of refraction. Rays of light are reflected from the interior surfaces of the facets several times before emerging, hence the flashing play of light.

Graphite. Graphite is a crystalline form of carbon differing noticeably from diamond. It is black, soft, and lighter than the diamond, having a density of only 2.25. Chemically it is quite inactive, yet it is possible to burn it at very high temperatures.

When any form of carbon is heated in the electric furnace, it turns into graphite; in fact carbon volatilizes at 3537° without melting and on cooling condenses as graphite.

HARRY N. HOLMES

5. *The Bessemer Process.*[7] William Kelly, an American, proved in 1852 that the impurities in melted pig iron could be burned out by a blast of air. It was three years later that Bessemer, the Englishman, discovered and patented the same process. Although Kelly did not apply for patents until 1857, almost two years after Bessemer's English patent was granted, his application was allowed because he was able to prove that he had worked out the idea as early as 1847. This invention enormously increased the world's steel production and thus made possible the great era of railroad building that marked the latter half of the past century.

The Bessemer converter for iron is a huge steel egg lined with dolomite or siliceous rock, as desired. In a false bottom are many small holes. Below is the wind box into which air is forced through a hollow trunnion. The whole converter can be tilted to any angle. Molten iron is poured in while the converter is nearly horizontal, air turned on, and the converter raised. Air bubbling up from the small holes at 20 to 30 lbs. pressure oxidizes the carbon, silicon, sulfur, phosphorus, and manganese with so much evolution of heat that the iron becomes even more fluid. A dazzling flame and showers of sparks present a magnificent spectacle. After 15 minutes of blowing to oxidize the impurities, the converter is tilted to pour its contents into a ladle, from which it is poured into a series of ingot molds. At the moment of pouring, the desired amount of carbon, together with manganese or other elements, is added to the ladle. Since there is much air trapped in pouring, there is danger of weak places in steel rails where such bubbles are found. It is customary to add deoxidizers, which unite with oxygen and form a light slag floating to the top. Manganese as spiegel iron has long been used for this purpose, but aluminum shot has become popular with the steel maker, as has silicon or rather ferrosilicon. Sometimes the deoxidizer is added just as the metal is poured.

HARRY N. HOLMES

[7] From *Introductory College Chemistry*, 3rd ed., by Harry N. Holmes. Copyright 1939 by Harry N. Holmes. Reprinted by permission of The Macmillan Company.

6. Books are the best of things, well used; abused, among the worst. What is the right use? What is the one end which all means go to effect? They are for nothing but to inspire. I had better never see a book than to be warped by its attraction clean out of my own orbit, and made a satellite instead of a system. The one thing in the world, of value, is the active soul. This every man is entitled to; this every man contains within him, although in almost all men obstructed and as yet unborn. The soul active sees absolute truth and utters truth, or creates. In this action it is genius; not the privilege of here and there a favorite, but the sound estate of every man. In its essence it is progressive. The books, the college, the school of art, the institution of any kind, stop with some past utterance of genius. This is good, say they — let us hold by this. They pin me down. They look backward and not forward. But genius looks forward; the eyes of man are set in his forehead, not in his hind head: man hopes: genius creates. Whatever talents may be, if the man create not, the pure efflux of the Deity is not his: — cinders and smoke there may be, but not yet flame. There are creative manners, there are creative actions, and creative words; manners, actions, words, that is, indicative of no custom or authority, but springing spontaneous from the mind's own sense of good and fair.

RALPH WALDO EMERSON

7. There is a time in every man's education when he arrives at the conviction that envy is ignorance; that imitation is suicide; that he must take himself for better or for worse as his portion; that though the wide universe is full of good, no kernel of nourishing corn can come to him but through his toil bestowed on that plot of ground which is given to him to till. The power which resides in him is new in nature, and none but he knows what that is which he can do, nor does he know until he has tried. Not for nothing one face, one character, one fact, makes such impression on him, and another none. This sculpture in the memory is not without pre-established harmony. The eye was placed where one ray should fall, that it might testify of that particular ray. We but half express ourselves, and are ashamed of that divine idea which each of us represents. It may be safely trusted as proportionate and of good issues, so it be faithfully imparted, but God will not have his work made manifest by cowards. A man is relieved and gay when he has put his heart into his work and done his best; but what he has said or done otherwise shall give him no peace. It is a deliverance which does not deliver. In the attempt his genius deserts him; no muse befriends; no invention, no hope.

Trust thyself: every heart vibrates to that iron string. Accept the place the divine providence has found for you, the society of your contemporaries, the connection of events. Great men have always done so, and confided themselves childlike to the genius of their age, betraying their perception that the absolutely trustworthy was seated at their heart working through their hands, predominating in all their being. . . .

RALPH WALDO EMERSON

8.   from *A History of Western Philosophy* [8]

Modern Physics and physiology throw a new light upon the ancient problem of perception. If there is to be anything that can be called "perception," it must be in some degree an effect of the object perceived, and it must more or less resemble the object if it is to be a source of knowledge of the object. The first requisite can only be fulfilled if there are causal chains which are, to a greater or less extent, independent of the rest of the world. According to physics, this is the case. Light-waves travel from the sun to the earth, and in doing so obey their own laws. This is only roughly true. Einstein has shown that light-rays are affected by gravitation. When they reach our atmosphere, they suffer refraction, and some are more scattered than others. When they reach a human eye, all sorts of things happen which would not happen elsewhere, ending up with what we call "seeing the sun." But although the sun of our visual experience is very different from the sun of the astronomer, it is still a source of knowledge as to the latter, because "seeing the sun" differs from "seeing the moon" in ways that are causally connected with the difference between the astronomer's sun and the astronomer's moon. What we can know of physical objects in this way, however, is only certain abstract properties of structure. We can know that the sun is round in a sense, though not quite the sense in which what we see is round; but we have no reason to suppose that it is bright or warm, because physics can account for its seeming so without supposing that it is so. Our knowledge of the physical world, therefore, is only abstract and mathematical.

BERTRAND RUSSELL

9.   from *The Miracle of Language* [9]

On the whole, language lives and grows as spoken language — even though parts of a dead language may be preserved in writing — and this principle is true in more ways than may at first appear. . . . Language was invented as a spoken language, and during the greater portion of its existence, it was only a spoken language, because only in relatively recent times could anybody read or write. Originally, and therefore basically, language was spoken language.

Furthermore, language has remained mainly spoken language. The bulk of the human race remains illiterate, except in the most elementary sense. Even in the more sophisticated countries, only a very few people spend any large part of their time reading or writing. A novelist, whose business is writing, does not tell his wife his soft-boiled egg is practically raw by writing notes to her. A college professor, who is presumably producing learned matter, emits hundreds or thousands of spoken words for every one he writes. Most of us read or write very little, and talk altogether too much. Written words have always been relatively rare, and with radio and television they have become rarer.

Nor is this all. Not only are the foundations of language oral, the foundation of each person's speech is oral. We learn our languages, all the elementary parts of language, from our mothers, from our brothers and sisters who have learned the language from our mothers, and from the neighbor kids who learned their language from their mothers. Thus it happens that women are the great arbiters of language. Mommy stays home, and Daddy does not — it is as simple as that. Women transmit the language, and they do it by oral means. Some of this transmission is deliberate; the mother tries to teach the child to speak. Most of it is unconscious. The mother has to try to get the child to drink his orange juice, and the child wants to tell his mother that the animal outside the window is a kitty. Then when the child learns that the "kitty" is a dog, that there are two furred animals, both with names, he tries to show off by babbling what he has heard. In the process, language is being transmitted and reborn, preserved and changed. . . . The enduring language lives on the breath of men, especially the breath of women; we learn it and we alter it almost as naturally as we breathe.

CHARLTON LAIRD

10.   from *What We Must Know About Communism* [10]

The Communist ideology, we must realize, is divisive not because Stalin had an insatiable thirst for power, not because Molotov, in his international dealings, was a scowling recalcitrant. Nor is it made less divisive by the fact that Khrushchev smiles where his predecessors would have been more likely to frown. It is *divisive at the core* because it denies to the individual any significant role outside the class struggle, and because it flatly denies that any moral law transcends this struggle, binding together as human beings those whom economic warfare has put asunder. Lenin's blunt statement on this score is no less "correct" today than it was when he made it: "We say that our morality is entirely subordinated to the interests of the class struggle. . . . Our morality is deduced from the class struggle."

HARRY AND BONARO OVERSTREET

11.   from *The Makers of Mathematics* [11]

The Pythagoreans regarded *ten* as the "perfect" number. Ten is the sum of 1, 2, 3 and 4. These numbers include the ratios giving the musical intervals discovered by Pythagoras or one of his followers. They were 2/1 (the octave), 3/2 (the fifth) and 4/3 (the fourth). They also represented to this brotherhood a point (1), a line located by 2 points, a triangle, or plane figure located by 3 points, and a pyramid, or solid figure located by 4 points. . . .

They associated certain numbers with the various signs of the Zodiac, observing that a certain number of stars made up a shape which they thought looked like a bull, another group of stars a shape like an archer, and so on.

Thus it came about that the Pythagoreans at first believed that everything in the universe was connected in some way with a number which had something in common with every other number. Thus, they believed that any two lengths must have some definite length common to each. Thus, if a length of $3\frac{1}{2}$ inches is divided into seven equal parts, and another length, of 5 inches, is divided into ten equal parts, each of the seven equal parts and the ten equal parts will be equal to each other. In other words, $3\frac{1}{2}$ and 5 have a *common measure* $\frac{1}{2}$. It had been taken for granted that any lengths (or the numbers representing those lengths) could be expressed in the same units, provided the process of subdivision were carried sufficiently far.

ALFRED HOOPER

PART THREE • Vocal Pitch and Intonation

PITCH

Pitch of the voice at any given moment in speech or singing is the musical note which the voice produces. If you strike the Middle C key on a piano and copy its sound, you will sing the pitch Middle C (C_4). You can probably also speak a sentence such as "I am tálking on the same pítch that I pláyed," matching the pitch of all the words (except those stressed) to Middle C. The changes in pitch on the stressed words will be discussed later. For now, it is enough to recognize that your voice has a pitch characteristic which is subject to certain voluntary control.

Students sometimes use the term *pitch* rather loosely with reference to other characteristics of voice. A girl suffering from laryngitis may say that her voice is "low" today. Actually, she means that the quality of her voice is not clear, that she sounds *hoarse*; but the term "low" implies that the pitch is low. Her pitch may not have changed at all, though her quality has. On the other hand, someone may say that a person's high-pitched voice annoys him, when in reality the voice may not be excessively high in pitch, but definitely is strident in quality and over-loud. We shall use the term *pitch* exclusively in reference to a musical note.

Frequency

Frequency of vibration at the source of a sound determines the pitch which we identify when we hear that sound. Suppose we strike Middle C on the piano. Inside the piano, a felt-covered hammer strikes a metal string. That string is of a certain length and diameter and has been tightened to a particular degree of tension, so that when it is struck it will vibrate (move back and forth) at the exact rate, or frequency, of 256 times per second. When a piano is tuned, each string is tightened until its frequency of vibration is correct for the pitch it should produce.

Pitch Discrimination

Some individuals are said to have perfect pitch. If asked to sing a given note on the musical scale, they can produce it spontaneously and unerringly. The advantage they have over countless other individuals is that their auditory association is very highly developed.

Research has shown that tone-deafness is extremely rare. Most individuals can discriminate between two musical notes which are a full tone apart. (F and G on the piano keyboard are a full tone apart, since there is a black key between them.) Many individuals tested can distinguish between two notes a half tone apart (as between F and F♯ — from a white key to a black key).

Perhaps your own auditory discrimination is not as good as you would like it to be. Do you say you "couldn't carry a tune in a bucket"? Did you ever get shushed when there was group singing because you tended to sing off key? If so, your plight is not hopeless. Experiments have shown that those with poorest pitch discrimination are actually the most trainable. This means that the associative aspect of your hearing can be improved with stimulation.

One of the best devices for improving your pitch discrimination is to work with a piano. Play two notes which are three tones apart, e.g., F - B, until you are certain they sound different. Then play two notes two tones apart, e.g., F - A, until you hear them as distinctly different. Then play a one-tone interval, e.g., F - G, until you really hear that difference. Finally play a half tone interval, e.g., F - F♯, until you hear that difference. Daily repetition of this procedure will improve your discrimination of pitch in a remarkably short time.

There is a psychological stumbling block in the way of a person who considers himself tone-deaf. Perhaps from early childhood he has been singled out as the poor singer by his parents, teachers, or friends. He has been "labelled" and identifies himself by that label. He may even use it as a defense to rationalize his lack of expressiveness in speaking. It may actually be more comfortable for him to hide behind the label than to do anything positive about developing his pitch discrimination. It is easier to say "I can't" than to prove you can.

An encouraging fact is that the pitch changes in speech encompass several tones. Even the person who never achieves good enough pitch discrimination for artful singing can still be quite an adequate speaker. Pitch changes are just as necessary in speaking as in singing, but the changes in speaking are more gross.

Use of Pitch in Speaking

You need only listen to your friends talking for a few minutes to become aware of three simple facts about vocal pitch. First, practically nobody talks on the same pitch all the time. An individual's pitch moves up and down almost continuously as he talks.

Second, you will notice that different people do not necessarily use the same pitch levels in their speech. Tom's voice sounds generally lower than Jane's. His lowest pitch is lower than her lowest pitch, and his highest pitch is also lower than her highest pitch.

Third, you will observe that each person uses one pitch much more frequently than any other. If he begins a sentence with an unemphasized word, he begins on that favorite pitch. He tends to stay on that pitch pretty constantly until he emphasizes a word or ends a sentence.

MODAL PITCH

If you recorded a one-minute extemporaneous speech, and then listened to your recording and identified the exact pitch on which you said each syllable, you would discover that you have a favorite pitch — one which occurs much more frequently than any other. It is like a base line from which you vary. You will hear it on unemphasized words, and even on the unemphasized syllables of an emphasized word (you emphasize only one syllable, not the whole word). Many phrases end on this same pitch, though some phrase endings are marked by a drop to a lower pitch or a rise to a higher one.

In statistics, we label a score which occurs most frequently as the *mode*. It is an actual score, unlike the *mean* (average) which might not actually occur at all. Nor is it the *median*, which would be exactly halfway between the highest and lowest scores. We are not interested in a hypothetical pitch which is the average (the mean) of all the pitches you use. Nor are we interested in a hypothetical median pitch which is exactly half way between the highest and lowest pitch levels you use. The actual pitch which you use most often, the one you vary from and return to repeatedly during speech, is your *modal* (moe-d'l) *pitch.*

Factors Which Influence Your Modal Pitch

An individual's modal pitch is likely to change somewhat under varying conditions. Some people observe that at different times of the day their modal pitch is different. Perhaps your modal pitch is lower when you first get up in the morning, before you are thoroughly awake, or when you become tired. Illness or inebriation can also change modal pitch.

Emotion affects modal pitch. A person who is sad or stunned is likely to use a lower modal pitch. Excitement and gaiety are normally shown by higher modal pitch. The "quietly" angry individual may use a low pitch, while the volatile type of anger may be high-pitched. We tend to associate low pitch with affection between sexes, but higher pitch with talking to babies.

Modal pitch often varies with intensity of the voice. Many people raise the pitch when cheering at a football game, or shouting across a yard, or making a speech to a large audience.

Deliberate changes of modal pitch between successive sentences can serve the purpose of punctuation. For instance, a parenthetical statement is clearly identified if said at a lower modal pitch than the sentence which it interrupts. For example, you might say, "Mother was talking to Harry (our gardener, not your husband) about transplanting the peonies," if you were talking to someone whose husband was named Harry and you wanted to avoid confusion. If you pitched the parenthetical part of the sentence lower than what preceded or followed it, you made the meaning quite clear.

Many accomplished public speakers use a rise in modal pitch to indicate a new paragraph. It is an effective device for helping your listeners follow the organization of your speech. After the first sentence in the new paragraph, the modal pitch returns to its previous level.

A topic sentence gains prominence by changing modal pitch. Normally, the sentence gains emphasis if said at a higher modal pitch than those sentences which amplify or develop the idea stated in the topic sentence. But if the gravity or soberness of an idea is to be impressed, the topic sentence may be said at a lower modal pitch than the rest of the paragraph.

Relation of Modal Pitch to Sex

Modal pitch for men and women is normally quite different. Researchers [12] have found that modal pitch for superior adult male speakers is close to C_3, one octave (eight notes or six full tones) below Middle C (C_4) on the musical

[12] W. Pronovost, "An Experimental Study of Methods for Determining Natural and Habitual Pitch," *Speech Monographs*, IX (1942), 111–123.

J. C. Snidecor, "The Pitch and Duration Characteristics of Superior Female Speakers During Oral Reading," *Journal of Speech and Hearing Disorders*, XVI (1951), 44–52.

scale, while for superior adult female speakers the modal pitch is about G_3, or two full tones (two and a half notes on the musical scale) below Middle C. This is a difference of four full tones between the modal pitch of superior male and female speakers.

Some difference in the average modal pitch for men and women is to be expected. Vocal fold length averages three-quarters to one inch in men, but only one-half to three-quarters inch in women.[13] One of the determinants of pitch in a vibrating string is its length. The longer string vibrates at a lower frequency than the shorter one. Lower frequency of vibration produces lower pitch. Hence, on the average, a man's vocal folds are capable of producing somewhat lower pitch levels than a woman's.

Each person is an individual, however, not an average. Some women have longer vocal folds than some men. Thus, if we were to examine the modal pitch of all men and women, we would discover that some men use a modal pitch higher than some women. What is more to the point, the optimum pitch of some men is higher than the optimum pitch of some women. This is a fact which must be accepted realistically. If you discover that your optimum pitch differs from the average for your sex, you will do yourself an injustice if you insist on conforming to the average. Using a modal pitch which is not optimum can result in quality distortion or inadequate projection. It can even injure the vocal folds. Use the pitch which is right for you — right for your particular vocal equipment.

Relation of Modal Pitch to Age

Usually between the sixth grade and high school graduation, a boy's modal pitch changes considerably. The process is more dramatic in some boys than in others. With some it is "yesterday a soprano, today a baritone." With others the voice change is so gradual that it is practically unnoticed. Boys who have difficulty "shifting gears" to their adult voice often find it hard to control pitch. They frequently experience "voice breaks," during which the pitch shifts unpredictably as much as a full octave upward or downward. On the other hand, some youngsters never have voice breaks.

Change of modal pitch, and of pitch range, is a secondary sex characteristic produced by puberty. Girls as well as boys experience a change of vocal pitch at this stage in their development. The average boy's lowest pitch level drops eight notes and his highest pitch drops six notes. The average girl's lowest pitch drops about two notes and her highest pitch rises about two notes.[14] A girl's voice change is less noticeable than a boy's because the amount of her pitch change is so much less. Also, voice breaks are much less common with girls than with boys.

[13] V. E. Negus, *Mechanism of the Larynx*, William Heinemann (Medical Books), Ltd. London, 1929, p. 257. Negus' measurements in millimeters (17–23 mm. in the adult male; 12.5–17 mm. in the adult female) have been converted into inches.

[14] D. A. Weiss, "The Pubertal Change of the Human Voice," *Folia Phoniatrica* II (1950), 127–158.

Having discussed average development, let us now consider individual differences. All individuals do not mature at the same rate. According to anthropologists, the people of southern Europe mature earlier than Scandinavians, and South Sea Islanders earlier still. Certain families mature more slowly than others. If a boy is a sophomore in college, and his voice has not completed its pitch change, he might simply be slow in this particular aspect of maturation.

There are other possible reasons why a person's voice may, according to popular standards, sound immature in pitch. If he grew up in a geographical area where high modal pitch is a dialectal characteristic, he may have unconsciously copied it. Conceivably, he might have made a deliberate choice during puberty to keep a high pitch in order to avoid the embarrassment of pitch breaks. Possibly he used a higher pitch during some prolonged illness (when his throat was sore, for instance, or he was very weak) and simply kept on speaking at that high pitch after he recovered. Maybe he sang in a boy's choir and found it a happy, rewarding experience; when his voice started changing, he attempted to keep it as it was in order to continue in the choir. The purpose of this discussion is not to psychoanalyze you, if *you* are a young man who thinks his modal pitch is too high. The exercises you will find in this section are intended primarily for the person who has not maintained adequate sensitivity to the sound of his own voice and who has drifted (largely through imitation) into poor habits of pitch control.

It must be reiterated, however, that your subjective evaluation of your voice as "too high" is not necessarily correct. Your modal pitch may not be as high as you think it is. Perhaps you control resonance in such a manner that the tone sounds strident or thin. If so, the *apparent* pitch will seem higher than the actual pitch of your tone. In that case, you should work on resonance to improve the fullness and richness of the tone instead of changing your modal pitch.

Few students diagnose their own modal pitch as too low. Too many of them, on the contrary, yearn for and strive toward as low pitch as possible. This reflects the cultural standards in America generally. For years, one important basis for success as a radio or television announcer was a low-pitched voice. Actors (and actresses), especially in movies, set a standard of low-pitched speaking. The fact that certain highly popular performers have not had low-pitched voices has apparently not impressed the population in general. Further, the significance of vocal pitch has been magnified out of all proportion. Some individuals have overlooked the fact that at such low pitch their voices fade to inaudibility at the ends of sentences, or scrape down to glottal fry. They have strained to force pitch down as low as they could, no matter what the sacrifice in tone quality and projection.

Finding Your Modal Pitch

Read the following sentences in a normal, unemotional manner. If possible, record them on tape. Emphasize only the italicized words. Concentrate on *hearing* the pitch level at which you speak the words which are not italicized. Modal pitch occurs on the unitalicized words, except at the ends of sentences.

1. It is a *voice* exercise.
2. I am listening to the *pitch* of my voice.
3. I must *listen* to my pitch.
4. I am trying to *locate* my *modal* pitch.
5. The words which are *not italicized* are at my *modal* pitch.
6. I believe now I can *hear* my modal pitch.

Now, try to hum your modal pitch. This should be easy, because most people automatically hum on modal pitch unless they deliberately plan to sing some other note. Say "ah" on your modal pitch and prolong it. If you recorded the six sentences above, you can replay them to help you hear your modal pitch. If you have a piano at your disposal, find the note on the piano which most nearly matches your modal pitch. Make a notation of the pitch you used.

Finally, do this. Sing down the scale, beginning on your modal pitch. Call modal pitch "one" and count down scale, "one, two, three, four, five, six, etc." How many notes down the scale can you sing before your voice fades out or shows glottal fry? Remember how many notes you can sing below your modal pitch when you proceed to the exercises on optimum pitch in the next section.

OPTIMUM PITCH

Optimum pitch is the best or most favorable pitch for speaking. By definition, optimum pitch is an ideal — yet one which a great many individuals have attained quite unconsciously. It is entirely possible that your modal pitch is already your optimum pitch. Using optimum pitch as your modal pitch is highly desirable. But naive tampering and uninformed experimentation will more likely move your modal pitch away from optimum rather than toward it.

Too many young men have adopted one of the lowest pitch levels they can phonate as their modal pitch, in the mistaken notion that a low pitch is manly and adult-sounding. In their eagerness to accelerate (or force) voice change, they abuse the vocal mechanism. The vogue for low pitch motivates some girls to "push" their modal pitch down to a sultry baritone, with unfortunate results. There are a few of both sexes who for some reason maintain juvenile voices into adolescence, but the chief offenders are those who attempt to maintain a modal pitch which is below their optimum pitch.

The chief reason students give for using a modal pitch which is not optimum shows confusion in their thinking between pitch and quality. In selecting a model voice to copy, these students honestly assume that the rich, mellow beauty of the voice they admire results from low pitch. Now, let us assume that you received as a gift a valuable violin. Assume that a friend of yours plays the cello beautifully. You would like to produce violin tones as mellifluous as those of the cello. You tune your violin to play the same pitch values as the cello. But it does not sound like a cello. Nor does it sound like a well-played violin. In violating the essential character of the violin — the size and length of its strings, the shape and construction of its resonance chamber — you have spoiled the beauty of its tones. The music of either a cello or a violin is lovely, if well played, but neither of them can assume the pitch levels of the other without sacrificing tonal beauty. Your vocal mechanism, too, has certain inherent characteristics which affect the pitch levels it can produce well. You should learn to "play" your voice with respect for its natural potential.

Characteristics of Optimum Pitch

Optimum pitch permits the voice to function most efficiently. Hence it has three practical characteristics:

1. Optimum pitch is *easiest* to phonate. In reality, each person has not one but several pitch levels, clustered together, at which production of a vocal tone is easiest and most free of strain. At optimum pitch, the muscular adjustment of the larynx is nearest a point of rest than at any other time.[15] At very high pitch the vocal folds must be stretched to maximum length, and the muscles within the folds must also be tensed. For extremely low pitch the vocal folds must be shortened and thickened as much as possible. Therefore, the pitch levels of easiest phonation will be neither the lowest nor the highest notes a person can sing, but somewhere in between.

2. Optimum pitch has greater intensity, with less effort. The vocal folds, being in a more "normal" state at optimum pitch, are more elastic than when extremely stretched or extremely thickened. Being more elastic, they are more responsive to the force of sub-glottic breath pressure. They can swing more widely apart and pull back together more quickly. Intensity of the vocal tone depends on amplitude of the vibration (the width of the opening when the vocal folds are pushed apart by sub-glottic breath pressure) and the duration of the glottal closure (resulting from quicker closure of the vocal folds).

As we noted earlier, the intensity of the tone you hear is also affected by resonance. Resonance tubes such as your own pharyngeal cavity and oral cavity have individual dimensions and acoustic characteristics best suited to amplification of particular pitches. In the chapter on Resonance we discussed ways of changing the size, shape, and wall texture of these resonating tubes. Such conscious control is still somewhat limited, however, by the basic physiological characteristics of your neck and mouth. Your optimum pitch levels fall within the frequencies which your resonance cavities can amplify most efficiently.

3. Optimum pitch is so located within the total range of the voice as to permit effective variation in pitch for intonations. By *total range* we mean all of the frequencies at which a person can produce a vocal tone. Total range

[15] Von Wolfgang Zenker and Adolf Zenker, "Uber die Regelung der Stimmlippenspannung durch von auben eingreifende Mechanismen," *Folia Phoniatrica*, Vol. 12, No. 1 (1960), 1–36.

extends from the lowest pitch a person can sing to the highest, including falsetto. Intonation in English (discussed in detail later in this chapter) involves changes of pitch both upward and downward from modal pitch. With good speakers, upward pitch changes are greater in extent than downward pitch changes. This means that optimum pitch will be somewhat lower than the midpoint in the entire singing range.

Symptoms of Inefficient Modal Pitch

Several vocal symptoms may suggest the possibility that your modal pitch is not optimum. In themselves, they are not conclusive. However, if you notice any of these problems in your own voice, and especially if your instructor has called them to your attention, find your optimum pitch and compare it with your modal pitch.

1. *Glottal fry or fading on downward shifts in pitch* at the end of a statement may indicate that you are attempting to produce such a low pitch at sentence endings that you cannot achieve a clear, strong tone. On the other hand, either glottal fry or fading may result from inadequate breath support.

2. *Weak tones throughout speech* might indicate that you are speaking at pitch levels where you cannot use resonance well to produce adequate intensity. This problem could also result from poor control of breath force and insufficient elasticity of the vocal folds.

3. *Nasal, strident,* or *thin quality* frequently occur with too-high modal pitch. Since the best use of resonance is achieved at optimum pitch, these resonance problems are often reduced when the speaker achieves optimum pitch.

4. *Harsh, hoarse, breathy,* or *throaty quality* may be at least partly related to speaking at a too-low modal pitch. Strain to produce pitch below normal range can contribute to laryngeal hypertension in harshness and hoarseness, and can cause hypertension in the lower pharynx to cause throatiness. On the other hand, speaking at a pitch too low for adequate closure of the glottis can produce breathiness.

5. *Special strain in producing high notes used for emphasized words* may mean that your modal pitch is too high. Occasionally, however, such strain results from the speaker's failure to develop flexibility in muscular adjustments necessary for pitch changes.

6. *Inadequate changes in pitch for intonation* often suggest a modal pitch which is not optimum. If modal pitch is too near the lower extremity of the total range, downward pitch changes are curtailed. If modal pitch is too near the upper limit of the total range, the amount of pitch change upward is reduced. But the same limitation of pitch changes may result from faulty auditory memory for normal intonation, or from inhibited oral expressiveness.

Finding Your Optimum Pitch

A. THE STRENGTH AND EASE TEST. Start at any pitch which seems comfortable for you, and sing "ah" in as easy and relaxed manner as you can.

Repeat "ah" on the same pitch, prolonging the vowel and increasing the loudness. Listen to the fullness and the loudness of the tone. Feel the degree of ease with which you produced the tone. If possible, play this same note on the piano, so that you can identify which note it is.

Singing "ah," move up the scale several notes and then down the scale for several notes, swelling the loudness on each. Select the one note, or more than one, on which your voice is produced with the greatest ease, strength, and fullness. You may discover one optimum pitch which can be produced loudest with ease. On the other hand, you may identify several notes in sequence that are equally easy to produce in a strong, full tone, any one of which would be an optimum pitch for you.

B. The Fourth-of-Total-Range Test

1. Sing "ah" in a relaxed manner, at an easy loudness level, beginning anywhere you wish on the musical scale. Sing down the scale to the very lowest note you can produce audibly and clearly. Identify that note by matching it on the piano, if possible.

2. Sing "ah" on successive notes upward until you reach the highest note you can produce audibly and clearly — to the very top of your falsetto range if you can sing falsetto. Identify the top note in your range.

3. Measure the extent of your total range. You could count the number of notes between your lowest and your highest pitch. In a musical scale, however, the interval between notes is not always the same. A scale played on all white notes begins at C and ends at C an octave higher. On Figure 1, you will see that from D to E is a full tone (since D to D♯ is a half tone and D♯ to E is a half tone); but from E to F is only a half tone. The interval between C_3 and C_4 is twelve half tones. The most accurate measure of your range, then, is in half tones. Count the half-tone intervals between the lowest and highest notes you sang.

4. Divide the number of half tones in your total range by four. For instance, if your total range is twenty-eight half tones, twenty-eight divided

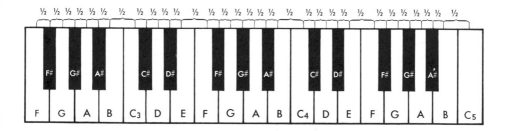

Fig. 1 Counting Half Tones on the Piano Keyboard

(For Exercise B, The Fourth of Total Range Test)

by four equals seven half tones. If your range is twenty-three half tones, then twenty-three divided by four equals approximately six half tones.

5. On the piano keyboard, count up from the lowest clear note in your total range the number of half tones which represent one-fourth of your range. For instance, if your lowest note was G below C_3, then seven half tones above that would be D above C_3. Or if your lowest note was F above C_3, then six half tones above that would be B below C_4. This one-fourth of range point has been represented as *the* optimum pitch by some authors. While we believe other pitches nearby will likely also be optimum for you, this is certainly one good pitch for you to use.

C. Count Up From Lowest Pitch

1. On any note you find comfortable, sing the word ONE, as relaxed and easily as possible. Sing ONE on each pitch as you go down the musical scale, continuing downward until you reach the first note which is strained, scrapes, or exhibits glottal fry. That "bad" note marks the lower limit of your range. You could not use that note in speaking effectively, but you could use the note just above it. Now sing up scale, calling the "bad" bottom note ONE, the next higher note TWO, etc., until you reach FIVE.

Test note FIVE to see if you can increase the intensity on it with minimal effort and strain. Then attempt to sing an octave higher than note FIVE, either as a "giant step" or singing up the scale eight notes higher. Was the note at the top of the octave relatively clear and unstrained?

Repeat this test for notes SIX and SEVEN. Was any one of the three — FIVE, SIX, or SEVEN — stronger and easier than the others? From which of these could you best go an octave higher? Either the fifth, sixth, or seventh note above the bottom of your range is likely to be optimum pitch for you. Testing of college students has shown note SIX to be the average optimum pitch.

2. The note you located as optimum pitch fulfills the following requirements: (a) It is within the pitch band where your tones are strongest with least effort, for use as your modal pitch. (b) You will have at least four notes below your modal pitch for downward intonations. (Less than four notes downward would sound as if a sentence did not end.) (c) You will have as much as an octave above modal pitch for upward intonations. (You will need this much pitch change for really emphatic stress on a word.)

3. You will find this test of optimum pitch easy to perform. You need not use a piano, or a pitch pipe. All you need is your own vocal apparatus and your own auditory attention.

Once having decided which note is your optimum pitch, in relation to the bottom of your range, you can re-find it at any time. Suppose note SIX is your optimum pitch. Then whenever you wish to check your pitch, simply sing down scale to your first scraping note, call that ONE, and count up scale to SIX. You have a reliable reference point with you at all times.

Comparing Modal Pitch to Optimum Pitch

When you located your own modal pitch, you were asked to sing down scale to the bottom of your range. You counted how many notes below modal pitch you could phonate. Then you tested your optimum pitch. How many notes above the bottom of your range is your optimum pitch? How does your modal pitch compare with the optimum pitch you discovered?

Should you change your modal pitch if it does not agree with the optimum pitch you located? *Yes,* if either one of these conditions applies:

1. If your modal pitch is less than *four notes above the lowest note* you can clearly phonate, learn to use optimum pitch as your modal pitch. Otherwise, you will either fail to drop your pitch adequately at sentence ends to indicate completion of the thought, or you will have glottal fry or strain when you try to force the pitch below the lower limit of your range.

2. If your modal pitch is as much as *two notes* from optimum, it is usually wiser to adopt optimum pitch as modal. If modal pitch is two notes *below* optimum, you will have trouble with downward intonations, as stated in item 1 above. If modal pitch is two notes *above* optimum, you might have difficulty reaching a note an octave higher for strong emphasis. Also, you will not use resonance effectively for quality and strength of tone if your modal pitch is several notes from optimum.

Stabilizing Optimum Pitch as Modal

If you need to change your modal pitch to optimum, be sure to establish the new pitch reliably in your everyday speech. When you have exercised conscious control of your pitch until you *automatically* use optimum pitch as your modal pitch, you have stabilized the pitch. Stabilizing the new pitch involves two processes which must be synchronized.

First, you must establish a new reference point for pitch in your auditory memory. Second, you must train your laryngeal musculature to produce that pitch reliably. Exercises must be performed frequently and continually until your new pitch reference (optimum) becomes dominant over your old modal pitch.

Since using a book for practice limits you as to the times and places you can practice, you will do better if you learn the following procedure well enough to follow it without the book. If you can run through this routine for two or three minutes at a time, as frequently as once an hour during the waking day, you will stabilize the new pitch remarkably fast. The frequency of repetition influences your pitch for ordinary speaking between practice periods. Follow this procedure each time you practice:

1. Find the optimum pitch you first discovered. (Sing ONE down the scale to the first note on which you have glottal fry or scraping. Count up the scale to the number which represents your optimum pitch. Was it FIVE, SIX, or SEVEN?) Never trust your memory of the pitch in this phase of practice. Re-find optimum pitch *every* time you practice.

2. Prolong an "ah" on your optimum pitch. Count slowly from 1 to 5 on optimum pitch as loudly as conditions allow, so that the pitch will "drum" into your hearing.

3. Sing "ah" on optimum pitch. Then chant a short sentence on optimum pitch, e.g., "Ah, this is my optimum pitch." Chanting means saying every word on the same pitch. It will sound dull, to be sure, but it will bombard your ears with *your* optimum pitch. Make up several sentences and chant them on optimum pitch. Listen to your pitch as you chant.

4. Sing "ah" on optimum pitch. Then *begin* a short sentence on that same pitch, changing pitch within the sentence for normal expressiveness. The only restriction on sentences you use for this exercise is that they *cannot begin* with an emphasized word. When you emphasize a word strongly, you say it at a higher than modal pitch. To keep your modal pitch at optimum, then, begin each sentence with an unemphasized word.

Sample sentences: (Emphasized words are underlined.)

> It is my coat.
> It is a brown desk.
> It is a blue rug.
> Stay in my room awhile.
> Listen to this pitch.

5. Take this warning seriously. Be absolutely *sure* that you begin every one of the sentences in #4 on your *optimum* pitch. There is a strong danger that you will drift away from it. In the first place, you will end each sentence with a drop in pitch. If your old pitch was lower than your optimum, you will be tempted to begin the next sentence lower — closer to the low pitch which ended the preceding sentence. If your old pitch was higher than optimum, the high pitch you use for the emphasized word of one sentence will tend to draw your pitch upward for the beginning of the next. Whenever you are in doubt about the pitch on which you should begin a new sentence, re-find your optimum pitch and chant the sentence on it before saying the sentence with normal intonation.

Remember, the whole intent of this exercise is to establish a pitch in your auditory memory which you will learn to pre-hear and match when you produce a vocal tone for speech. The real value of the exercise is in giving you auditory stimulation for auditory memory of your optimum pitch.

INTONATION

The English language uses three pitch levels for intonations. The most frequently used is modal pitch, the easy in-between pitch level we have already discussed. A higher pitch than modal and a lower pitch than modal are also commonly used. We shall designate these three pitch levels as *low pitch* (#1), *modal pitch* (#2), and *high pitch* (#3). These designations indicate their relative positions on the musical scale. We cannot prescribe the exact musical value of each of them, because individual voices differ. Whatever modal pitch (#2) is, low pitch (#1) will be lower than modal and high pitch (#3) will be higher than modal. Normally, the space between #2 and #3, in number of musical notes, will be greater than that between #2 and #1. We shall discuss ideals for these intervals, and how to achieve them, later.

Now, let us examine the uses of these pitch levels in English intonation. Intonation involves two functions: (1) pitch change on a particular syllable as an adjunct of stress, and (2) pitch change at the end of a phrase to indicate the intention or purpose in speaking it.

Use of Pitch for Emphasis

Suppose you said, "Give me *that* one." There is a reason (in the meaning intended) for emphasizing the word **that**. Basically, emphasis involves stress (produced by greater duration and loudness) on a particular syllable. To increase emphasis still more, we use a *higher* pitch on the word which is important to meaning. In the sentence "Give me *that* one," we assume that the speaker has a choice of objects and that the nature of the objects is agreed on, since **one** is used rather than a specific noun. Suppose he said, "Give me that bóok," in a situation where he might choose from books and other objects, too. Now he needs to stress **book** to tell what kind of thing he wants, and **that** to tell which specific one he wants. Therefore, he needs to emphasize two words. He will give greater duration and loudness to both **that** and **book** than to the preceding words. But how can he make **book** more emphatic than **that**? By using higher pitch on **book** in addition to increased duration and energy. The most emphasized word in any phrase (as far as meaning is concerned) has *high pitch* in addition to duration and stress.

Phrase Terminal Intonation

The second important function of intonation is to indicate the speaker's purpose in speaking. The intention of his words is conveyed by the pitch level on which he completes the sentence. Suppose you saw the words "That's my hat" on a page, unpunctuated. Do they make a statement, or ask a question? What if a question mark followed? It would become a question, of course. Try saying "That's my hat?" as a question. How did you convey a questioning intention? Your pitch went up at the end of the sentence. Now say "That's my hat" as a statement. Your pitch should have dropped to low (#1), so that the sentence sounded positive and completed. Pitch contours which end phrases can also convey other meanings, as we shall see presently.

Intonation Contours

To illustrate intonations graphically, we shall superimpose intonation contours on sentences. The pitch line will be directly beneath all words spoken on modal pitch. When the line drops a space below the word, it indicates low (#1) pitch level. When the line is drawn above a word or syllable, it indicates high (#3) pitch level.

STATEMENTS. At the end of a statement, the pitch drops to low (#1) to indicate finality. The drop in pitch is a signal to the listener that the idea is completed, so that his attention may "let go" the content of the statement just finished and be free to grasp the following idea as a fresh concept not dependent on the preceding one. Read these short sentences to perceive the two uses of pitch: (1) the most emphasized word in the sentence is spoken at high pitch (#3); (2) each sentence which is a statement ends at low pitch (#1).

SIMPLE QUESTIONS REQUIRING YES OR NO ANSWERS. Suppose you spoke the same sentences above as questions. It is not even necessary to rephrase them or to reverse the order of words. All you need do is raise the pitch at the end of the sentence, and it becomes a question. As you read the sentences below, note that to indicate a question, the pitch continues upward from high pitch (#3) on the emphasized word to a higher pitch (#3+). The upward glide in pitch at the end marks the sentence as a question.

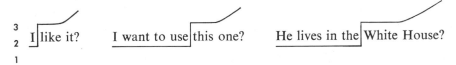

Did you observe that each of the foregoing questions could appropriately be answered with a simple "yes" or "no," requiring no informative answer? That is an important aspect of the rising terminal contour. As we shall see presently, not *all* questions have a rising pitch at the end. If a question can be answered with "yes" or "no," the rising contour is required. Even when word order is reversed, as in the following sentences, the intonation contour shows a terminal rise to #3+ because a "yes" or "no" answer suffices.

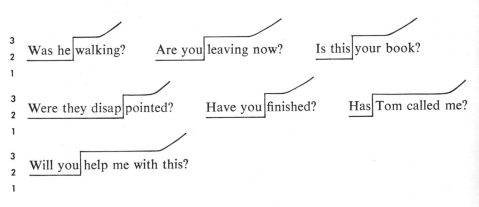

QUESTIONS INTRODUCED BY INTERROGATIVE WORDS. A terminal pitch rise is one marker of a question, and a very necessary one when it is the only indication that the words spoken comprised a question, as in the examples above. Many questions in English, however, do not end with a pitch rise. If a question begins with an interrogative word, **how, what, when, where, which, who, whose, whom,** or **why,** the interrogative word marks it as a question, and a terminal pitch rise is not needed. As you read each of the following examples, note that the most emphasized word is said at high pitch (#3), but that the pitch drops to low (#1) at the end of the question. One significant characteristic of interrogative-word questions is that they cannot be answered simply "yes" or "no," but require informative answers.

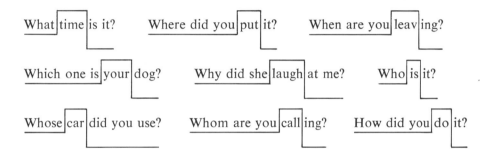

With special intention, these same questions may be spoken with a rising terminal intonation. If an interrogative-word question ends like a statement, with a drop to low pitch (#1), it calls for a straightforward, informative answer. But if it ends with a rising pitch (#3+), it calls for repetition or confirmation of an answer already given, or it may be a rhetorical question the speaker intends to answer himself.

Suppose you asked "What time is it?" You would expect an answer like "Four

o'clock." But suppose you had an appointment at 3:30 and realize that if it is now 4:00 you are half an hour late, you might well ask again incredulously,

"What time is it?" Or suppose you asked "Where did you put it?" about the book

you lent your roommate, you would expect an answer like, "On your desk." If your roommate answered, "In the shower," you might wonder if your ears deceived

you and ask again, "Where did you put it?"

Sometimes a speaker asks a rhetorical question to heighten the impact of his statement, posed as the answer to his question. "What did I say to him?" might

be the introduction to a blow-by-blow account of how the speaker won an argu-

ment. "What is he doing about it?" may well be the springboard for a diatribe

against someone's ineptitude and inefficiency. The rising pitch at the end of
these questions marks them as special interrogative-word questions, not to be
answered with ordinary information.

INTONATION OF FRAGMENTARY SENTENCES.   In informal speech, fragmentary sen-

tences are common. To the question, "What have you been doing all afternoon?"

you might answer simply "Typing," which has the same intonation contour as the

grammatically complete sentence, "I have been typing all afternoon." If asked,

"Who is going to the prom Friday night?" you could answer either "Jean is" or

"Jean is going to the prom Friday night." And that last question could be ab-

breviated to "Who is going?" or even to "Who is?" if its reference is clearly

established by what was previously said. In each case, the fragmentary sentence
has the same intonation contour as if it were expanded into a grammatically complete sentence in more formal speech.

INTONATION OF PHRASES WITHIN SENTENCES. So far, we have been discussing
intonation as if every sentence were a single phrase. In each example you
have read, there has been a single word with strong stress on which the pitch
rose to high (#3). There has been only one spot — the end of the sentence —
where the terminal intonation was considered. In actuality, each sentence we
speak may consist of several phrases, and each phrase will have an intonation
contour of its own.

To lay down hard and fast rules for phrasing is impossible. Your phrasing
must depend on what you intend to say. One helpful rule is that each phrase
has exactly one heavily stressed word, and that heavily stressed word is said

at a high pitch. This principle is best illustrated in the following expanded sentences. As you read the (a)-(b)-(c) versions aloud in sequence, you will see that each one is a further expansion of the idea in the preceding sentence. Each idea which is increased in prominence demands a strong stress, and with strong stress a high pitch is needed. The intonation contour is superimposed, as before. Division into phrases is marked by a heavy slash /. Note that when high pitch for emphasis occurs on the last syllable in the phrase, the pitch must change within the space of one syllable from high to modal (#3–2) or from high to low (#3–1); e.g., in the sentences below, **home** in 1.(a), (b), (c), **eat** in 2.(c), **Marine** in 3.(a), (b), (c), **John** in 3.(b), (c). A pitch change on a single syllable, though quite rapid, moves continuously and gradually through all intervening pitch levels (marked in the intonation contour as a curved line). Such a gradual pitch change on a single syllable is called a *glide*.

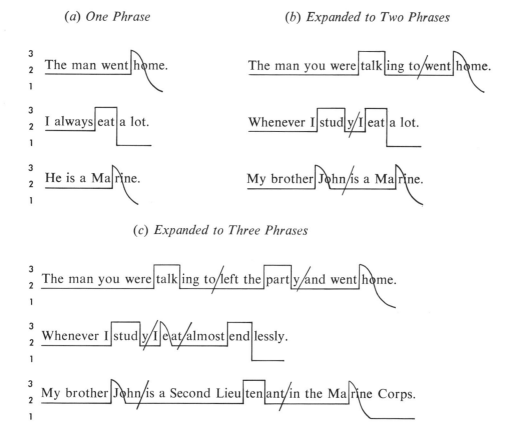

(a) One Phrase

(b) Expanded to Two Phrases

(c) Expanded to Three Phrases

The return to modal pitch (#2) at the end of phrases in the sentences above is noteworthy. When a phrase does not complete the statement, its ending at modal pitch implies that something more which is directly related will follow. In effect, when the pitch is "left in the air," the hearer's attention is kept up.

Read the following examples aloud, noting the "incomplete" sound of modal pitch at phrase endings within the sentences, and the sense of finality and completion implied by the drop to low pitch (#1) at the ends of sentences.

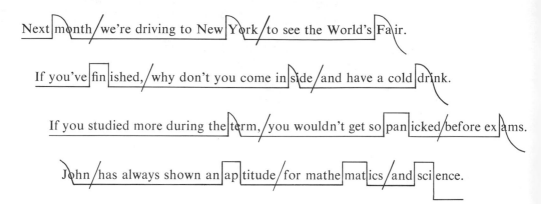

If your sentence lists a series of items or events, each of the items or events comprises a phrase. The intonation on such phrases may be of two types, each of which has specific significance. Read the following sentences aloud, as marked. Note that the (a) versions sound entirely communicative but matter-of-fact, with a return to modal pitch (#2) at the end of each phrase. You will probably think the (b) versions, with a rise to higher pitch (#3+) at the end of each phrase, sound more exciting. Which intonation contour you would use at a particular time would be governed by the attitude you wanted to express.

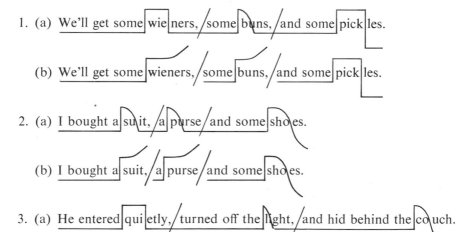

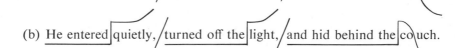

4. (a) I pressed a dress, wrote a letter, and washed my hair.

(b) I pressed a dress, wrote a letter, and washed my hair.

A common type of sentence is one which presents two choices to the listener. It asks if someone wants this or that, if someone intends to do this or that, if someone thinks or feels this or that. The sentences which follow are of this type. Intonation makes the difference between the implied meaning in the (a) and (b) versions. As spoken in (a), both propositions may be refused or accepted, but the intonation of a (b) question assumes the listener to be agreeable to one proposition or the other. Each (a) question is really two separate questions, and can be answered separately or collectively either "yes" or "no." But the intonation of a (b) question presupposes that one or the other alternative will be acceptable. As you read each question, first with the (a) intonation and then with the (b) intonation, think of the answer which would be appropriate. For instance, to refuse 1.(a) you would need only say, "No, thanks"; that would cover both choices. But to refuse 1.(b), you would need to say, "Neither, thanks," because the intonation presumes your answer to be either "pie" or "cake."

(a) Either Can Be Rejected   *(b) Must Choose One of Them*

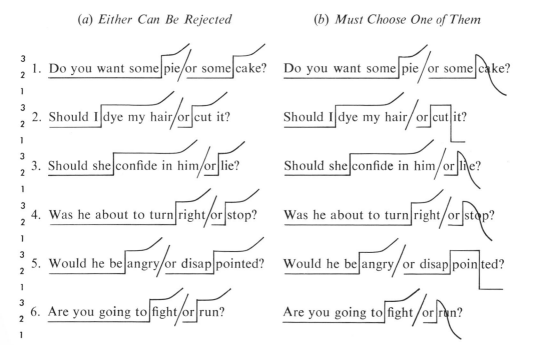

1. Do you want some pie or some cake?   Do you want some pie or some cake?

2. Should I dye my hair or cut it?   Should I dye my hair or cut it?

3. Should she confide in him or lie?   Should she confide in him or lie?

4. Was he about to turn right or stop?   Was he about to turn right or stop?

5. Would he be angry or disappointed?   Would he be angry or disappointed?

6. Are you going to fight or run?   Are you going to fight or run?

Intonation Problems

Mistakes which you might make in intonation fall into two categories: (1) kind of intonation, and (2) extent of intonation.

Kind of intonation means the nature of the pitch changes. *Where* does the pitch rise? *Where* does it stay on modal pitch? *Where* does it fall? Your pitch variations should reinforce meanings and increase the intelligibility of your speech. They should correctly convey your attitudes and feelings towards what you are saying, and the person or persons to whom you are talking. Whatever intonations you use, good or poor, they assuredly do convey information. Either they reinforce your meanings, or they obscure and confuse them.

(a) Are you using high pitch to coincide with heavy stress? Obviously, if you are stressing the wrong words and using high pitch to reinforce your incorrect stress, you are not speaking effectively. The essence of that problem, however, is in your choice of words to stress. But what if you do stress the words which carry strong meaning, yet fail to add high pitch to stressed words for emphasis? Then you should concentrate on hearing the words which are emphasized and raising your pitch on those words.

(b) Are your intonations at phrase endings appropriate to your intention in speaking? Is it possible that your intonations are stereotyped, repeating the same pattern over and over, regardless of the type of phrase you have spoken? If this is your problem, you need increased auditory awareness of the different terminal intonations in relation to their meanings. You will benefit from continual practice in hearing the intonation contours presented in the foregoing section.

Extent of intonation means the amount of change in pitch you use when you change pitch. Even if you use appropriate intonation contours, you may fail to communicate if your pitch changes are so slight that your listener has difficulty in perceiving them. If you used no pitch changes at all, you would be a monotone. A true monotone is extremely rare. But some speakers use such small intervals of pitch change that their listeners hear them as monotones. On Figure 2, the range of the "apparent monotone" is actually five notes on the musical scale. Perhaps your pitch changes perceptibly, but so little that your listeners judge you to be unemotional and dull. Appraise the extent of your pitch changes realistically.

Are your high notes, which you use for emphasis, high enough? Are your low notes, which you use to end statements, low enough (and clear)? Concentrate your effort on the aspects of your intonation which need improvement.

Speaking Range

Speaking range is a measure of the musical interval (the number of notes) between the high pitch (#3) and the low pitch (#1) which you use in speaking.

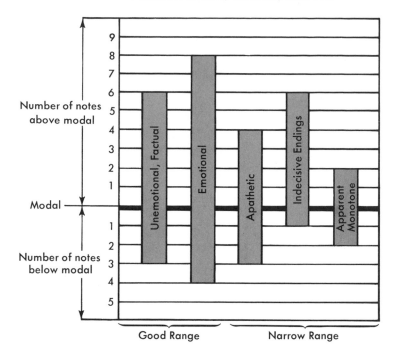

Fig. 2 Range Evaluations

Your range is made up of two parts: (a) the interval between your modal pitch (#2) and your low pitch (#1), and (b) the interval between modal pitch (#2) and high pitch (#3). Criticizing your total range may be unrealistic. Perhaps your low interval is entirely adequate, but your high interval is insufficient. In Figure 2, the third bar labelled "Apathetic" shows this type of range. If your stressed words do not sound emphatic enough, this may be the trouble. On the other hand, it may be that your high interval is fine, but your low interval is inadequate, like the fourth bar in Figure 2, labelled "Indecisive Endings." If you sound as if your sentences don't really end, this is your type of range. The fifth bar in Figure 2, "Apparent Monotone," represents your type of range if you have a combination of inadequate highs and lows.

Adequate Range

Adequate range for speech is a subject about which much has been said and written. At one extreme, you will find advice to try to develop a range of an octave. This is remarkable, since speakers with *less* than an octave range have rarely been reported in research studies of pitch. What is more, we have discovered, on the basis of students' appraisals of voices, that an octave range is not adequate for expressive speech. On Figure 2 the graphs labelled both "Apathetic" and "Indecisive Endings" have precisely a one-octave (eight notes) range.

At the other extreme, you can find advice to extend your range as much as possible — the more the better. Actually, students tend to be wary of this advice, and with reason. All of us have encountered a "gusher," the overly effusive and patently insincere type of speaker. One of the "gusher's" chief characteristics is extremely wide swoops of intonation.

How much range, then, is enough? First, let us discuss the needs for everyday, unemotional, factual speech. That is the sort we do most of. Students' judgments indicate that three notes below modal pitch is *minimal* — the least you can afford to use if your sentences are to sound finished. If emphasized words are to be reinforced by high pitch, those same students chose six notes above modal pitch as the *minimal* interval for high pitch. This adds up to ten notes *minimal range* for factual speech: three notes below modal, plus the modal pitch, plus six notes above modal.

Measure your own range in factual speaking. Read the preceding paragraph for tape recording. Then replay your recording. As you listen to each sentence, hum the high note you used and then the modal pitch. Sing up scale from your #2 to your #3 pitch. How many notes above your modal pitch was your high pitch? Perhaps your high pitch differed slightly from sentence to sentence. Measure the interval between modal and high pitch for each sentence, and then average it for the whole paragraph. Was your average high pitch as much as six notes above your modal pitch? Now hum the low note (#1) on which you ended sentences. Sing down scale from your modal pitch to your low pitch. Count the notes in that interval. If your low pitch varied somewhat during this paragraph, measure the interval each time it occurred, and average them all. Was your interval between modal and low pitch at least three notes? If your high or low interval was *less* than the minimal intervals stated, you should start increasing your range. If either part of your range exceeded the minimal intervals slightly, this is all to the good.

Emotional speech normally uses a wider range than factual speech. The minimal intervals indicated for "Emotional" on Figure 2 show this increase in range over "Factual" speech. Students' listening judgments have indicated that the speaker's apparent conviction, sincerity, and emotional involvement in his subject, and with his audience, *increases in direct relation to the upper interval of his range.* Variation in the lower interval of the range has much less effect on these factors of judgment, except that a low pitch which is less than three notes below modal sounds indecisive. For most speakers, an increase in the upper range interval (from modal pitch to high pitch) will increase effectiveness of speech more surely than any other one device.

Increasing Your Range

If you have performed the exercises in this chapter up to this point, you have already laid the groundwork for increasing your range. Have you measured your singing range? It is necessary to discover how many notes there are in your total range, since all of them are potentially usable for your speaking range. Have you located your modal pitch? Remember that if your modal pitch is too near either limit of your total range, your range will be somewhat curtailed. Have you discovered your optimum pitch? Have you started exercises to move your modal pitch to optimum, if necessary? If your upper-range interval is inadequate, you are not raising pitch enough to reinforce emphasis. Were you to attempt remedying this deficiency without specific training in pitch changes, you might simply increase the energy and duration of stressed syllables without moving the pitch higher. You need to *hear* an adequate interval between modal pitch and high pitch, and to establish this interval in your auditory memory, in order to produce it reliably in speaking. Also, you need to "limber up" your laryngeal muscles to enable you to hit a note high enough for emphasis without strain.

STEP EXERCISE. The diagrams below show you the technique for coaxing your high pitch (#3) higher. Diagram (a) represents what you already say, if you stress the word **like**. When you say the sentence diagrammed in (b), the second **like** should move up a note higher (another *step* higher) than the first **like**. In (c) say **like** on the top note. In (d) you move **like** up a note still higher, and in (e) you say **like** on the top note. Continue up successive steps until you can achieve an octave (8 notes) interval between **I** (at modal pitch) and **like** at high pitch.

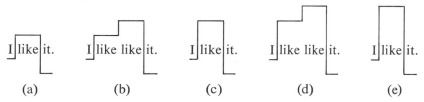

| (a) | (b) | (c) | (d) | (e) |

Any exercise in this chapter which is marked with an intonation contour can be used for the step exercise. Read a phrase with pitch #3 at your normal interval above pitch #2. Repeat the phrase just as you repeated "I like it" above, raising pitch #3, step by step, until the interval between #2 and #3 is adequate.

Mark intonation contours on a practice reading selection at the end of this chapter, or any one you choose. Practice the step exercise on each phrase, until your interval between pitch #2 and pitch #3 is adequate.

Tape recording of this exercise will afford you additional auditory training. At first, recording is necessary to be sure you really are raising pitch #3 on successive repetitions of a given phrase. Until your hearing becomes more sensitive to musical intervals, there is real danger that, instead of actually raising the #3 pitch higher and higher, you simply think you do. Perhaps you only increase the loudness and duration of the emphasized word, without increasing the height of pitch #3. The tape recorder allows you to check your performance, to see if you actually raised the pitch as you intended to.

Keep this thought in mind as you practice: Only when the desired interval between modal pitch (#2) and high pitch (#3) is memorized and accepted as the norm of performance, *only then* will you use this interval reliably in your everyday speech. This interval is as specific as the distance between two successive notes in a song you may be learning. You cannot sing the song reliably until you memorize the melody.

SLIDE-DOWN EXERCISE. If your intonation problem involves inadequate *lowering of pitch* at ends of statements, you need the slide-down exercise. The first purpose of this exercise is to train your auditory discrimination for an adequate interval between modal pitch (#2) and low pitch (#1). Its second purpose is to train your auditory memory to retain this musical interval as an internal "model" for your pitch drops at the ends of sentences.

Before practicing this exercise, re-check your modal pitch and make sure that it is within your optimum band of pitches. Sing down the scale from modal pitch. Do you have four clear notes lower than your modal pitch? Listening to a tape recording of your voice will help you make sure that you actually do sing four notes down scale from modal pitch, and that the notes are all clear. Finding your modal pitch on the piano, and playing successive notes down scale as you sing, will help you make sure that you actually sing down four notes.

Read each of the following sentences, matching your intonation to the drawn contour. The first time you read a sentence, sing down four notes on the last word. The second time, step down four notes from modal pitch on the last word.

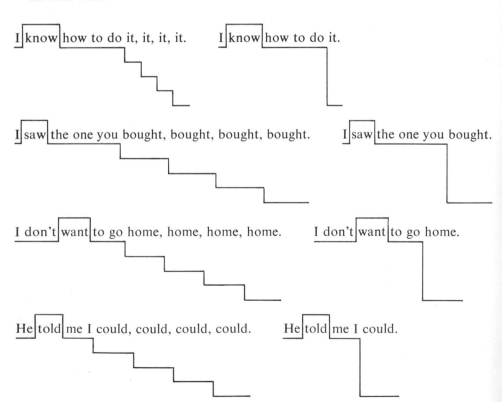

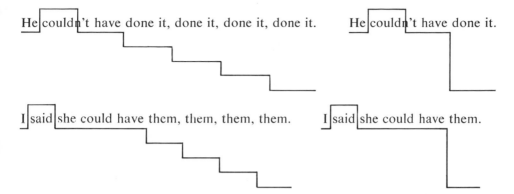

The sentences you have just practiced are "tailor-made" to help you learn the interval between pitch #2 and pitch #1, because they allow you to speak on pitch #2 just before you step down to pitch #1. Hearing modal pitch just before low pitch is ideal for helping you to hear the interval between them. Until you are fairly secure in your ability to produce an adequate interval between #2 and #1, use these or similar sentences for practice.

The test of your auditory memory for an adequate interval between pitch #2 and pitch #1 is a sentence which requires a pitch change all the way from pitch #3 to pitch #1 at its end. When the last word in a sentence is emphasized strongly, pitch #3 must be used for emphasis, and pitch #1 must be used to signal the completion of the statement — both on the same word. When the last word has more than one syllable, as in sentences (a, b, c, d, e) you make a *step* down from pitch #3 to pitch #1. But when the last word is a single syllable, as in (f, g, h, i, j), you make a *glide* down from pitch #3 to pitch #1.

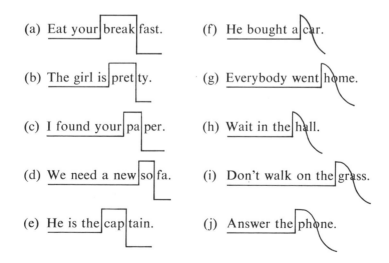

Increasing Pitch Flexibility

The speaker who uses adequate intervals in pitch for intonation must be able to produce the required high pitch (#3) and the required low pitch (#1). Even though he hears the inadequacy of his own intervals and recognizes that greater intervals are more effective, he may be hampered by the inflexibility of his vocal musculature in effecting the needed pitch changes.

Pitch changes require a delicate control of the length and tension of the vocal folds, balanced carefully by the sub-glottal breath pressure. If you have not used certain pitch levels commonly, you may be awkward at exercising the necessary controls. Strain in producing either an adequate high pitch (#3) or an adequate low pitch (#1) may indicate simple lack of exercise in producing these pitches. Just as a dancer does certain "limbering up" exercises to maintain suppleness of muscles, so does a singer or speaker need to "limber up" muscles required for vocal pitch changes. The exercises here, which are really singing exercises, will help you acquire and maintain greater agility and ease in producing the pitch changes which effective speaking requires.

RELAX. Before beginning these exercises, make sure that you are working under optimum conditions. Your vocal mechanism should be as relaxed as possible. Sit in a comfortable chair (but an erect one, not the sort that bends you into a pretzel shape) with a head rest. Or lie down on your bed. Even practice in a tub of warm water, if this relaxes you. Prepare for exercising by relaxing the neck with the head rotation exercise, the open-throat exercise, or the sighing exercise (from Chapter 3). Your larynx should be as near a condition of rest as possible when you begin.

SING SCALES. Sing "ah" lightly and softly, beginning on any comfortable note (optimum for you) and proceeding note by note up the musical scale. You might prefer singing "hah" on each note, since this reduces laryngeal strain. Be sure to stop every few notes to inhale, since running short of breath will produce hypertension in the larynx. As you get fairly high up the scale, you might be tempted to "reach up" for high notes, by extending your neck and pulling your chin upward. Deliberately keep your neck relaxed. Reach the high notes by *thinking* them, and let your voice "float up" to the right pitch. Straining for high pitch defeats your purpose. When you go as high as possible without strain, begin again and see if you can go any higher the next time. Successive repetitions should help you reach higher notes without strain, as your laryngeal muscles acquire greater flexibility through exercise.

Reverse the process. Sing a scale downward, as low as you can phonate without strain. As you approach your lowest notes, be careful to avoid pulling your chin downward. Remember here, too, that good breath support will reduce laryngeal strain.

SING ARPEGGIOS. An arpeggio is a singing exercise particularly suited to speaking, because it comprises larger intervals than single notes in the scale.

For a scale, you sing notes 1, 2, 3, 4, 5, 6, 7, 8, etc. For an arpeggio, you sing notes 1, 3, 5, 8. You might need to play the notes on a piano in order to sing them. You would play C, E, G, C and then return to G, E, and C. You can begin an arpeggio at any comfortable note, but the intervals between successive notes are the same.

SELECTIONS FOR INTONATION PRACTICE

The literary excerpts which follow are varied in style and content, but they share the common feature of high saturation of meaning. As you prepare a selection for oral reading, make up your mind about the author's purpose in writing this piece, his attitude, and point of view. Decide which words deserve stress and where phrases should end to best convey the meanings inherent in the selection. It would be helpful to mark ' over the syllables to be stressed and / between phrases.

By now you are well aware that pitch #3 should accompany strong stress. *If* you are using stress to emphasize meaning, your pitch #3 will be appropriately used. On the other hand, if you stress the wrong words, your intonation will also be incorrect. Stereotyped stress will be reflected in a singsong type of intonation. Remember, too, that your pitch #3 must be high enough above #2 to sound high. Perhaps you need to apply the step exercise to some phrases to widen the musical interval between #2 and #3.

Intonation at phrase endings usually poses the greater problem. Stereotyped intonations most often consist of repeating the same pitch contour (a drop to #1, for instance) at every pause, whether it is appropriate to meaning or not. Think of the various pitch contours which would be logical at each pause; then experiment with possible intonations until you discover the one at each phrase ending which best interprets the author's intention. When you have decided on the most appropriate intonation contour, draw the line-contour on your copy of the reading, to guide you when you re-read the selection.

Record your reading and re-listen critically. Did your reading project the author's ideas and attitudes clearly and faithfully? Did your reading vivify the selection, making it more meaningful and emotionally significant than a silent reading?

1.   from *Please Don't Eat the Daisies* [16]

The twins are four now, and for several years we have had galvanized iron fencing lashed onto the outside of their bedroom windows. This gives the front of the house a rather institutional look and contributes to unnecessary rumors about my mental health, but it does keep them off the roof, which is what we had in mind.

[16] From the book, *Please Don't Eat the Daisies* by Jean Kerr. Copyright © 1954, 1955, 1956, 1957, by Jean Kerr. Reprinted by permission of Doubleday & Company, Inc.

For twins they are very dissimilar. Colin is tall and active and Johnny is short and middle-aged. Johnny doesn't kick off his shoes, he doesn't swallow beer caps or tear pages out of the telephone book. I don't think he ever draws pictures with my best lipstick. In fact, he has none of the charming, lighthearted "boy" qualities that precipitate so many scenes of violence in the home. On the other hand, he has a feeling for order and a passion for system that would be trying in a head nurse. If his pajamas are hung on the third hook in the closet instead of on the second hook, it causes him real pain. If one slat in a Venetian blind is tipped in the wrong direction he can't have a moment's peace until somebody fixes it. Indeed, if one of the beans on his plate is slightly longer than the others he can scarcely bear to eat it. It's hard for him to live with the rest of us. And vice versa.

Colin is completely different. He has a lightness of touch and a dexterity that will certainly put him on top of the heap if he ever takes up safe-cracking. Equipped with only a spoon and an old emery board, he can take a door off its hinges in seven minutes and remove all of the towel racks from the bathroom in five.

JEAN KERR

2.   *Mending Wall* [17]

Something there is that doesn't love a wall,
That sends the frozen-ground-swell under it,
And spills the upper boulders in the sun;
And makes gaps even two can pass abreast.
The work of hunters is another thing:
I have come after them and made repair
Where they have left not one stone on a stone,
But they would have the rabbit out of hiding,
To please the yelping dogs. The gaps I mean,
No one has seen them made or heard them made,
But at spring mending-time we find them there.
I let my neighbor know beyond the hill;
And on a day we meet to walk the line
And set the wall between us once again.
We keep the wall between us as we go.
To each the boulders that have fallen to each.
And some are loaves and some so nearly balls
We have to use a spell to make them balance:
"Stay where you are until our backs are turned!"
We wear our fingers rough with handling them.

[17] From *Complete Poems of Robert Frost.* Copyright 1923, 1930, 1939 by Holt, Rinehart and Winston, Inc. Copyright 1951, © 1958 by Robert Frost. Reprinted by permission of Holt, Rinehart and Winston, Inc.

Oh, just another kind of outdoor game,
One on a side. It comes to little more:
There where it is we do not need the wall:
He is all pine and I am apple-orchard.
My apple trees will never get across
And eat the cones under his pines, I tell him.
He only says, "Good fences make good neighbors."
Spring is the mischief in me, and I wonder
If I could put a notion in his head:
"*Why* do they make good neighbors? Isn't it
Where there are cows? But here there are no cows.
Before I built a wall I'd ask to know
What I was walling in or walling out,
And to whom I was like to give offence.
Something there is that doesn't love a wall,
That wants it down." I could say "Elves" to him,
But it's not elves exactly, and I'd rather
He said it for himself. I see him there,
Bringing a stone grasped firmly by the top
In each hand, like an old-stone savage armed.
He moves in darkness as it seems to me,
Not of woods only and the shade of trees.
He will not go behind his father's saying,
And he likes having thought of it so well
He says again, "Good fences make good neighbors."

ROBERT FROST

3. from *To Turn the Tide* [18]

We dare not forget today that we are the heirs of that first revolution. Let the word go forth from this time and place, to friend and foe alike, that the torch has been passed to a new generation of Americans, born in this century, tempered by war, disciplined by a hard and bitter peace, proud of our ancient heritage, and unwilling to witness or permit the slow undoing of those human rights to which this nation has always been committed, and to which we are committed today at home and around the world.

Let every nation know, whether it wishes us well or ill, that we shall pay any price, bear any burden, meet any hardship, support any friend, oppose any foe to assure the survival and the success of liberty.

JOHN F. KENNEDY

[18] From p. 7 of *To Turn the Tide* by John F. Kennedy, edited by John W. Gardner (Harper & Row, 1962). Reprinted by permission of Harper & Row, Publishers.

4.   from *To Turn the Tide* [19]

History will not judge our endeavors, and a government cannot be selected, merely on the basis of color or creed or even party affiliation. Neither will competence and loyalty and stature, while essential to the utmost, suffice in times such as these.

For of those to whom much is given, much is required. And when at some future date the high court of history sits in judgment on each of us, recording whether in our brief span of service we fulfilled our responsibilities to the state, our success or failure, in whatever office we hold, will be measured by the answers to four questions:

First, were we truly men of courage, with the courage to stand up to one's enemies, and the courage to stand up, when necessary, to one's associates, the courage to resist public pressure as well as private greed?

Second, were we truly men of judgment, with perceptive judgment of the future as well as the past, of our own mistakes as well as the mistakes of others, with enough wisdom to know what we did not know, and enough candor to admit it?

Third, were we truly men of integrity, men who never ran out on either the principles in which we believed or the people who believed in us, men whom neither financial gain nor political ambition could ever divert from the fulfillment of our sacred trust?

Finally, were we truly men of dedication, with an honor mortgaged to no single individual or group, and compromised by no private obligation or aim, but devoted solely to serving the public good and the national interest?

JOHN F. KENNEDY

5.   from *The Stones of Venice*

And now I wish that the reader, before I bring him into St. Mark's Place, would imagine himself for a little time in a quiet English cathedral town, and walk with me to the west front of its cathedral. Let us go together up the more retired street, at the end of which we can see the pinnacles of one of the towers, and then through the low grey gateway, with its battlemented top and small latticed window in the centre, into the inner private-looking road or close, where nothing goes in but the carts of the tradesmen who supply the bishop and the chapter, and where there are little shaven grass-plots, fenced in by neat rails, before old-fashioned groups of somewhat diminutive and excessively trim houses, with little oriel and bay windows jutting out here and there, and deep wooden cornices and eaves painted cream colour and white,

---

[19] From pp. 4–5 of *To Turn the Tide* by John F. Kennedy, edited by John W. Gardner (Harper & Row, 1962). Reprinted by permission of Harper & Row, Publishers.

and small porches to their doors in the shape of cockle shells, or little, crooked, thick, indescribable wooden gables warped a little on one side; and so forward till we come to larger houses, also old-fashioned, but of red brick, and with gardens behind them, and fruit walls, which show here and there, among the nectarines, the vestiges of an old cloister arch or shaft, and looking in front on the cathedral square itself, laid out in rigid divisions of smooth grass and gravel walk, yet not uncheerful, especially on the sunny side, where the canon's children are walking with their nursery maids. And so, taking care not to tread on the grass, we will go along the straight walk to the west front, and there stand for a time, looking up at its deep-pointed porches and the dark places between their pillars where there were statues once, and where the fragments, here and there, of a stately figure are still left, which has in it the likeness of a king, perhaps indeed a king on earth, perhaps a saintly king long ago in heaven; and so higher and higher up to the great mouldering wall of rugged sculpture and confused arcades, shattered, and grey, and grisly with heads of dragons and mocking fiends, worn by the rain and swirling winds into yet unseemlier shape, and coloured on their stony scales by the deep russet-orange lichen, melancholy gold; and so, higher still, to the bleak towers, so far above that the eye loses itself among the bosses of their traceries, though they are rude and strong, and only sees like a drift of eddying black points, now closing, now scattering, and now settling suddenly into invisible places among the bosses and flowers, the crowd of restless birds that fill the whole square with that strange clangour of theirs, so harsh and yet so soothing, like the cries of birds on a solitary coast between the cliffs and sea.

JOHN RUSKIN

6. The changes wrought by death are in themselves so sharp and final, and so terrible and melancholy in their consequences, that the thing stands alone in man's experience, and has no parallel upon earth. It outdoes all other accidents because it is the last of them. Sometimes it leaps suddenly upon its victims, like a Thug; sometimes it lays regular siege and creeps upon their citadel during a score of years. And when the business is done, there is sore havoc made in other people's lives, and a pin knocked out by which many subsidiary friendships hung together. There are empty chairs, solitary walks, and single beds at night. Again, in taking away our friends, death does not take them away utterly, but leaves behind a mocking, tragical, and soon intolerable residue, which must be hurriedly concealed. . . .

ROBERT LOUIS STEVENSON

7.   from *The Edge of Tomorrow* [20]

When it was obvious that delivery will soon ensue the father called for all family members to come to the house and help. A birth was a family affair. The mother was put over in a corner, in a certain part of the house, facing the south, towards the religious capitol, Luang Prabang. Some old snag-tooth sorceress was the mid-wife. When she entered the house she was given, as an offering, a small silver bowl with three fruits. Later, when we Americans became assistants to the sorceress, we got the fruits.

The first thing the witch doctor did was to rub betel nut oil, perfumes, orange rinds, and other "medicaments" onto the mother's abdomen and forehead in hopes of helping the obstetrical procedure. All the neighboring women came and sat in one part of the house chatting, and occasionally moaning, groaning, grunting and gasping, in order to help the poor mother.

The men sat outside the house around a huge fire. The only men allowed inside were the wise men of the village who set up musical instruments in a corner. They lit candles, and banged on the drums throughout the whole delivery. The hut was packed to suffocation. The stifling odors that arose from the sweating bodies blended with the smoke from the indoor fire. . . .

During the last few minutes of labor all the women in the hut (and me too) would begin to shout "bing bing bing!" And the woman bings and bings, "pushing" as hard as she can. The child was born, to the great relief of the family, doctor, husband and oh yes, mother too. . . .

Now custom demands the village elder to cut the baby's cord with two pieces of sharp bamboo. I did not object to this at all. We had learned by now. I first clipped the cord and tied it off with sterile ligature. From that point outward, the village elder can do all he wants. After he cut it with bamboo, he then rubbed ashes on the ends of the umbilical cord. All this of course is distal to my sterile knot. Black, red and white cotton cords were tied around the wrists of the mother and child, invoking specific phantoms to come with their blessings. . . .

. . . The rice alcohol was then passed around, and everyone rejoiced. The husband gave us four coconuts as our payments. We kept two and gave two to our "assistant" the sorceress. This husband, as at home, managed to look as exhausted as his wife, but I think it was only show (in both instances). It is said that there are some tribes over in Burma that get the husband into the act in a more meaningful way. During the wife's labor, the husband is hung by his feet, outside of the house.

THOMAS A. DOOLEY, M.D.

8.   *Ozymandias*

    I met a traveler from an antique land
    Who said: "Two vast and trunkless legs of stone
    Stand in the desert. Near them, on the sand,
    Half sunk, a shattered visage lies, whose frown,
    And wrinkled lip, and sneer of cold command,
    Tell that its sculptor well those passions read
    Which yet survive, stamped on these lifeless things,
    The hand that mocked them and the heart that fed:
    And on the pedestal these words appear:
    'My name is Ozymandias, King of Kings:
    Look on my works, ye Mighty, and despair!'
    Nothing beside remains. Round the decay
    Of that colossal wreck, boundless and bare.
    The lone and level sands stretch far away."

                            PERCY BYSSHE SHELLEY

9.   from *Mark Twain's Autobiography* [21]

. . . I can see the farm yet, with perfect clearness. I can see all its be-
longings, all its details; the family room of the house, with a "trundle"
bed in one corner and a spinning-wheel in another — a wheel whose
rising and falling wail, heard from a distance, was the mournfulest
of all sounds to me, and made me homesick and low-spirited, and
filled my atmosphere with the wandering spirits of the dead; the vast
fireplace, piled high, on winter nights, with flaming hickory logs from
whose ends a sugary sap bubbled out, but did not go to waste, for
we scraped it off and ate it; the lazy cat spread out on the rough
hearthstones; the drowsy dogs braced against the jambs and blinking;
my aunt in one chimney corner, knitting; my uncle in the other, smok-
ing his corncob pipe; the slick and carpetless oak floor faintly mirror-
ing the dancing flame tongues and freckled with black indentations
where fire coals had popped out and died a leisurely death; half a
dozen children romping in the background twilight; "split"-bottomed
chairs here and there, some with rockers; a cradle — out of service,
but waiting, with confidence; in the early cold mornings a snuggle
of children, in shirts and chemises, occupying the hearthstone and pro-
crastinating — they could not bear to leave that comfortable place
and go out on the wind-swept floor space between the house and
kitchen where the general tin basin stood, and wash.

                               SAMUEL CLEMENS

[21] "Life on the Farm" from *Mark Twain's Autobiography* by Samuel Clemens, edited by
Charles Neider. Reprinted by permission of Harper & Row, Publishers.

10.   from *The Hills Beyond*[22]

He was said to have been, particularly in his earlier years, a man of a hot temper, who liked a fight. There is a story of his fight with a big blacksmith: a quarrel having broken out between them over the shoeing of a horse, the blacksmith brained him with an iron shoe and knocked him flat. As William started to get up again, bleeding and half conscious, the blacksmith came at him again, and Joyner hit him while still resting on one knee. The blow broke the blacksmith's ribs and caved in his side as one would crack a shell.

He was known in his own day to be a mighty hunter; and old men who remembered him used to tell of the time he "chased the dogs the whole way over into Tennessee, and was gone four days and nights, and never knowed how fer from home he was."

There is also the story of his fight with a grizzly bear: the bear charged him at close quarters and there was nothing left for him to do but fight. A searching party found him two days later, more dead than living — as they told it, "all chawed up," but with the carcass of the bear: "and in the fight he had bit the nose off that big b'ar and chawed off both his ears, and that b'ar was so tored up hit was a caution."

                                                    THOMAS WOLFE

11.   When, in the course of human events, it becomes necessary for one people to dissolve the political bands which have connected them with another, and to assume, among the powers of the earth, the separate and equal station to which the laws of nature and of nature's God entitle them, a decent respect to the opinions of mankind requires that they should declare the causes which impel them to the separation.

We hold these truths to be self-evident, that all men are created equal, that they are endowed by their Creator with certain unalienable rights, that among these are life, liberty, and the pursuit of happiness. That, to secure these rights, governments are instituted among men, deriving their just powers from the consent of the governed; that, whenever any form of government becomes destructive of these ends, it is the right of the people to alter or to abolish it, and to institute a new government, laying its foundation on such principles, and organizing its powers in such form, as to them shall seem most likely to effect their safety and happiness.

                                                    THOMAS JEFFERSON

[22] P. 179 in *The Hills Beyond* by Thomas Wolfe. Copyright 1937, 1941 by Maxwell Perkins as Executor. Reprinted by permission of Harper & Row, Publishers.

12.   from *Home Front Memo* [23]

Freedom is a habit
and a coat worn
some born to wear it
some never to know it.
Freedom is cheap
or again as a garment
is so costly
men pay their lives
rather than not have it.
Freedom is baffling:
men having it often
know not they have it
till it is gone and
they no longer have it.
What does this mean?
Is it a riddle?
Yes, it is first of all
in the primers of riddles.
To be free is so-so:
you can and you can't:
walkers can have freedom
only by never walking
away their freedom:
runners too have freedom
unless they overrun:
eaters have often outeaten
their freedom to eat
and drinkers overdrank
their fine drinking freedom.

CARL SANDBURG

13.   . . . With malice toward none; with charity for all; with firmness in
the right, as God gives us to see the right, let us strive on to finish the
work we are in; to bind up the nation's wounds; to care for him who
shall have borne the battle, and for his widow, and his orphan — to do
all which may achieve and cherish a just and lasting peace among ourselves, and with all nations.

ABRAHAM LINCOLN

[23] From *Home Front Memo*, copyright, 1943, by Carl Sandburg. Reprinted by permission
of Harcourt, Brace & World, Inc.

14.   from *The Agony and the Ecstasy* [24]

He was determined to get a teeming humanity up on the Sistine ceiling, as well as the God who created it; mankind portrayed in its breathless beauty, its weaknesses, its indestructible strengths: God in His ability to make all things possible. The center space, running the full length of the vault, he would use for his major works: Dividing the Waters from the Earth; God Creating the Sun, the Moon; God Creating Adam and Eve; Expelling Adam and Eve from the Garden; the legend of Noah and the Deluge. Ideas now came tumbling over each other tumultuously. On the ends and sides he would show Prophets and Sibyls, each sitting on a marble throne. Connecting the thrones would be a cornice painted like marble. . . .

For thirty days he painted from light to darkness, completing the Sacrifice of Noah, the four titanic male nudes surrounding it, the Erythraean Sibyl on her throne, and the Prophet Isaiah opposite. For thirty days he slept in his clothes; and when, at the completion of this section, utterly spent, he had Michi pull his boots off, bits of skin came away with them.

He grew dizzy from painting standing with his neck arched so that he could peer straight upward; he had learned to blink his eyes with each brush stroke, but they still blurred from the dripping paint. He had Rosselli make him a still higher platform on top of the scaffolding. He painted sitting down, his thighs drawn up tight against his belly for balance, his eyes a few inches from the ceiling, until the unpadded bones of his buttocks became so bruised and sore he could no longer endure the agony. Then he lay flat on his back, his knees in the air, doubled over as tightly as possible against his chest to steady his painting arm. His beard became a catchall for the constant drip of paint. No matter which way he leaned, crouched, lay or knelt, he was always in strain.

Then he thought he was going blind. A letter arrived from Buonarroto. He could not decipher a word. He threw himself on his bed. What was he doing to himself? Sleepless, racked with pain, homesick, lonely, he rose in the inky blackness, lit a candle, and on the back of an old sketch tried to lighten his mood by pouring out his woes:

> "My beard turns up to heaven; my nape falls in,
> fixed on my spine: my breastbone visibly
> grows like a harp: a rich embroidery
> bedews my face from brush drops thick and thin.
> . . . foul I fare and painting is my shame."

When he walked from his house to the chapel and back he did so almost blinded by paint, his head lowered, seeing no one. Passers-by often thought him crazy.

He forced himself to see his only reality: the life and the people on his ceiling. His intimates were Adam and Eve in the Garden of Eden. He portrayed them not as timid, delicate creatures, but powerful, handsome, accepting temptation in calm strength rather than weak stupidity. This was the mother and father of man, created by God, and he, Michelangelo Buonarroti, brought them to life in noble mien and proportion.

Irving Stone

15. from *To Turn the Tide* [25]

A few statistics will illustrate the depth of the problems of Latin America. This is the fastest-growing area in the world. Its current population of 195 million represents an increase of about 30 per cent over the past ten years, and by the 1980's the continent will have to support more than 400 million people. At the same time the average per capita annual product is only $280, less than one-ninth that of the United States; and in large areas, inhabited by millions of people, it is less than $70. Thus it is a difficult task merely to keep living standards from falling further as population grows.

Such poverty inevitably takes its toll in human life. The average American can expect to live seventy years, but life expectancy in Latin America is only forty-six, dropping to about thirty-five in some Central American countries. And while our rate of infant mortality is less than 30 per thousand, it is more than 110 per thousand in Latin America.

Perhaps the greatest stimulus to our own development was the establishment of universal basic education. But for most of the children of Latin America education is a remote and unattainable dream. Illiteracy extends to almost half the adults, reaching 90 per cent in one country. And approximately 50 per cent of school-age children have no schools to attend.

In one major Latin-American capital a third of the total population is living in filthy and unbearable slums. In another country 80 per cent of the entire population is housed in makeshift shacks and barracks, lacking the privacy of separate rooms for families.

It was to meet these shocking and urgent conditions that the Act of Bogotá was signed.

John F. Kennedy

[25] From pp. 170–171 of *To Turn the Tide* by John F. Kennedy, edited by John W. Gardner (Harper & Row, 1962). Reprinted by permission of Harper & Row, Publishers.

16.   from *Please Don't Eat the Daisies* [26]

But let's get to the heart of the matter. All these diets that appear so monotonously in the flossy magazines — who are they for? Are they aimed at men? Certainly not; most men don't read these magazines. Are they intended for fat teen-agers? Probably not; teen-agers can't afford them. Do not ask for whom the bell tolls. It tolls for you, Married Woman, Mother of Three, lumpy, dumpy, and the source of concern to practically every publication in the country. And why, why is the married woman being hounded into starvation in order to duplicate an ideal figure which is neither practical nor possible for a person her age? I'll tell you why.

First, it is presumed that when you're thinner you live longer. (In any case, when you live on a diet of yogurt and boiled grapefruit, it *seems* longer.) Second, it is felt that when you are skin and bones you have so much extra energy that you can climb up and shingle the roof. Third — and this is what they're really getting at — when you're thin you are so tasty and desirable that strange men will pinch you at the A&P and your husband will not only follow you around the kitchen breathing heavily but will stop and smother you with kisses as you try to put the butter back in the icebox. This — and I hope those in the back of the room are listening — is hogwash.

Think of the happy marriages you know about. How many of the ladies are still wearing size twelve? ... What I have discovered — attention, Beauty Editors everywhere! — is that the women who are being ditched are one and all willowy, wand-like, and slim as a blade. ...

That the fourteen divorcees, or about-to-be divorcees, whom I happen to know personally are thin may be nothing more than a coincidence. Or it may just prove that men don't divorce fat wives because they feel sorry for them. ...

The real reason, I believe, that men hang onto their well-endowed spouses is because they're comfy and nice to have around the house. In a marriage there is nothing that stales so fast as physical beauty ... What actually holds a husband through thick and thick is a girl who is fun to be with. And any girl who has had nothing to eat since nine o'clock this morning but three hard-boiled eggs will be about as jolly and companionable as an income-tax inspector.

JEAN KERR

[26] From the book, *Please Don't Eat the Daisies* by Jean Kerr. Copyright © 1954, 1955. 1956, 1957, by Jean Kerr. Reprinted by permission of Doubleday & Company, Inc.

Part Two

ARTICULATION

CHAPTER **5**

Improvement of Articulation and Pronunciation of Vowel Phonemes

PART ONE • An Introduction to English Phonetics

PHONETICS

Speech is a mode of communication which uses auditory signals. Many types of signals impinge upon the intelligence of a human being. If you are driving a car, you receive information from visual signals, such as the hand motions of the traffic officer, the changing colors of traffic lights, highway signs, the turn-signal light, or the hand signal of the motorist ahead of you. If you see a road sign with an arrow ↱, you interpret it as a signal for a right turn in the road. No matter what language you speak, the sign has meaning for you, because it represents an idea without words. You simply supply the words of your language to suit the idea. A written symbol like % or $ or 231 signals an idea without reference to the sound of the words of a particular language which would express that idea. These, then, are *ideographs*, because they signal ideas without reference to the sound of spoken words. Certain languages like Chinese and Japanese use ideographic characters in their writing. English, like European languages, uses written symbols for a word which relate to the sound of the spoken word. If you saw the words LEFT TURN on a road sign, you would think of the way those words sound, as well as the meaning they express. *Phonetic writing* uses written symbols to represent the sound of the words spoken. It happens, as we shall discuss presently, that English has less accurate phonetic spelling than certain other languages, such as Italian or Spanish. However, English spelling is classified as phonetic since it relates, however imperfectly and inconsistently, to the sound of the spoken words.

A point which may need clarification is the difference between phonetics and phonics. Occasionally a parent says his elementary school child is studying phonetics. This is highly unlikely. *Phonetics* is the study of the sounds of spoken language. It includes several fields of study, among them the following: sounds which distinguish meaning within a given language or dialect; how individual sounds of a language are produced by the speech mechanism; the acoustic characteristics of the sounds of speech. Since English is ostensibly a phonetically spelled language, though its spelling is phonetically inaccurate, one device used in teaching children to read and spell is to make them aware of correspondences between spelling and the sounds of speech. The teaching of spelling in relation to the sounds they represent is called *phonics*.

The Phoneme

If you were asked to name the most basic element which signals meaning in speech, you might say it is the word, because we put words together to produce meaningful utterances. But how do we form words? Compare the sound of the words **hat** and **cat**. Are there any common features in the two words, any reusable elements which carry over from **hat** to **cat**? Of course. The vowel and final consonant of both words not only look the same in print, but they sound identical. To change the meaning from **hat** to **cat**, all we need to change is the first consonant. What is the minimal change required to transform **cat** into **coat**? Only the sound of the vowel. The consonants remain the same. What is the minimal distinction between **cat** and **cap**? The last consonant changes from /t/ to /p/. Now let us do some counting. We can say that each of the words we have used as examples (**hat, cat, coat, cap**) has three signal elements, any one of which is significant in establishing the meaning of the word. The smallest segment of spoken sound which is capable of signalling a distinctive meaning is a *phoneme*. Do not assume that a phoneme equals a letter used in spelling a word, simply because in these particular samples (except in **coat**) there was a one-to-one relationship. Some letters are silent, and a letter is not always pronounced the same way in English. Pronounce the following words, all of which begin and end with the same consonant sounds but differentiate meaning on the basis of the vowel phoneme in between: **beet, bit, bait, bet, bat, bought, boat, boot, but, Bert, butte, bite, bout**. Observe the change in meaning as the consonant phoneme changes in the final position in these words: **bet, bed, Beth, Bess, bell, Ben, beck, beg**. Meaning changes with a change of the initial consonant phoneme in these words: **bet, pet, met, wet, whet, vet, debt, net, let, set, yet,**

get. In each of these lists all the words are identical except for a single segment of sound. For that reason, we identify the phoneme as the minimal sound segment which distinguishes the meaning of a word.

The Allophone

Within specified limits, any signal can be varied and still serve its function. For instance, every amber traffic light need not be the identical shade of yellow as every other one, so long as it clearly conveys the idea of CAUTION to the approaching driver. The amber light may vary in color without changing its signal value so long as it is not confusable with red or green. Again, within certain limits, a driver may vary the hand signal he uses for a right turn without confusing another driver. He may raise his hand higher or less high, point his finger to the right or up, or make a fist, and still signal a right turn. If, however, he half-raises, half-extends his hand, the other driver is not sure whether he is turning right or left, or simply waving to a friend.

A phoneme also has numerous varieties. Because the physical dimensions of the speech mechanism vary from person to person, there must necessarily be some variation in the sound of a particular phoneme produced by different people. An individual does not produce a phoneme the same way each time simply because it is extremely difficult to reproduce identically the muscular adjustments used before, just as he does not always write a **t** exactly the same way. The position of a phoneme in a syllable and the phonemes which adjoin it produce variations in its production. For instance, the /t/ commonly used initially in a word, as in **take**, has more aspiration (release of breath following) than final /t/ as in **hot**, or in an initial /st/ cluster, as in **stop**. It has even less aspiration in a phrase like **hot cakes** or **hot night**. To articulate /t/, the tongue tip normally touches the gum tissue back of the upper front teeth, but if the next word begins with **th**, in a phrase like **hit the ball** or **do not think**, the tongue tip touches the upper front teeth. All of these varieties of /t/, which are perceptibly different from one another, are still classifiable within the phoneme /t/ because they convey a /t/ signal to differentiate meaning. Each variety of the phoneme is an *allophone* of that phoneme. We write a phonemic symbol in / / and an allophonic symbol in [ ]. Thus we could say that [t̪] is the variety of /t/ which is articulated against the teeth.

Standard allophones are those varieties of a phoneme which good usage has established as acceptable. Substandard allophones are those which, compared with established good usage, are used inappropriately (like using an unaspirated /t/ initially) or are outside the limits of variability (like an /ɛ/ vowel in **pen** which is so much like an /ɪ/ that the word is confused with **pin**).

The Trouble with English Spelling

Though English spelling was originally intended to be phonetic, it was not entirely so even at first, and its imperfections have increased with time.

Dictionary makers have effected some small improvements in spelling during the last two centuries, but much of our spelling is obsolete and inaccurate. Four types of phonetic inaccuracies in spelling exist in modern English.

1. *Silent letters* are letters which appear in written words but are not pronounced. They are much too commonplace in English. Examples are: silent **t** in **hasten, listen, soften, moisten,** and similar words; silent **g** in **gnat, gnaw, reign, diaphragm,** etc.; silent **k** in **knee, knight, knew,** etc.; silent **p** in **pneumonia, pneumatic, ptomaine, receipt,** etc.; silent **l** in **half, calf, chalk, talk, calm, palm,** etc.; silent **b** in **limb, climb, dumb, plumber, debt,** etc.; silent **w** in **write, wrestle, wrong,** etc.; silent **h** in **hour, honest, heir,** etc.; silent **gh** in **through, thought, bought, fought,** etc.; silent **e** in **time, gone, take, home,** etc. Obviously, a letter which is silent in some words is correctly pronounced in others. Inconsistency produces most of the confusion.

2. *More than one spelling of a single phoneme* produces confusions both in spelling and in pronunciation. Examples are: /f/ is spelled **f** in **fine, gh** in **rough,** and **ph** in **physics**; /t/ is spelled **t** in **to, ed** in **passed,** and **th** in **Thomas**; the /i/ vowel phoneme is spelled **e** in **be, ee** in **keep, ea** in **beam, ie** in **believe, ei** in **receive, eo** in **people, oe** in **subpoena, ae** in **Caesar,** and **uay** in **quay**; the /e/ vowel phoneme is spelled **a** in **late, ay** in **say, ea** in **steak, ei** in **freight, ai** in **straight,** and **au** in **gauge.** Here again English demonstrates unfortunate inconsistency.

3. *More than one phoneme may be spelled alike,* in different words. For instance, **ea** represents /e/ in **break,** /ɛ/ in **breakfast,** /i/ in **sea**; the letter **a** represents /e/ in **late,** /æ/ in **hat,** /ɑ/ in **calm,** /ɔ/ in **chalk**; **o** represents /o/ in **go,** /ɑ/ or /ɒ/ in **hot,** /ɔ/ or /ɒ/ in **dog,** /ə/ [1] in **come**; **s** represents /s/ in **bus,** /z/ in **has.**

4. *A single phoneme may be spelled with two or more letters.* Ideally, a single phoneme should be spelled with a single letter. Examples of digraph (two-letter) spellings: /f/ is spelled **ff** in **off, gh** in **laugh, ph** in **phrase**; both /θ/ and /ð/ are always spelled with the same two letters **th,** as in **think, then**; /ʃ/ is spelled **sh** in **she, ss** in **tissue, ti** in **action, ch** in **chaperone**; the vowel /ɔ/ is spelled **aw** in **law, au** in **caught, ou** in **bought**; /u/ is spelled **oo** in **food, ue** in **blue, ew** in **flew, ou** in **you.**

Why English Spelling Is Phonetically Inaccurate

To understand how English has arrived at its present state of confused spelling, we must review briefly some of its history.

1. Latin spelling for a Germanic language started the confusion. Apparently the Roman missionaries of the sixth century gave a written form to Anglo-Saxon dialects which comprised a Germanic language. Since Latin did not have some of the sounds of Old English, they improvised as best they

---

[1] The International Phonetic Alphabet represents this vowel sound with /ʌ/ when it occurs in a stressed syllable, and /ə/ in an unstressed syllable. We have simplified symbolization by using /ə/ for this vowel sound whenever it occurs because no distinctive contrast between its stressed and unstressed occurrence can be established.

could. The **th** spelling for /θ/, as in **thin**, and /ð/, as in **then**, is an example.

2. Word borrowings from various languages have compounded the confusion in spelling. When Norsemen invaded the British Isles, they introduced new words. The Roman invaders added Latin words to English. The largest body of borrowings came with the Norman Conquest; it is estimated that approximately 25 per cent of our present vocabulary stems from French. In more modern times we have appropriated words from many sources: Spanish, Italian, Greek, etc. The tendency has been to preserve original spellings of borrowed words. In some cases the pronunciations were kept unchanged. Other borrowed words gradually changed in pronunciation although their spellings remained the same. Since the various source-languages of our borrowings had different phonetic systems of writing, inconsistencies in spelling the same sounds in modern English inevitably arose.

3. Archaic spellings have persisted even after pronunciations changed. It is normal for pronunciations to undergo gradual change through centuries of use. Evidence from old manuscripts suggests that English spelling was once reasonably fluid, reflecting changes in pronunciation with fair accuracy. The invention of the printing press and the wholesale printing of books and papers tended to stabilize spelling. Public education, involving a tremendous popularization of literacy, also tended to arrest the free revision of spelling to suit changing pronunciations. Many of our spellings are fairly accurate representations of pronunciations current two centuries ago.

The Need for a Phonetic Alphabet

The study of articulation and pronunciation depends basically on auditory identification and comparison of the sounds of speech. Perceiving allophones and relating them to phonemes as auditory reference points require that allophones and phonemes be identified as positive entities. It is conceivable that a chemist could work without symbols for chemical elements, but it is certain that his work is facilitated by having symbols. It is conceivable that a student of speech could improve his articulation without phonetic symbols to identify the elements (allophones, phonemes) which he perceives, but his work is easier and more direct if he uses them. Particularly in a class, phonetic symbols enable one person to communicate to another the sounds he is talking about.

The choice of symbols to represent perceived segments of spoken sound is arbitrary. Several phonetic alphabets have been used for various purposes. Dictionaries use phonetic symbols called diacritical markings to indicate pronunciations of words. You should learn what sounds are intended by the diacritical markings in your dictionary if you expect to use it intelligently. However, various dictionaries use different diacritical markings. Also, certain markings in most dictionaries have deliberately ambiguous implications, intended to indicate possible variations in good pronunciation rather than specific values of sounds. The most widely used phonetic alphabet today is the International Phonetic Alphabet, which we use in this book with certain modifications. This alphabet, correctly abbreviated as IPA, has two powerful arguments in its favor:

1. Each symbol of IPA represents a particular speech sound, always the same speech sound; and that sound is never represented by a different symbol. This fulfills a primary requirement for establishing each speech sound as a positive entity: one symbol per sound, and only one sound per symbol.

2. IPA has universal application. As a universal alphabet, it is used for any language you know or may study. Since we are studying English, all of the symbols needed for another language may not be included in the symbols you will learn in this book. A symbol you learn here, however, identifies the same perceived unit of spoken sound in any language where it occurs.

How to Make IPA a Useful Tool

Bear in mind that learning IPA is not an end in itself. IPA provides you with a frame of reference for identifying the sounds of language which you perceive. It enables you to discuss pronunciations in terms of positive entities of sound. Your facility in using IPA will grow as you study this chapter and Chapter 6. But before you can begin studying vowels or consonants in detail, you need a working knowledge of the symbols you will be using in your study. These suggestions for learning the phonemic symbols should prove helpful:

1. Identify the *sound* represented by each symbol. Each phoneme has a different sound from every other phoneme. On the basis of class exercises in auditory stimulation, and by perceiving your own pronunciation of key words furnished, single out and recognize the specific sound value for each phoneme. If two phonemes appear at first to be the same, differentiate them on the basis of how they are articulated or by the words in which they appear. This auditory identification of phonemes is comparable to visual identification of colors. If you were learning color names, you would follow a similar process of differentiating between reds and oranges, for instance, or various values of red such as bluish-reds and orange-reds, intense and pale values, etc. Phonemic symbols are meaningful only as they represent auditory identifications of speech sounds. After pronouncing a phoneme in a key word, isolate the sound of that phoneme by repeating it several times as a single sound. Verify the sound of each phoneme by comparing your production of it with that of your instructor and classmates.

2. Memorize the symbol for each phoneme. Repeat the sound of the phoneme as you write its symbol over and over. List words in which that phoneme occurs, writing the IPA symbol for it above the regular spelling of that phoneme. Pronounce each word you write, listening to the sound of the phoneme you are memorizing as you write the phonemic symbol.

3. If the association of sound and symbol is difficult for you, perhaps you would profit from flash-card practice. Write each symbol on a small file card or a page from a small memo pad. On the back of each card or slip, list several key words to remind you of the sound of that phoneme. Then, as you

look at each symbol, attempt to say the sound, checking your accuracy by looking at the key words on the back. As you become proficient in identifying some phonemes, you can eliminate those cards from your drill packet, continuing to repeat those which are troublesome.

4. When you have learned all the phonemic symbols, practice writing ordinary short words completely in IPA symbols as you pronounce them aloud. (Writing words in IPA is called *phonetic transcribing*.) Recheck your use of symbols against the text when in doubt. This exercise is doubly beneficial if you practice with a classmate, taking turns dictating words and comparing your transcriptions.

5. Interpret the pronunciation system of your dictionary in relation to IPA. Before you can use your dictionary as a pronunciation reference, you must understand its pronunciation system. The only dictionary which uses IPA symbols is the Kenyon and Knott *Pronouncing Dictionary of American English* (Merriam-Webster), which is concerned solely with pronunciation. Popular dictionaries generally use diacritical markings to indicate pronunciations. You should read thoroughly whatever explanation of its symbols the dictionary provides, in order to use those symbols intelligently. Some of them are deliberately ambiguous, referring not to a specific sound but to a possible choice of two or more different sounds. The editors assume that you will interpret such symbols according to the best usage in your environment. Some of the dictionary symbols are duplicative, in that they use more than one symbol for the same phoneme. The discussions of pronunciations included in this and the following chapter should enable you to clarify your dictionary's symbols as they apply to your particular dialect. If you write appropriate IPA symbols alongside the diacritical markings in the dictionary's pronunciation guide, you can be sure of the phonemes intended and use your dictionary as a reliable guide to pronunciation.

IPA Symbols

In English there are forty-four phonemes — nineteen vowels and twenty-five consonants. To represent each phoneme with a separate symbol requires more than the twenty-six letters of the conventional English alphabet. Some new symbols must be learned, but many of them are already quite familiar to you.

Of the twenty-five consonant phonemes, you know sixteen of the symbols. All you need to do is remember that each of them has a single specific value.

1. /b/   as in **baby.**
2. /d/   as in **did, ladder.**
3. /f/   as in **fluff, rough, physics.**
4. /g/   as in **go, egg, beg.**
5. /h/   as in **help, ahead, who.**
6. /k/   as in **keep, take, cool, ache, back.**

7. /l/ as in **leap, pool, call, allow.**
8. /m/ as in **me, came, summer.**
9. /n/ as in **no, can, winner.**
10. /p/ as in **pay, cup, supper.**
11. /r/ as in **run, car, drink, grow, arrow.**
12. /s/ as in **sit, city, bus, miss, passing.**
13. /t/ as in **take, hit, letter, missed.**
14. /v/ as in **vine, wave, ever.**
15. /w/ as in **we, wind, one, quit.**
16. /z/ as in **zero, does, his, easy.**

Of the remaining nine consonants, #17 is a familiar letter with an un-expected sound value, the next six symbols are modifications of familiar letters, and #24 and #25 are the Greek letter theta and an Old English letter called "ethe" /ɛð/.

17. /j/ as in **you, yellow, onion, canyon.**
18. /ŋ/ as in **sing, long, coming, ink, bank.**
19. /ʃ/ as in **she, cash, tissue, option.**
20. /ʒ/ as in **vision, azure, rouge.**
21. /tʃ/ as in **chew, each, church, catch.**
22. /dʒ/ as in **jump, joke, George, edge, page.**
23. /ʍ/ as in **what, when, somewhere.**
24. /θ/ as in **think, bath, ether.**
25. /ð/ as in **these, bathe, either.**

The nineteen vowel symbols include fifteen simple vowels and four diph-thongs (vowels which change their sound during production). Since our con-ventional alphabet has only five vowel letters, many of the IPA vowel symbols are special adaptations of familiar letters.

1. /i/ as in **machine, be, seem, meat, believe, receive, people.**
2. /ɪ/ as in **sit, pick, bicycle, near, women.**
3. /e/ as in **cake, name, paid, say, break.**
4. /ɛ/ as in **bet, red, breakfast.**
5. /æ/ as in **sat, glad, happy,** and as most Americans pronounce **half, pass, can't,** and **path.**
6. /a/ as many Easterners pronounce **half, pass, can't, path.** This vowel sounds like a compromise between /æ/ and /ɑ/. The vowels /a/ and /ɑ/ are not separate phonemes in most American speech.
7. /ɑ/ as in **father, car, heart,** and as most Americans pronounce **not, lock, doll, hop.**

8. /ɒ/   as some Easterners pronounce **not, lock, doll, hop** (with lips slightly rounded).   You may also use this vowel sound (which is formed with a more open mouth than /ɔ/) in words such as **sorry, orange, bought, taught, dog, log, water, wash.**

9. /ɔ/   as in **warm, fall, law, dawn,** and possibly also in **sorry, orange, bought, taught, dog, log, water, wash.**   In some dialects /ɒ/ and /ɔ/ are not separate phonemes.

10. /o/   as in **go, home, omit, coat, hoe.**

11. /ʊ/   as in **foot, book, pull, push, woman.**

12. /u/   as in **do, move, food, boot,** and as many Americans pronounce **tune, due, new.**

13. /ə/   as in **cut, up, us, come, mother, above, sofa, connect, circus,** and for those Easterners and Southerners who "drop the /r/" also in **after, winter, permit, dollar.**   (IPA uses the symbol /ʌ/ for this vowel sound when it occurs in a stressed syllable, and /ə/ for the same sound in an unstressed syllable.   A single symbol is entirely adequate.)

14. /ɚ/   as in **bird, hurt, worse, earn, after, winter, permit, dollar, doctor** when pronounced with the sound of /r/.   (IPA uses the symbol /ɝ/ for this vowel sound when it occurs in a stressed syllable and /ɚ/ for the same sound in an unstressed syllable.   A single symbol is entirely adequate.)

15. /ɜ/   as "/r/-dropping" speakers pronounce **bird, hurt, worse, earn.**

16. /ju/   as in **use, few, view, music, beauty, cube.**

17. /aɪ/   as in **ice, fly, tie, side, I.**

18. /aʊ/   as in **out, loud, how, down.**

19. /ɔɪ/   as in **coin, boy, voice, enjoy.**

THE ORGANS OF ARTICULATION

Articulation is the act of bringing the movable parts of the speech mechanism into contact (or near contact) to produce phonemic segments of speech. Articulation produces distinguishing characteristics of phonemes in several ways.   Movements of the articulators change the shape and size of the vocal tract to vary its resonance characteristics, to produce additional noise elements, or to insert stopgaps (spaces of dead silence) in the speech continuum.

The *articulators for speech phonemes* are shown in Figure 1, which is a simplified drawing of the head and neck in midsagittal section (cut from front to back at the midline).   You will see the *nasal cavity*, the *oral cavity*, and the *pharyngeal cavity*, which make up the vocal tract, and the *larynx*, where the vocal tone originates.   As the vocal tone or the unphonated breath moves up from the larynx through the vocal tract, it is shaped and molded into phonemes by movements of the articulators.

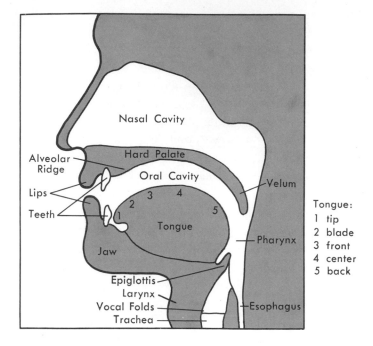

Fig. 1 Organs of Articulation

(Diagrammatic midsagittal section of the head and neck)

The *lips* may touch together, as in **be, pea, me**; the lower lip may touch the upper teeth, as in **few** and **view**; or the lips may round, as in **we, why, rude, look, owe, ought.**

The *teeth* (front teeth), though not themselves movable, serve as articulators when the other articulators move into contact with them. The lower lip touches the upper teeth in **few** and **view**, while the tongue tip touches the upper teeth in **thin** and **then.**

The *tongue* is the most mobile of all the articulators, capable of the most delicate and precise adjustments in shape and movement. The tongue *tip* touches the upper front teeth for **thin** and **then**; it makes contact with the alveolar ridge for **tip, dip, lip,** and **nip.** The tongue *blade* touches the alveolar ridge for **bus** and **buzz,** and just behind the alveolar ridge for **she** and **vision.** The *front* of the tongue moves close to the hard palate for **you, beet,** and **bit.** The *center* of the tongue articulates the vowels in **cut** and **curt.** The *back* of the tongue articulates the vowels in **food, foot, foe.** The *sides* of the tongue are raised to make contact with side teeth for **to, do, new, sue, zoo, shoe**; but the sides of the tongue lower to emit air from the sides of the mouth for **look.**

The *lower jaw* is lowered to make a wide mouth opening for **opposite** or **apple,** but is almost closed for **even** or **ooze.**

The *velum* (soft palate) rises to close off the nasal passage for all the sounds of English except three. For the three nasal consonants in **me, no,** and **sing,** the velum lowers to allow the sound to be resonated in the nasal cavity.

Information about the movement of articulators for the production of speech sounds serves two practical purposes. First, it is often helpful to examine your production of a phoneme to discover whether you are forming it correctly. Especially if you have been criticized for misarticulating a specific phoneme, you should attempt to discover the particular aspect of your articulation which is at fault. Second, when you practice that phoneme, concentrate on correcting that part of the articulation which is incorrect. For personal application to speech improvement, there is no special virtue in memorizing the articulation of every phoneme in English. There is, however, much value in examining and correcting the incorrect aspect of your articulation.

PART TWO • Vowel Phonemes of English

ARTICULATION OF VOWELS

A vowel phoneme derives its identifying sound from its particular resonance characteristics. Four factors in articulation affect vowel resonance:

1. *The height of the tongue in the mouth* varies the resonance of the vocal tone. As a part of the tongue is lifted high toward the hard palate, it creates a narrow connecting passageway between the cavities behind and in front of that point. If the tongue is lowered, the coupling (connecting passageway) between the cavities grows more open. To observe how height of the tongue affects vowel production, compare the vowels in **feed, fade, fad.**

2. *The position in the mouth of the highest point of the tongue* affects the resonance of the vocal tone. If the front part of the tongue is lifted, the cavity in front of the coupling is short, but the cavity behind the coupling is long. If the back of the tongue is lifted, the forward cavity is relatively long, the back cavity relatively short. To test the effect of changing the position of the tongue, compare **feed** and **food, gay** and **go.** (The shape of your lips will probably change, as well as the position of your tongue. This factor is discussed in item 4.)

A diagram of vowel articulations is shown in Figure 2. It represents schematically the relative height of the tongue for each vowel (high, mid, or low) and the relative position of the highest point of the tongue in the mouth (front, central, or back). Obviously, the oral cavity is not shaped like a trapezoid, but this diagram furnishes a convenient scheme for showing relative positioning of the tongue for the various vowel phonemes. We cannot realistically designate an exact measurement from the humped-up tongue to the hard palate, or from the raised part of the tongue to the teeth or the lips, because each person's mouth is somewhat different, and some variation in articulation is inevitable.

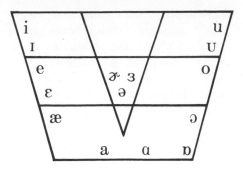

Fig. 2 Vowel Diagram

(Schematic representation of the relative position and
height of the tongue for the articulation of vowels)

3. *The degree of tension in the tongue* affects identification of vowel phonemes. The tongue muscles are more tense for the vowel in **feet** than in **fit**,
in **gate** than in **get**, in **food** than in **foot**.

4. *The shape of the lips* affects the quality of vowel phonemes. The vowel
sounds in **food, foot, foe, fought** are normally produced with the lips rounded,
as is the diphthong in **use**. The diphthong in **now** ends with lip-rounding, and
the diphthong in **joy** begins with lip-rounding. All the other vowel sounds are
produced without lip-rounding.

CHARACTERISTICS OF VOWELS

All vowel phonemes of English share certain characteristics. They are
voiced, i.e., they are produced from vocal tone created by vibration of the
vocal folds. They are produced with some degree of *mouth opening* and with
the *velum raised*, so that the tone is emitted from the mouth rather than the
nose.

The variable characteristics of vowels, other than those determined by
articulation, are duration and degree of purity. *Duration* is the length of time
a sound is held. Do not confuse it with dictionary diacritics of "long" and
"short" vowels, which indicate the quality of vowels (e.g., ē is /i/ as in **beet**,
while ĕ is /ɛ/ as in **bet**). In actual duration in time, a given vowel may be
prolonged or shortened, depending on two factors: (1) Increased stress on a
syllable lengthens the duration of the vowel in that syllable. For instance,
contrast the lengthened and shortened varieties of /o/ in **go** and **window**, of
/ɪ/ in **pin** and **include**, of /ə/ in **love** and **about**, of /ɚ/ in the two syllables of
murder. (2) The vowel's position in a word affects its duration. In a final
position, as in **pay** or **so**, or when its syllable ends with a voiced consonant,
as in **pays** or **sewn**, the vowel is longer in duration than when the syllable ends
with a voiceless consonant, as in **pace** or **soap**.

Purity of a vowel sound refers to its quality — whether it maintains the same resonance characteristic (the same sound) throughout its production or changes quality (shifts to a different sound) while it is being produced. Certain vowel sounds are called *diphthongs* because they do change articulation and quality during their production. The diphthongs /aɪ/ as in **side**, /aʊ/ as in **south**, /ɔɪ/ as in **coin**, and /ju/ as in **use**, are called *phonemic diphthongs*, because they would not signal the same meaning if they were changed to pure vowels. When the tense vowels are long in duration they become *non-phonemic diphthongs* (so called because they do not signal a different meaning when they become diphthongs): /i/ becomes [ɪi] when prolonged as in **seed**; /e/ becomes [eɪ] when prolonged as in **paid**; /u/ becomes [ʊu] when prolonged as in **food**; /o/ becomes [oʊ] when prolonged as in **rode**. We expect other vowels to remain essentially pure. If a speaker drawls or slurs his vowels, he probably changes many vowels to unacceptable non-phonemic diphthongs.

VOWEL PHONEMES IN DETAIL

/i/ as in be

Spellings of /i/: ea as in **beat**, **ee** as in **keep**, **e** as in **be**, **ie** as in **believe**, **ei** as in **receive**, **i** as in **machine**, **eo** as in **people**, **oe** as in **subpoena**, **ey** as in **key**, **uay** as in **quay**, **ae** as in **Caesar**.

Description of /i/: The front of the tongue is raised very high toward the hard palate. The jaw is almost closed. Muscles of the tongue are tense. The lips are unround. In a stressed syllable, when /i/ is prolonged, the non-phonemic diphthong [ɪi] normally occurs, especially if the vowel is final in the syllable or followed by a voiced consonant.

EXERCISES

A. Pronounce each word with a clear, bright /i/.

be	eager	grieve	believe	illegal	alleviate
seen	meager	sleep	receive	machinery	conceivable
keep	clean	please	relief	appreciate	displeasing
meek	seat	recent	either	achieve	deceit

B. When /l/ follows, there is danger of changing /i/ to the unacceptable diphthong [iə]. Transfer practice: read the following pairs of words, copying the vowel /i/ from the first word to the second word of each pair:

read — reel	wheat — wheel	heat — heal
steed — steel	meat — meal	repeat — repeal
feed — feel	seat — seal	conceit — conceal

C. Sentences for practicing /i/.

1. Keep the reel clean and neat.
2. People keep the greenest leaves to eat.
3. The thief feels ashamed of stealing.
4. We need only tea and cheese this week.
5. I believe the teams on the field are evenly matched.
6. He concealed the wheel until he could appeal for help.
7. We eat veal for at least three meals a week.

D. Reading selections for /i/ practice.

1.   You steal green apples from the Tree
                Of Life, miscalling greenness pleasure.

                                    LEE W. DODD

2.   We are the music-makers,
                And we are the dreamers of dreams . . .
                World-losers and world-forsakers,
                On whom the pale moon gleams;
                Yet we are the movers and shakers
                Of the world forever, it seems.

                                    ARTHUR O'SHAUGHNESSY

3.   To be prepared for war is one of the most effectual means of preserving
     peace.
                                    GEORGE WASHINGTON

4.   You write with ease to show your breeding,
                But easy writing's curst hard reading.

                                    RICHARD BRINSLEY SHERIDAN

5.   Teach me to feel another's woe,
                To hide the fault I see;
                That mercy I to others show,
                That mercy show to me.

                                    ALEXANDER POPE

| I |

                         /ɪ/ as in **sit**

Spellings of /ɪ/: i as in **sit**; **ea** as in **dear**; **e** as in **here**, **pretty**; **u** as in **busy**; **ee** as in **been**; **o** as in **women**; **ei** as in **forfeit**; **y** as in **bicycle**.

Alternate Correct Pronunciations: The unstressed **y** as in **happy**, **ey** as in

donkey, ee as in **coffee, e** as in **describe** are correctly pronounced as either /i/ or /ɪ/. Use whichever sounds familiar to you.

The unstressed **a** in **village** or **palace, u** in **lettuce, e** in **chicken, i** in **Alice** are correctly pronounced as either /ɪ/ or /ə/. Use whichever you prefer.

Description of /ɪ/: The front of the tongue is raised high toward the palate. Muscles of the tongue are lax. Lips are unround. This vowel has a clear quality, and is pure and undiphthongized in standard usage.

EXERCISES

A. Pronounce each word with a pure /ɪ/ vowel.

fit	which	dinner	been	dear
bit	wrist	rinse	pretty	near
skip	slipped	this	women	here
dim	him	thin	busy	appear

B. Avoid substituting /ɛ/ for /ɪ/, especially when /l/ follows. Transfer practice: copy the /ɪ/ you use in the first word of each line in all the words on that line.

> sit — sill — silk — silver
> mitt — mill — milk — million
> wit — will — willing — William
> it — ill — Illinois

C. In prefixes spelled with e, use either /ɪ/ or /i/, but do not substitute /ə/. Pronounce each of the following words, giving attention to the vowel sound in the prefix.

believe	beside	defend	detail	defend	prefer
behave	become	describe	deceive	decide	prevent
behind	before	deliberate	demand	deplore	pretend

D. Avoid substituting /i/ for /ɪ/. Transfer exercise: pronounce each pair of words, copying the vowel from the first word to the second word of the pair.

drip — drink	thin — think	wit — wish
it — ink	sick — sing	dip — dish
sit — sink	pit — pinch	fit — fish
pit — pink	it — inch	mitten — mission

E. Contrast /i/ with /ɪ/. If you have learned English after another language, you may have difficulty distinguishing between /i/ and /ɪ/. Pronounce each pair of words, producing a tense /i/ in the first word and a lax /ɪ/ in the second.

beet — bit	seek — sick	peak — pick	leave — live
leak — lick	steal — still	seat — sit	feel — fill
each — itch	keen — kin	heat — hit	feet — fit
week — wick	seen — sin	green — grin	eat — it

F. Sentences for practicing /ɪ/.

1. The milk is in the deep dish on the window sill.
2. We will be busy until six o'clock this evening.
3. His sister lives in Illinois but visits here often.
4. I wish we could get some silk that is tissue thin.
5. Billy, when you drink, don't let it drip on your chin.
6. He lives near the mill stream.
7. This reading is easy, isn't it?
8. Is Edith sitting in a seat near here?
9. The city police are busy in the Christmas season.
10. We will just heap the dishes in the sink.

G. Reading selections for /ɪ/ practice.

1. It is easy for men to talk one thing and think another.

   PUBLILIUS SYRUS

2. True hope is swift, and flies with swallow's wings;
   Kings it makes gods, and meaner creatures kings.

   WILLIAM SHAKESPEARE

3. Spring, the sweet spring, is the year's pleasant king;
   Then blooms each thing, then maids dance in a ring,
   Cold doth not sting, the pretty birds do sing.

   THOMAS NASH

4. A little learning is a dangerous thing;
   Drink deep, or taste not the Pierian spring:

   ALEXANDER POPE

5. I wish I hadn't broke that dish,
   I wish I was a movie-star,
   I wish a lot of things, I wish
   That life was like the movies are.

   SIR ALAN HERBERT

6. Do you want an image of the human will or the self-determining principle, as compared with its pre-arranged and impassable restrictions? A drop of water, imprisoned in a crystal; you may see such a one in any mineralogical collection. One little fluid particle in the crystalline prism of the solid universe!

OLIVER WENDELL HOLMES

7.   "Beside," quoth the Mayor with a knowing wink,
"Our business was done at the river's brink:
We saw with our eyes the vermin sink,
And what's dead can't come to life, I think.
So, friend, we're not the folks to shrink
From the duty of giving you something for drink, . . .
Beside, our losses have made us thrifty,
A thousand guilders! Come, take fifty!"

ROBERT BROWNING

/e/ as in **name, chaotic**

e

Spellings of /e/: a as in **name**; **ai** as in **aid**; **ay** as in **day**; **ei** as in **weigh**; **ey** as in **obey**; **ea** as in **steak**; **ue** as in **risqué**; **e** as in **fiancé**; **ee** as in **entrée**; **au** as in **gauge**.

Though **ay** in **day, birthday**, and **holiday** is pronounced /e/, it may also be pronounced [ɪ] or [i] in the days of the week, i.e., **Monday, Friday**.

Description of /e/: The front of the tongue is raised mid-high toward the palate. Muscles of the tongue are tense. Lips are unround.

A diphthong [eɪ] (non-phonemic) usually occurs in stressed syllables, especially if final in the syllable (as in **pay, payment**) or preceding a voiced consonant (as in **paid**).

EXERCISES

A. When an /l/ follows, there is danger of changing /e/ to an unacceptable [eə] diphthong. Transfer exercise: use the same /e/ vowel in the second word as in the first word of each pair.

say — sail	may — mail	ray — rail
pay — pale	whey — whale	fate — fail

B. Contrast /i/ and /e/.

pea — pay	me — may	we — way
plea — play	see — say	mean — main

C. Opening the mouth too widely changes /e/ to [æɪ] or [aɪ]. Contrast /e/ and /aɪ/.

pay — pie	main — mine	pain — pine
say — sigh	paint — pint	take — tyke

D. Pronounce each word with a clear /e/ vowel.

cake	naked	radiator	tornado
take	break	aviator	regalia
steak	grateful	vacation	pathos
snake	state	oration	risqué

E. Sentences for practicing /e/.

1. The mail is late today.
2. Mary is afraid of snakes.
3. Don't fail to mail us a letter on your vacation.
4. I can't make those brakes work lately.
5. We went to a play on State Street on my birthday.
6. Bake me a cake and put my name on it.
7. At the lake it rains every day.
8. Kate waited in the shade until the parade passed.
9. Eight law-makers made speeches today.
10. Nail the gray sail to the frame.

F. Reading selections for /e/ practice.

1.   The rain in Spain falls mainly on the plain.

                   GEORGE BERNARD SHAW

2.   Break, break, break,
          On thy cold grey stones, O Sea!

                   ALFRED, LORD TENNYSON

3. Some are born great, some achieve greatness, and some have greatness thrust upon them.

                   FRANCIS BACON

4.   Why so pale and wan, fond lover?
          Prithee, why so pale?
          Will, when looking well can't move her,
          Looking ill prevail?
          Prithee, why so pale?

                   SIR JOHN SUCKLING

5.   For he who fights and runs away
                    May live to fight another day:
                    But he who is in battle slain
                    Can never rise and fight again.

OLIVER GOLDSMITH

6.   It is easy to be brave from a safe distance.

AESOP

/ɛ/ as in bet

                                                ɛ

Spellings of /ɛ/: e as in **bet**; ea as in **breath**; a as in **any, dictionary**; ie as in **friend**; ei as in **heifer**; eo as in **Leonard**.

Alternate Correct Pronunciations: Preceding an **r**, ea as in **bear**, a as in **marry**, ai as in **hair**, e as in **there**, ei as in **their** are correctly pronounced as either /ɛ/ or /æ/, though /ɛ/ is more common in most areas except in the Southern dialect.

In the particular words **dairy, Mary, vary, various,** and **again** the stressed vowel is correctly pronounced either /ɛ/, /e/, or /æ/. The /ɛ/ pronunciation has widest use, while /e/ is popular chiefly in Southern and Eastern dialects, and /æ/ occurs chiefly in New York City.

Description of /ɛ/: The front of the tongue is raised mid-high toward the palate. Muscles of the tongue are lax. Lips are unround.

EXERCISES

A. Avoid substitution of /ɪ/ for /ɛ/ before a nasal consonant.

(1) Transfer exercise: copy the vowel /ɛ/ from the first to the second word of each pair.

pet — pen	Ted — ten	head — hem
met — men	petty — penny	stead — stem
met — many	dead — den	met — member
whet — when	met — meant	ebb — emphasis

(2) Contrast /ɪ/ in the first word with /ɛ/ in the second word of each pair.

pin — pen	tin — ten	Minnie — many
wind — wend	tint — tent	lint — lent

(3) Practice a clear /ɛ/ vowel in each word.

tenth	intention	tension	them	membrane
then	pretense	plenty	Memphis	emphasis
when	intense	any	empty	member

B. The words **get** and **forget** should be pronounced with /ɛ/, not /ɪ/.

C. Use /ɛ/, not /ɪ/ or /e/, in **length** and **strength**.

D. Avoid substituting /e/ for /ɛ/ before /g/ or /ʒ/. Transfer exercise: copy the sound of /ɛ/ from the first to the second word of each pair.

Ed — egg	kept — keg	tread — treasure
bed — beg	pet — peg	met — measure
led — leg	pet — Peggy	pled — pleasure

E. Avoid changing /ɛr/ to /ɚ/ in the following.

very	American	there	dictionary
cherry	somewhere	where	library

F. Sentences for /ɛ/ practice.

1. There was a terrible wreck in Memphis on the tenth of December.
2. Twenty men said the cherry pie was best.
3. Peggy broke her leg at the Easter egg hunt.
4. Americans emphasize the value of inventions.
5. It is a pleasure to forget the ten pennies he lent me.
6. He begged us to measure the length again.
7. Ted keeps pens and pencils in his desk.
8. The treasure map was sketched on a page from an old ledger.
9. That is the tenth time he has mentioned his pension.
10. He went inside the tent and opened the keg.

G. Reading selections for /ɛ/ practice.

1.   As an egg, when broken, never
       Can be mended, but must ever
       Be the same crushed egg for ever — . . .

                THOMAS H. CHIVERS

2. . . . I gained an immense advantage over the cleverer boys. . . . I got into my bones the essential structure of the ordinary British sentence — which is a noble thing. . . .

                WINSTON CHURCHILL

3. Crimes are not to be measured by the issue of events, but from the bad intentions of men.

Cicero

4. Lay up for yourselves treasures in heaven.

Matthew, vi

5. If you call a tail a leg, how many legs has a dog? Five? No; calling a tail a leg don't make it a leg.

Attributed to Abraham Lincoln

6. Good health and good sense are two of life's greatest blessings.

Publilius Syrus

7.   My strength is as the strength of ten,
       Because my heart is pure.

Alfred, Lord Tennyson

/æ/ as in **hat**

/a/ as used in **ask** by some Easterners

æ
a

Spellings of /æ/: a as in **hat**; **ai** as in **plaid**.

Alternate Correct Pronunciations: When the spellings **a** or **ai** precede a final /s/ as in **class**, /f/ as in **half**, /θ/ as in **path**, or /n/ + another consonant as in **can't, command, aunt,** correct pronunciation favors /æ/ in American usage. In parts of New England and in New York City, /a/ and occasionally /ɑ/ are also used in these words.

Description of /æ/: There is a very slight elevation of the front part of the tongue. The jaw is widely opened. Lips are unround.

Description of /a/: The same as for /æ/ except that the tongue is pulled slightly back from the /æ/ position, and the jaw may be even more widely opened than for /æ/.

EXERCISES

A. Auditory discrimination. Learn to identify unacceptable allophones of /æ/ and to recognize your own errors and where they are most likely to occur. (Read a formula [ɛ/æ] as "[ɛ] is substituted for [æ].")
   1. [ɛ/æ] if the tongue and jaw are raised too high.
   2. [e/æ] if the tongue is tense and raised and the jaw is too closed.

3. [a/æ] (on words not included in alternate pronunciations) if the tongue is drawn back.

4. [æə/æ, æɪ/æ, æi/æ] if the shift of articulators to the following consonant is too slow.

5. [ɛə/æ, ɛɪ/æ] if the tongue and jaw are raised and the shift to the following consonant is too slow.

6. [ɪæ/æ, əæ/æ] if the shift from the preceding consonant is too slow.

B. Transfer exercises. The word which begins each line below is one in which good /æ/ articulation is normally most predictable. As you pronounce successive words in a line your chances of error increase. Control your production of /æ/ by copying in each successive word the sound of /æ/ you produced in the first word of that line. Circle the words you find most difficult and practice them repeatedly, transferring the vowel sound from a "safe" word in that line to your troublesome word.

1. at add ant aunt act actor actual
2. bat bad bath bass bash batch balance back bag bang bank
3. fat fad fan fast fact fang fashion
4. sat sad sand sash sack sang sank
5. hat had half hand hash hatch hack hang hank
6. pat pad pan path pass patch pack pang
7. cat cad can cash catch can't
8. mat mad matter mass man mash match mangle
9. lad laugh lass lash latch lap lab lamb lamp lank
10. dad Dan dash dab dam damp dank
11. tat tan tap tab tam tack tag tang tank
12. rat radish rather raft wrap rash ran ram rang rank
13. gap gaff gander gallon gash gag gang
14. gnat nab nap nasty gnash knack nag
15. vat vast van vacuum
16. chat chatter chap chastise champion chant
17. plait plaid plan plant plaque
18. blab bland blast black blank
19. clap clam clamp clad clan clank
20. glad glass gland glance
21. grad grab grand grass gramp
22. trap tramp trash track
23. stab stamp stand staff stash stack stank
24. slap slab slash slant slam slack slang
25. snap snack snatch snag

26. flat flap flab flash flask flack flag flank
27. exact example examine examination

C. Contrast of /ɛ/ and /æ/. Read each pair of words with a clear distinction between the quality of /ɛ/ and /æ/, and not simply a difference in vowel duration.

pet — pat	bet — bat	heck — hack	said — sad
pen — pan	bend — band	hem — ham	peck — pack
met — mat	set — sat	left — laughed	lest — last
men — man	send — sand	pest — passed	then — than

D. Contrast of /æ/ and /ɑ/. If you have learned English after some other language, you may have trouble distinguishing between /æ/ and /ɑ/. It may help to remember that the letter **a** has to be pronounced /ɑ/ only when it precedes **r** as in **park** or silent **l** as in **calm**, and in the word **father**. Pronounce the following pairs of words, using /æ/ in the first and /ɑ/ in the second of each pair. (Easterners often prefer /ɒ/ in the second word.)

hat — hot	sack — sock	map — mop	tags — togs
cat — cot	lack — lock	tap — top	battle — bottle
rat — rot	rack — rock	plaid — plod	sadden — sodden
pat — pot	knack — knock	band — bond	packet — pocket
gnat — not	cam — calm [2]	panned — pond	Sam — psalm [2]

E. Sentences for /æ/ practice.

1. Sam ran into the First National Bank with the sack of cash in his hand.
2. That was our last chance for a camping trip.
3. Thanks for stacking those bags of sand on the planks.
4. My aunt demanded that we clean the trash out of the attic.
5. Alice was so angry that she had a tantrum.
6. Do you plan to have the actors stand on that platform in the last act?
7. He acted as if these hats and caps were grand values.
8. Frank has a passion for having his back scratched.
9. These damaged lamps can be had at half price on Saturday.
10. Is the last chapter of *Anthony Adverse* happy or sad?
11. Practically half this class can't pass the algebra examination.
12. That man has asked to see the plant manager.
13. After the accident her hand had to be in a plaster cast.
14. Actually, "philatelist" is just a fancy name for a stamp collector.
15. Has the champion answered Max's demands for a return match?

[2] The contrast here presumes a pronunciation of **calm** and **psalm** with silent "l".

F. Reading selections for /æ/ practice.

1. A man should always consider how much he has more than he wants and how much more unhappy he might be than he really is.

> JOSEPH ADDISON

2. Those who'll play with cats must expect to be scratched.

> MIGUEL DE CERVANTES

3. Man is a reasoning animal.

> SENECA

4. Romantic plays with happy endings are almost of necessity inferior in artistic value to true tragedies. Not, one would hope, simply because they end happily; happiness in itself is certainly not less beautiful than grief; but because a tragedy in its great moments can generally afford to be sincere, while romantic plays live in an atmosphere of ingenuity and make-believe.

> GILBERT MURRAY

5.   Whom unmerciful Disaster
            Followed fast and followed faster.

> EDGAR ALLAN POE

6.   Great rats, small rats, lean rats, brawny rats,
            Brown rats, black rats, gray rats, tawny rats, . . .
            From street to street he piped advancing,
            And step for step they followed dancing, . . .

> ROBERT BROWNING

7. His [Ishmael's] hand will be against every man, and every man's hand against him. . . .

> GENESIS, XVI

8.   Rats!
            They fought the dogs and killed the cats,
            And bit the babies in the cradles,
            And ate the cheeses out of the vats,
            And licked the soup from the cooks' own ladles,
            Split open the kegs of salted sprats,
            Made nests inside men's Sunday hats,
            And even spoiled the women's chats,
            By drowning their speaking
            With shrieking and squeaking
            In fifty different sharps and flats.

> ROBERT BROWNING

9.   Know then thyself, presume not God to scan;
      The proper study of mankind is man.

ALEXANDER POPE

/ɑ/ as in **father, calm, car**
/ɒ/ as sometimes used in **not, orange, office**
/ɔ/ as in **law, war**

α
ɒ
ɔ

Spellings of /ɑ/: a as in **father**; **ea** as in **heart**.

Alternate Correct Pronunciations: The "short o" as in **not** is pronounced /ɑ/ by the vast majority of American speakers. An alternate correct pronunciation using /ɒ/, called the "rounded short **o**," occurs chiefly in the Eastern dialect. Reasonable consistency in pronunciation is desirable (see Exercise A).

In most words where the dictionary diacritical marking equates with the vowel /ɔ/, except those where an **r** follows (e.g., **warm**), good usage varies between /ɔ/ and /ɒ/ (see Exercise D).

The letter **o**, when it precedes either a medial /r/, as in **orange**, or a fricative consonant, as in **office**, and the letter **a** following **w** in many words (e.g., **wash**), are correctly pronounced either /ɑ/, /ɒ/, or /ɔ/ (see Exercise E).

Descriptions of /ɑ/, /ɒ/ or /ɔ/: For these three vowels the highest point of the tongue is in the back of the mouth. For /ɑ/ and /ɒ/ the tongue is held as low in the mouth as possible and the jaw is lowered. For /ɔ/ the tongue is raised slightly, and the jaw is not quite as open as for /ɑ/ and /ɒ/. Tongue muscles are relaxed for all these vowels. For /ɑ/ the lips are unrounded. For /ɒ/ the lips are very slightly rounded. For /ɔ/ the lips are more rounded.

Some people use all three of these vowels, while some others use only two of them. Examine your own pronunciation of the key words listed, comparing your articulation with the description above, to discover your own usage. Otherwise, you may identify these vowels incorrectly.

EXERCISES

A. In "short **o**" words, most Americans use /ɑ/, though many Easterners use /ɒ/. Be sure that you do not substitute /a/ for /ɑ/. Pronounce these words with either /ɑ/ or /ɒ/.

hot	not	doll	pocket	doctor	dollar
shot	box	rock	deposit	proper	knock
pot	fox	lock	possible	probable	block

B. Pronounce the following words with /ɑ/. Do not substitute either /a/ or /ɒ/.

car	heart	harsh	charm	cart	father
far	art	harm	part	sharp	calm
star	arm	march	park	smart	palm
start	arc	garage	mark	bark	qualms

C. Transfer exercise: if you use /ɑ/ in **pot** and **hot**, then both words of each pair following should have the same /ɑ/ vowel.

pot — par	shot — sharp	hot — are
hot — heart	chop — chart	stop — star
cot — car	pot — part	hod — hard

D. You may pronounce the following words with either /ɒ/ or /ɔ/. Do not substitute either /ɑ/ or /o/. Be careful to keep the vowel pure. If you shift the articulation to the following consonant too gradually, you are likely to change the vowel to an unacceptable diphthong, such as [ɒə], [ɔə], [ɔʊ] or [ɑo].

dog	cough	fraud	cause	song	caught
frog	soft	broad	because	long	bought
log	off	cost	pause	wrong	thought
hog	often	lost	clause	taught	fought

E. Some words are correctly pronounced with either /ɔ/, /ɒ/, or /ɑ/, and consistency in using a particular vowel in all these words is not necessary. Do not substitute either /a/ or /o/ or change the vowel to an unacceptable diphthong, e.g., [ɔə], [ɔɪ], [ɒə], [ɒɪ], [ɑə], [ɑɪ].

orange	tomorrow	Florida	on	closet	want
sorry	borrow	quarrel	laundry	squash	water
horrible	incorrigible	faucet	office	squalid	wash

F. Contrast of /ɑ/ and /ɔ/. If you tend to confuse /ɑ/ and /ɔ/, pronounce the following pairs of words, contrasting /ɑ/ in the first with /ɔ/ in the second of each pair.

farm — form	darn — dormitory	knotty — naughty
far — for	mart — mortify	pond — pawned
barn — born	tart — tort	pod — pawed
car — corn	nod — gnawed	cot — caught

G. Contrast of /ɔ/ and /o/. If you confuse /ɔ/ and /o/, pronounce the following pairs of words, contrasting /ɔ/ in the first with /o/ in the second of each pair.

hall — hole	walk — woke	pause — pose
horse — hoarse	war — wore	law — low
bought — boat	call — coal	lawn — loan
born — borne	warn — worn	morning — mourning

H. Unstressing and Restressing. Certain words, like **of, from, for, was, because,** because of their meaning, rarely occur except in an unstressed position in a phrase. When a word becomes unstressed, normally its vowel shifts to a more "neutral" quality, becoming a /ə/ or /ɚ/, whichever fits. Then two problems develop: (1) When a speaker needs to stress one of these words which he usually unstresses, he is unsure of the appropriate vowel to use in the stressed form. (2) A "careful" but unsure speaker might avoid the normal unstressed form because he fears it sounds careless, thereby giving more stress to the word than it deserves and over-pronouncing the vowel. Read the following exercise, observing the indicated word stresses as marked with ', noting the difference in the unstressed and correctly stressed forms.

	Correct Unstressed Form	*As in this sentence*	*Incorrect Restressed Form*	*Correct Restressed Form*	*As in this sentence*
of	/əv/	I thóught of you.	/əv/	/ɑv/	I was speaking óf you, not tó you.
from	/frəm/	This is a létter from Tóm.	/frəm/	/frɑm/	This is a letter fróm Tom, not tó him.
was	/wəz/	I was plánning to go.	/wəz/	/wɑz/	I wás planning to go, but I chánged my mind.
for	/fɚ/	Is this for mé?	/fɚ/	/fɔr/	If this is fór me, why can't I háve it?
because	/bɪkəz/	He díd it because he didn't knów he shóuldn't.	/bɪkəz/	/bɪkɔz/	He did it becáuse he knéw he shóuldn't.

I. Sentences for practicing /ɑ/, /ɒ/, /ɔ/. If you are unsure which vowel is correct in any word, recheck its pronunciation and write the IPA symbol above it to guide you when you practice the sentence where it occurs.

1. Carl parked the car in his yard.
2. Tom's father went to Harvard.
3. Was the doctor alarmed about Father's heart?
4. It was after dark when Bob started through the park.
5. The marble from that rock quarry is used for monuments.

6. That barrage of shot probably hit the garage.
7. Mark put the palm fronds in a box by the altar.
8. Florida and California are famous for their oranges.
9. The closet door at my office is not locked.
10. The water from these faucets is hardly hot enough for laundry.
11. Possibly the office supplies were lost.
12. He sat down on a mossy log, with his arm around the dog.
13. All our chalk is bought at Morton's Shop.
14. Don't let the ball fall off the edge of the walk.
15. We thought he fought extraordinarily well.
16. There was a bad storm in northern Arkansas.
17. Gargle with warm salt water every morning.
18. We paused often on our long walk.

J. Reading selections for /ɑ/ practice.

1.
> When we are parted, let me lie
> In some far corner of thy heart,
> Silent, and from the world apart,
> Like a forgotten melody.
>
> CHARLES H. AIDE

2.
> As a beauty I'm not a great star,
> Others are handsomer far;
> But my face — I don't mind it
> Because I'm behind it;
> It's the folks out in front that I jar.
>
> ANTHONY EUWER

3.
> Hark, hark! The lark at Heaven's gate sings, . . .
>
> WILLIAM SHAKESPEARE

4.
> Two men look out through the same bars;
> One sees the mud and one the stars.
>
> ANONYMOUS

5.
> The perfection of art is to conceal art.
>
> QUINTILIAN

6.
> Soon shall thy arm, unconquer'd stream! afar
> Drag the slow barge, or drive the rapid car;
>
> ERASMUS DARWIN

K. Reading selections for /ɒ/ and /ɔ/ practice.

1.   But all the dwarfs and giants tall,
            Working till doomsday shadows fall
            Can't make a blade of grass.

                              JULIAN S. CUTLER

2.   Genius must be born, and never can be taught.

                              JOHN DRYDEN

3.   When to the sessions of sweet silent thought
            I summon up remembrance of things past,
            I sigh the lack of many a thing I sought.

                              WILLIAM SHAKESPEARE

4.   He is all fault who hath no fault at all.

                              ALFRED, LORD TENNYSON

5.   If to her share some female errors fall,
       Look on her face, and you'll forget 'em all.

                              ALEXANDER POPE

6.   Unlike my subject now shall be my song;
            It shall be witty, and it sha'n't be long.

                              LORD CHESTERFIELD

/o/ as in go   **O**

Spellings of /o/: o as in **go**, **omit**; **oa** as in **loan**; **ow** as in **low**, **window**; **oe** as in **doe**; **ou** as in **shoulder**, **thorough**; **eau** as in **beau**; **oo** as in **brooch**; **au** as in **chauffeur**.

Description of /o/: The back of the tongue is raised mid-high toward the palate. The jaw is half lowered. The tongue muscles are tense. The lips are rounded.

A standard allophone of /o/ is the non-phonemic diphthong [oʊ], produced as a glide toward a higher tongue and jaw position with gradually relaxing muscles. The [oʊ] allophone results from prolongation of /o/ in a stressed syllable, especially when it is final in the syllable as in **go**, or when /o/ precedes a voiced consonant as in **load, loan, coal**. The undiphthongized [o] is more predictable in unstressed syllables, as in **omit** or **piano**, or in a stressed syllable which ends in a voiceless consonant, as in **coat, broke, hope,** or preceding /r/ as in **core, pork**.

EXERCISES

A. Pronounce the following words with /o/ in the unstressed syllable. Do not substitute /ə/.

omit	hotel	location	pillow	shadow	thorough
obey	convocation	cooperate	yellow	mellow	window
oration	ovation	piano	fellow	follow	willow

In the following words, however, the **o** spelling is correctly pronounced /ə/ To use /o/ in these words would be an over-pronunciation.

occasion	occur	o'clock	officious
occasionally	occurrence	official	opinion

B. Before /r/, the pure vowel /o/, or even /ɔ/ is normally used in preference to the non-phonemic diphthong [ou].

oar	shore	bore	spore	door	implore
tore	store	snore	roar	floor	explore
more	core	swore	pour	restore	story

C. Keep the lips round throughout the production of [ou]. When a consonant precedes, as in **go** or **foe**, you should round the lips while making the initial consonant. When a consonant follows, as in **own** or **load**, keep the lips rounded until after the final consonant is formed. The diphthongs [ɛo], [əo], [ɔə] are unacceptable allophones of /o/. Pronounce each word with careful attention to keeping the lips rounded.

own	cone	loan	coast	coat	both
bone	grown	shown	most	boat	sofa
flown	known	alone	boast	soak	soap

D. In pronouncing /o/ before /l/, be especially careful to keep the lips rounded until after the /l/ is formed, lest you change the vowel to [ɔə]. Transfer exercise: pronounce each pair of words, copying the [ou] diphthong from the first word to the second.

owe — old	hoe — hole	foe — foal
go — goal	hoe — hold	foe — fold
go — gold	toe — toll	show — shoal
so — soul	toe — told	code — coal
so — sold	row — roll	code — cold

E. Sentences for practicing /o/.

1. Both our boats have holes in them.
2. Please go and close the window by the piano.

3. That is an old story from the African Gold Coast.
4. Coal is worth more than it was four years ago.
5. Cut out the core and pour honey into the hole.
6. That old oarsman knows these shoals thoroughly.
7. He won't condone being told less than the whole truth.

F. Reading selections for /o/ practice.

1.
> It fortifies my soul to know
> That, though I perish, Truth is so.
>
> ARTHUR H. CLOUGH

2.
> I grow old. . . . I grow old. . . .
> I shall wear the bottoms of my trousers rolled.
>
> T. S. ELIOT

3.
> Oh, this is the joy of the rose:
> That it blows,
> And goes.
>
> WILLA CATHER

4.
> Fame is the scentless sunflower, with gaudy crown of gold:
> But friendship is the breathing rose, with sweets in every fold.
>
> OLIVER WENDELL HOLMES

5.
> Man proposes, but God disposes.
>
> THOMAS À KEMPIS

6.
> Better to bind your brow with yellow
> And follow, follow until you die,
> Than to sleep with your head on a golden pillow,
> Nor lift it up when the hunt goes by.
>
> ELINOR WYLIE

7.
> In words, as fashions, the same rule will hold,
> Alike fantastic if too new or old: . . .
>
> ALEXANDER POPE

8.
> Build thee more stately mansions, O my soul,
> As the swift seasons roll!
>
> OLIVER WENDELL HOLMES

U
u

/ʊ/ as in **foot**
/u/ as in **food**

Spellings of /ʊ/: **oo** as in **foot**; **u** as in **pull**; **ou** as in **would**; **o** as in **wolf**; **or** as in **worsted**.

Spellings of /u/: **oo** as in **food**; **u** as in **rule**; **ue** as in **blue**; **ew** as in **grew**; **o** as in **move**; **ou** as in **bouquet**; **oe** as in **shoe**; **ui** as in **fruit**; **wo** as in **two**.

Alternate Correct Pronunciations: In **roof** and certain other specific words (see Section D), the **oo** spelling may be pronounced either /ʊ/ or /u/. This does not apply to all **oo** spellings.

Descriptions of /ʊ/ and /u/: Both these vowels are articulated with the back of the tongue raised very high toward the palate. Muscles of the tongue are lax for /ʊ/ but tense for /u/. Lips are rounded for both vowels but more tightly rounded for /u/ than /ʊ/.

The /u/ vowel usually becomes a non-phonemic diphthong [uʊ] when it is prolonged, occurring in a stressed syllable, especially if the vowel is final in the word as in **shoe**, or followed by a voiced consonant as in **food**.

EXERCISES

A. Be sure to keep the lips rounded for the vowel /ʊ/, to prevent confusion with /ə/. Contrast the sound of /ʊ/ and /ə/ in the following pairs of words.

book — buck	shook — shuck	put — putt
look — luck	took — tuck	pull — pulverize

B. Pronounce the following words with /ʊ/, not /u/. Keep the lips rounded to avoid confusion with /ə/. Keep the tongue pulled far back in the mouth, to make a clear distinction from /ɪ/. Unacceptable allophones are the diphthongs [ʊɪ], [ʊə], [ɪʊ], [əʊ].

put	book	should	would	full	good
push	bush	could	wool	pull	cook

C. Contrast of /o/ and /ʊ/. When /r/ follows, there is danger of confusing /o/ and /ʊ/. Pronounce these pairs of words, with /ʊ/ in the first word and /o/ in the second of each pair. (Be careful also not to substitute /ɚ/ for /ʊr/.)

tour — tore	moor — more	boor — bore
poor — pore	sure — shore	your [3] — yore

[3] In New York City and parts of the South, **your** is acceptably pronounced with either /ʊ/ or /o/.

D. A few words spelled with **oo** are correctly pronounced with either /ʊ/ or /u/. Pronounce the following with either /u/ or /ʊ/, as they sound familiar to you.

room   roof   root   coop   hoof   hoop   whoop

E. Pronounce /u/ in the following words, keeping the tongue far back in the mouth and rounding the lips quickly and tightly. The diphthong [ʊu] is a correct allophone of /u/, but [ɪu] and [əu] are not.

blue	who	groom	food	youth	croon
you	whom	broom	mood	truth	spoon
two	bloom	loom	fruit	noon	soon
grew	gloom	doom	shoot	moon	June

F. When pronouncing /u/ before /l/, be especially careful to keep the tongue muscles tense and hold the vowel sound until the /l/ is formed. Do not substitute /ʊ/ or the diphthong [uə]. Transfer exercise: pronounce the following pairs of words, copying the sound of /u/ from the first to the second word of each pair.

food — fool	spoon — spool	stoop — stool
cooed — cool	scoot — school	droop — drool
too — tool	rude — rule	pooch — pool

G. Foreign students often encounter difficulty distinguishing between /ʊ/ and /u/. To differentiate the two vowels, pronounce the following pairs of words, contrasting the kinesthesia of lax muscles for /ʊ/ and tense muscles for /u/, as well as noting the difference in the sounds.

look — Luke	would — wooed	pull — pool
could — cooed	should — shooed	full — fool

H. Sentences for practicing /ʊ/ and /u/. If you are unsure which vowel is correct in any word, recheck its pronunciation and write the IPA symbol above it to guide you when you practice the sentence where it occurs.

1. The wood box should be full.
2. If you could push the broom, I could pull it.
3. A good-looking woman should have had the lead in the movie.
4. Worsted is a good woolen material for suits.
5. Would you like to move your books to school?
6. Who put a hook on the door of the chicken coop?
7. How much Worcestershire sauce should we put in the pudding?
8. Whose cookbook did you put in the bookshelf?
9. The water in the pool at school is too cool.

10. Those cool, gloomy days will be here soon.
11. The glue on these shoe soles is loose.
12. Did you lose the two spools of blue thread?
13. The troops followed this route, moving cautiously through the woods.
14. We were looking at the blooms in the moonlight.
15. Could the tool shed be moved away from the pool?
16. Your blueberry bushes should be in full bloom soon.

I. Reading selections for /ʊ/ practice.

1.   Finds tongues in trees, books in the running brooks,
    Sermons in stones, and good in everything.

WILLIAM SHAKESPEARE

2. As good almost kill a man as kill a good book: who kills a man kills a reasonable creature, God's image; but he who destroys a good book kills reason itself.

JOHN MILTON

3. The cook was a good cook, as cooks go; and as cooks go she went.

H. H. MUNRO (SAKI)

4. You cannot put the same shoe on every foot.

PUBLILIUS SYRUS

5. I would my horse had the speed of your tongue, and so good a continuer.

WILLIAM SHAKESPEARE

6. The English Bible, — a book which if everything else in our language should perish, would alone suffice to show the whole extent of its beauty and power.

LORD MACAULAY

7.   The halls of fame are open wide
    And they are always full;
    Some go in by the door called "push,"
    And some by the door called "pull."

STANLEY BALDWIN

8.   Dreams, books, are each a world, and books, we know,
    Are a substantial world, both sure and good.

WILLIAM WORDSWORTH

J. Reading selections for /u/ practice.

1.   Better no rule than cruel rule.

                                            AESOP

2.   Who think too little and who talk too much.

                                            JOHN DRYDEN

3. From *Cat Naps Are Too Good for Cats* [4]

                    .   .   .   .   .   .

            I would not sell my daily swoon
            For all the rubies in Rangoon.
            What! sell my swoon? My lovely swoon?
            Oh, many and many's the afternoon
            I've scoured the woods with Daniel Boone,
            Or sipped a julep with Lorna Doone
            And former Governor Ruby Laffoon.
            I'll sell my soul before my swoon,
            It's not for sale, my swoon's immune.

            From two to three each afternoon
            Mine are the Mountains of the moon,
            Mine a congenital silver spoon.
            And I can lead a lost platoon
            Or dive for pearls in a haunted lagoon,
            Or guide a stratosphere balloon.
            Oh, where the schooner schoons, I schoon,
            I can talk lion or baboon,
            Or make a crooner cease to croon.
            I like to swoon, for when I swoon
            The universe is my macaroon.
            Then blessings on thee, my afternoon torpor,
            Thou makest a prince of a mental porpor.

                                            OGDEN NASH

4.   'Tis an old maxim in the schools
                       That flattery's the food of fools.

                                            JONATHAN SWIFT

5.   Health that mocks the doctor's rules,
                       Knowledge never learned in schools.

                                JOHN GREENLEAF WHITTIER

[4] From *Verses From 1929 On* by Ogden Nash, by permission of Little, Brown and Co. Copyright 1936 by Ogden Nash.

ǝ

/ə/ as in **above**

Spellings of /ə/: In stressed syllables,[5] this vowel is spelled **u** as in **cut, o** as in **come, ou** as in **trouble, oe** as in **does,** and **oo** as in **flood.** In unstressed syllables /ə/ is spelled with **a** as in **sofa, o** as in **connect, u** as in **circus, io** as in **connection, ou** as in **mischievous,** and usually **ie** as in **mischievous, ai** as in **mountain, e** as in **absent,** and **i** as in **terrify.** A final unstressed syllable spelled **le,** as in **able, apple, cackle, giggle,** is usually pronounced with /ə/ before the /l/.

Description of /ə/: The central part of the tongue is lifted mid-high toward the palate. The muscles of the tongue are lax. Lips are unround. This vowel has a neutral quality, as if it were a blend of all vowels, comparable to grey on a color wheel. Any vowel is likely to become /ə/ when it is unstressed, so that this is the most frequently occurring vowel in the English language. It is called schwa ("shvah" /ʃvɑ/), a name which came from Hebrew via German (related to Ger. **schwach,** meaning "weak").

Alternate Correct Pronunciations: In a final unstressed syllable, either /ə/ or /ɪ/ is correct for **i** as in **Alice, u** as in **lettuce, e** as in **business, president, a** as in **salad, ai** as in **mountain.**

A medial, unstressed **e** as in **telephone, i** as in **nullify, ie** as in **mischievous** is usually pronounced /ə/ in America, but is sometimes pronounced /ɪ/.

EXERCISES

A. If you formerly spoke a language which does not have /ə/, you may confuse /ə/ with /ɑ/. Contrast these two vowels in the following pairs of words, differentiating between /ɑ/ in the first word and /ə/ in the second word of each pair.

cot — cut	lock — luck	don — done
not — nut	sock — suck	calm [6] — come
rob — rub	dock — duck	psalm [6] — some

B. In the Southern dialect, /ə/ is sometimes confused with /ɜ/ (the "/r/-less" pronunciation of the **ur** in **hurt**). Transfer exercise: the first word of each pair below is a "safe" word, i.e., the /ə/ vowel is commonly undistorted there. The second word of each pair is one in which the substitution of

---

[5] The IPA uses the /ʌ/ symbol to designate this vowel in stressed syllables and /ə/ in unstressed syllables. Since the vowel sounds the same whether stressed or unstressed (except for longer duration with stress) and cannot be contrasted to establish different meanings, it is logical and practical to use a single symbol for the vowel wherever it occurs.

[6] See footnote 2, page 225.

/ɜ/ for /ə/ is likely. Listen carefully to your vowel in the first word and copy it in the second word of each pair.

mutt — mother	luck — love	putt — punish
mutt — money	truck — trouble	mutt — much

C. In an unstressed syllable /ə/ is so weak that there is danger of its being dropped altogether. In words such as the following, good usage demands the pronunciation of /ə/.

about	suppose	cruel	diary	corridor	telephone
around	account	quiet	audience	possible	editor
along	period	jewel	society	president	policy
afraid	absolutely	jewelry	liable	poem [7]	vanity
occasionally	naturally	riot	miracle	poetry [7]	similar
police	violent	lion	mystery	charity [7]	terrible [7]

D. In the process of linguistic change, the dropping of unstressed syllables in certain words has gradually become more acceptable. The underlined letter in the following words represents /ə/ if you pronounce it. In most careful speech, particularly in formal usage, /ə/ would be pronounced. However, many good speakers omit the /ə/ in these words, especially in casual or informal speech.

accidentally	vegetable	camera	federal	interesting	several
bachelor	visitor	considerably	gallery	liberal	slippery
cabinet	bakery	delivery	generally	literally	temperament
definitely	battery	different	grocery	memorable	tolerable
family	beverage	drapery	history	memory	veteran
sophomore	boisterous	elementary	honorable	miserable	victory
traveler	boundary	favorable	inseparable	recovery	wondering

E. Over-carefulness sometimes results in the incorrect insertion of /ə/ where it does not belong. Make sure of the following pronunciations.

1. athlete /æθ-lit/ not /æθ-ə-lit/
2. bracelet /bres-lɪt/ not /bres-ə-lɪt/
3. burglar /bɝg-lɚ/ not /bɝg-ə-lɚ/
4. business /bɪz-nɪs/ not /bɪz-ə-nɪs/
5. disastrous /dɪs-æs-trəs/ not /dɪs-æs-tə-rəs/
6. evening (p.m.) /iv-nɪŋ/ not /iv-ə-nɪŋ/
7. hindrance /hɪn-drəns/ not /hɪn-də-rəns/
8. lightning /laɪt-nɪŋ/ not /laɪt-ə-nɪŋ/
9. rigmarole /rɪg-mə-rol/ not /rɪg-ə-mə-rol/
10. ticklish /tɪk-lɪʃ/ not /tɪk-ə-lɪʃ/

[7] You may prefer /ɪ/ to /ə/ in these words, but be sure not to omit the unstressed vowel.

F. Sentences for /ə/ practice:

1. We dug up the roots and cut them apart.
2. Run up and see if she has enough butter for the buns.
3. We put some money in the monkey's cup.
4. Mother cut up one onion and I cut up the others.
5. He was punished for all the trouble he caused us.
6. The dove is often a symbol of brotherly love.
7. With luck, we should get the truck loaded before sun-up.
8. Bud shoved his lunch bucket under his bunk.
9. The visitor started an argument about politics.
10. We keep the telephone on a table by the sofa.
11. The president's cabinet assists in executive functions of government.
12. The federal government controls several different territories.

G. Reading selections for /ə/ practice.

1. Government is a trust, and the officers of the government are trustees; and both the trust and the trustees are created for the benefit of the people.

HENRY CLAY

2. No member needs so great a number of muscles as the tongue; this exceeds all the rest in the number of its movements.

LEONARDO DA VINCI

3. Put not your trust in money, but put your money in trust.

OLIVER WENDELL HOLMES

4. 'Tis with our judgments as our watches, none
   Go just alike, yet each believes his own.

ALEXANDER POPE

5. The love of justice is simply, in the majority of men, the fear of suffering injustice.

DE LA ROCHEFOUCAULD

6. And doubly dying shall go down
   To the vile dust from whence he sprung,
   Unwept, unhonored and unsung.

SIR WALTER SCOTT

7. Love in a hut, with water and a crust,
   Is — Love, forgive us! — cinders, ashes, dust.

JOHN KEATS

/ɚ/ as in **murder**
/ɜ/ as in **burn** (with a silent **r**),
as many Southerners and
Easterners pronounce it.

Spellings of /ɚ/: In stressed syllables,[8] this vowel is spelled **ur** as in **urge**, **er** as in **merge**, **ir** as in **bird**, **ear** as in **learn**, **or** as in **work**, **our** as in **journey**. In unstressed syllables, /ɚ/ is spelled **er** as in **after**, **or** as in **actor**, **ar** as in **dollar**, **ure** as in **treasure**, **ur** as in **murmur**, **yr** as in **zephyr**, **oar** as in **cupboard**.

Description of /ɚ/: The central part of the tongue is raised mid-high toward the palate. The tip of the tongue is either lifted toward the front part of the palate or pulled backward along the floor of the mouth. Muscles of the tongue are tense. The lips are normally unround.

To explain the varied spellings of /ɚ/ requires a consideration of the historical development of /ɚ/ in English. At one time in our language, **ur** in **hurt** would have been pronounced /u/ followed by a trilled /r/ very much like Spanish /r/, **ir** in **bird** would have been /i/ plus a trilled /r/, **or** in **work** would have been /ɔ/ plus a trilled /r/, etc. Gradually /r/ took on the quality it has in modern English. Then, by a process called assimilation, the /r/ overpowered and absorbed the preceding vowel, so that modern English /ɚ/ is essentially a vowel /r/, like a prolonged consonant /r/.

Spellings of /ɜ/: The same as for stressed /ɚ/.

Description of /ɜ/: The same as for /ɚ/, except that the tip of the tongue is relaxed and lies on the floor of the mouth behind the lower front teeth. /ɜ/ has the sound of /ɚ/ with the /r/-quality deleted.

/ɜ/ has developed in the Southern and Eastern dialects (as in southern England) by the same process that has resulted in the "dropping" of /r/ in words like **far, fear, fourth.** Usually, a speaker who does not pronounce /r/ at the end of a word or before a consonant sound will also use /ɜ/ instead of /ɚ/ in stressed syllables. /ɜ/ is neither more nor less correct than /ɚ/. It is a dialectal variation in standard pronunciation.

If you use /ɜ/ in stressed syllables instead of /ɚ/, then you will probably also use /ə/ instead of /ɚ/ in unstressed syllables, as in **mother, doctor, dollar.** This is also a dialectal variation in standard pronunciation.

EXERCISES

A. If you "drop" the **r**, be careful that you do not confuse /ɜ/ with /ə/. Contrast the following pairs of words, pronouncing /ə/ in the first and either /ɜ/ or /ɚ/ in the second of each pair.

[8] The IPA uses the /ɜ/ symbol to designate this vowel in stressed syllables and /ɚ/ in unstressed syllables. Since the vowel sounds the same whether stressed or unstressed (except for longer duration with stress) and cannot be contrasted to establish different meanings, it is logical and practical to use a single symbol for the vowel wherever it occurs.

bust — burst	ton — turn	hut — hurt
bun — burn	cub — curb	gull — girl

B. While /ɜ/ is a correct pronunciation for those who "drop" the **r**, the diphthongs [ɜɪ], [ɜi], [əɪ], [əi] are considered substandard allophones of /ɜ/. Pronounce the following with either a pure /ɜ/ vowel or /ɚ/.

birth	deserve	first	nerve	reverse	verb
burn	dirt	furnace	nurse	skirt	verse
burst	disturb	girl	purse	squirm	word
confirm	earn	hurt	rehearse	term	work
curb	earth	jerk	reserve	third	worse
curve	firm	learn	return	turn	worth

C. Confusion of /ɚ/ with /rɪ/ or /rə/ in syllables with reduced stress can be avoided by more careful attention to the spelling of words.

(a) In the following words /ɚ/ is correct (/ə/ or /ɜ/ in Southern or Eastern dialects).

perspire	perhaps	per cent	modern	northern	eastern
perspiration	perverse	perform	southern	western	pattern

(b) Pronounce the following words with /rə/ or /rɪ/ in the unstressed syllable. Do not substitute /ɚ/ or /ə/.

children	apron	hindrance
hundred	kindred	entrance

(c) In the following words use /rɪ/ or /ri/ in the prefix, not /ɚ/ or /ə/.

prevent	prescribe	pretend	preclude
prevention	prescription	preserve	prevail

D. If you normally pronounce /ɚ/ in a word like **after**, be sure you also use /ɚ/ in the words which follow. The fact that these words contain two /ɚ/'s in succession, or /ɚ/ following an /r/, makes them difficult for some people.

mirror	bearer	fairer	northerner	westerner	governor
terror	wearer	rarer	southerner	easterner	laborer

E. Over-carefulness can trick you into artificial, pedantic pronunciations. The same /ɚ/ vowel belongs in the unstressed syllables of the following words, even though it is spelled **or, ar,** or **ure.**

actor	director	forget	senator	pillar	mixture
benefactor	doctor	forgive	tailor	scholar	murmur
comfort	editor	forgotten	victor	sugar	picture
contractor	effort	governor	collar	fixture	pleasure

corridor	elector	labor	dollar	lecture	rapture
curator	factor	mirror	dullard	leisure	seizure
debtor	favor	razor	mallard	measure	texture

F. Sentences for /ɚ/ or /ɜ/ practice.

1. The early bird deserves to get the worm.
2. Myrtle works in a shirt factory in New Jersey.
3. Insert a verb in the first verse.
4. Herbert is learning to assert himself.
5. The girls are going to a birthday party after rehearsal.
6. Let's measure this pattern for the collar before we use it.
7. The actor ruined the performance when he forgot his lines.
8. Mother permitted us to begin supper before father arrived.
9. Robert thought there was another corridor on the other side.
10. Perhaps it's paper instead of leather if it costs only a dollar.
11. This is an interesting history of furniture manufacture.
12. With effort, memory can be considerably improved.

G. Reading selections for /ɚ/ or /ɜ/ practice.

1. Curiosity is one of the permanent and certain characteristics of a vigorous mind.

    SAMUEL JOHNSON

2. A man travels the world over in search of what he needs and returns home to find it.

    GEORGE MOORE

3.   All the little boys and girls,
       With rosy cheeks and flaxen curls,
       And sparkling eyes and teeth like pearls, . . .

    ROBERT BROWNING

4.   Of ancient race by birth, but nobler yet
       In his own worth.

    JOHN DRYDEN

5.   To hold, as 'twere, the mirror up to nature.

    WILLIAM SHAKESPEARE

6.   We poets are (upon a poet's word)
       Of all mankind the creatures most absurd: . . .

    ALEXANDER POPE

THE PHONEMIC DIPHTHONGS

A *diphthong*, you remember, is a vowel sound which changes articulation — and quality — during its production. You have already encountered [ɪi] as a diphthongal allophone of /i/, [eɪ] as an allophone of /e/, [ʊu] as an allophone of /u/, [oʊ] as an allophone of /o/. These *allophonic diphthongs*, although common and acceptable, do not distinguish meaning from the simple vowels of which they are allophones. They, and the numerous unacceptable diphthongs which occur as allophones of these and other vowels, do not need to be diphthongs in order to signal distinctive meaning in words.

Four diphthongs of English are phonemic in all dialects: /ju/, /aɪ/, /aʊ/, and /ɔɪ/. These are called *phonemic diphthongs* because if they were changed to simple vowels, the meaning of words in which they occur would be changed. If /ju/ in **beauty** were reduced to /u/, the word would change to **booty**. If /aɪ/ in **kite** were reduced to /ɑ/ (the closest vowel to /a/ occurring in all dialects), the word would change to **cot**. If /aʊ/ in **pout** were reduced to /ɑ/, the word would become **pot**. If /ɔɪ/ in **oil** were reduced to /ɔ/, the word would become **all**.

ju	/**ju**/ as in **use**

Spellings of /ju/: u as in **use**, **ue** as in **value**, **eu** as in **eulogy**, **ew** as in **few**, **iew** as in **view**, **eau** as in **beauty**, **ewe** as in **ewe**, **ueue** as in **queue**. (This diphthong is never spelled **oo**.)

Description of /ju/: The tongue glides from a high-front to a high-back articulation. The muscles of the tongue are tense. The lips are rounded at the completion of the diphthong.

The allophone [ɪu] often occurs as a variation of /ju/ when a consonant precedes, as in **pupil, beauty, music, few, view, cube.** The [ɪu] allophone of the diphthong differs from /ju/ only in more relaxed tongue muscles at the start of the glide.

Usually when **r** follows, as in **pure**, or in an unstressed syllable, as in **regular**, the diphthong [jʊ] is the allophone of /ju/ most likely to occur.

Alternate Correct Pronunciations: The spellings **u, ue, eu, ew, ui** may be pronounced as either the diphthong /ju/ or the simple vowel /u/ when preceded by the consonants **d, n,** or **t,** as in **due, new, tune** (see Exercise C).

EXERCISES

A. Pronounce the initial vowel in each word as /ju/.

use	usual	universal	uranium	euphony
unit	utility	utensil	university	eulogy
union	unify	uniform	Unitarian	euphonic

B. Pronounce the following words with the diphthong /ju/ or its allophone [ɪu].

abuse	cube	human	mute	puma	refuse
amuse	few	humiliate	mutilate	pupil	refute
beauty	funeral	humor	puberty	putrid	review
bugle	huge	music	pugilist	refusal	view

C. Following a /d/, /n/, or /t/, it is equally correct to pronounce either the diphthong /ju/ or the simple vowel /u/. Use whichever sounds most familiar to you. Consistency is desirable but not obligatory.

due	duplex	nude	nucleus	tube	Tuesday
dew	duplicate	numeral	nuclear	tune	tutor
duty	new	numerous	enumerate	tulip	attitude
duly	newel	nuisance	pneumonia	tumor	attuned

D. In general, Americans prefer to use the simple vowel /u/ when preceded by /s/, /z/, /l/, or /θ/. Some Americans mistakenly assume that the British use of /ju/ in these words is superior and copy it. Use of /u/ in these words is less obtrusive and more familiar in the United States.

suit	suitor	lute	absolutely	dissolute
suitcase	resume	Lutheran	resolutely	enthusiasm

E. Before an **r** the diphthong /ju/ normally relaxes to [jʊ]. Substitution of /jɚ/ for /jʊr/ is substandard, however.

bureau	curate	Europe	furious	pure
bureaucratic	cure	European	infuriate	secure
curable	curious	figure	mercury	tenure

F. In an unstressed syllable, the diphthong /ju/ may be relaxed to [jʊ], or in casual speech to /jə/. But avoid substituting /ə/ for /ju/ in unstressed syllables.

accumulate	communist	municipal	reputable	tabulate
accurate	cumulative	mutation	ridiculous	tuberculosis
annual	cumulus	popular	soluble	tubular
argument	fabulous	regular	speculate	valuable

G. Sentences for /ju/ practice.

1. Eunice was curious about security regulations.
2. Culinary programs are usually popular on radio.
3. He was incredulous that the mercury might drop so regularly.
4. Her argument was ridiculous and amusing.

5. The newspaper enumerated duties of our bureaus in Europe.
6. Are these figures about tuberculosis accurate?
7. He was the dupe of popular communist propaganda.
8. Uranium is used in nuclear fission.

H. Reading selections for /ju/ practice.

1.   The union of lakes, the union of lands,
            The union of States none can sever,
            The union of hearts, the union of hands,
            And the flag of our Union forever!

                                    GEORGE P. MORRIS

2. Ignorance of the law excuses no man; not that all men know the law, but because 'tis an excuse every man will plead, and no man can tell how to refute him.

                                    JOHN SELDEN

3.   To seek the beauteous eye of heaven to garnish,
            Is wasteful and ridiculous excess.

                                    WILLIAM SHAKESPEARE

4. No woman should ever be quite accurate about her age. It looks so calculating.

                                    OSCAR WILDE

5. He that prefers the beautiful to the useful in life will, undoubtedly, like children prefer sweetmeats to bread, destroy his digestion, and acquire a very useless outlook on the world.

                                    FRIEDRICH NIETZSCHE

aɪ   /aɪ/ as in **ice**

Spellings of /aɪ/: **i** as in **ice**, **y** as in **my**, **uy** as in **buy**, **ei** as in **height**, **eye** as in **eye**, **ui** as in **guide**.

Description of /aɪ/: Because this sound is used as the name of the single letter **i**, students sometimes find it difficult to accept it as a diphthong. It is a phonemic diphthong in all dialects except Southern (where the simple vowel /a/, prolonged, substitutes for /aɪ/ without confusion of meaning). Even in Southern dialect, use of /aɪ/ as a diphthong is widely preferred.

The /aɪ/ diphthong begins with the front of the tongue held quite low and the jaw very open, and glides to a high-front tongue position. Tongue muscles are relaxed, and lips are unround.

A standard allophone of /aɪ/ is [ɑɪ], which begins with a low-back tongue position. Occasionally [ai] or [ɑi] occur as standard allophones also.

EXERCISES

A. If you substitute a prolonged /a/ for the diphthong /aɪ/, you must first learn to hear the changing quality of the diphthong.

  (a) In each word below, –**ing** /ɪŋ/ follows the diphthong /aɪ/. Say each word first as written. Then repeat it, leaving off the final consonant /ŋ/, listening carefully to the /ɪ/ with which you completed the second pronunciation. This /ɪ/ is the correct completion of the /aɪ/ diphthong.

buying	dying	frying	plying	sighing
crying	flying	lying	prying	tying

  (b) Transfer exercise. In each line below, the first word ends in /aɪ/, giving you a good opportunity to listen to the completion of the diphthong. As you read the other words on a line, copy the diphthong from the first word, being sure each time that you hear /ɪ/ at the end of the diphthong.

die — dime — died — dial   pie — pied — pine — pile
eye — ice — isle — iron   rye — right — ride — rhyme
fie — fight — fine — file   sigh — sight — side — siphon
lie — light — lied — line   tie — time — tide — tile
my — might — mine — mile   why — white — whine — while

B. /aɪ/ does not involve lip-rounding. The unacceptable allophone [ɒɪ] is a diphthong which begins with the lips rounded. Practice reading the first word of each line below while actually smiling, to keep the lips unrounded. When you have learned to unround the lips in the first word of a line, copy that diphthongal sound in all the words of that line. (Also practice words in Section C.)

eye — tie — die — try — shy — lie — cry — my — pie — buy — why
ice — dice — lice — nice — rice — mice — bison
isle — tile — lisle — style — Nile — mile — file — pile — bile
ire — tire — dire — lyre — shire — briar — pyre — fire — wire — squire
I'd — tied — died — lied — shied — fried — cried — pied — wide

C. The mouth should be wide open at the beginning of the /aɪ/ diphthong, with the tongue held very low in the mouth. Inadequate tongue and jaw lowering produces an unacceptable allophone [əɪ], [æɪ], or [ɛɪ]. Read the words on each line below, copying the sound of /aɪ/ from the first word in the line. Be especially careful to open the mouth wide after an initial consonant which requires the tongue tip to touch the alveolar ridge. (Also practice words which appear in Section B.)

I've — dive — alive — strive — drive — thrive — arrive
I — sky — try — dry — apply — deny — imply — supply — certify — rely
height — tight — right — bright — night — light — fight — fright — might
eyes — ties — dies — tries — lies — shies — cries — pies — buys
Ike — tyke — dike — like — strike — Mike — pike — bike

D. Sentences for practicing /aɪ/.

1. I like to fly kites high in the sky.
2. I try to do it right every time.
3. Mine is higher on the right side.
4. I shall arrive at the mine tonight at nine.
5. A white light is shining brightly outside.
6. I might buy some ice on the island.
7. Mr. White has finally decided to retire.
8. I tried to change the tire by myself.
9. Iva is tired of ironing.
10. These wider pliers might have a tighter grip.

E. Reading selections for /aɪ/ practice.

1. Dictators ride to and fro upon tigers which they dare not dismount. And the tigers are getting hungry.

WINSTON CHURCHILL

2.
The night has a thousand eyes,
And the day but one:
Yet the light of the bright world dies,
With the dying sun.

FRANCIS BOURDILLON

3.
She walks in beauty, like the night
Of cloudless climes and starry skies;
And all that's best of dark and bright
Meet in her aspect and her eyes;
Thus mellow'd to that tender light
Which Heaven to gaudy day denies.

LORD BYRON

4.
Tiger, tiger, burning bright
In the forests of the night.
What immortal hand or eye
Could frame thy fearful symmetry?

WILLIAM BLAKE

5. I will follow the right side even to the fire, but excluding the fire if I can.

    MICHEL DE MONTAIGNE

6.   But what am I?
                An infant crying in the night:
                An infant crying for the light:
                And with no language but a cry.

    ALFRED, LORD TENNYSON

7. I think you will find it true, that, before any vice can fasten on a man, body, mind, or moral nature must be debilitated. The mosses and fungi gather on sickly trees, not thriving ones; and the odious parasites which fasten on the human frame choose that which is already enfeebled.

    OLIVER WENDELL HOLMES

/aʊ/ as in **out**

aU

Spellings of /aʊ/: **ou** as in **out**, **ow** as in **cow**, **au** as in **kraut**.

Description of /aʊ/: This phonemic diphthong begins exactly like /aɪ/, with the tongue low in the front of the mouth, muscles relaxed, and lips unrounded. Articulation glides to a high-back, lax, rounded vowel.

A standard allophone of /aʊ/ is [ɑʊ], which begins with a low-back articulation.

EXERCISES

A. Be sure your mouth opens wide and the tongue is held low in the mouth at the start of /aʊ/. A tense jaw or bunching the tongue too high in the mouth can produce unacceptable allophones [æʊ], [ɛʊ], [əʊ]. Practice the first word in each line below until you control the mouth opening and tongue lowering at the start of /aʊ/. Then read each line, copying the sound of /aʊ/ from the first word to all the other words on that line.

    out — doubt — shout — bout — pout — lout— kraut — scout
    ouch — couch — pouch — crouch — vouch
    house — mouse — louse — douse — blouse*
    hound — round — mound — pound — ground — sound — wound
    how — now — brow — cow — scow — prow — vow — wow

    * In Southern dialect, **blouse** ends in a /z/ and would not rhyme in this line.

B. The /aʊ/ diphthong ends with a rounded /ʊ/ glide. The unacceptable allophones [aə], [ɑə], and [ɑ] result from carelessness in lip-rounding and occur chiefly when an **r** or an **l** follows. Another unacceptable allophone of /aʊ/ in these words is the triphthong [awə].

(a) Pronounce /aʊ/ preceding /r/ or /ɚ/.

our　ours　tower　sour　shower　bower　flower　power　glower　cower

(b) Pronounce /aʊ/ preceding /l/ or /əl/.

owl　cowl　scowl　foul　prowl　growl　dowel　towel　trowel

C. Sentences for /aʊ/ practice.

1. How many brown houses are around here?
2. I doubt that she would allow us to go downtown.
3. Shout loudly to get the cows out of the field.
4. The owl looked down with great round eyes.
5. We found a mouse cowering on the ground near the tower.
6. How can you account for a deficit of this amount?
7. Down South the flowers are blooming outside now.
8. A loud shout from the scow made him turn around.

D. Reading selections for /aʊ/ practice.

1. A huge gap appeared in the side of the mountain. At last a tiny mouse poked its little head out of the gap. . . .

   Much outcry, little outcome.

   AESOP

2. Getting and spending, we lay waste our powers:
   Little we see in Nature that is ours.

   WILLIAM WORDSWORTH

3. Till like one in slumber bound,
   Borne to ocean, I float down, around,
   Into a sea profound of everlasting sound.

   PERCY BYSSHE SHELLEY

4. The owl looked down with his great round eyes
   At the lowering clouds and the darkening skies,
   "A good night for scouting," says he,
   "With never a sound I'll go prowling around.
   A mouse or two may be found on the ground
   Or a fat little bird in a tree."

So down he flew from the old church tower,
The mouse and the birdie crouch and cower,
Back he flies in half an hour,
"A very good supper," says he.

UNKNOWN

5.   Ye gods! how he talk'd! What a torrent of sound,
His hearers invaded, encompass'd and — drown'd!

AUSTIN DOBSON

6.   He who doubts from what he sees
Will ne'er believe, do what you please.
If the Sun and Moon should doubt,
They'd immediately go out.

WILLIAM BLAKE

/ɔɪ/ as in **coin**   **ɔɪ**

Spellings of /ɔɪ/: oi as in **coin**; **oy** as in **boy**.

Description of /ɔɪ/: This phonemic diphthong begins with the back of the tongue raised almost mid-high, the muscles lax, and the lips rounded. From this articulation it glides to a high-front tongue position, with muscles lax and lips unrounded.

EXERCISES

A. Lip-rounding at the start of the /ɔɪ/ diphthong is essential. Unrounding the lips produces the unacceptable allophone [əɪ] or [ɜɪ], either of which might be confused with the /ɚ/ phoneme. A more openmouthed, unrounded articulation results in the [ɑɪ] allophone, which is confusable with the phoneme /aɪ/. Pronounce the first word on each line below with a lip-rounded beginning of the diphthong /ɔɪ/. Then copy the sound of that /ɔɪ/ in each word on that line.

boy — boisterous — voice — choice
joy — rejoice — joist — hoist — moist — oyster
coy — coin — join — joint — loin
toy — toys — noise — poise — boys

B. When /ɔɪ/ precedes /l/, the unacceptable allophones [ɔə], [ɔɪə], or [ɔjə] may occur. A helpful device for **oil**-type words is to practice "splitting" the diphthong into [ɔ-ɪl], and gradually blending the parts in successive repetitions. Try this system on the following words.

oil	oiling	broil	coil	foil	soil
oiled	boil	broiled	coiled	foiled	soiled
oily	boiled	broiling	embroiled	recoil	toil

C. Sentences for /ɔɪ/ practice.

1. Noisy boys annoy him.
2. Do you enjoy boiled oysters?
3. There is oil in this soil.
4. Avoid loitering in noisy places.
5. What an adroit maneuver to avoid royal displeasure!
6. My first choice is voice lessons, but I would enjoy piano, too.

D. Reading selections for /ɔɪ/ practice.

1.
> I thank you for your voices: thank you,
> Your most sweet voices.
>
> WILLIAM SHAKESPEARE

2.
> Coining words in the quick mint of joy.
>
> LEIGH HUNT

3. Thanksgiving, like ambassadors, cabinet-officers and others smeared with political ointment,
   Depends for its existence on Presidential appointment.
>
> OGDEN NASH

4.
> The anointed sovereign of sighs and groans,
> Liege of all loiterers and malcontents.
>
> WILLIAM SHAKESPEARE

5.
> For just experience tells, in every soil,
> That those that think must govern those that toil.
>
> OLIVER GOLDSMITH

VOCABULARY EXERCISES

A. Don't Omit Syllables. The dropping out of an unstressed vowel is a very natural process in English. There are innumerable words in which vowels that were pronounced in Chaucer's day, for instance, are now silent in Modern

English. If left unchecked, the process of vowel-dropping would doubtless continue rapidly. Many words in Modern English are now in the process of change. For instance, in **bakery, family, vegetable,** and similar words, the omission of medial /ə/ has grown so popular that many dictionaries admit the two-syllable pronunciation alongside the three-syllable pronunciation. The words listed below, however, are not at present open to argument. Omission of syllables in the following words still suggests careless or uninformed pronunciation. The pronunciation of each word is transcribed in IPA. A symbol written above another represents an alternate correct pronunciation.

	Correct Pronunciation	*Don't Omit*			*Correct Pronunciation*	*Don't Omit*
1. actually	/ǽktʃu̍ɪəli/	/ʊ-u/	20. orange	/ɔ́ɒ̍rɪndʒ/	/ɪ-ə/
2. believe	/bilɪ́ˌiv/	/i-ɪ/	21. physical	/fɪ́ɪzəkəl/	/ə-ɪ/
3. cereal	/sɪ́ɪriəl/	/i-ɪ/	22. popular	/pɑpjulɒ̍˞/	/ju/
4. cruel	/krúəl/	/ə/	23. proverbial	/prəvɝ̍ˑbiəl/	/ɪ-i/
5. deteriorate	/dɪtíriˌəret/	/i/	24. regular	/régjulɚ/	/ju/
6. eventually	/ɪvéntʃu̍ɪˌʊˌəli/	/u-ʊ/	25. seriously	/sɪ́riˌɪəsli/	/ɪ/
7. factually	/fǽktʃu̍ʊˌɪəli/	/u-ʊ/	26. ruin	/rúɪn/	/ɪ/
8. figurative	/fɪ́gju̍rətɪv/	/ə/	27. stereotype	/stɪrɪ́ˌíˌiətaɪp/	/ɪ-i/
9. finally	/fáɪnˌɪəli/	/ə/	28. strenuous	/strénjuəs/	/ə/
10. fuel	/fjúəl/	/ə/	29. suppose	/səpóz/	/ə/
11. geography	/dʒiágˌɪrəfi/	/i/	30. terrible	/térəbəl/	/ə/
12. geometry	/dʒiámˌɪətri/	/i/	31. theory	/θɪ́ˌíɪˌɪri/	/ə/
13. gradually	/grǽdʒu̍ʊˌɪəli/	/u-ʊ/	32. trivial	/trívˌiɪəl/	/ɪ-i/
14. horrible	/hɔ́ɒ̍rəbəl/	/ə/	33. usually	/júʒu̍ʊˌɪəli/	/u-ʊ/
15. idea	/aɪdíˌiə/	/ə/	34. valuable	/vǽljuəbəl/	/ə/
16. individual	/ɪndəvɪ́ˌɪdʒuˌʊəl/	/u-ʊ/	35. variable	/véˌériˌɪəbəl/	/i-ɪ/
17. jewel	/dʒúəl/	/ə/	36. variegated	/véˌériˌɪ əˌgetɪd/	/i-ɪ/
18. lion	/láɪən/	/ə/	37. various	/véˌériˌɪəs/	/i-ɪ/
19. nuclear	/núkliˌjú˞/	/i/	38. violent	/váɪələnt/	/ə/

B. Don't Add Syllables. Mispronunciation by inserting an extra vowel sound (producing an extra syllable) sometimes occurs because of false analogy to another word. Check your own pronunciation of each word in the following list, examining both the spelling and the pronunciation carefully.

		Correct	*Incorrect*
1.	athlete	/ǽθlit/	/ǽθəlit/
2.	athletic	/æθlétɪk/	/æθəlétɪk/
3.	bracelet	/bréslɪt/	/brésəlɪt/
4.	burglar	/bɝ́·glɚ/	/bɝ́·gələˣ/
5.	business	/bíznɪs/	/bízɪnɪs/
6.	disastrous	/dɪzǽstrəs/	/dɪzǽstərəs/
7.	elm	/ɛlm/	/ɛ́ləm/
8.	evening (p.m.)	/ívnɪŋ/	/ívənɪŋ/
9.	fibrous	/fáɪbrəs/	/fáɪbərəs/
10.	film	/fɪlm/	/fíləm/
11.	foundry	/fáʊndri/	/fáʊndərⁱ/
12.	gorgeous	/gɔ́rdʒəs/	/gɔ́rdʒⁱəs/
13.	grievance	/grívəns/	/grívⁱəns/
14.	grievous	/grívəs/	/grívⁱəs/
15.	heart-rending	/hɑ́rt-réndɪŋ/	/hɑrt-réndɚɪŋ/
16.	hindrance	/híndrəns/	/híndərəns/
17.	laundry	/lɒ́ˢndri/	/lɒ́ˢndərⁱ/
18.	lightning	/láɪtnɪŋ/	/láɪtənɪŋ/
19.	lovely	/lʌ́vli/	/lʌ́vəli/
20.	luncheon	/lʌ́ntʃən/	/lʌ́ntʃⁱən/
21.	massacring	/mǽsəkrɪŋ/	/mǽsəkərɪŋ/
22.	mischievous	/místʃəvəsᴵ/	/mɪstʃívⁱəs/
23.	momentous	/moméntəs/	/moméntⁱəs/
24.	monstrous	/mɑ́ⁿstrəs/	/mɑ́ⁿstərəs/
25.	rigmarole	/rígmərol/	/rígəmərol/
26.	stupendous	/stⁱᵘpéndəs/	/stⁱᵘpéndⁱəs/
27.	ticklish	/tíklɪʃ/	/tíkəlɪʃ/
28.	umbrella	/əmbrélə/	/əmbərélə/
29.	varied	/vɛ́rɪd/	/vɛ́rⁱɪd/

C. Vowel Pronunciations. Some of the words in this section are familiar ones which are occasionally mispronounced. Some of these words may be in your reading vocabulary but not in your speech vocabulary. Some may be useful additions to your vocabulary. To make a word a practical part of your speaking vocabulary, you should: (1) learn its correct pronunciation, (2) learn its meaning, (3) experiment with using it in practice sentences, (4) make a conscious effort to use it in actual conversation several times immediately.

1. **acumen** /əkjúmən/ (noun) keenness or acuteness in mental or practical endeavors; e.g., his business acumen; his acumen in mathematics.

2. **askew** /əskjú/ (adj. and adv.) turned to one side, crooked; e.g., her hat was askew; the tablecloth was askew.

3. **awry** /ərái/ (adj. and adv.) not straight, turned to one side; aside from the truth, perverse; e.g., her hat was awry; he sat awry as if he were about to slip from the saddle.

4. **bucolic** /bjukɑlɪk/ (adj.) rustic, pastoral, of country life; e.g., a bucolic poem; bucolic pleasures; a bucolic scene.

5. **caprice** /kəprís/ (noun) sudden change in feeling, attitude or action governed by whim; whim or fancy which prompts unpredictable action; e.g., he was a slave to her caprice; a caprice of fashion.

6. **chic** /ʃik/ (adj.) fashionable; e.g., a chic dress; a chic young lady.

7. **cliché** /kliʃé/ (noun) an over-used expression, a trite or hackneyed statement; e.g., a tiresome conversation of clichés; she talks in clichés; that old cliché, "it never rains but it pours."

8. **clique** /klik/, /klɪk/ (noun) a small, exclusive group of associates; e.g., the student body is divided into cliques.

9. **column** /kɑləm/ (noun) a supporting pillar or something resembling a pillar; a line or procession of things; a vertical section of newsprint separated from another by a blank space or line; e.g., the porch had four columns; a column of soldiers filed past; he writes a sports column for the paper.

10. **culinary** /kjúlənɛri/ (adj.) having to do with cooking or the kitchen; e.g., this pie is a culinary masterpiece; her interests are chiefly culinary.

11. **cumulus** /kjúmjuləs/ (noun) a piled-up, rounded cloud form with a flat base; e.g., a sunny day with cumulus clouds banked against blue skies.

12. **cupidity** /kjupídəti/ (noun) greed; overwhelming desire for wealth; e.g., the avarice and cupidity of money lenders who charge exorbitant interest.

13. **cupola** /kjúpələ/ (noun) a miniature tower; e.g., a cupola with a weathervane enhances the roof line of the garage.

14. **dais** /déɪs/ (noun) a slightly raised platform which elevates dignitaries above the audience; e.g., on the dais with the President were Senator Black and Mayor Schultz.

15. **data** /détə/ (noun, plural of **datum**) facts which are presented as the basis for inferences; e.g., data regarding voter preferences were collected randomly.

16. **err** /ɚ/ (verb) to make a mistake or error; e.g., to err is human.

17. **eugenics** /judʒénɪks/ (noun) the science relating to improvement of hereditary characteristics, especially human; e.g., in the interest of eugenics, intelligent people should be encouraged to have larger families.

18. **euphemism** /júfəmɪzəm/ (noun) the substitution of an inoffensive expression for a word one wishes to avoid; e.g., "passed away" is a euphemism for "died."

19. **euphoria** /jufóriə/ (noun) a sense of well-being, sprightliness, "walking on air"; e.g., overcome with euphoria, she broke into a happy song; this drug may give you a false sense of euphoria.

20. **euthanasia** /juθənéʒə/ (noun) painlessly putting to death a person suffering from an incurable disease; e.g., no matter how merciful, euthanasia violates all religious precepts.

21. **facade** /fəsád/ (noun) the front of a building, or a person; e.g., they modernized this building chiefly by adding a new facade; he hid his insecurity behind a facade of arrogance.

22. **fatigue** /fətíg/ (noun) weariness from activity and work; e.g., overcome with fatigue, he lay down to rest.

23. **fiancé** (mas.), **fiancée** (fem.) /fiɑnsé/ or /fiánse/, (noun) a man or woman engaged to be married; e.g., he met his fiancée in Rome.

24. **furor** /fjúrɔr/ (noun) an outburst of excitement or anger; e.g., a great furor and shouting from the mob.

25. **gauge** /gedʒ/ (noun) a measuring device; e.g., a gasoline gauge; (verb) to measure, estimate, or judge; e.g., gauge the strength of your opponent; gauge the value of the article; gauge the volume of a silo.

26. **grimace** /grɪmés/ (noun) a facial contortion; (verb) to twist the face into a contorted shape; e.g., his expression was more a grimace than a smile; he grimaced with disgust.

27. **imbue** /ɪmbjú/ (verb) to saturate, penetrate; e.g., he was imbued with wisdom.

28. **infuse** /ɪnfjúz/ (verb) to instill, soak, imbue, penetrate; e.g., infuse this with a water solution; infuse some school spirit into the class.

29. **oblique** /oblík/ (adj.) slanting, inclined; indirect, underhand; e.g., the oblique line of the roof; he made an oblique reference to her age.

30. **pathos** /péθɔs/ (noun) characteristic of literature or music which evokes sympathy or pity; e.g., a scene of touching pathos.

31. **pique** /pik/ (noun) offense at being slighted, resentment; e.g., voicing her pique at not being invited to the reception.

32. **piqué** /piké/ (noun) cotton fabric having ribbed or waffled weave; e.g., a white piqué collar.

33. **placate** /pléket/ (verb) to calm, pacify, or satisfy (an angry person); e.g., she feigned agreement only to placate George.

34. **puerile** /pjúɛrəl/ (adj.) childish, foolish; e.g., a puerile argument.

35. **pugilist** /pjúdʒəlɪst/ (noun) a prize-fighter; e.g., Jack Dempsey was a pugilist of world renown.

36. **pulverize** /pə́lvəraɪz/ (verb) to crush into minute particles; e.g., the powder must be pulverized before liquid is added.

37. **regalia** /rɪgéljə/ (plural noun) insignia pertaining to a high office; e.g., at the head of the procession the regalia of the queen were carried.

38. **risqué** /rɪské/ (adj.) daring, bordering on impropriety; e.g., a risqué bathing suit; a risqué story.

39. **sadist** /sedɪst/ (noun) one who derives pleasure from inflicting cruel treatment on someone else; e.g., anyone who gives examinations like that is a sadist.

40. **savory** /sévəri/ (adj.) pleasant or agreeable in taste or smell; e.g., a savory stew; a savory sauce.

41. **shirr** /ʃɚ/ (verb) to gather material, as in ruffles; e.g., the gown is shirred onto a yoke.

42. **suave** /swɑv/ (adj.) smoothly agreeable or polite, applied to speech or manners; e.g., he has a suave manner; he made a suave reply in spite of her rudeness.

43. **tornado** /tɔrnédo/ (noun) a whirling wind accompanied by a funnel-shaped cloud which creates destruction in a narrow path; e.g., a tornado lifted the roofs off several houses.

44. **unique** /juník/ (adj.) without equal, one of a kind, without comparison; e.g., a unique appearance; a unique attitude; a unique experience.

45. **usurp** /jusɚp/ (verb) to take or hold possession by force or unrightfully; e.g., Prince John usurped the throne in King Richard's absence; he usurped the prerogative of a husband and began to order her about.

46. **vagary** /vəgéri/ (noun) an eccentric or capricious notion, action, or manifestation; e.g., a vagary of fashion; the vagaries of fate; the vagaries of her imagination.

47. **Worcestershire** /wústɚʃɚ/ (adj.) a sharp sauce made of soy, vinegar, and spices, formerly from Worcester, England; e.g., put Worcestershire sauce on the roast.

48. **worsted** /wústɪd/ (adj. or noun) firmly twisted wool yarn, or material woven from such yarn or thread, having a smooth surface; e.g., worsted suits wear well.

D. Don't Confuse Words. Each group of words in the following list is enough alike in spelling or pronunciation to present some confusion, but is quite different in meaning. Learn the spelling and pronunciation to match each meaning.

1. (a) **affect** /æfékt/ (verb) to cause a change; influence; to assume or feign (something); e.g., damp weather affects my joints badly; he affects a French accent.

   (b) **effect** /ɛfékt/ (noun) a result, consequence; e.g., an effect of the war. (verb) to produce, cause to happen; e.g., effect a change.

2. (a) **amenable** /əménəbəl/ (adj.) can be influenced or caused to submit; e.g., he is amenable to argument.

   (b) **amiable** /émiəbəl/ (adj.) friendly, good-natured; e.g., an amiable fellow.

3. (a) **bravery** /brévəri/ (noun) courage; e.g., bravery beyond the call of duty.

   (b) **bravado** /brəvádo/ (noun) boastful action to appear brave; e.g., a great show of bravado to hide his cowardice.

4. (a) **causal** /kɔ́zəl/ (adj.) relates to cause (and effect) relationship; e.g., a causal relationship between fluoridation of water and the reduction of caries.

   (b) **casual** /kǽʒuəl/ (adj.) not formal or structured; e.g., only a casual knowledge of algebra; a casual friendship.

5. (a) **confidant** /kɑnfədǽnt/ (noun) a person in whom one confides; e.g., I was my son's confidant until recently.

   (b) **confident** /kɑ́nfədənt/ (adj.) self-reliant; e.g., he is confident of success.

6. (a) **consul** /kɑ́nsəl/ (noun) representative of a foreign government in a city; e.g., the Japanese consul in Chicago.

   (b) **council** /káʊnsəl/ (noun) a deliberative or governing group; e.g., the City Council met with the mayor.

   (c) **counsel** /káʊnsəl/ (noun) an advisor, lawyer; e.g., the counsel for the defense.

   (d) **counsel** /káʊnsəl/ (noun) advice; e.g., heed my counsel for your behavior.

   (e) **counsel** /káʊnsəl/ (verb) to advise; e.g., he was counselled to plead guilty.

   (f) **console** /kɑ́nsol/ (noun) a cabinet; e.g., a TV in a maple console.

   (g) **console** /kənsól/ (verb) to comfort; e.g., he consoled me in my grief.

7. (a) **imply** /ɪmpláɪ/ (verb) to leave an impression; to suggest; e.g., what I said was not meant to imply that you are fat.

(b) **infer** /ɪnfɚ/ (verb) to assume a meaning from what someone else has said; e.g., I infer that you think I am fat.

8. (a) **incredible** /ɪnkrɛ́dəbəl/ (adj.) unbelievable; beyond belief; e.g., an incredible number of people on relief rolls.

(b) **incredulous** /ɪnkrɛ́dʒʊləs/ (adj.) unable to believe or to accept as true; e.g., his excuse was so thin that I am incredulous.

9. (a) **inimical** /ɪníməkəl/ (adj.) unfriendly, hostile; e.g., I sensed in him an inimical opponent.

(b) **inimitable** /ɪnímətəbəl/ (adj.) surpasses imitation; e.g., the inimitable detective, Sherlock Holmes.

10. (a) **poor** /pʊr/ (adj.) not having wealth; of inferior quality; e.g., a poor man; a poor imitation; a poor excuse.

(b) **pour** /por/ (verb) to empty from a container; e.g., pour water from a pitcher.

11. (a) **timidity** /tɪmídəti/ (noun) a lack of courage or self-assurance; e.g., his timidity keeps him from asking for a raise.

(b) **temerity** /təmɛ́rəti/ (noun) boldness, rashness, contempt for danger; e.g., I don't have the temerity to try bob-sledding.

12. (a) **veracious** /vərɛ́ʃəs/ (adj.) habitually truthful; e.g., he is absolutely veracious and trustworthy.

(b) **voracious** /vorɛ́ʃəs/ (adj.) ravenous; having an insatiable appetite; e.g., he has a voracious appetite; he is a voracious reader.

E. Word Prefixes, Suffixes, and Roots. One of the most profitable ways to build your vocabulary is to study prefixes and suffixes. A tremendous number of words in English are derived either immediately or ultimately from Latin or Greek. One root word from Latin or Greek, you will discover, occurs repeatedly in our language, taking on new meanings as it is altered by the addition of a prefix or suffix. Learning a few of these roots, prefixes, and suffixes will increase your vocabulary by literally hundreds of words. What is more, this study will disclose a technique which will make it easy for you to acquire thousands of new words.

Follow this method in studying root words, prefixes, and suffixes:

(1) Look up each word listed below in the dictionary, noticing the varied relationships possible between derivation and definition. Then look up each prefix and suffix. The dictionary entry will help fix meanings in your mind, and will often indicate assimilative changes.

(2) Quickly list at least ten words containing the prefix or suffix, checking each with the dictionary to avoid mistakes. Some prefixes and suffixes are as changeable as chameleons. For instance, the prefix **com** (meaning **with** or **together**) sometimes appears as **con** (e.g., **constant**), sometimes as **cor** (e.g., **correlation**), sometimes as **col** (e.g., **collaboration**), sometimes as **coun**

(e.g., **council**), to mention only a few. In each of those examples, the prefix **com** has changed its consonant ending by assimilation to become more easily pronounced with the consonant which begins the root word. A suffix, too, may change slightly in spelling without changing meaning. For instance, the suffix **able** (e.g., **comfortable**) occurs also as **ible** (e.g., **edible**). Noting these changes by adaptation to various root words will help you to understand similar changes in other prefixes and suffixes.

(3) List at least ten words containing the root, checking each carefully in the dictionary. Try to discover less common forms by some intelligent guessing. Each discovery of a variant form adds to your background and understanding of the large family of words for which that root is a key.

Remember that these are only a few of the roots, prefixes, and suffixes which English uses to build words. Having mastered these, use your technique to try to understand the composition of every word you see or hear. The possibilities for increasing your vocabulary are limitless.

PREFIXES AND ROOTS

Word	Prefix	Meaning of Prefix	Latin or Greek Root	Meaning of Root
1. absent	ab–; a–	from; away	esse	to be
avert			vertere	to turn
2. abridge	a–; ad–	to; toward	brevis	short
admit			mittere	to send
3. combine	com–; con–	with; together	bini	two and two; double
concur			currere	to run
4. contradict	contra–	against	dicere	to say
5. depart	de–	from; down; away	partire	to leave
depend			pendere	to hang
6. extend	ex–	out	tendere	to stretch
7. hypersensitive	hyper–	over; above; extra	sentire	to perceive; to feel
8. hypothesis	hypo–	under; below	tithenai	to put
9. insist	in–	into	sistere	to stand
10. inactive	in–; ir–	not	agere	to do
irreparable			reparabilis	reparable
11. intervene	inter–	between	venire	to come
12. monograph	mono–	one	graphein	to write
13. nonadhesive	non–	not	haerere	to stick
14. prevent	pre–; pro–	before; forward	venire	to come
produce			ducere	to lead
15. repair	re–	back; again	parare	to prepare
16. submit	sub–; suf–	under	mittere	to send
sufficient			facere	to make; to do
17. transcribe	trans–	over; across	scribere	to write

SUFFIXES AND ROOTS

Word	Suffix	Meaning of Suffix	Latin or Greek Root	Meaning of Root
1. capable	–able	tendency; fit to be	capere	to take; to contain
2. final	–al; –ial	relating to; act of	finis	the end
filial			filius	son
3. intermediary	–ary	one who; place where	medius	middle
primary			primus	first
4. liberate	–ate	to make	liber	free
5. agent	–ent	one who; that which	agere	to do
6. testify	–fy; –ify	to make	testis	a witness
7. demonic	–ic; –ical	like unto	daimon	evil spirit
spherical			sphaira	sphere; ball
8. mission	–ion	act of; state of	mittere	to send
9. baptism	–ism	act of; doctrine of	baptein	to dip in water
10. locality	–ity	state of being	locus	place
11. restive	–ive	quality; tendency	restare	to stay back; remain
12. advertisement	–ment	act or state of	vertere	to turn
13. donor	–or; –er	one who; that which	donare	to give
courier			currere	to run
14. verbose	–ose; –ous	full of; like	verbum	word
precious			pretium	price
15. magnitude	–tude	state or quality of	magnus	great; big
16. veracity	–ty	state or condition	verus	true
17. picture	–ure	process; result of	pingere	to paint

Test in Identifying Prefixes, Suffixes, and Roots. Every prefix and suffix in the following words has been identified in the exercise above, as have most of the roots. For each word below, identify the prefix or suffix and the root, and discover how the present meaning of the word has been derived.

1. abbreviate	12. brevity	22. hemisphere	32. present
2. adhere	13. capable	23. immediate	33. pretest
3. adventure	14. cogent	24. instant	34. primer
4. adverb	15. cohesion	25. magnanimous	35. reverse
5. affiliate	16. contest	26. manufacture	36. sensory
6. affinity	17. convert	27. meridian	37. submissive
7. aggressive	18. current	28. pendulous	38. subtend
8. avenue	19. dictator	29. photograph	39. suffice
9. aversion	20. facile	30. pigment	40. tendon
10. atmosphere	21. graphic	31. prescribe	41. thesis
11. binocular			42. verify

6

Improvement of Articulation and Pronunciation of Consonant Phonemes

ARTICULATION OF CONSONANTS

A major factor in the production of clear and distinct speech is the accurate articulation of consonant phonemes. Identifying, distinctive features of consonant sounds are produced by three variable characteristics:

1. *Voicing* distinguishes nine pairs of consonants out of the total twenty-five consonant phonemes of English. When we say that a consonant is *voiced*, we mean that it is formed of vocal tone resulting from vibration of the vocal folds. When we say that a consonant is *voiceless*, we mean that it is formed of breath, without a tone produced by vocal fold vibration. Two consonants differing only in voicing are called *cognates*. Voiceless /f/ and voiced /v/ are cognates, because they are produced identically except for the difference in voicing. Voiceless /k/ and voiced /g/ are cognates. The other voiceless-voiced cognate pairs are: /t/ and /d/; /θ/ and /ð/; /s/ and /z/; /ʃ/ and /ʒ/; /tʃ/ and /dʒ/; /p/ and /b/; /ʍ/ and /w/. The voiceless consonant /h/ does not have a voiced cognate. The six voiced consonants /m/, /n/, /ŋ/, /l/, /r/, /j/ have no voiceless cognates. Any voiceless consonant in English tends to be produced more vigorously (with more forceful muscular activity) and more breathily (with a greater quantity of breath release) than its voiced cognate.

2. *Place of articulation* is often the single distinctive difference between two consonant phonemes. For instance /t/ and /k/ are alike except for their place of articulation: /t/ is formed by touching the tongue tip to the alveolar ridge; /k/ is formed by touching the back of the tongue to the velum. The distinction between /m/ and /n/ is in place of articulation: /m/ is bilabial (two lips touching together); /n/ is tip-alveolar. Articulation is a moving of two parts of the vocal apparatus to make contact with each other or to nearly contact each other. Clear diction requires quick, exact movements of the articulators for individual consonants and for sequential movements in groups of consonants.

3. *Manner of formation* is sometimes the single distinctive difference between two consonant phonemes. Some consonants are formed as *stops*. For the stop consonants /p, b, t, d, k, g/ the articulators make a tight seal to hold air in the mouth while the velum is lifted to prevent escape of air through the nasal passage. The air, continuing to move upward from the larynx, is dammed up or compressed within the mouth and pharynx before being released. Other consonants are formed as *fricatives*. The fricatives /f, v, θ, ð, s, z, ʃ, ʒ/ are formed by bringing articulators quite close (but not completely) together to constrict the air passage. Forcing breath through a narrowly constricted passage causes friction and produces noise elements which help to identify these phonemes. *Nasal consonants* /m, n, ŋ/ are formed by lowering the velum and diverting the breath stream through the nasal passage rather than the oral cavity. The consonant /l/ is a *lateral consonant*, because it is formed by lowering the sides of the tongue and diverting the air stream to be emitted from the sides rather than the front of the mouth. The *glide consonants* are like vowels in motion, with resonance characteristics like vowels. /w/ is like "the tail end" of /u/; if you say /u-i/, you can hear /w/ between the /u/ and the /i/. /j/ is the glide away from /i/, which you can hear between the /i/ and the /u/ if you say /i-u/. /r/ is a glide away from the vowel /ɚ/ in a word like **run** and a glide toward /ɚ/ in a word like **fear**.

Confusion in manner of formation can damage speech clarity considerably. For instance, /l/ and /n/ are both voiced, and both have tip-alveolar articulation. But if you change a lateral to a nasal, you change /lɛt/ to /nɛt/. The chief difference between /t/ and /s/ is the manner of formation. They are both voiceless. Since /t/ is tip-alveolar and /s/ is blade-alveolar, their articulation is quite similar. But change the stop to a fricative and you have changed English /bɛtɚ/ to German /bɛsɚ/.

AGILITY IN ARTICULATION

Correct articulation of consonants requires speed and agility in muscular movements. Labored, "slow-motion" articulation is inadequate for the quick transitions from phoneme to phoneme in an utterance. The exercises which follow have been found useful in developing facility in precise, quick articulation.

Here are three rhythm patterns, formed of a simple syllable-nucleus using a consonant plus the vowel /ɑ/ (useful because it requires lowering the jaw and tongue, in contrast to the close articulation of the preceding consonant). The consonant /t/ is used in this example, but any consonant requiring practice may be substituted for /t/. The stressed syllables are longer in duration than the unstressed ones. Repeat each pattern a number of times, at first slowly (in the proper rhythm) and gradually faster, but preserving the exactness of articulation. Do not sacrifice precision to speed.

1. /tá tɑ tá tɑ tá tɑ tá/
2. /tá tɑ tɑ tá tá/
3. /tá tɑ tɑ tɑ tá tá/

If you sometimes confuse two phonemes, e.g., /d/ and /ð/, /w/ and /v/, or /l/ and /r/, it will be profitable to practice alternating the two in these rhythm patterns. As an example, let us use /w/ and /v/ in alternation, thus:

1. /wá vɑ wá vɑ wá vɑ wá/
2. /wá vɑ vɑ wá wá/
3. /wá vɑ vɑ vɑ wá wá/

CONCENTRATED PHRASE PRACTICE

A technique which musicians commonly use can accomplish much in speech practice. When you come upon a difficult phrase, extract it from the sentence in which it occurs and concentrate on it, repeating it at first slowly, then more quickly, over and over, until your articulation is precise, facile, and quick. Remember, though, that the rhythm of the syllables as they would occur in the sentence must be preserved if the facility is to be retained when the phrase is restored to its context in the sentence.

For example, suppose you have had trouble with /ð/, tending to make it a stop instead of a fricative (so that it sounds like a variety of /d/). A phrase such as "to the door" would be tricky, since both the syllable preceding **the** and the one following it begin with a stop. But observe that **the** is usually said quite fast in such a phrase; the stress should fall on **door**. When you practice slowly, keep the proper rhythmic relationship of syllables; maintain the same rhythm when you develop speed. When you can easily maintain precision at a normal rate, practice the whole sentence containing the phrase. If you misarticulate the phrase in the sentence, return to phrase practice. Mastery of a single phrase effects better carry-over into your daily speech than stumbling through great quantities of exercises.

CONSONANT PHONEMES IN DETAIL

/t/ as in **to**

/d/ as in **do**

/t/

/d/

Spellings of /t/: **t** as in **to**; **tt** as in **better** (pronounced as a single /t/); **ed** (following a voiceless phoneme) as in **slipped**; **th** as in **Thomas**.

Spellings of /d/: d as in **do**; **dd** as in **muddy** (pronounced as a single /d/); **ed** (following a voiced phoneme) as in **showed, begged.**

Description of /t/ and /d/: These consonants are cognates: /t/ is voiceless; /d/ is voiced. They are both tip-alveolar stops. Voiceless /t/ has stronger aspiration (more breath expulsion) and greater energy in articulation than /d/, especially noticeable when it occurs initially in a word.

Acceptable Variation: In a phrase such as **hit that** or **had this**, where /t/ or /d/ precedes /ð/, or in a phrase such as **that theme** or **had thought**, where /t/ or /d/ precedes /θ/, the correct articulation of /t/ or /d/ is tip-dental [t̪], [d̪] (i.e., the tip of the tongue touches the upper front teeth) because it anticipates the tip-dental articulation of /θ/ or /ð/. This is the only situation in which a dental [t̪] or [d̪] is correct, for in all other cases, /t/ and /d/ have tip-alveolar articulation.

EXERCISES

A. Contrast initial /t/ with /d/. Initially, voiceless /t/ is more aspirate (breathy) and energetic in articulation than /d/.

to — do	till — dill	told — doled
tie — die	time — dime	tam — dam
toe — dough	tame — dame	tea — D
ten — den	tip — dip	Tim — dim
tell — dell	tick — Dick	tot — dot

B. Contrast final /t/ with /d/. The vowel preceding voiced /d/ is characteristically longer in duration than a vowel preceding voiceless /t/.

beat — bead	tight — tide	bet — bed
right — ride	hat — had	wet — wed
wrote — rode	bat — bad	wait — wade
hit — hid	mate — made	lit — lid
let — led	root — rude	cat — cad

C. Medial /t/ is commonly changed to /d/ (sometimes a quite weakly contacted /d/). While this substitution seldom changes the meaning of the word in which it occurs, careful speakers are likely to consider /d/ for /t/ unacceptable. On the other hand, if your attempt to correct this substitution makes /t/ too prominent, it will become /tt/ as in **hit Tom.** To pronounce **better** with /tt/ is probably more obtrusive than the /d/t/ substitution. The chief audible difference between medial /t/ and medial /d/ is the greater breath emission following /t/. The /t/ requires no longer contact of the articulators than /d/, nor any change in the place of articulation. The necessary breath emission following medial /t/ can be produced by inserting a slight /h/ after /t/. (The consonant /h/ is simply breath emitted from the larynx.) As you pronounce each of the following phrases, listen to the breath emission on /h/. Then copy the /h/-like breath emission after /t/ in the word opposite.

bet her — better	dirt he — dirty	mat her — matter
bet he — Betty	eight he — eighty	pit he — pity
bit her — bitter	hot her — hotter	visit hid — visited
but her — butter	let her — letter	wit he — witty

D. Changing /t/ to /d/ is just as likely when one word in a phrase ends in /t/ and the word which follows it begins with a vowel. The same technique as in Section C above can be used to assure you of using /t/ in the following phrases. Carry over a slight /h/ after the /t/ from the first phrase to the second of each pair.

it his — it is easy   what his — what is that   that his — that is easy

Practice these phrases, making sure that a slight /h/ (breath emission) follows the final /t/ when the next word begins with a vowel.

hit a ball	sit on a chair	laughed at a joke
thought I would	his hat in his hand	can't ever hit it
a lot of these	put on his coat	hit at it every time

E. Omission of final /t/ following another consonant may be one of your errors. If so, practice the following words, making sure that you complete each one with /t/. Remember that –**ed** is pronounced /t/ when added to a word ending in a voiceless consonant.

/st/	/st/	/ft/	/pt/	/kt/
last	against	lift	hoped	effect
past	oldest	left	ripped	exact
best	insist	loft	slapped	expect
trust	kissed	raft	slipped	fact
paste	missed	laughed	wrapped	inspect
worst	passed	bereft	flapped	reject

F. Medial /t/ is sometimes omitted when it follows another consonant. When you practice the following words, it might help you to pronounce the /t/ if you think of pronouncing the preceding consonant at the end of one syllable and the /t/ at the beginning of the next.

enter	frantic	renting	distance	history	resisting
interest	lantern	twenty	faster	mustard	sister
interlining	panting	wanting	fastest	pester	western

G. Omission of final /d/ following another consonant may be one of your errors. If so, practice the following words, making sure that you complete each word with /d/.

/nd/	/nd/	/md/	/ŋd/	/ld/	/dʒd/
bend	friend	ashamed	belonged	gold	judged
behind	hand	blamed	hanged	piled	bulged
bound	intend	dreamed	longed	sealed	arranged
end	land	rammed	winged	told	changed
find	pretend	wormed	wronged	yield	hinged

H. Medial /d/ is sometimes omitted when it follows another consonant. When you practice the following words, it might help you to pronounce the /d/ if you think of pronouncing the preceding consonant at the end of one syllable and the /d/ at the beginning of the next.

/nd/	/nd/	/nd/	/nd/	/ld/	/ld/
Anderson	finding	spending	understand	boldest	holding
candle	handle	spindle	winding	children	older
candy bar	hundred	under	wonder	coldest	oldest
ending	pretending	underneath	wondering	folding	wildest

I. Omission of /t/ between two other consonants, as in **expects** and **insists**, is an even greater danger than omitting /t/ after another consonant, as in **last** or **winter**. An inadequate pronunciation of the consonant clusters /kts/ or /sts/, which is sometimes heard, breaks the word between the /t/ and the following /s/, e.g., **expect-s, insist-s**. Such a "split-word" pronunciation probably attracts more attention than omitting the /t/ because it appears so difficult and overdone.

(1) The least obtrusive way to articulate a cluster such as /kts/ or /sts/ is to produce the /ts/ as a blended unit, and then pronounce the word as if it were **expec-ts** or **insis-ts**. To master the /ts/ blend, try this procedure: say CATS several times to perceive the sound and feel of the blending. Next say CAT'S EYE as a continuous word (with no pause between); repeat until you hear /ts/ at the beginning of EYE. Now say CA–TSEYE (keep the same /æ/ vowel in CAT, but make the word break before /ts/ rather than after it). Repeat this until it is easy. Now cut off the /kæ/ beginning, saying simply /tsaɪ/. To be sure you are using /ts/ and not simply /s/ initially, contrast /tsaɪ/ — /saɪ/. Now pronounce /ts/ alone. Contrast /ts/ with /s/. Use /ts/ as a blended unit to end the words in this list.

/s-ts/	/s-ts/	/k-ts/	/k-ts/	/f-ts/	/p-ts/
insists	pests	acts	facts	gifts	disrupts

lists	tastes	affects	inspects	lifts	erupts
pastes	trusts	effects	rejects	sifts	interrupts

(2) Use the same technique when /t/ occurs between two other consonants at the juncture of two words in a phrase, e.g., **sts** in **last summer**. Instead of separating the two words, make a /ts/ blend of the final /t/ in the first word and the /s/ beginning the next word, thus: **las-tsummer**.

/s-ts/	/k-ts/	/f-ts/	/p-ts/
first semester	expect Sam	laughed suddenly	chipped six cups
last summer	exact salary	left side	hoped something
last Sunday	reject some	left suddenly	roped seven cows
lost something	the fact seems	shift some	wept sadly

J. To avoid omitting /d/ in a word like **hands** requires blending /dz/ in the same manner as the /ts/ blend in Section I above. To master the /dz/ blend, substitute CAD'S EYE for CAT'S EYE in the /ts/-blend procedure. In the following words the final –s is pronounced /z/. Pronounce each word with /dz/ as a blended unit, e.g., **han-ds** /hæn-dz/.

/n-dz/	/n-dz/	/n-dz/	/n-dz/	/n-dz/	/l-dz/
bands	demands	finds	hands	pretends	fields
bends	ends	friends	intends	rinds	holds
bounds	extends	grounds	lends	winds	shields

K. When /t/ occurs between another consonant and /l/, there is danger of omitting it. A word like **exactly**, with a /ktl/ cluster, is especially tricky. To release breath in a puff after the /t/, as if it were final, and then to add on –ly, sounds affected and artificial. The best solution is to learn to produce a /tl/ blend and to pronounce the word as **exac-tly**. Try this technique for learning to articulate a /tl/ blend: practice saying RIGHTLY and observe the transition between /t/ and /l/. Say /raɪ-tli/ until a perception of /tl/ as a blend is established. Then practice /tli/ contrasted with /kli/ to be sure there is no confusion. Observe that in /tli/ there is a perceptible puff of breath over the sides of the tongue as /t/ is released into the /l/. Now pronounce **exactly** as /ɛgzæk-tli/. Use the same method with all of the words below.

/s-tl/	/k-tl/	/f-tl/	/p-tl/
costly	correctly	deftly	abruptly
mostly	exactly	softly	aptly
listless	perfectly	swiftly	corruptly

L. To avoid omitting /d/ in a /ndl/ or /ldl/ cluster, you need to produce /dl/ as a blend. To master the /dl/ blend, practice BADLY, BA–DLY, etc.,

as you practiced RIGHTLY in Section K above. Practice the following
words with /dl/ as a blend, e.g., **en-dless.**

/n-dl/	/n-dl/	/n-dl/	/l-dl/
blandly	friendless	kindly	boldly
endless	groundling	roundly	coldly
fondly	handling	soundless	wildly

M. Changing the articulation of /t/ is an error that results from assimilation
(changing one phoneme to be more like another which occurs close to it
in a word or phrase). Remember that /t/ is correctly articulated with the
tip of the tongue touching the alveolar ridge. The one allowable exception
is in a phrase like **at the** or **might think**, in which /t/ may be tip-dental
(tongue tip touching the upper teeth) to agree with the articulation of the
/ð/ or /θ/ which begins the next word. In careful speech, /t/ must remain
/t/, and does not change to /p/, /k/, or some other consonant. Note the
unacceptable assimilations below and guard against using similar ones.

Phrase	*Incorrectly Assimilated Pronunciation (in IPA)*	*Error (in IPA)*	*Explanation*
(1) that proves	ðæp pruvs	p/t	same articulation as the following /p/
(2) it can	ɪk kæn	k/t	same articulation as the following /k/
(3) it fits	ɪp fɪts	p/t [1]	same articulation as the following /f/
(4) it was	ɪʔ wəz	ʔ/t	[ʔ] is a glottal stop — made by closing the vocal folds and then "exploding" the breath. This error "saves effort" in tongue movements.
(5) it uses	ɪʔ juzɪz	ʔ/t	same as #4
(6) that looks	ðæʔ lʊks	ʔ/t	same as #4
(7) street cleaner	strik klinɚ	k/t	same articulation as the following /k/
(8) hot potato	hɑp pəteto	p/t	same articulation as the following /p/
(9) light brown	laɪp braʊn	p/t	same articulation as the following /b/
(10) write Fred	raɪp *frɛd†	p/t	same articulation as the following /f/

N. Incorrect assimilations of /d/ also occur, similar to the process of /t/
assimilations explained in Section M. Here are some examples:

---

[1] [p] and [b] are symbols added to IPA to represent /p/ and /b/ which are articulated with
teeth and lip (like /f/ or /v/) rather than with two lips. The [ˌ] modifier, meaning "dental,"
has been borrowed from [t] and [d] which are tip-dental articulations of normally tip-alveolar
/t/ and /d/.

† A proper noun is written in IPA with an asterisk preceding.

Phrase	Incorrectly Assimilated Pronunciation (*in IPA*)	Error (*in IPA*)	Explanation
(1) had gone	hæg gɔn	g/d	same articulation as the following /g/
(2) Dad bought	*dæbʈ bɔt	b/d	same articulation as the following /b/
(3) red flannel	rɛḇ flænḷ	ḇ/d [1]	same articulation as the following /f/

O. In a word like **little** the final /l/ is a syllabic [ḷ], and in a word like **cotton** the final /n/ is a syllabic [ṇ], because this [ḷ] or [ṇ] forms the final syllable without a vowel sound. Since /l/ and /n/ are articulated like /t/, with the tongue tip touching the alveolar ridge, this tip-alveolar articulation should be held from the /t/ to the following syllabic [ḷ] or [ṇ] rather than released and rearticulated in the same place. Four kinds of errors may occur in words of this type: (1) omission of the /t/; (2) substitution of /d/ for /t/; (3) substitution of a glottal stop [ʔ] for the /t/ (closing the vocal folds and then releasing the compressed breath from the glottis as [ʔ] instead of articulating /t/ with the tongue tip); (4) inserting /ə/ between the /t/ and the /l/, or between the /t/ and the /n/.

To insure correct production of /t/ before [ḷ] or [ṇ], test your articulation thus: (1) *feel* the contact of the tongue tip against the alveolar ridge for /t/ in **little** as in **lit**, in **cotton** as in **cot**; (2) maintain the articulation of /t/ for the [ḷ] or [ṇ]. If you release the /t/ and rearticulate /l/ or /n/, you will say /əl/ for [ḷ] and /ən/ for [ṇ]. Be sure to keep the tongue tip in continuous contact from /t/ to [ḷ] or [ṇ]; (3) *listen* for an explosive release of breath over the sides of the tongue (through the [ḷ]) in **little**, through the nasal passage (in the [ṇ]) in **cotton**. The puff of breath following /t/ should not precede the [ḷ] or [ṇ] but should occur *with* the [ḷ] or [ṇ]. This breath expulsion which characterizes /t/ would not be heard if you substituted /d/ for /t/.

kettle	metal	settle	bitten	cotton	rotten
little	rattle	whittle	certain	kitten	written

P. When /d/ precedes syllabic [ḷ] or [ṇ], be sure that the tongue tip articulation is held continuously from /d/ through the syllabic [ḷ] or [ṇ]. Do not insert /ə/ between. Be sure /d/ is not omitted or replaced by [ʔ].

medal	paddle	riddle	couldn't	shouldn't	widen
middle	poodle	saddle	hadn't	wouldn't	sudden

Q. Silent **t** and **d** occur in certain words. It is possible to become so careful in pronunciation that you overdo it. In the following words, **t** is not correctly pronounced.

bristle	chestnut	fasten	hustle	mortgage	thistle
castle	Christmas	glisten	listen	mustn't	whistle
chasten	epistle	hasten	moisten	soften	wrestle

The **d** is correctly silent in the following words:

grandfather grandmother handkerchief handsome Wednesday

R. Sentences for /t/ and /d/ practice.

1. Handle that antique table delicately.
2. The old lady sat down on the divan and held sister's hand.[2]
3. Betty will be at the party until exactly two this afternoon.
4. Mr. Kindly can boast of his youngest son's record.
5. An artist visited here in the past.
6. The officer promised to arrest the first vagrant he saw.
7. Daddy begged Sam to withhold the lists.
8. He inspects hundreds of ladles every day, but rejects few of them.
9. She insists that my friends' visiting disrupts our practice periods.
10. We begged Susie to take an interest in pictures last winter.
11. He used some of the paste simply for its decorative effect.
12. She said she would expect Sam to take the last seat.
13. A hundred and twenty students registered for history last semester.
14. She arranged some candles amidst flowers to make an interesting centerpiece.

S. Reading selections for /t/ practice.

1. It is better to have a little than nothing.

    PUBLILIUS SYRUS

2. City that breathes of things too large for books, that is too beautiful for poets, too terrible for drama, too true for testimony. . . .

    FELIX RIESENBERG

3. How oft the darkest hour of ill
    Breaks brightest into dawn.

    EURIPIDES

4. They say best men are moulded out of faults,
    And, for the most, become much more the better
    For being a little bad.

    WILLIAM SHAKESPEARE

---

[2] The **d** which ends **and** need not be pronounced if the following word begins with a consonant sound.

5. We talk little if we do not talk about ourselves.

    HENRY HAZLITT

6. She took to telling the truth; she said she was forty-two and five months. It may have been pleasing to the angels, but her elder sister was not gratified.

    H. H. MUNRO (SAKI)

7. From *Word Power Made Easy* [3]

    Titillate comes from a Latin verb meaning *tickle*, and may be used both literally and figuratively. That is (literally), you can *titillate* someone by stroking him gently in strategic places; you are then causing an actual (and always very pleasant) physical sensation; or you can (figuratively) *titillate him*, or *his mind*, or *his fancy*, or *his palate* (and this is the more common use of the word), by your *charm, brilliance, cuteness, attractive appearance*, or by any other device your imagination can conceive. And I hope you have a good imagination. The noun is *titillation*.

    NORMAN LEWIS

T. Reading selections for /d/ practice.

1. Let us, to the end, dare to do our duty as we understand it.

    ABRAHAM LINCOLN

2. Continued dependence upon relief induces a spiritual and moral disintegration fundamentally destructive to the national fibre. To dole out relief in this way is to administer a narcotic, a subtle destroyer of the human spirit.

    FRANKLIN D. ROOSEVELT

3. Delusions, like dreams, are dispelled by our awakening to the stern duties of life.

    MARIANNA MAHRT

4. It is a double pleasure to deceive the deceiver.

    JEAN DE LA FONTAINE

5.   And the Devil did grin, for his darling sin
          Is pride that apes humility.

    SAMUEL TAYLOR COLERIDGE

[3] From *Word Power Made Easy* by Norman Lewis. Copyright 1949 by Norman Lewis. Reprinted by permission of Doubleday & Company, Inc.

n

/n/ as in **no**

Spellings of /n/: n as in **no**: **nn** as in **dinner** (pronounced as a single /n/); **pn** as in **pneumonia**; **kn** as in **knew**; **gn** as in **gnaw**.

Description of /n/: This is a voiced, tip-alveolar, nasal semi-vowel. The tongue closes off the passage of breath from the mouth, while the velum lowers to allow the passage of the breath through the nasal cavity.

Syllabic /n/ (IPA symbol [ņ]) forms a syllable without a vowel phoneme, therefore serving the purpose of a vowel in a syllable. In order to produce a syllabic [ņ], there must be no "break" in articulation between the preceding consonant and the [ņ]. The most common occurrence of [ņ] is following a /t/ or /d/ (as in **cotton, sudden**), when the tongue-tip articulation for /t/ or /d/ is maintained for the /n/, or when the /n/ is articulated during the articulation of a preceding consonant like /s/ or /z/ (as in **hasten, reason**).

EXERCISES

A. Changing the place of articulation of /n/ to that of whatever consonant follows the /n/ is the most common error with this phoneme. This process, called *assimilation*, is not inherently bad, for some assimilations of /n/ are entirely correct. Long ago cultivated usage changed the **n** ending the prefix in **congress** and **congregate** to an /ŋ/, to be articulated like the /g/ which follows. In words like **combine** and **composite**, this same prefix ends in **m** because the roots of these words begin with /b/ and /p/ (articulated with the lips, as is /m/). In most English words, however, if a prefix ends in the letter **n**, it is preferably pronounced as /n/, no matter what consonant begins the root to which the prefix attaches. Remember that /n/ is articulated with the *tip* of the tongue contacting the *alveolar ridge*. As you pronounce words in the following lists, depend on the tactile sense (feeling the contact of tongue tip on alveolar ridge) to be certain you pronounced /n/ rather than another nasal consonant in substitution.

(1) Substitution of /ŋ/ for /n/ should be avoided in the following words. Each has a prefix ending in **n**, attached to a root which begins with either a /k/ or a /g/. Since /k/ and /g/ are articulated with the back of the tongue touching the velum, you will be tempted to articulate /ŋ/ preceding, with the back of the tongue touching the velum. Keep /n/ at the end of the prefix a tip-alveolar articulation.

concave	incomparable	incontestable	incumbent	unconditional
congratulate	incompatible	inconvenience	ingrown	unconscious
congruity	incompetence	incorporated	inquest	unconstitutional
inclement	incomplete	incorrect	inquisition	uncounted

inclination	incomprehensible	incorrigible	inquire	uncouth
inclined	inconceivable	incorruptible	uncanny	uncovered
enclose	inconclusive	increase	unclean	ungainly
include	incongruous	incredible	uncoil	ungovernable
incognito	inconsequential	increment	uncomfortable	ungracious
incoherent	inconsiderate	incriminate	uncommon	ungrateful
income	inconsistency	incubator	uncompromising	unguarded
incommunicado	inconspicuous	inculcate	unconcerned	ungodly

(2) The substitution of /m/ for /n/ threatens when a prefix ending in /n/ attaches to a root which begins with /b/ or /p/. Since /b/ and /p/ are articulated with the two lips, it would be easier (but unacceptable) to articulate a bilabial /m/ just before the /b/ or /p/. Keep a tip-alveolar articulation of /n/ at the end of each prefix in the following words.

inboard	unbend	unborn	unpack	unpredictable
inborn	unbent	unbowed	unpaid	unprejudiced
inbred	unbiased	unbridled	unparalleled	unprincipled
unbalanced	unbidden	unbroken	unpin	unprintable
unbecoming	unbind	unbuckle	unpleasant	unprofessional
unbelievable	unblushing	unburden	unpopular	unproved
unbeliever	unbolt	unbutton	unprecedented	unprovoked

(3) The substitution of [m̪] [4] for /n/ is a danger when /n/ ends a prefix attached to a root beginning with /f/ or /v/. The fricatives /f/ and /v/ are articulated with the lower lip against the upper teeth (labio-dental). Less effort would be required to make a labio-dental [m̪] ahead of a labio-dental /f/ or /v/, but the substitution is unacceptable. Keep the tip-alveolar articulation of /n/ at the end of each prefix in the following words.

confection	infamy	infirmary	invalidate	invocation
confederacy	infancy	inflammable	invaluable	involuntary
conference	infantile	inflammatory	invasion	involve
confession	infantry	inflated	invective	unfailing
confidence	infatuated	inflection	inveigle	unfair
configuration	infection	inflexible	invent	unfaithful

[4] In the interest of consistency and simplicity, the [m̪] symbol is used here for the labio-dental nasal continuant which IPA symbolizes as [ɱ]. From the [t̪] and [d̪] symbols of IPA, which represent tip-dental articulations of normally tip-alveolar /t/ and /d/, the modifier has been borrowed to mean "dental," extending its use to any allophone articulated with teeth though the most common variety of that phoneme does not involve the teeth as an articulator. Thus [m̪] represents a teeth-lip articulation of /m/ which is normally formed with two lips, just as [p̪] and [b̪] represent a teeth-lip articulation of normally bilabial /p/ and /b/.

confined	inference	inflict	inventory	unfamiliar
confirmation	inferior	influence	invert	unfasten
confiscate	infernal	inform	investment	unfavorable
conflagration	infidelity	information	investigate	unfit
conflict	infield	infraction	inveterate	unflinching
conform	infiltrate	infrequent	invidious	unforgettable
confound	infinite	infuriated	invincible	unfortunate
confront	infinitive	invade	invisible	unfounded
confuse	infinity	invalid	invitation	unfurl

(4) [ɲ] is an unacceptable allophone of /n/ articulated with the front part of the tongue against the hard palate (very much like the /j/ in **yes**). The substitution of [ɲ] for /n/ is a danger when **n** is followed by /s/ or /ʃ/, which are formed with the blade of the tongue against or just back of the alveolar ridge, or by a /j/, which is formed with the front of the tongue held closed to the hard palate, or by an /r/, which is formed with the central part of the tongue held high toward the hard palate. By assimilation, the articulation of /n/ would copy /s, ʃ, j, r/. What should be a tip-alveolar /n/ may become a blade-alveolar [ɲ]. Maintain a tip-alveolar articulation of /n/ in the following words.

/ns/	/ns/	/ns/	/nʃ/	/nr/
consecrate	incipient	insulate	censure	unravel
consecutive	incite	insult	conscience	unreal
consensus	insanity	uncertain	conscientious	unreality
consent	insect	unscrew	conscious	unreasonable
consequence	insensitive	unsociable	expansion	unregenerate
conservative	inseparable	unsophisticated	insure	unrelenting
consider	insert	unsuitable	insurance	unremitting
consist	inside		mansion	unreserved
console	insignificant	/nj/	mention	unresponsive
consolidate	insincere	bunion	pension	unrest
consonant	insipid	canyon	sunshine	unrestrained
consul	insist	companion	tension	unrighteous
consume	insolent	onion	unsure	unrivaled
incentive	inspect	union		unroll
incident	inspiration	unused		unruffled
incinerator	insufficient	unyielding		unruly

(5) Any of the /n/ assimilations described above can, but should not, occur in phrases where /n/ ends one word and a consonant with articulation different from /n/ begins the next word. Practice the following phrases, guarding against the errors noted.

Phrase	Incorrectly Assimilated Pronunciation (*in IPA*)	Error (*in IPA*)	Explanation
(1) can be	kæm bi	m/n	Articulation like /b/
(2) in case	ɪŋ kes	ŋ/n	Articulation like /k/
(3) in front	ɪɱ frənt	ɱ/n	Articulation like /f/
(4) can sit	kæɲ sɪt	ɲ/n	Articulation like /s/
(5) in fact	ɪɱ fækt	ɱ/n	Articulation like /f/
(6) can cook	kæŋ kʊk	ŋ/n	Articulation like /k/
(7) hen pecked	hɛm pɛkt	m/n	Articulation like /p/
(8) can view	kæɱ vju	ɱ/n	Articulation like /v/
(9) in yours	ɪɲ jʊrz	ɲ/n	Articulation like /j/
(10) can go	kæŋ go	ŋ/n	Articulation like /g/

B. There is danger of omitting /n/ or changing /n/ to /m/ when /n/ precedes /m/. Since these two consonants are both nasal continuants, it may be difficult for you to hear whether you have said /nm/, /mm/, or /m/ in words and phrases like those which follow. In your practice, depend on tactile awareness of the tip-alveolar articulation of /n/.

adjournment	learn more	can move
discernment	earn more	can make
environment	rain more	have been made
government	win more	yours an(d) mine

C. Erroneous insertion of /n/ sometimes occurs in these words.

Word	Correct (*IPA*)	Incorrect (*IPA*)	Reason for Error
united	ju-náɪ-tɪd	ju-náɪn-tɪd	Possible analogy to **nine**
veterinarian	vɛt-ɚ-ə-nɛ́r-i-ən	vɛnt-ɚ-ə-nɛ́r-i-ən	Possible analogy to **vent**

D. Syllabic [n̩] should be used in the unstressed syllable of each word in the following list. In each word, the [n̩] is preceded by a syllable ending in /t/ or /d/. Syllabic [n̩] forms a syllable without a vowel. Production of syllabic [n̩] requires its articulation before the release of the articulation for the preceding consonant. Since /t/ and /d/ have tip-alveolar articulation, like /n/, the articulation of the preceding /t/ or /d/ should be simply held in place for the syllabic [n̩].[5]

[5] Syllabic [n] can also be produced following /s/ as in **listen**, /z/ as in **season**, /ʃ/ as in **mission**, or /ʒ/ as in **vision**; such words are equally correct with either [n] or /ən/. Following /nt/ as in **mountain, fountain**, many good speakers prefer to use /ən/ because it sounds clearer, though [n̩] is also correct in these words. Only when /t/ or /d/ precedes, is [n̩] definitely preferable over /ən/.

bitten	cotton	didn't	laden	sadden	wooden
button	curtain	hadn't	ridden	shouldn't	wouldn't
certain	couldn't	kitten	rotten	sudden	written

E. Sentences for /n/ practice.

1. I inferred that she found no information in books she consulted.
2. Her inconsiderate behavior isn't as infuriating as her infrequent visits.
3. The government doesn't give information very informally.
4. In Mother's opinion, the investment was unsound.
5. I am confident he was knocked unconscious by the sudden jolt.
6. Inlaid linoleum is an unwise choice, at our present income.
7. The kitten is chasing insects out in the sunshine.
8. It isn't safe to fasten cotton to this wooden form.

F. Reading selections for /n/ practice.

1. Free trade, one of the greatest blessings which a government can confer on a people, is in almost every country unpopular.

    LORD MACAULAY

2. We have learned that we cannot live alone, in peace; that our own well-being is dependent on the well-being of other nations, far away. We have learned that we must live as men, and not as ostriches, nor as dogs in the manger. We have learned to be citizens of the world, members of the human community.

    FRANKLIN D. ROOSEVELT

3.   Where is the knowledge we have lost in information?
    The cycles of Heaven in twenty centuries
    Bring us farther from God and nearer to the Dust.

    T. S. ELIOT

4. No man is an island, entire of itself; every man is a piece of the continent, a part of the main.

    JOHN DONNE

5. The West begins where the average annual rainfall drops below twenty inches. When you reach the line which marks that drop — for convenience, the one hundredth meridian — you have reached the West.

    BERNARD DE VOTO

6. Never trouble another for what you can do yourself.
    Never spend your money before you have it.

Never buy what you do not want because it is cheap.
Nothing is troublesome that we do willingly.
Take things always by the smooth handle.
When angry, count ten before you speak; if very angry, a hundred.

THOMAS JEFFERSON

/l/ as in **late**

1

Spellings of /l/: l as in **late**; **ll** as in **tall.**

Description of /l/: This is a voiced, tip-alveolar, lateral semi-vowel. The tip of the tongue makes contact with the alveolar ridge, while the sides of the tongue are lowered (not in contact with the back teeth), so that the breath stream is emitted laterally, i.e., over the sides of the tongue.

Two types of /l/ occur regularly in English. The articulation described above holds for both, but the position of the back of the tongue differs in the two types: The allophone [l], called "clear" /l/, is articulated with the back of the tongue held low in the mouth. "Clear" /l/ occurs initially, especially if followed by a front vowel /i, ɪ, e, ɛ, æ, a/. The allophone [ɫ], called "dark" /l/, however, has as a secondary articulation the lifting of the back of the tongue toward the velum (soft palate), approximately in the position required for the vowel /o/ or /ʊ/. In all dialects "dark" /l/ occurs finally in words. Most commonly, "dark" /l/ occurs in the medial position also, though many Southerners use a "clear" /l/ medially if a front vowel precedes it.

Syllabic [l̩] forms a syllable without a vowel phoneme, therefore serving the purpose of a vowel in the syllable. If the tongue-tip contact for a preceding /t/, /d/, or /n/ (as in **little, saddle, funnel**) is maintained for the /l/, or when the /l/ is articulated before releasing the articulation of a preceding consonant (such as /s/ or /z/ as in **whistle, muzzle**), a syllabic [l̩] is formed.

EXERCISES

A. Pronounce the following pairs of words to perceive the difference in "clear" /l/ and "dark" /l/. For both "clear" and "dark" /l/ you should *feel* the tongue tip touch the alveolar ridge. For "clear" /l/ the back of the tongue is held low; for "dark" /l/ the back of the tongue is held high. The first word of each pair *begins* with "clear" /l/, while the second word *ends* with "dark" /l/.

lace — sail	lean — kneel	lick — kill
lap — pal	least — steal	loop — pool
leaf — feel	life — file	lost — stall

B. Omission of "dark" /l/, or distortion of its articulation, is an error which is most likely to occur when another consonant follows the /l/. A similar problem with "clear" /l/ is highly unlikely. Because "dark" /l/ involves lifting the back of the tongue in addition to touching the tongue tip to the alveolar ridge, a careless speaker is likely to make only the back-tongue articulation and neglect the tip-alveolar articulation, producing a vowel /o/ or /ʊ/ instead of /l/. When "dark" /l/ is followed by /r/ as in **already**, /j/ as in **will you**, or /w/ as in **all week**, a careless speaker may omit the /l/ entirely. Sometimes the error involves combining /l/ and /j/ to form a [λ] (as in Spanish **caballo**), which is an /l/ articulated with the front of the tongue (like /j/) instead of the tongue tip. Practice the following pairs of words, concentrating on the tactile sensation of the tongue tip touching the alveolar ridge, both when the /l/ is final and when another consonant follows it.

all — almost	goal — gold	sell — self
all — already	mill — milk	sell — sell you
all — all right	hell — help	shoal — shoulder
bowl — bolt	mill — million	sill — silk
civil — civilian	mill — Milwaukee	well — welcome
coal — cold	rail — railroad	will — William

C. Students who learned an Oriental language before English usually have difficulty distinguishing between /l/ and /r/, since their only similar consonant has some characteristics of both sounds. Practice in contrasting /l/ and /r/ in the following pairs of words should involve *visual* and *tactile* monitoring for these features: for /l/ the tongue tip touches the alveolar ridge *flatly* and *firmly;* for /r/ the tongue is bunched up in the center of the mouth *tensely*, and the tongue tip points upward but *does not* touch the palate.

lace — race	led — red	blue — brew
laid — raid	lid — rid	bled — bread
lag — rag	limb — rim	climb — crime
lake — rake	lip — rip	flame — frame
lamp — ramp	list — wrist	flee — free
lane — rain	liver — river	flute — fruit
lap — wrap	load — road	fly — fry
late — rate	lobe — robe	gland — grand
lay — ray	long — wrong	glaze — graze
lead — read	lose — ruse	glue — grew
leak — reek	lung — rung	glow — grow
leaf — reef	alive — arrive	play — pray

D. Syllabic [l̩] should be used in a final unstressed syllable when the preceding consonant is /t/ or /d/. Rather than releasing the articulation of /t/ or /d/ and rearticulating /l/ in the same place (tip-alveolar), which would make the syllable /əl/, it is better to hold the tip-alveolar articulation from the /t/ or /d/ to the [l̩]. A syllabic [l̩] can occur following any fricative consonant if the [l̩] is articulated before the release of the articulation of the preceding consonant. In words such as **waffle, evil**, and **whistle,** you may correctly use either /əl/ or [l̩]. If a stop consonant other than /t/ or /d/ precedes the /l/, most good speakers prefer to use /əl/ rather than [l̩], for greater clarity.

Use [l̩]	*Use* [l̩]	*Use* [l̩] *or* /əl/	*Use* [l̩] *or* /əl/	*Use* /əl/	*Use* /əl/
cattle	nettle	awful	raffle	apple	tickle
kettle	pedal	dazzle	ruffle	dabble	tackle
ladle	petal	evil	shovel	nipple	opal
little	saddle	lawful	sizzle	pickle	wiggle
medal	settle	muscle	waffle	shackle	wriggle
metal	turtle	muzzle	whistle	frugal	mogul

E. The letter l is preferably silent in certain English words. Practice the silent-l words below to make sure your eagerness to pronounce carefully does not cause you to over-pronounce.

almond	palm	behalf	halve	chalk	walk
balm	psalm	calf	salve	solder	could
calm	qualm	calve	balk	stalk	should
embalm	salmon	half	calk	talk	would

F. Sentences for /l/ practice.

1. I'll tell you the value of that article.
2. Let me sell you a million copies of "Colliers."
3. Will you come over and tell William to help?
4. I need a bottle of purple ink, please.
5. William was watching the cattle from the saddle.
6. Billy has already learned to hold a glass of milk.
7. Surely you didn't spill salt on this pillow.
8. Twelve elves played in the open glade.
9. The silk dress is almost ready for Lillian to try on.
10. All the boys helped to load the gold bullion.
11. He told us that there was a wolf on the golf course.
12. It is all right to let the baby play with the little rattle.
13. Are trains on the Milwaukee Railroad always late?
14. Let's count the little turtles in the pool.

G. Reading selections for /l/ practice.

1.   In the past we have had a light which flickered, in the present we
     have a light which flames, and in the future there will be a light which
     shines over all the land and sea.

                                                    WINSTON CHURCHILL

2.   God helps them that help themselves.

                          BENJAMIN FRANKLIN

3.   Light, God's eldest daughter, is a principal beauty in a building.

                                                    THOMAS FULLER

4.   Be not afraid of life. Believe that life is worth living, and your belief
     will help create the fact.

                                                    WILLIAM JAMES

5.   Borrowers are nearly always ill-spenders, and it is with lent money
     that all evil is mainly done, and all unjust war protracted.

                                                    JOHN RUSKIN

6.   You roll my log, and I will roll yours.

                          SENECA

7.   All men think all men mortal but themselves.

                          EDWARD YOUNG

8.   Faith is like a lily lifted high and white,
              Love is like a lovely rose the world's delight.

                                        CHRISTINA ROSSETTI

9.   Faultily faultless, icily regular, splendidly null.

                                   ALFRED, LORD TENNYSON

10. Sensual pleasures are like soap bubbles, sparkling, evanescent. The
     pleasures of intellect are calm, beautiful, sublime, ever-enduring and
     climbing upward to the borders of the unseen world.

                                                    AUGHEY

11.   The gray sea and the long black land;
              And the yellow half-moon large and low;
              And the startled little waves that leap
              In fiery ringlets from their sleep, . . .

                                   ROBERT BROWNING

/r/ as in **rat**

r

Spellings of /r/: r as in **rat**; **rr** as in **arrow**; **wr** as in **write**.

Description of /r/: This is a voiced, tip-central, glide semi-vowel. The central part of the tongue is tensed and raised toward the palate. The tip of the tongue varies in its articulation, being either lifted toward (but not touching) the hard palate, or drawn back somewhat from the lower teeth. This phoneme is called a glide because the tongue is in motion during its production. When /r/ occurs before a vowel, the glide is from the position of the vowel /ɚ/ and toward the vowel which follows. When /r/ occurs after a vowel, it is a glide toward the position of the vowel /ɚ/. In an initial /tr/ or /dr/ cluster, as in **try** or **dry**, the tongue is in near enough contact with the alveolar ridge for /r/ that it has fricative characteristics. In an initial /θr/ cluster, as in **three**, many speakers use a tip-trilled /r/ (like the /r/ in Spanish), though trilled /r/ is not used otherwise in English.

EXERCISES

A. Initial /r/, which occurs at the beginning of a syllable, is a glide away from the articulation of the vowel /ɚ/. If you have difficulty pronouncing /r/, concentrate on lifting the central part of the tongue tensely, "stiffen" the tongue, and point the tongue tip upward but do not let it touch the palate. At the beginning of each word below, first hold this articulation briefly before completing the word so that **rat** sounds like /ɚræt/, to help to reinforce the feel of /r/ articulation. Then repeat the word with a faster "take-off" from /ɚ/ but still monitoring the kinesthesia of tense bunching up of the tongue as /r/ begins.

read	race	rack	rock	roof
real	raid	ran	rot	room
reap	rain	rat	raw	root
reason	rate	wrap	wrong	rude
rich	red	rub	robe	rhyme
rid	rent	run	roll	right
rip	reptile	rung	rose	round
risk	wreck	rush	row	rouse

B. When a /pr/, /br/, or /fr/ cluster is initial in a syllable, the /r/ is articulated exactly the same way as initial /r/ described in Section A above. However, the /r/ is *not* articulated *after* the /p/, /b/, or /f/. Instead, the tongue articulates /r/ *at the same time* that the lips articulate the /p/, /b/, or /f/, so that when the articulation of the /p/, /b/, or /f/ is released, the /r/ glide is already in progress.

/pr/	/pr/	/br/	/br/	/fr/	/fr/
approach	pretend	abrasion	broom	afraid	fright
approve	price	brash	brought	frame	fritter
practice	pride	brew	brow	frantic	from
prattle	prim	bride	brown	free	front
prepare	probe	bright	brush	freeze	frown
present	prove	broad	brusque	friend	fry

C. When a /kr/ or /gr/ cluster begins a syllable, the /r/ is articulated with the tongue pulled back in the mouth very near the position of /k/ or /g/, to permit a close blending between /k/ and /r/, or /g/ and /r/. Speakers who have habitually used a uvular trilled /r/ (e.g., French) must give attention to releasing the articulation of the /k/ or /g/ quickly to form the glide /r/, since maintaining the back-velar contact is likely to induce the uvular trilled /r/.

/kr/	/kr/	/kr/	/gr/	/gr/	/gr/
cram	crepe	crow	grain	grass	groan
cramp	crew	cruel	grand	great	grope
crate	crisp	crumb	grant	green	ground
crawl	crop	crust	grape	grew	group
creep	cross	cry	grasp	grind	growl

D. The articulation of /r/ in a /tr/ or /dr/ blend is different from the other /r/'s discussed above. The tongue tip makes firm contact with the alveolar ridge for /t/ or /d/. For the following /r/, the tongue-tip contact releases in a slightly backward "scrape," producing a fricative /r/ as the breath is released through the constricted slit above the tongue tip. A tongue-tip trilled /r/, such as Spanish uses, has this same articulation, but with the tongue tip relaxed to allow it to flutter as the breath passes over it. For the fricative /r/ in /tr/ and /dr/ clusters the tongue tip is "stiffened" tensely.

/tr/	/tr/	/tr/	/tr/	/dr/	/dr/
track	travel	trip	construct	address	drip
trade	treat	trough	construe	drain	drive
train	tree	truce	destroy	drape	droop
trap	trim	true	patriotic	dream	drop
trash	trinket	try	string	drink	dry

E. When **r** follows a vowel sound, either finally in a word or preceding another consonant phoneme, correct usage varies. In the General American dialect,

/r/ is pronounced in this as in all other positions. But in the standard Eastern and Southern dialects /ə/ commonly replaces /r/ after all vowel phonemes except /ɑ/ (as in **far**), when a prolongation of the vowel usually replaces the /r/.

If you have difficulty pronouncing a glide /r/ at the end of a syllable, practice prolonging it as a vowel /ɚ/, lifting the center and tip of the tongue tensely but avoiding actual contact of the tongue tip against the hard palate.

appear	near	pair	war	acquire	bark
beer	severe	scare	door	desire	farm
cheer	sincere	share	floor	fire	heart
clear	air	stair	four	wire	part
dear	bear	wear	more	our	north
ear	care	car	store	sour	warm
fear	chair	far	poor	beard	fourth
here	fair	jar	your	stared	pork

F. Between two vowel sounds, /r/ should be pronounced in all dialects.

arrest	berry	erase	marry	orange	parrot
arrive	bereaved	garage	merry	parable	terrible
around	carry	horrible	miserable	parade	very

G. *Linking* /r/ is a final /r/ which is restored because the following word begins with a vowel sound. Though a final **r** may be "dropped" in cultivated speech of the South and East (see Section E), it should be pronounced as a link between vowels. In the sentences on the left below, /r/ may be correctly replaced by /ə/ or, after /ɑ/, by a lengthening of the vowel phoneme. But in the sentences to the right, the same words must have linking /r/ pronounced.

1. I won't go that far.
2. He has no fear.
3. Will these wear well?
4. I saw your kitten.
5. Our dog is lost.
6. She sat by the fire.
7. He fought in the war.

1. How far away is it?
2. What caused his fear of dogs?
3. Did he wear out his shoes?
4. Take your own luggage with you.
5. That is our only hope.
6. Did they put the fire out?
7. The War of the Roses was long ago.

H. People who "drop" /r/, but who pronounce linking /r/, should guard against adding a false linking /r/ finally in words such as **idea, sofa, madonna.** Do not insert /r/ between words in the following phrases:

the idea of it	Africa and Asia	the madonna of Raphael
a sofa and chair	Alabama and Georgia	stamina and vigor

I.   Sentences for /r/ practice.

1. Our garage is the fourth one on the right side of the driveway.
2. Ironing that intricate embroidery is tiresome.
3. The children tried to prove their courage on the camping trip.
4. These carrots are processed, frozen, and wrapped very promptly.
5. Harry was afraid to drive through the forest preserve after dark.
6. The three friends protested that the truck had not collected the trash.
7. Robert ran around the rose bush and across the grass.
8. Tomorrow may be a very rainy day.
9. We took a package of frozen fried fish from Mrs. Brown's freezer.
10. Crisp crackers are crunchy, but the crumbs are troublesome.
11. The trip by train was rough because the track was under construction.
12. The waitress tripped and dropped a tray of cold drinks.
13. The bride's brother disapproved of the groom's behavior at the reception.
14. Grasp the crate firmly to throw it into the refrigerator car.

J.   Reading selections for /r/ practice.

1. The tree of liberty must be refreshed from time to time with the blood of patriots and tyrants. . . .

    Thomas Jefferson

2. Every reform, however necessary, will by weak minds be carried to an excess, that itself will need reforming.

    Samuel Taylor Coleridge

3. The Miracles of the Church seem to me to rest not so much upon faces or voices or healing power coming suddenly near to us from afar off, but upon our perceptions being made finer, so that for a moment our eyes can see and our ears can hear what is there about us always.

    Willa Cather

4. Error of opinion may be tolerated where reason is left free to combat it.

    Thomas Jefferson

5.   Drip, drip, the rain comes falling,
               Rain in the woods, rain on the sea.

    Morse

6. A good reader is nearly as rare as a good writer. People bring their prejudices, whether friendly or adverse.

    Willmott

7. Reprove thy friend privately, praise him publicly.

SOLON

8. Oh, it offends me to the soul to hear a robustious periwig-pated fellow tear a passion to tatters, to very rags, to split the ears of the groundlings. . . .

WILLIAM SHAKESPEARE

/j/ as in yes

j

Spellings of /j/: **y** as in **yes**; **i** as in **onion**; **gn** /nj/ as in **monsignor**.

Description of /j/: This phoneme is a voiced, front-palatal, glide semi-vowel. It is called a glide because the tongue is in motion during its formation. The front part of the tongue is lifted high and tensely toward the palate, in the same position as for the vowel /i/, and then quickly glides from that position to the position of whatever vowel phoneme follows. /j/ occurs in English only preceding a vowel, never at the end of a syllable.

Alternate Correct Pronunciations: In certain words the letter **i**, preceding unstressed /ə/, is correctly pronounced either /j/ or /i/.

California	champion	genial	Lillian	spaniel	William

EXERCISES

A. Omission of /j/ is an error which occurs primarily when /j/ precedes or follows the vowel /i/. The similarity of the two phonemes accounts for the problem in producing them in sequence. If the tongue is held very tense ("stiffened") at the onset of /j/, its production is more certain.

beyond	year	yearly	yield
ye	yearling	yeast	yielding

B. Foreign students whose native languages do not have the phoneme /j/ are likely to omit it in English words or to substitute /dʒ/, as in **joke**. Since /j/ is a glide away from the articulation of the vowel /i/, you can perceive /j/ as the transition between /i/ and another vowel.

(1) For each word beginning with /j/ below, say an initial /i/ quite tensely, making a quick transition to the following vowel sound.

yawn	yellow	yesterday	you	young
yell	yes	yet	youth	yule

(2) Contrast /j/ with /dʒ/ in the following word pairs. For initial /j/, in the first word of each pair, the front of the tongue is lifted and tensed but does not touch the hard palate, and the tongue tip is held down behind the lower front teeth. For initial /dʒ/, in the second word of each pair, the tongue tip and blade touch the alveolar ridge firmly and then "scrape" away from the contact.

yet — jet	you — Jew
yell — jell	year — jeer

(3) Practice /j/ at the beginning of the final syllable in the following words. If you have difficulty articulating /j/, it should help to practice each word first with a slight pause before the /j/, to allow time to adjust the tongue in a tense /i/ articulation for the /j/.

billion	civilian	dominion	pavilion	opinion
bunion	communion	genius	million	stallion
canyon	companion	lawyer	onion	union

C. Sentences for /j/ practice.

1. Youths in the army often yearn for civilian life.
2. Our champion spaniel is lost in that canyon.
3. William is a very genial lawyer.
4. A genius has mental ability beyond his age.
5. Probably millions of young people have sat in that pavilion.

D. Reading selections for /j/ practice.

1.   Give me your tired, your poor,
       Your huddled masses yearning to breathe free, . . .

       EMMA LAZARUS

2.   The ambitious young man is like yeast in the unmade loaf.

       HENRY WARD BEECHER

3.   That time of year thou may'st in me behold
       When yellow leaves, or none, or few, do hang
       Upon those boughs which shake against the cold, . . .

       WILLIAM SHAKESPEARE

4.   What ye gave, ye have;
           What ye spent, ye had;
           What ye left, ye lost.

           Epitaph of EDWARD,
           EARL OF DEVON

5. If a single cell, under appropriate conditions, becomes a man in the space of a few years, there can surely be no difficulty in understanding how, under appropriate conditions, a cell may, in the course of untold millions of years, give origin to the human race.

HERBERT SPENCER

/θ/ as in thin
/ð/ as in then

Spellings of /θ/ **and** /ð/: Both phonemes are always spelled **th**.

Description of /θ/ **and** /ð/: These two cognate phonemes are tip-dental fricatives. /θ/ is voiceless; /ð/ is voiced. The tongue tip is held in very light contact with the upper front teeth, so that the breath passes through the constricted slit between tongue and teeth, with the sound of friction. The position of the tongue contact may be either underneath the upper teeth or against the back surfaces of the upper teeth. The most significant factor is that the articulation contact must be light, not firm.

EXERCISES

A. If you substitute /d/ for /ð/ and /t/ for /θ/, the error is not so much in *where* you place your tongue for the articulation as *how* you place it there. The /d/ which substitutes for /ð/ and the /t/ which substitutes for /θ/ are usually "dental" [d̪] and [t̪], articulated with the tongue tip touching the back surface of the upper teeth, the same as one of the acceptable articulations of /ð/ and /θ/. However, the tongue tip contact for [d̪] and [t̪] is *firm*, closing off the breath passage momentarily, while for /ð/ and /θ/ the contact is *light*, allowing the breath to hiss through the slit between the upper surface of the tongue and the teeth. If you are afraid that your habitual tongue position tempts you to make too firm a contact, change the articulation so that the tip of the tongue barely shows beneath the edges of the upper teeth. But changing the place of articulation does not correct the error. Whichever position you place your tongue in, you must make so light a contact that the breath continues to escape through the slit as a fricative and is not stopped for even an instant.

(1) Contrast /d/ in the first word of each pair with /ð/ in the second.

day — they	fodder — father	teed — teethe
den — then	breed — breathe	tide — tithe
dough — though	laid — lathe	seed — seethe

(2) Contrast /t/ in the first word with /θ/ in the second word of each pair.

taught — thought	tinker — thinker	boat — both
tie — thigh	tread — thread	oat — oath
tin — thin	bat — bath	rat — wrath

(3) To test your control of articulation for /θ/ and /ð/, practice the following phrases in which /t/ and /d/ occur with /θ/ and /ð/. At first say the phrases slowly, until you master the articulation. Then you may increase the speed without sacrificing precision.

to think	sold a wreath	to the door	take the food
ten themes	to eat with meat	take the dog	do the dishes
to throw	to thank Ted	do that today	take the handle
took both	bath tub	do the trick	did father tell

B. If you substitute /s/ for /θ/ and /z/ for /ð/, your place of articulation is incorrect. For /s/ and /z/ the tongue makes light contact against the alveolar ridge. For /θ/ and /ð/ the tongue tip makes light contact against the upper front teeth, either against the back surfaces or the lower edges of the teeth. Maintain the same light contact which you now use, but move the tongue forward to touch the upper teeth for /θ/ and /ð/.

(1) Contrast /s/ in the first word with /θ/ in the second word of each pair.

sank — thank	sin — thin	miss — myth
seem — theme	sink — think	mouse — mouth
sick — thick	sing — thing	pass — path

(2) Contrast /z/ in the first word with /ð/ in the second word of each pair.

Zen — then	lays — lathe	ties — tithe
breeze — breathe	rise — writhe	seize — seethe
close — clothe	tease — teethe	easy — either

(3) The best test of your control of the articulation of /θ/ and /ð/ is to say them in phrases also containing /s/ and /z/. Be very careful that when you correct your error you do not produce a lisp on your /s/ and /z/. Practice the following phrases slowly at first, until you master the necessary articulation shifts, and then more rapidly.

a safe path	slip through	saw them	sew these
six themes	has a tooth	say this	stamp them
some things	takes a bath	sit there	slice that roast
sad thoughts	say thanks	sell those	sing those songs

C. If you substitute /f/ for /θ/, your place of articulation is incorrect. For /f/ the lower lip touches the upper teeth lightly, while for /θ/ the tongue tip touches the upper teeth lightly. (Incidentally, /v/ is seldom substituted for /ð/ in American speech.)

(1) Contrast /f/ in the first word of each pair with /θ/ in the second word.

fie — thigh	free — three	laugh — lath
fin — thin	fret — threat	loaf — loath
first — thirst	frill — thrill	miff — myth
fought — thought	fro — throw	reef — wreath
Fred — thread	half — hath	sheaf — sheath

(2) To test your control of /θ/ production, practice the following phrases which contain both /f/ and /θ/. Pay close attention to differentiating between /f/ and /θ/.

different things	fix three fenders	firm earth surface
defend the truth	flew through fog	filled with laughter
fasten both cuffs	if we both laugh	Fred's third birthday
four thick folds	firm healthy teeth	birth of the fourth child
five birthdays	refuse both offers	fill your mouth full
fill the bathtub	the Catholic faith	fun with both of them

D. When /θ/ occurs in a consonant cluster, it becomes more difficult to pronounce. As you practice the following words, be careful not to substitute /t/ for /θ/ or to omit /θ/.

fourth /rθ/	depth /pθ/	seventh /nθ/	anesthetic /sθ/
fourths /rθs/	depths /pθs/	sevenths /nθs/	anesthesia /sθ/
sixth /ksθ/	fifth /fθ/	ninth /nθ/	anesthetist /sθ/
sixths /ksθs/	fifths /fθs/	ninths /nθs/	esthetic /sθ/

E. Sentences for /θ/ and /ð/ practice.

1. We thought that Thelma had both of them.
2. The other theater is farther away than that one.
3. Arthur would rather take another path into town.
4. Mother was pathetic in her grief over that author's death.
5. My brother hasn't bothered to write during the last three months.
6. Is this thistle plant worth taking with us?
7. Thursday is the birthday of his other brother.
8. Neither of the themes is on the table.
9. Is Ithaca in the southern part of the state?
10. Tommy, hit the ball this time.

11. Thelma ordered thirteen tables this morning.
12. Throw the shells into the sea.
13. Toss this stick to the dog.
14. Take the dead stalks to the trash heap.
15. Father, take this to the door.
16. Mother wanted to telephone the weather bureau.
17. Can he breathe better without the tube?
18. Convert the fourths and the fifths into twentieths.

F. Reading selections for /θ/ and /ð/ practice.

1. There's a time for some things, and a time for all things; a time for great things, and a time for small things.

MIGUEL DE CERVANTES

2. Then darkness enveloped the whole American armada. Not a pin-point of light showed from those hundreds of ships as they surged on through the night toward their destiny, carrying across the ageless and indifferent sea tens of thousands of young men, fighting for . . . for . . . well, at least for each other.

ERNIE PYLE

3. Theology is but science of mind. As schools change, theology must necessarily change. Truth is everlasting, but our ideas of truth are not. Theology is but our ideas of truth classified and arranged.

HENRY WARD BEECHER

4. Many thoughts are so dependent upon the language in which they are clothed that they would lose half their beauty if otherwise expressed.

JOHN RUSKIN

5. Whatever is worth doing at all is worth doing thoroughly.

LORD CHESTERFIELD

6.   Three silences there are: the first of speech,
          The second of desire, the third of thought.

HENRY WADSWORTH LONGFELLOW

7. To have a thing is nothing, if you've not the chance to show it,
   And to know a thing is nothing, unless others know you know it.

LORD NANCY

8. They come to see; they come that they themselves may be seen.

OVID

9. In order that people may be happy in their work, these three things are needed: They must be for it. They must not do too much of it. And they must have a sense of success in it.

    JOHN RUSKIN

10. If you give to a thief he cannot steal from you, and he is then no longer a thief.

    WILLIAM SAROYAN

11. There is nothing either good or bad, but thinking makes it so.

    WILLIAM SHAKESPEARE

12. Women upset everything. When you let them into your life, you find that the woman is driving at one thing and you're driving at another.

    GEORGE BERNARD SHAW

/s/ as in **sit**
/z/ as in **zoo**

S

Z

Spellings of /s/: s as in **sit**; c as in **city**; sc as in **science**; x /ks/ as in **box**.

Spellings of /z/: z as in **zoo**; zz as in **buzz**; s as in **has, dogs**; x as in **xylophone**; x /gz/ as in **exist**.

Description of /s/ and /z/: These two cognates are blade-alveolar fricatives. /s/ is voiceless; /z/ is voiced. The sides of the tongue are in continuous contact with the inside surfaces of the upper back teeth. The blade of the tongue is in contact with the alveolar ridge except for a small V-shaped groove along the midline of the tongue. No breath escapes except through this closely constricted, narrow groove in the tongue blade. As the breath is forced through this narrow groove under great pressure and strikes the upper edges of the lower front teeth, it produces the sound of friction. The tip of the tongue may be lowered or raised but must not touch the upper teeth or hard palate.

Alternate Correct Pronunciations: In the three words **blouse, grease** (verb), and **greasy,** either /s/ or /z/ is correct. /s/ is more widely used in these words, while /z/ is common chiefly in the Southern dialect.

EXERCISES

A. The **s** spelling of /z/ causes confusion in pronunciation. Applying certain established rules of pronunciation will resolve some of the confusion.

(1) When an **s**-ending is added to a verb (**takes, begs, buys**) or to a noun

(**hats, beds, bees, Jeff's, Tom's, Joe's**), the **s** is pronounced /s/ if the immediately preceding sound in that word is a voiceless consonant (/k/ in **takes**, /t/ in **hats**, /f/ in **Jeff's**). If the sound immediately preceding the s-ending is a voiced sound, either a vowel (/aɪ/ in **buys**, /i/ in **bees**, /o/ in **Joe's**) or a voiced consonant (/g/ in **begs**, /d/ in **beds**, /m/ in **Tom's**), then the **s** is pronounced as a /z/.

Verbs			*Noun Plurals and Possessives*		
/s/	/z/	/z/	/s/	/z/	/z/
breaks	calls	catches	banks	cars	boy's
hits	cares	judges	brakes	rugs	child's
jumps	comes	passes	maps	shoes	dog's
leaks	goes	misses	rats	horses	Alice's
laughs	loves	rises	Pat's	houses [6]	Gregg's
shuts	rubs	rushes	Dick's	pages	Joe's
winks	runs	seizes	Hope's	matches	Tom's

(2) In pairs of words like the following which are spelled alike, or essentially alike, the one which is a verb will be pronounced with /z/, while the one which is a noun or an adjective will be pronounced with /s/.

/s/	/z/	/s/	/z/
abuse (n.)	abuse (v.)	excuse (n.)	excuse (v.)
advice (n.)	advise (v.)	house (n.)	house (v.)
close (a.)	close (v.)	misuse (n.)	misuse (v.)
device (n.)	devise (v.)	spouse (n.)	espouse (v.)
diffuse (a.)	diffuse (v.)	use (n.)	use (v.)

B. Foreign students are likely to confuse /s/ and /z/ in almost any word, because the spelling does not indicate which phoneme should be used.
  (1) Note particularly that /z/ ends each of the following common words. Practice them until the pronunciations are memorized.

is	does	because	hers	yours	these
has	was	his	ours	theirs	those

  (2) Practice distinguishing between /s/ and /z/ in the following pairs of words. Remember that /s/ is voiceless, /z/ voiced. Remember, too, that the vowel sound preceding /s/ should be cut shorter than that preceding /z/.

---

[6] The medial /z/ in **houses** /hauzɪz/ is exceptional, because the final /s/ of the singular **house** changes to /z/ when the plural suffix is added.

/s/	/z/	/s/	/z/	/s/	/z/
accurse	occurs	dose	doze	niece	knees
averse	avers	face	phase	pace	pays
base	bays	fleece	flees	peace	peas
bus	buzz	fuss	fuzz	place	plays
cease	seize	hearse	hers	price	prize
deceased	diseased	ice	eyes	purse	purrs
decrease	decrees	lace	lays	rice	rise
dice	dies	lice	lies	sparse	spars
displace	displays	loose	lose	spice	spies

C. If /s/ is too prolonged, or has a whistling sound (like a doorman's whistle to call a taxi), it is unpleasantly noticeable.

  (1) If /s/ is too noticeable in your speech, not because you articulate it poorly but because there is too much of it, you should practice cutting /s/ shorter in duration. To reduce the length of initial /s/, practice "rushing through" the /s/ to accentuate the vowel which follows. Practice: **sigh** /saɪ/, **sew** /so/, **see** /si/, **say** /se/. To reduce the prominence of final /s/, cut it off sooner like this: **ice** /aɪs/, **race** /res/, **lease** /lis/, **loss** /lɔs/, **loose** /lus/.

  (2) For a whistling /s/ the remedy will likely be found in changing the articulation. The whistle is frequently caused by pointing the tongue tip upward too sharply for /s/. Experiment with forming /s/ while holding the tongue tip down behind the lower front teeth. Try shifting the lower jaw forward until the edges of the upper and lower front teeth come together as they would if you were biting a thread in two. Most important, if you simply hiss as you experiment with the positioning of tongue and jaw, listening carefully to the sound of the hissing, you should discover an articulatory adjustment which produces a satisfactory /s/. When you discover a good /s/ articulation, carefully reproduce that variety of /s/ in practicing the words **see, say, sigh, sew, sue.** Repeat these words several times in succession, at frequent intervals during the day, until you can reliably produce a clear /s/ without a whistle. Then practice any words in which /s/ occurs, carefully monitoring the sound of /s/ and your articulation of it.

D. A frontal lisp is the substitution of /θ/ for /s/ and /ð/ for /z/. Instead of touching the blade of the tongue to the alveolar ridge to articulate /s/ and /z/, the frontal lisper touches the tip of his tongue to his upper front teeth, producing /θ/ and /ð/.

  (1) Bite your upper front teeth against your lower front teeth edge-to-edge, as if you were biting a piece of thread or a fingernail. Hiss between your teeth /sssss/. Usually, without trying to relocate your

tongue articulation, this device will produce a clear, sharp /s/. You might have had to shift your lower jaw forward slightly to bring your lower teeth out even with your upper teeth. If so, observe this jaw shift as part of your necessary articulation of /s/. Practice the same technique to achieve a clear /z/ sound.

(2) If you did not get a clear /s/ by bringing the edges of your front teeth together, then try this: say **yes** several times, keeping your tongue in the same shape throughout the word. This means that you will be making /s/ with the tip of the tongue held *down* behind the lower front teeth instead of lifting it. It will force you to articulate /s/ with the blade of the tongue. Watch your articulation in a mirror. Be sure that your tongue does not bulge too far forward (against your teeth). Now repeat **yes** several times, prolonging the final /s/, as /jessss/. Listen carefully to the /s/, to be sure you produce a sharp clear /s/. Repeat the word **is**, prolonging the final /z/, as /ɪzzzz/. Listen to the /z/ to make sure that it is sharp and clear.

(3) When you can produce /s/ and /z/ reliably in isolation, as /ssss/ and /zzzz/, you are ready to combine them with vowels. Practice first the words having /s/ and /z/ in the final position, next those in initial position, and then the ones in medial position.

Final /s/	Initial /s/	Medial /s/	Final /z/	Initial and medial /z/
peace	see	piecing	bees	zero
miss	sip	missing	whiz	zeal
pace	say	pacing	pays	zip
yes	sell	blessing	has	zone
mass	sap	passing	buzz	zoo
bus	supper	fussing	pause	easy
boss	sought	bossing	pose	busy
use (n.)	sew	closer	use (v.)	lazy
ice	sue	looser	wise	buzzing
house	sigh	icing	bows	music

(4) Negative practice is necessary to reinforce the distinction between /θ/ and /s/ and between /ð/ and /z/. Pronounce the following words in pairs, contrasting /θ/ with /s/ and /ð/ with /z/.

/θ/	/s/		/ð/	/z/
bath	bass		bathe	bays
Beth	Bess		breathe	breeze
moth	moss		lathe	lays
myth	miss		lithe	lies
path	pass		seethe	seize

thank	sank	clothing	closing
theme	seem	teething	teasing
thick	sick	withered	wizard
thought	sought	writhing	rising

(5) After you master the /s/ and /z/ occurring next to a vowel, practice words containing /s/ in consonant clusters.

Initial		*Medial*		*Final*	
speak	school	also	instant	dance	hopes
spoon	skip	blister	lipstick	laughs	hats
sweet	stand	blissful	pastry	mix /ks/	facts
swell	stop	risky	whisper	pulse	disrupts

(6) Your most severe test of /s/ and /z/ will occur in phrases which also contain /θ/ and /ð/. Practice the following phrases slowly at first for accuracy. Then gradually assume a normal rate when you can do so without sacrificing accuracy.

the seventh	this easy theme	has the same thing
both sisters	those are the ways	six birthdays
sing the song	is this Thursday?	sell those stocks

E. A lateral lisp distorts /s/ and /z/ by articulating them like /l/. Instead of directing the breath stream from the front of the mouth, the lateral lisper touches his tongue tip firmly to the alveolar ridge and lowers the sides of his tongue (or only one side) to emit the breath stream between the sides of the tongue and the back teeth. A lateral lisp sounds less distinct and sharp than a normal /s/, and even sounds "slushy" at times when breath passes over saliva which has collected in the cheek. Besides sounding distorted, a lateral lisp looks bizarre, because it usually involves drawing the corners of the mouth far back to allow the breath to escape from the side of the mouth.

The goal in practice is to lift the sides of the tongue to make a firm contact against the inner surfaces of the back teeth, to prevent lateral emission of air, and to direct the air out of the front of the mouth.

(1) For the tactile sensation of lifting the sides of the tongue, repeat **tea** several times. Do you feel the sides of the tongue touching gum tissue or the inner surfaces of your jaw teeth? Now repeat **eat** several times, giving attention again to the feeling of firm contact of the sides of the tongue. Next, repeat **eats** several times, being careful to keep the sides of the tongue lifted for the /s/ just as for the /t/. Repeat each of the following lines several times, to experience the tactile sensation of closing the space at the sides of the tongue for /s/, and to hear the sharp "hissy" quality of /s/ when emitted properly from the front of the mouth.

eat — eats — eats — eatsss — eatsss — ssss — ssss
hit — hits — hits — hitsss — hitsss — ssss — ssss
date — dates — dates — datesss — datesss — ssss — ssss
debt — debts — debts — debtsss — debtsss — ssss — ssss
toot — toots — toots — tootsss — tootsss — ssss — ssss
dote — dotes — dotes — dotesss — dotesss — ssss — ssss

(2) Practice lifting the sides of the tongue for /z/, just as you have for /s/. Repeat each of the following lines several times, to experience the tactile sensation of closing the space at the sides of the tongue for /z/, and to hear the sharp quality of a properly articulated /z/.

need — needs — needs — needsss — needsss — /zzz/ — /zzz/
bid — bids — bids — bidsss — bidsss — /zzz/ — /zzz/
Ted — Ted's — Ted's — Ted'sss — Ted'sss — /zzz/ — /zzz/
mood — moods — moods — moodsss — moodsss — /zzz/ — /zzz/
toad — toads — toads — toadsss — toadsss — /zzz/ — /zzz/

(3) If you still have difficulty preventing the escape of air from the sides of the tongue for /s/ and /z/, even in exercises (1) and (2) above, perhaps you need to "block" the air passage from the sides of the mouth. Try rounding your lips as you say the following words. If necessary, hold the corners of your mouth with your fingers to prevent their pulling back at the sides.

you — use /jus/ — /jus/ — /jusss/ — /jusss/ — /sss/ — /sss/
you — use /juz/ — /juz/ — /juzzz/ — /juzzz/ — /zzz/ — /zzz/
doe — dose /dos/ — /dos/ — /dosss/ — /dosss/ — /sss/ — /sss/
doe — doze /doz/ — /doz/ — /dozzz/ — /dozzz/ — /zzz/ — /zzz/

(4) Negative practice is imperative. You must develop auditory discrimination between your old defective /s/ and a properly articulated /s/, between your old defective /z/ and a properly articulated /z/. Say each of the following words two ways: first, as you habitually do, with a lateral lisp; second, exercise as much control as possible, keeping the sides of the tongue up and directing the air stream out of the front of your mouth. Listen to the /s/ or /z/ carefully, noting the fine differences in the sounds when produced incorrectly and when produced correctly. Learn to produce reliable /s/ and /z/ in one position before attempting it in another.

Final position

/s/	peace	miss	pace	mess	pass	muss	moose	dose	toss
/z/	peas	'tis	pays	fez	fuzz	dues	doze	pause	

Initial position

/s/ see sit say set sat sup sue sew saw sigh

/z/ "z" zip zany Zen zoo zone

Medial position

/s/ piecing missing pacing guessing passing fussing
deducing dosing bossing bison

/z/ easy crazy buzzing using cruising posing rising

(5) Practice /s/ and /z/ in consonant clusters, as in **speak, sweet, stop, takes, pants, dogs, bibs.** (You will find more of these words in Exercise D.5 above.) But you will be wise to gain reliable control of /s/ and /z/ articulation first in Exercise E.4 above. You will experience most difficulty controlling either /s/ or /z/ when /l/ occurs next to it, as in **sleep, pulse, also, asleep, this looks, will sit, pals, has looked,** because your articulation of /l/ will tend to draw your /s/ or /z/ back into the lateral lisp. Remember this: conscious attention to the feel of the correct tongue position, and to the sound of the /s/ or /z/ you produce, will enable you to control the articulation and eventually to make the correct articulation a habit.

F. Perhaps you have a distortion of /s/ and /z/ which fits none of the types described above. In order to correct your lisp, you need first to analyze what you are doing incorrectly and then to exercise conscious control in establishing a new articulation pattern to achieve a good sharp /s/ and /z/.

(1) Analyze your articulation, not only listening to your /s/ and /z/, but feeling where your articulators make contact, and observing (in a mirror) what you are doing to produce these phonemes.

   (a) Is your lower jaw pulled back so that your upper teeth overlap your lower teeth when you say [s] and [z]?

   (b) Is your tongue tip making contact with the alveolar ridge to constrict the breath passage? This is the same kind of articulation used for /θ/ and /ð/ except that the tongue tip is touching just a bit farther back (against gum tissue instead of teeth).

   (c) Is your lower lip pulled up to the edges of your upper teeth, as if you were making /f/ at the same time you made /s/ or making /v/ at the same time you made /z/?

(2) Can you discover a reason for your lisp? You may have some slightly atypical dental characteristic for which you have been attempting to compensate. Do you have wide spaces between your upper front teeth, or a missing tooth? Do you have an "overbite," with the upper teeth lapping quite far over the lower teeth when you close your jaw? Do you have an "underjet," with the lower teeth lapping over the upper ones when you close your jaw? Do you have an "open bite," so that when you close your jaw there is still a considerable space between the

edges of your upper and lower teeth? Are there spaces between your lower front teeth, or is a tooth missing? Any of these problems can make the production of a clear /s/ and /z/ something of a problem. In many cases, however, a satisfactory /s/ and /z/ can be produced in spite of dental irregularities, if the speaker is willing to do some careful experimenting and subsequent readjusting of his articulation.

(3) Experiment with producing /s/, and when you have discovered a satisfactory production, copy that same articulation for /z/. As you experiment, try to remember what a good /s/ sounds like. Compare your /s/ objectively with /s/ in the speech of other people around you. Here are some suggestions for controls of articulation which often improve the sound of /s/.

(a) Pull your lower lip down slightly, so that the top edges of your lower teeth are entirely visible when you make an /s/.

(b) If you can, bring the edges of your upper and lower front teeth together for /s/, as if you were biting a thread in two. Such a position may require you to shift your lower jaw forward if you have an overbite. If you have an underjet or an open bite, this may be impossible.

(c) Try articulating /s/ with the tip of the tongue held down behind the lower front teeth. In that position the tongue acts like a "slide" to direct the air stream downward across the top edges of your lower teeth. Remember that the cutting of the air stream across the edges of your lower teeth is what makes the characteristically sharp sound of /s/.

(d) If you have a space between your front teeth, either upper or lower, you might find it practical to "point" the air stream a little to the side of front, where you do have upper and lower teeth which can be touched edge-to-edge. This requires moving the tongue tip slightly to that side, but it is not impossible to do.

(4) Master /s/ and /z/ initially in a word first, because in the initial position you have more opportunity to exercise conscious control over the articulation. Practice "initial" position words for /s/ and /z/ from Section E.4 above. At first, prolong the /s/ or /z/ before pronouncing the rest of the word, to allow time to examine the quality of the consonant and to get your articulation adjusted satisfactorily. Then, when you are more confident of success, gradually speed up the /s/ or /z/ production. After mastering initial /s/ and /z/, practice them in final position, then in medial position, then in consonant clusters, and finally in phrases and sentences. (Practice exercises in Sections D.3, D.5, and E.4 above.)

G. Sentences for /s/ and /z/ practice.

1. My sister sat silently in the swing.
2. Sam said he had to sit there in the snow for six hours.

3. Susan always cleans the house on Saturdays.
4. Mrs. Pierce promised to bake some pies for us.
5. What a pleasant surprise Santa had for the kiddies on Christmas!
6. Southern resort clothes are often a foretaste of the best styles for the next summer.
7. Y plus or minus x equals zero.
8. Esther stood beside the stone steps of her house.
9. Sledding was excellent last week after the snow storm.
10. We stood in line for hours before being served at the restaurant.
11. The tired student stifled a yawn as he closed his books.
12. Did you stop at the STOP sign at the corner of State Street?
13. The story told of stirring adventure on the high seas.
14. The dog snarled when he saw the thief sneaking down the stairs.
15. Mr. Smith says that he plays the zither and the xylophone.
16. She says that the thistles are soft in the summertime.
17. His theme is due Thursday, and he hasn't even started it.

H. Reading selections for /s/ and /z/ practice.

1. No one means all he says, and yet very few say all they mean, for words are slippery and thought is viscous.

   HENRY BROOKS ADAMS

2. Private beneficence is totally inadequate to deal with the vast numbers of the city's disinherited.

   JANE ADDAMS

3. Beware lest you lose the substance by grasping at the shadow.

   AESOP

4.   I have known the silence of the stars and of the sea,
       And the silence of the city when it pauses . . .

   EDGAR LEE MASTERS

5. There are books of which the backs and covers are by far the best parts.

   CHARLES DICKENS

6. Secret, and self-contained, and solitary as an oyster.

   CHARLES DICKENS

7. He [Shakespeare] was the man who of all Modern, and perhaps Ancient Poets, had the largest and most comprehensive soul.

   JOHN DRYDEN

8. The sewing-circle — the Protestant confessional, where each one confesses, not her own sins, but the sins of her neighbors.

CHARLES B. FAIRBANKS

9. The true use of speech is not so much to express our wants as to conceal them.

OLIVER GOLDSMITH

10. In all societies it is advisable to associate if possible with the highest; not that the highest are always the best, but because, if disgusted there, we can at any time descend. But if we begin with the lowest, to ascend is impossible.

WALTER COLTON

11. A little inaccuracy sometimes saves tons of explanation.

H. H. MUNRO (SAKI)

12.   Men seldom make passes
             At girls who wear glasses.

DOROTHY PARKER

13. Simplicity is the straightforwardness of the soul which refuses itself any regard to itself or its deeds. This virtue differs from and surpasses sincerity. We see many people who are sincere without being simple.

FRANÇOIS FÉNELON

14.   *Hester's Sister Sally*

Hester Smith has a sister whose name is Sally. Sally works as a salesgirl on the first floor of Carson's store. She sells girls' stockings and socks. She said her sales last Saturday totalled six hundred seventy-six dollars and sixty-three cents. She expects to receive the exceptional salesgirl's prize this September. At Carson's they choose the salesgirl with the highest gross sales each month to receive this special salesmanship prize. Sally said she hopes this month's prize is a box of silk stockings because she needs some. Of course, when she buys stockings at Carson's, she gets a twenty per cent discount.

15.   *Cynthia's Zebra*

My sister Cynthia has a strange distinction. She has a pet zebra she calls Zanzibar. The zebra is spoiled but exceptionally smart. Cynthia has taught him tricks and has also taught him to speak like a person.

Everyone knows it is silly to say that a horse can speak, so of course, a zebra can't speak. But Zanzibar speaks distinctly. Cynthia gives him speech exercises from six to seven-thirty every day. Seldom has such an amazing zebra been seen. He is able to recite the soliloquy from Shakespeare's "A Midsummer-Night's Dream." Consequently, he has reached the heights of success. Cynthia has displayed the talents of Zanzibar in performances before audiences all over the United States. The sports section of the Sunday Sun-Times tells the story of Cynthia's zebra, Zanzibar.

/ʃ/ as in **she**
/ʒ/ as in **vision**

ʃ
ʒ

Spellings of /ʃ/: **sh** as in **she**; **si** as in **mansion**; **ssi** as in **mission**; **ss** as in **tissue**; **ci** as in **special**; **ti** as in **nation**; **ch** as in **chauffeur**.

Spellings of /ʒ/: **z** as in **azure**; **si** as in **vision**; **s** as in **measure**; **ge** as in **rouge**; **j** as in **Bijou**.

Description of /ʃ/ and /ʒ/: These two cognates are blade, pre-palatal fricatives. /ʃ/ is voiceless; /ʒ/ is voiced. The sides of the tongue are in continuous contact with the inside surfaces of the back teeth, and the blade of the tongue is in firm contact with the front part of the palate (just back of the alveolar ridge), except for a shallow groove along the midline of the tongue. As the breath is emitted through this constricted passageway at the midline of the tongue blade and strikes the cutting edges of the lower front teeth, a fricative sound is produced.

EXERCISES

A. A lisp of any variety may operate to distort the /ʃ/ and /ʒ/ phonemes. The same technique used to improve /s/ and /z/ may be applied to /ʃ/ and /ʒ/.

B. Some foreign students confuse /s/ with /ʃ/, and /z/ with /ʒ/. Others confuse /tʃ/ with /ʃ/ and /dʒ/ with /ʒ/. Practice the following sets of words to establish these contrasts.

/tʃ/	/ʃ/	/s/		/ʒ/	/z/		/ʒ/	/dʒ/
chew	shoe	sue		vision	visible		rouge	rage
chip	ship	sip		pleasure	pleasant		pleasure	pledging
cheap	sheep	seep		glazier	glazing		beige	page
match	mash	mass		usual	using		massage	message

C. Practice /ʃ/ in the following words.

Initial		Medial		Final	
shall	shoot	anxious	issue	ash	fresh
she	shop	condition	mission	cash	gnash
sheep	shout	confession	motion	clash	mash
sheer	show	direction	social	dash	vanish
sheet	shy	dishes	special	famish	varnish
shine	sugar	fashion	tissue	flash	wash
ship	sure	fishing	washer	flesh	wish

D. Note that **ch** represents /ʃ/ in certain words of French origin, as in the following words.

champagne	chaperone	chauffeur	chiffon	machine
chandelier	charades	Chicago	chivalrous	mustache

E. Final /ʒ/, which occurs in some words of French origin, is often confused with /dʒ/. Be sure that for /ʒ/ you do not feel tongue-tip contact, which occurs with /dʒ/. Pronounce the following words in pairs to differentiate between the final /ʒ/ and /dʒ/.

/ʒ/	/dʒ/	/ʒ/	/dʒ/	/ʒ/	/dʒ/
beige	page	barrage	lodge	massage	lodge
rouge	huge	garage	lodge	mirage	lodge

F. Practice medial /ʒ/ in the following words.

amnesia	conclusion	illusion	Persian	treasure
anesthesia	evasion	leisure	persuasion	usual
collision	hosiery	measure	pleasure	vision

G. Sentences for /ʃ/ and /ʒ/ practice.

1. She is anxious about the condition of her Chevrolet since the collision.
2. This fashion creation is appropriate for such a special occasion.
3. Surely the chauffeur wouldn't store the champagne in the garage.
4. Charlotte operates a machine at the Chicago Cash Box Company.
5. She has the notion that rouge creates the illusion of youthfulness.
6. What a pleasure it is to wash these sheer chiffon dresses!
7. Mrs. Shaw wishes to buy some hosiery in a greyish-beige shade.
8. She usually puts fresh fruit in this dish and sprinkles sugar on top.

H. Reading selections for /ʃ/ practice.

1. From *Word Power Made Easy*[7]

    To *condone* is to *forgive:* a *donation* is a *gift* — you can see the connection. *Condone* comes from the Latin verb *donare*, to give (as does *donation*); when you *condone* an act, you *give* freedom from punishment, almost mild approval, to the perpetrator of that antisocial act. Of course you only *condone* such actions as other people are likely to disapprove of.

    NORMAN LEWIS

2. Nicholas Chauvin,[7] soldier of the French Empire, so vociferously and unceasingly aired his veneration of Napoleon Bonapart that his name became the laughingstock of all Europe. Thereafter, an exaggerated and blatant patriot was known as a chauvinist — and still is today. . . .
    To be patriotic is to be normally proud of and devoted to one's country — to be chauvinistic is to carry such pride and devotion to an obnoxious and pathological point. . . .

    NORMAN LEWIS

3. Marriage resembles a pair of shears, so joined that they cannot be separated; often moving in opposite directions, yet always punishing anyone who comes between them.

    SYDNEY SMITH

4. The victory of socialism in Russia is not complete because the danger of intervention from capitalist countries continues.

    JOSEPH STALIN

5. The island of Sardinia, consisting chiefly of marshes and mountains, has from the earliest period to the present been cursed with a noxious air. . . . The convulsions produced by its poisonous plants gave rise to the expression of sardonic smile, which is as old as Homer (*Odyssey*, xx. 302).

    LORD MAHON

I. Reading selections for /ʒ/ practice.

1.   Rich the treasure,
                            Sweet the pleasure,
                            Sweet is pleasure after pain.

    JOHN DRYDEN

---

[7] From *Word Power Made Easy* by Norman Lewis. Copyright 1949 by Norman Lewis. Reprinted by permission of Doubleday & Company, Inc.

2. No man is happy without a delusion of some kind. Delusions are as necessary to our pleasures as realities.

BOVEE

3. Do you know that conversation is one of the greatest pleasures in life? But it wants leisure.

SOMERSET MAUGHAM

/tʃ/ as in **chew**
/dʒ/ as in **joke**

Spellings of /tʃ/: ch as in **chew**; **tch** as in **catch**; **ti** as in **question**; **t** as in **picture.**

Spellings of /dʒ/: j as in **joke**; **g** as in **gem**; **dj** as in **adjourn**; **ge** as in **college**; **dge** as in **edge**; **di** as in **soldier**.

Description of /tʃ/ and /dʒ/: These two cognates are tip and blade-alveolar affricates. /tʃ/ is voiceless; /dʒ/ is voiced. An affricate is a closely blended stop and fricative, occurring as a single phoneme. For /tʃ/ or /dʒ/ the tip and blade of the tongue first make firm contact with the alveolar ridge and the area just back of it, stopping the flow of breath; and then very rapidly the midline of the tongue is pulled downward slightly to form a shallow groove, through which the compressed breath is released with the sound of friction. The sides of the tongue maintain contact with the inner surfaces of back teeth to prevent lateral emission of breath.

EXERCISES

A. A speaker who lisps on /s/ and /z/ might also lisp on /tʃ/ and /dʒ/ with a similar type of distortion. The same general technique used for correcting a faulty articulation of /s/ will probably be effective for improving a faulty /tʃ/ and /dʒ/.
B. Substitution of /ts/ for /tʃ/ and of /dz/ for /dʒ/ is an error some foreigners make. To develop an awareness of the difference between /ts/ and /tʃ/, and between /dz/ and /dʒ/, contrast the following pairs of words.

/ts/	/tʃ/	/dz/	/dʒ/
arts	arch	aids	age
cats	catch	raids	rage
watts	watch	wades	wage
wits	witch	weds	wedge

C. Foreigners of Scandinavian language backgrounds are likely to substitute /ʃ/ for /tʃ/ and /j/ for /dʒ/. To distinguish between these pairs of phonemes, practice the following word pairs.

/ʃ/	/tʃ/		/ʃ/	/tʃ/		/j/	/dʒ/
cash	catch		sheet	cheat		yell	jell
mash	match		ship	chip		yellow	Jello
share	chair		shoe	chew		yet	jet
sheep	cheap		shoes	choose		yoke	joke
she's	cheese		shop	chop		you	Jew

D. Some speakers who have no trouble pronouncing /tʃ/ in most positions find it difficult to pronounce /tʃ/ after another consonant. In the words listed below, /ʃ/ is often substituted for /tʃ/. This is partly a confusion in pronunciation, for it is difficult to identify the /tʃ/ sound in these spellings. The **tu** in these words, pronounced /tju/ a long time ago, gradually developed into /tʃu/. Additionally, the unstressed **ture** ending has been changed to /tʃɚ/. To help you with these pronunciations, each word is written in IPA alongside the regular spelling.

actual /ǽk-tʃu-əl/	fracture /frǽk-tʃɚ/	rapture /rǽp-tʃɚ/
capture /kǽp-tʃɚ/	lecture /lɛ́k-tʃɚ/	rupture /rʌ́p-tʃɚ/
factual /fǽk-tʃu-əl/	mixture /míks-tʃɚ/	scripture /skríp-tʃɚ/
fixture /fíks-tʃɚ/	picture /pík-tʃɚ/	texture /tɛ́ks-tʃɚ/

E. Unvoicing of final /dʒ/ changes it to /tʃ/. Contrast final /tʃ/ with /dʒ/ in the following pairs, listening both to the longer duration of the vowel before the /dʒ/ and to the voice accompanying /dʒ/.

/tʃ/	/dʒ/		/tʃ/	/dʒ/		/tʃ/	/dʒ/
batch	badge		larch	large		perch	purge
cinch	singe		leech	liege		rich	ridge
etch	edge		lunch	lunge		search	surge

F. Additional words for /tʃ/ practice.

chafe	champion	chastise	archbishop	catch	much
chain	chaplain	check	bachelor	church	peach
chalk	charge	cherry	preacher	hatch	reach
challenge	chase	chicken	teacher	lurch	which

G. Additional words for /dʒ/ practice.

gem	jaw	adjacent	courageous	age	judge
generous	jealous	adjourn	legislature	badge	page
genius	joke	adjustment	magic	cage	rage

gesticulate	journey	adjective	margin	damage	wage
gesture	just	collegiate	wager	edge	wedge

H. Sentences for /tʃ/ and /dʒ/ practice.

1. Judge James attended college in Georgetown.
2. The Jewish and Christian religions actually have much in common.
3. Jim journeyed to Natchez during the garden pilgrimage.
4. Catch the pitcher before it falls off the edge of the kitchen table.
5. The teacher touched the shoulder of each child who was to march to the gymnasium.
6. A picture of the Magi with Mary, Joseph, and the infant Jesus was featured on the front page of the journal.
7. James chose a watch with a jeweled band to give Janet.
8. Cheddar cheese has a rich, pungent flavor.

I. Reading selections for /tʃ/ practice.

1. Old men have need to touch sometimes with their lips the brow of a woman or the cheek of a child, that they may believe again in the freshness of life.

   MAURICE MAETERLINCK

2. The death of each day's life, sore labour's bath;
   Balm of hurt minds, great nature's second course,
   Chief nourisher in life's feast.

   WILLIAM SHAKESPEARE

3. The play's the thing
   Wherein I'll catch the conscience of the king.

   WILLIAM SHAKESPEARE

4. A good name is rather to be chosen than great riches.

   PROVERBS

5. To a mother, a child is everything; but to a child, a parent is only a link in the chain of her existence.

   LORD BEACONSFIELD

6. Consistency is a paste jewel that only cheap men cherish.

   WILLIAM ALLEN WHITE

J.   Reading selections for /dʒ/ practice.

1.   Books are the legacies that a great genius leaves to mankind, which are delivered down from generation to generation, as presents to the posterity of those yet unborn.

Joseph Addison

2.   Many religious people are deeply suspicious. They seem — for purely religious purposes, of course — to know more about iniquity than the Unregenerate.

Rudyard Kipling

3.   The magic of the tongue is the most dangerous of all spells.

Edward Bulwer-Lytton

4.   Those who compare the age in which their lot has fallen with a golden age which exists only in imagination, may talk of degeneracy and decay. . . .

Lord Macaulay

5.   Cauliflower is nothing but cabbage with a college education.

Mark Twain

6.   It is good to jest — to turn a joke — but not to make a trade of jesting.

Queen Elizabeth I

7.   The jewel, genius, is mainly energy.

Sir Thomas Browne

8.   Be just before you're generous.

Richard B. Sheridan

/p/ as in **pay**
/b/ as in **be**

p
b

Spellings of /p/: p as in **pay**; **pp** as in **dipping**; **gh** as in **hiccough**.

Spellings of /b/: b as in **robe**; **bb** as in **rubber**; **pb** as in **cupboard**.

Description of /p/ and /b/: These two cognates are bilabial stops. /p/ is voiceless; /b/ is voiced. The lips touch firmly together, stopping the flow of breath, which is compressed before its release. /p/ is more aspirate (breathy) and more energetic in articulation than /b/.

When /p/ or /b/ is followed by another stop consonant, the sound of the stop, but not an explosion, for /p/ or /b/ is heard; e.g., **cupcake, Bob took, jump down.** If the same stop consonant ends one word and begins the next, as in **hip pocket, grab bag,** the stop is prolonged (i.e., its release is delayed) rather than repeated.

EXERCISES

A. Omission of /b/ at the beginning of an unstressed syllable is a danger when it immediately follows an /m/, or when the preceding syllable contains either a /p/ or another /b/. Practice the following words, making sure you pronounce /b/ clearly.

capably	encumber	lumber	probably	remember
combination	encumbering	members	numbering	September
December	limber	membership	number	slumber

B. Changing the articulation of /p/ or /b/ to that of a following consonant is an unacceptable assimilation. The most common error of this kind affects /p/ or /b/ preceding /f/ or /v/, making /p/ and /b/ labiodental (lips touching teeth) [p] and [b̪] like the /f/ or /v/. A less common error (though not rare) involves changing /p/ to /t/ or /b/ to /d/ when the following consonant is a /t/, /d/, /s/, or /ʃ/. As you practice the following words and phrases, be sure that you articulate /p/ and /b/ with the lips touching together firmly.

/p/	/p/	/b/	/b/	/b/
cupcake	rope fell	obvious	subsidize	Bob fell
cupful	sip from	subversive	substance	cab full
hopefully	top value	subversion	substantiate	cab veered
optimum	stop fast	subdivide	subtract	rub firmly
upset	up front	subjective	substantial	robe fits
cap fits	wrap first	subscription	substitute	rub first
help find	clasp firmly	subsidiary	subterfuge	tub full

C. Foreigners often confuse /p/ and /b/. Initial /p/ particularly should be more aspirate (with greater breath emission) than /b/. Be sure that /p/ is voiceless and /b/ voiced, and that a vowel preceding /b/ is more prolonged than one preceding /p/. Contrast /p/ with /b/ in the following pairs.

/p/	/b/	/p/	/b/	/p/	/b/
pay	bay	pill	bill	lap	lab
pall	ball	pig	big	mop	mob
pear	bear	cup	cub	rip	rib

D. Some foreigners substitute a bilabial fricative for medial /b/. Native English speakers with careless articulation are likely to make this same error by incompletely closing the lips for medial /b/.

(1) Contrast /b/ with /v/ in the following pairs:

habit — have it   robing — roving   saber — saver

(2) Practice the following words, making the medial /b/ with firm lip closure.

baby	bobbing	hobnobbing	robber	rubber	stabbing
barber	flabby	obeying	robbing	rubbing	stubbing

E. Medial /p/ must be articulated with firm lip closure, or it reduces to a fricative sound. Practice the following words, giving special attention to firm lip closure for medial /p/.

dapper	dripping	helping	pepper	slipper	upper
dipper	gripping	hoping	popping	slipping	weeping
dipping	happy	paper	puppy	supper	wrapping

F. In your care to pronounce /p/ and /b/, bear in mind that **p** and **b** are sometimes correctly silent. Fortunately, there are rules governing such situations:

Silent **p** preceding **b** medially, e.g., **cupboard, clapboard.**
Silent **p** preceding **n** initially, e.g., **pneumatic, pneumonia.**
Silent **p** preceding **t** initially, e.g., **ptomaine.**
Silent **b** following **m** finally, e.g., **comb, dumb, lamb, limb, numb, womb.**
Silent **b** following **m** finally, even when a suffix is added, e.g., **plumber, combing.**

G. Sentences for /p/ and /b/ practice.

1. Bob is buying a pump to put in the basement.
2. Probably the boys upset that basket.
3. Obviously it would be better to lay a pipe beneath it.
4. Babies love to play with puppies.
5. A big black bear jumped into the pit.
6. Peter Piper picked a peck of pickled peppers.
7. Betty Brown bought a big pat of butter.
8. Papa was happy to sleep in the upper berth.
9. A substantial number of boys belong to boys' clubs.

H. Reading selections for /p/ and /b/ practice.

1. Power tends to corrupt; absolute power corrupts absolutely.

LORD ACTON

2. Papa, potatoes, poultry, prunes, and prism, are all very good words for the lips: especially prunes and prism.

CHARLES DICKENS

3. We have an innate propensity to get ourselves noticed, and noticed favorably, by our kind. No more fiendish punishment could be devised, were such a thing physically possible, than that one should be turned loose in society and remain absolutely unnoticed by all the members thereof.

WILLIAM JAMES

4. Beat an empty barrel with the handle of a broom,
    Hard as they were able,
    Boom, boom, Boom,
    With a silk umbrella and the handle of a broom,
    Boomlay, boomlay, boomlay, Boom.

VACHEL LINDSAY

5. The Puritan hated bear-baiting, not because it gave pain to the bear, but because it gave pleasure to the spectators.

LORD MACAULAY

6. Painting is silent poetry, and poetry is a speaking picture.

SIMONIDES

7. There was another little boy with whom I walked to school in the same fortuitous fellowship; a very prim and proper little boy, as became the son of the venerable and somewhat ponderous clergyman who held one of the highest scholastic posts in the school. He also was very neat, he also was quite an industrious pupil; and he also had a peculiarity. He was the most fertile, fluent and really disinterested liar I have ever had the pleasure of knowing.

G. K. CHESTERTON

8. There is no absurdity so palpable but that it may be firmly planted in the human head if you only begin to inculcate it before the age of five, by constantly repeating it with an air of great solemnity.

ARTHUR SCHOPENHAUER

/m/ as in **me**

m

Spellings of /m/: m as in **me**; **mb** as in **dumb**; **mn** as in **solemn**.

Description of /m/: This phoneme is a voiced, bilabial, nasal semi-vowel. The lips are closed firmly to prevent the passage of breath from the mouth. The velum is lowered to permit the breath to pass through the nasal cavity.

EXERCISES

A. Touch the lips firmly together to form /m/.

Initial		*Medial*		*Final*	
may	my	army	hammer	balm	name
me	mock	climbing	mama	calm	poem
mine	more	coming	summer	came	some

B. One of the most common errors with /m/ is the changing of its articulation to be like a consonant which follows it. The substitution for /m/ may take several forms, depending on the consonant to which /m/ is assimilated.

(1) The substitution of /n/ for /m/ is a danger when /m/ is final in a syllable or a word, and is followed by a consonant articulated with the tongue tip against the teeth or alveolar ridge. Practice the following words and phrases, giving special attention to articulating /m/ with contact of the two lips.

something	I'm discussing	I'm looking	I'm talking	I'm turning
sometimes	I'm doing	I'm not	I'm testing	some things
come through	I'm leaving	I'm taking	I'm through	some thoughts

(2) When an **ed** suffix is added to a verb which ends with /m/, there is a danger of substituting /n/ for /m/. In each of the following words, make a firm bilabial contact for /m/.

acclaimed	boomed	combed	exclaimed	named	roomed
aimed	calmed	creamed	flamed	proclaimed	seemed
beamed	chimed	declaimed	framed	rammed	shamed
bloomed	claimed	doomed	maimed	roamed	tamed

(3) When /m/ which ends a syllable or a word is followed by /f/ or /v/ at the beginning of the next syllable or word, there is danger of articulating the /m/ as [ɱ], with the lower lip against the upper teeth, like /f/ or

/v/. The labiodental [ɱ] [8] is an unacceptable assimilation. Maintain firm closure of the lips for /m/ in the following words and phrases.

comfort	come first	I'm finding	I'm very well	Tom fell
comfortable	I'm feeling	I'm frank	name four	warm fire
climb fast	I'm filling	I'm friendly	room full	warm friendship

(4) When /m/ is final in a word, and is followed by a word beginning with /k/ or /g/, the substitution of /ŋ/ for /m/ is a danger. Like /k/ and /g/, the /ŋ/ is formed by contact of the back of the tongue against the velum. In the following phrases, be careful to form /m/ with contact of the two lips.

come give	I'm cold	I'm covering	I'm giving	make him give
home cooking	I'm cooking	I'm keeping	I'm going	let him go

(5) When /m/ at the end of a syllable or word is followed by /s/, /ʃ/, /j/, /w/, or /ʍ/ at the beginning of the next syllable or word, the substitution of [ɲ] for /m/ sometimes occurs. ([ɲ] is a nasal continuant formed by contact of the tongue blade behind the alveolar ridge.) In the following words and phrases, be sure to produce /m/ by firm contact of the two lips.

clumsy	homespun	somewhat	themselves	I'm sure
himself	homework	somewhere	I'm saying	I'm using
homesick	someone	teamwork	I'm sick	I'm used to it

C. Sentences for /m/ practice.

1. Martha missed a number of meetings last summer.
2. Teamwork might improve the game.
3. My companions in the army are homesick for their mothers' home-cooking.
4. Chambray is more like gingham than homespun.
5. The plumber calmly moved the steampipe somewhere else.
6. Come look at something Jim did all by himself.
7. Are you comfortable by the warm fire?

D. Reading selections for /m/ practice.

1. Some of mankind's most terrible misdeeds have been committed under the spell of certain magic words or phrases.

                                        JAMES B. CONANT

---

[8] The [ɱ] symbol is used for the labiodental allophone of /m/ here (rather than [ɱ] which IPA uses), for conformity with other "dental" articulations of phonemes not normally articulated with teeth: [t̪], [d̪], [p̪], [b̪].

2. From *Word Power Made Easy* [9]

    When you call a man a monomaniac you imply that he carries his interest in some one thing to such a point that it scarcely makes sense. It may not be the same thing all his life or for any great length of time — but whatever it is, and for however long it engages his attention, nothing else in the world matters, and everything else in the world is subordinated to it.

    NORMAN LEWIS

3. How convenient it would be to many of our great men and great families of doubtful origin, could they have the privilege of the heroes of yore, who, whenever their origin was involved in obscurity, modestly announced themselves descended from a god.

    WASHINGTON IRVING

4. From *Word Power Made Easy* [9]

    Bloomers: Mrs. Elizabeth Smith Miller invented them in 1849, and showed a working model to a famous woman's rights advocate, Amelia J. Bloomer. Amelia was fascinated by the idea of garments that were both modest (they then reached right down to the ankles) and convenient — and promptly sponsored them. . . .

    NORMAN LEWIS

/ʍ/ as in **when**
/w/ as in **we**

Spelling of /ʍ/: wh as in **when.**

Spellings of /w/: w as in **we**; **u** as in **queer**; **o** /wə/ as in **one.**

Description of /ʍ/ and /w/: These two cognates have dual articulation: lip-rounded and back-velar, glide semi-vowels. /w/ is voiced; /ʍ/ is voiceless, with some friction component. These phonemes are called glides because the articulators are in motion during their formation. The back of the tongue is raised high toward the palate, with the lips rounded as for the vowel phoneme /u/; then there is a rapid shift or glide from this position to the articulation of whichever vowel phoneme follows. These two phonemes occur only preceding a vowel sound.

---

[9] From *Word Power Made Easy* by Norman Lewis. Copyright 1949 by Norman Lewis. Reprinted by permission of Doubleday & Company, Inc.

EXERCISES

A. In the speech of many individuals the /ʍ/ phoneme is not differentiated, and in some dialect areas the substitution of /w/ for /ʍ/ is not considered confusing or objectionable. If you have difficulty producing /ʍ/, here is a suggestion for overcoming it. Form the articulation of /w/ and blow breath from the rounded lips at the start of the syllable. You may hear /ʍ/ as /hw/, or you may hear it as a voiceless /w/ with some friction noise as the breath passes from the lips.

(1) Contrast /w/ with /ʍ/ in the following pairs of words.

way — whey	weather — whether	wine — whine
weal — wheel	were — whir	witch — which
wear — where	wet — whet	Y — why

(2) Practice these words for the /ʍ/ sound.

anywhere	somewhere	whale	wheat	while	whisper
nowhere	whack	what	when	whiskers	whistle

B. Some foreigners confuse /w/ with /v/ (a labiodental fricative), in some cases using a bilabial fricative (articulated like a /b/) for both /w/ and /v/. Practice the following pairs of words to establish a clear contrast between lip-rounded /w/ and labiodental /v/.

wail — veil	weal — veal	west — vest
wane — vane	wend — vend	worse — verse
wary — very	went — vent	wine — vine

C. For those foreigners who have not acquired the /w/ phoneme, it will be helpful to pronounce /u/ with very tense articulation as the beginning of the /w/ glide. As you learn to hear the /w/ glide as the transition between /u/ and another vowel, you can gradually reduce the duration of /u/, leaving only the /w/ glide as the initial consonant of the word. Practice the following words with initial /w/.

one	water	wear	went	wild	wise
once	wave	weave	west	will	won't
waste	wax	web	wet	wind	wood
wait	way	wedding	wicked	wine	wool
wash	weak	weed	wide	wing	word
watch	wealth	well	wiggle	wink	work

D. The tendency to relax the articulation of /w/ occurs chiefly in the word *forward* and in initial /kw/ clusters. Pronounce the following words with special care in rounding the lips for /w/.

forward	qualify	quarantine	quartz	question	quip
quack	quality	quarrel	quaver	quick	quirk
quail	qualms	quarry	queen	quiet	quit
quaint	quandary	quart	queer	quilt	quiver
quake	quantity	quarter	quench	quinine	quote

E. It is as important to know when *not* to pronounce /w/ and /ʍ/ as when *to* pronounce them.

    (1) **wh** represents /h/, not /ʍ/, in **who, whose, whom, whole.**

    (2) **w** is silent in **toward** /tord/ and **answer.**

    (3) Initial **w** before **r** is always silent, as in **write, wreck, wrench, wrestle, wretched, wring, wrist, wrap, wreath, wrong.**

    (4) Final /w/ does not exist in English. In **window, yellow, below,** the **ow** spells the vowel /o/. In **how, now, cow,** the **ow** spells the diphthong /aʊ/.

F. Sentences for /ʍ/ and /w/ practice.

    1. Why does Miss Watson wear white everywhere she goes?

    2. Walter wanted to know whether the weather had improved.

    3. I wonder if wheat is grown anywhere in West Virginia.

    4. Will the tire wear worse on the right wheel or on the left wheel?

    5. We are waiting for some water to wash these white woolens.

    6. Lord Whiteside went somewhere out West on a quest for the queen.

    7. Which one of these queer questions will you answer?

G. Reading selections for /ʍ/ practice.

1.
        Oh, what a tangled web we weave,
        When first we practise to deceive!

              Sᴛʀ Wᴀʟᴛᴇʀ Sᴄᴏᴛᴛ

2.
        What's in a name? That which we call a rose
        By any other name would smell as sweet.

              Wɪʟʟɪᴀᴍ Sʜᴀᴋᴇsᴘᴇᴀʀᴇ

3.
        What will you say when the world is dying?
        What, when the last wild midnight falls.

              Aʟғʀᴇᴅ Nᴏʏᴇs

4.
        Every why hath a wherefore.

              Wɪʟʟɪᴀᴍ Sʜᴀᴋᴇsᴘᴇᴀʀᴇ

H. Reading selections for /w/ practice.

1.   Men must work, and women must weep.

CHARLES KINGSLEY

2.   But war's a game, which, were their subjects wise,
      Kings would not play at.

WILLIAM COWPER

3. If I am not worth the wooing, I surely am not worth the winning.

HENRY W. LONGFELLOW

4.   Make us a wind
      To shake the world out of this sleepy sickness
      Where flesh has dwindled and brightness waned! . . .

CECIL DAY LEWIS

5.   A boy's will is the wind's will.

HENRY W. LONGFELLOW

6.   No man is born into the world whose work
      Is not born with him; there is always work,
      And tools to work withal, for those who will; . . .

JAMES RUSSELL LOWELL

f
v

/f/ as in **fill**
/v/ as in **van**

Spellings of /f/: f as in **fill**; **ff** as in **off**; **ph** as in **phase**; **gh** as in **cough**.

Spellings of /v/: **v** as in **very**, **love**; **f** as in **of**; **ph** as in **Stephen**.

Description of /f/ and /v/: These two cognates are labiodental fricatives. /f/ is voiceless; /v/ is voiced. Normally, the articulation is a light contact between the lower lip and the edges of the upper teeth, so that the breath stream is forced through this constricted slit, resulting in the sound of friction.

EXERCISES

A. A common careless error is to omit the /v/ from the preposition **of** when the word it precedes begins with a consonant. At the fast rate a preposition is normally spoken, a speaker tends to drop the /v/ from **of** because he is anticipating the articulation required for the consonant at the start of the next word. This is another unacceptable assimilation of consonants. Practice the following phrases, at first slowly and then at normal rate, giving attention to the sound of /v/ and the feel of the lower lip touching the upper teeth to form the /v/ in **of**.

bag of beans	dish of fruit	half of those	pair of shoes
bag of candy	fact of the matter	handle of the ax	pair of slippers
bag of dates	field of clover	head of the class	pile of leaves
bag of prunes	flock of geese	Jack of Clubs	pound of steak
bag of sand	front of the house	land of lakes	seat of the car
book of notes	full of flowers	line of cars	sheaf of papers
box of pins	full of grease	loaf of bread	stack of letters
box of salt	game of darts	lots of clothes	think of me
box of things	gang of boys	lots of reasons	thought of one
box of toys	glass of milk	lots of talking	thought of you
can of worms	group of friends	lots of time	tired of dusting
cause of the trouble	group of girls	package of figs	top of the building

B. Any /v/ occurring in a final position in a syllable or word is subject to unacceptable assimilation to the consonant which begins the next syllable or word. Usually the error is an omission of /v/. If the next consonant after the /v/ is /m/, /p/, or /b/, the /v/ often changes to a /b/, which has bilabial articulation like /m/, /p/, and /b/. Practice each of the following words and phrases, at first slowly and then at normal rate, giving careful attention to the sound of /v/ and to its lip-to-teeth articulation.

bereavement	five men	have more	leave this
evening	five months	have my	leave me
improvement	five more	I've come	love me
involvement	five pounds	I've decided	relieve me
pavement	five times	I've delivered	save money
believe me	give me	I've done	save more
five buttons	give you	I've dressed	they've begun
five children	have made	I've practiced	they've gone
five days	have many	I've thought	they've started
five dollars	have mentioned	I've told	they've taken

C. Some foreigners confuse /f/ and /v/. If this is your problem, practice the following pairs of words to contrast /f/ and /v/. Remember to make /f/

voiceless and /v/ voiced. Also, remember that the vowel should be longer in duration preceding a final /v/ than before a final /f/.

Initial		Medial		Final	
/f/	/v/	/f/	/v/	/f/	/v/
face	vase	define	divine	calf	calve
fast	vast	infest	invest	grief	grieve
fan	van	raffle	ravel	half	have
fail	veil	reference	reverence	leaf	leave
feel	veal	refuse	reviews	life	live
few	view	rifle	rival	plaintiff	plaintive
file	vile	shuffle	shovel	safe	save
fine	vine	sniffle	snivel	shelf	shelve
foil	voile	surface	service	surf	serve
folly	volley	wafer	waiver	waif	wave

D. If you have difficulty distinguishing between /v/ and /w/, refer to Exercise B, p. 316.

E. Some speakers, either because of careless articulation or because of the influence of some other language on their pronunciation of English, articulate /f/ and /v/ as bilabial fricatives (with the air passing between the slit formed by contact of the lips). Practice the following words, giving special attention to the articulation of lower lip against upper teeth.

/f/

fill	phase	baffle	definition	if	off
fine	pheasant	coffee	difference	graph	puff
food	physical	defend	diphthong	laugh	rough
forget	physics	deference	diphtheria	life	tough

/v/

vacant	veteran	avoid	heavy	above	love
vague	victim	driver	Heaven	behave	move
varnish	vivid	ever	never	forgive	prove
very	vowel	giving	seven	have	starve

F. Sentences for /f/ and /v/ practice.

1. I forgot to give David some coffee.
2. Have very many offers been made?
3. Stephen avoided having himself photographed on his vacation.
4. I never saw a finer finish on furniture.
5. You will have to move over before you jump off the platform.

6. The Governor was afraid of subversive elements in the government.

7. The pavement on Seventh Avenue is very rough.

G. Reading selections for /f/ and /v/ practice.

1. The first and worst of all frauds is to cheat Oneself.

PHILIP J. BAILEY

2. In Franklin Roosevelt there died the greatest American friend we have ever known — and the greatest champion of freedom who has ever brought help and comfort from the new world to the old.

WINSTON CHURCHILL

3. I love Vermont because of her hills and valleys, her scenery and invigorating climate, but most of all because of her indomitable people. They are a race of pioneers who have almost beggared themselves to serve others. If the spirit of liberty should vanish in other parts of our Union . . . it could all be replenished from the generous store held by the people of this brave little State of Vermont.

CALVIN COOLIDGE

4. Within him, as he hurled himself forward, was born a love, a despairing fondness for this flag which was near him. It was a creation of beauty and invulnerability.

STEPHEN CRANE

5. Four freedoms: The first is freedom of speech and expression — everywhere in the world. The second is freedom of every person to worship God in his own way, everywhere in the world. The third is freedom from want . . . everywhere in the world. The fourth is freedom from fear . . . anywhere in the world.

FRANKLIN D. ROOSEVELT

6. 　　　The gift without the giver is bare;
　　　Who gives himself with his alms feeds three, —
　　　Himself, his hungering neighbor, and me.

JAMES RUSSELL LOWELL

7. Failure is more frequently from want of energy than from want of capital.

DANIEL WEBSTER

8. Provided a man is not mad, he can be cured of every folly but vanity.

JEAN JACQUES ROUSSEAU

9.   At thirty, man suspects himself a fool;
       Knows it at forty, and reforms his plan;
       At fifty chides his infamous delay,
       Pushes his prudent purpose to resolve;
       In all the magnanimity of thought
       Resolves, and re-resolves; then dies the same.

                                        EDWARD YOUNG

10. To everything there is a season, and a time to every purpose under the
     heaven.

                                        ECCLESIASTES

k
g

/k/ as in **key**
/g/ as in **go**

Spellings of /k/: k as in **key**; **c** as in **cow**; **ck** as in **sack**; **cc** as in **tobacco**; **ch** as in **echo**; **q** as in **quick**; **que** as in **clique**; **x** /ks/ as in **box**.

Spellings of /g/: g as in **go**; **gg** as in **egg**; **gh** as in **ghost**; **gue** as in **rogue**; **x** /gz/ as in **exact**.

Description of /k/ and /g/: These two cognates are back-velar stops. /k/ is voiceless; /g/ is voiced. The back of the tongue makes firm contact with the velum to stop the breath stream momentarily while breath pressure is built up and then suddenly released in a puff or explosion. /k/ is more aspirate and has a more energetic articulation than /g/.

When another stop consonant follows /k/ or /g/, the arrest of breath for /k/ or /g/, but not an explosion, is heard; e.g., **work day, big dogs.** If the same stop consonant ends one word and begins the next, as in **make cookies** and **big game**, the stop consonant is prolonged rather than repeated.

EXERCISES

A. Be sure that your articulation of /k/ and /g/ is a *firm* contact of the back of the tongue and the velum. Careless speakers tend to articulate medial /k/ and /g/ inadequately, with the result that they are changed from stop consonants to fricatives. Practice the following words with firm contact in articulating /k/ and /g/.

Medial /k/

aching	chicken	knocking	packing	rocky	shocking
attacking	cookie	locker	picking	taking	wicked
backing	docking	locking	rocker	talkative	worker
blocking	kicking	lucky	rocking	talking	working

Medial /g/

again	begin	foggy	jagged	nagging	rugged
ago	bigger	gagging	jigger	nugget	sagging
baggage	buggy	haggle	lagging	ragged	tugging
begging	digging	hugging	luggage	rigging	wiggle

B. Foreign students may sometimes confuse /k/ and /g/. If you have this problem, practice the following pairs of words, making /k/ voiceless and /g/ voiced, remembering, too, to make the vowel longer in duration before /g/ than before /k/.

Initial	*Medial*	*Final*
/k/ — /g/	/k/ — /g/	/k/ — /g/
came — game	backing — bagging	caulk — cog
card — guard	bicker — bigger	duck — dug
cash — gash	hackle — haggle	leak — league
come — gum	lacking — lagging	peck — peg
could — good	sacking — sagging	pick — pig
curl — girl	tucking — tugging	pluck — plug

C. Various spellings of /k/ occur in the following words for practice.

k /k/	**c** /k/	**ch** /k/	**ch** /k/	**q** /k/	**ck** /k/
keen	cabinet	archangel	choreography	brusque	attack
keep	cadence	archeology	chorus	grotesque	block
key	calendar	architect	chloride	picturesque	clock
kind	caliber	archives	chlorine	quarrel	kick
kitten	can	chaos	chloroform	quick	package
strike	come	character	echo	quality	rock
talk	doctor	chasm	epoch	quantity	sick
took	lecture	choir	monarchy	quarry	ticket
worker	picture	chord	patriarch	quarter	wicker

D. When another stop consonant follows a /k/ or a /g/, as in **backed** /bækt/ or **begged** /bɛgd/, the /k/ or /g/ sounds different than when final, as in **back** or **beg**. For a final /k/ or /g/ there is usually a sound of the breath "exploding" in a little puff when it is released. For the /k/ in **backed**, the breath is stopped by the contact of the back of the tongue touching the velum and is compressed; then, before the /k/ articulation is released, the /t/ is articulated with the tongue tip touching the alveolar ridge, and the breath which was "dammed up" for /k/ is transferred to the space which is now stopped off for the /t/. There is no sound of breath "explosion" following the /k/ in /kt/. For the /gd/ in **begged** the same process occurs, and there is no sound of breath release after the /g/.

As you pronounce the following words with final /kt/ and /gd/ clusters, be aware of the feeling of the tongue touching first in the back for /k/ or /g/ and then at the tip for /t/ or /d/, with no release of breath between.

/kt/	/kt/	/kt/	/kt/	/gd/	/gd/
act	detect	liked	rocked	bagged	lagged
affect	elect	locked	soaked	begged	nagged
backed	exact	looked	talked	flagged	rigged
choked	expect	packed	walked	gagged	sagged
compact	fact	react	worked	hugged	tagged
contact	leaked	reject	wrecked	jogged	wagged

E. When /k/ or /g/ is final in a word, and the next word in the phrase begins with a consonant, there is a temptation to articulate /k/ or /g/ like the consonant which follows. In the phrases below, just as in the words in Section D, you should feel the back of the tongue make contact for /k/ or /g/ and then make contact for the next consonant before releasing the /k/ or /g/. There should not be a puff of breath released after the /k/ or /g/. Be careful not to substitute /p/ for /k/ or /b/ for /g/.

back porch	black board	pick berries
bake bread	black blouse	stick bent
bag broke	black puppy	take back
beg Mother	chalk broke	walk by
big baby	pack melons	walk past

F. The cc spelling in the following words represents /ks/ pronunciation. As you pronounce these words, be sure that the /k/ is not omitted.

accept	accelerate	accessory	accent	acceptance	accession
acceptable	accelerator	accede	accentuate	access	accident

G. When a word ends in /sk/, /skt/ or /sks/, there is a temptation to omit the /k/. As you practice the following words, make sure of the /k/ pronunciation, both by its sound and the tactile sensation of its articulation.

ask	basked	desk	flask	risk	tasks
asked	basks	desks	flasks	risked	tusk
asks	cask	disc	husk	risks	tusks
bask	casks	discs	husks	task	whisk

H. The x spelling often causes confusion in pronunciation. Fortunately, there is a practical rule to guide your pronunciation.

   (1) If a vowel sound immediately following the x is stressed (accented), the x has a voiced pronunciation, usually /gz/. (When a silent h follows the x, the next sound is the following vowel.) Words in this list are pronounced with /gz/.

					Silent *h*
exact	examination	executive	exertion	exuberant	exhaust
exactly	examine	exemplary	exist	exuberance	exhibit
exaggerate	example	exempt	existence	exult	exhilarate
exalt	exasperate	exert	exotic	exultant	exhort

(2) When **x** occurs in a final position, or a pronounced consonant follows the **x**, or the stress is on any vowel except the one immediately following the **x**, the **x** has a voiceless pronunciation, usually /ks/. The following words are pronounced with /ks/.

ax	except	exclamation	expand	explain	extend
box	exception	exclude	expatriate	explanation	extenuating
fix	excerpt	excuse	expect	explode	external
fox	excess	execute	expediency	exploit	extinct
mix	exchange	exercise	expedition	explosion	extinguish
wax	excise	exhale	expel	export	extort
excavate	excite	exhume	expendable	exposition	extra
exceed	excitable	exigency	expensive	express	extraneous
excel	excitement	exit	experience	exquisite	extraordinary
excellent	exclaim	exodus	experiment	extemporaneous	extravagant

(3) **Luxury** /lə́kʃəri/ and **anxious** /ǽŋkʃəs/ have voiceless pronunciation of **x** like the words in Section 2. **Luxurious** /ləgʒúrɪəs/ and **anxiety** /æŋzáɪəti/ have voiced pronunciation of **x** like the words in Section 1.

I. The **ng** spelling, as in **sing** and **singing**, represents the back-velar nasal consonant /ŋ/ alone, without the sound of /g/. But /g/ should be pronounced after /ŋ/ when the **ng** occurs medially in the root word (the irreducible word, with all prefixes and suffixes removed).

(1) In the following words **ng** occurs medially in the root word, and therefore should be pronounced /ŋg/.

finger	jingle	mangle	angry	anguish	singular
single	English	fungus	dangle	tingle	distinguish
linger	England	tangle	hunger	language	flamingo
anger	ingot	jungle	angle	kangaroo	extinguish

(2) /g/ should never be pronounced after final /ŋ/ and is normally silent even when a suffix is added to final /ŋ/. The following words should logically follow this rule, but they are exceptions. The **ng** in these particular words should be pronounced /ŋg/.

longer	stronger	younger	elongate
longest	strongest	youngest	

J. When a **kn** or **gn** cluster begins a word, the **k** or **g** is silent, as in the following words.

Silent k	Silent k	Silent k	Silent k	Silent g	Silent g
knack	knell	knighthood	know	gnarled	gnome
knapsack	knew	knit	knowledge	gnash	gnostic [10]
knave	knickknack	knob	knuckle	gnat	gnu
knead	knife	knock		gnaw	
knee	knight	knot			

K. A **g** which precedes a final **n** or **m** is silent. The **g** remains silent when some suffixes are added. But when certain others are added, the /g/ is pronounced as the end of one syllable, and the /n/ or /m/ begins the following syllable. In the list below, related words are in parallel columns, arranged according to whether the /g/ is silent or pronounced.

Silent g	Silent g	Pronounced /g/		Silent g	Silent g	Pronounced /g/
align	alignment			deign	deigning	dignity
	aligning			design	designing	designation
arraign	arraignment				designer	
	arraigning			diaphragm		diaphragmatic
assign	assignment	assignation		ensign		insignia
	assigning			feign	feigning	
benign		benignant		malign	maligning	malignant
		benignity		reign	reigning	
campaign	campaigning			resign	resigning	resignation
champagne				sign	signing	signal
consign	consignment				signer	
	consigning					

L. Sentences for /k/ and /g/ practice.

1. Could Gertrude go to the bakery to get the cakes?
2. Put the eggs for cooking in this basket.
3. Katherine talked excitedly about the luxury of baroque furnishings.
4. Mrs. Gordon didn't recognize her cook in the crowd at the ball game.
5. Dig the hole bigger before you sink the bucket.
6. The architect took longer with the sketches than we had expected.
7. I suspect that English is an extremely difficult language.

[10] But in **agnostic** the [g] is pronounced because the prefix **a** is added.

8. The chiropractor cured the crick in her neck with a quick jerk.
9. He was angry that the choir lingered to talk with the congregation.
10. That kangaroo crouching in the corner has evoked considerable curiosity.
11. Kim can make a quilt of the scraps of green and gray calico we gave her.
12. I can't explain exactly how the crab nets got so tangled.
13. Could a chiropodist cut out these corns completely?
14. The accelerator got stuck and the car crashed into a plate glass window.
15. The lecture about arctic exploration was accompanied by excellent pictures.

M. Reading selections for /k/ and /g/ practice.

1. A good cigar is as great a comfort to a man as a good cry to a woman.

    EDWARD BULWER-LYTTON

2. Grass is the forgiveness of nature — her constant benediction. Fields trampled with battle, saturated with blood, torn with the ruts of the cannon, grow green again with grass, and carnage is forgotten. Forests decay, harvests perish, flowers vanish, but grass is immortal.

    JOHN J. INGALLS

3.
    Life is too short to waste
    In critic peep or cynic bark,
    Quarrel or reprimand:
    'Twill soon be dark.

    RALPH WALDO EMERSON

4. Times of general calamity and confusion have ever been productive of the greatest minds.

    COLTON

5. There grows all over what was once the child a sort of prickly protection like hair; a callousness, a carelessness, a curious combination of random and quite objectless energy with a readiness to accept conventions. . . .

    G. K. CHESTERTON

/ŋ/ as in **sing**   ŋ

Spellings of /ŋ/: ng as in **sing**; n as in **ink**; ngue as in **harangue**.

Description of /ŋ/: This phoneme is a voiced, back-velar, nasal semi-vowel. Firm closure of the back of the tongue with the velum prevents emission of

the breath stream from the mouth and diverts it through the nasal passage
as the velum is lowered.

EXERCISES

A. A common error involves changing the articulation of final /ŋ/ in the –**ing**
suffix, as in **coming**. This mistake is popularly called "dropping the *g*,"
a designation which is quite misleading. Actually, the **ng** in an –**ing** suffix
represents the single phoneme /ŋ/ and has no /g/ sound to "drop." The
error is a substitution for /ŋ/ of either /n/ or [ɲ] (a nasal consonant articulated with the front of the tongue against the hard palate, the same tongue
positioning as used for /j/ in **young**). In addition, some speakers change
the vowel of the suffix, so that the word ends in /ɪn/ or /ɪɲ/ instead of
/ɪŋ/.

(1) To perceive the difference between the articulation of /n/ and /ŋ/, say
the following pairs of words, giving attention to the feel of the tongue
tip articulating the /n/ and the back of the tongue articulating the /ŋ/.

/ɪn/	/ɪŋ/	/ɪn/	/ɪŋ/	/in/	/ɪŋ/	/in/	/ɪŋ/
sin	sing	kin	king	seen	sing	bean	bing
win	wing	been	bing	keen	king	ween	wing

(2) Even if you have difficulty saying /ŋ/ in the –**ing** suffix, you probably
say /ŋ/ perfectly in a word like **sing** or **king**. If you practice a word
like **blessing** as if it were **bless-sing**, you can say /ŋ/ in the ending
correctly. Pronounce each word in the following list as if it were
"broken in the middle," with **sing** as the second half. Then repeat it,
putting the two parts together. Listen to the /ŋ/ and *feel* its articulation in the split word; then make sure that the recombined word has
the same sound and feeling for final /ŋ/.

blessing	casing	cursing	erasing	missing	racing
bossing	chasing	dancing	facing	nursing	rejoicing
bracing	creasing	dosing	lacing	passing	romancing
caressing	crossing	dressing	leasing	prancing	tossing

(3) Practice each word in the following list with a split in the middle and
king as the second half. Then repeat the word, combining the two
halves. Keep the /ŋ/ articulation the same at the end of the recombined
word as it was in **king** when the word was divided.

aching	breaking	dunking	making	raking	talking
baking	choking	joking	marking	shaking	walking
booking	cooking	leaking	parking	taking	working

(4) Practice each of the following words, at first "broken" with a **–ring** ending, and then with the two parts put together. Be sure that /ŋ/ at the end of the recombined word sounds and feels like the /ŋ/ at the end of **ring** in the split word.

bearing	curing	flowering	mooring	securing	tearing
blurring	daring	hearing	nearing	showering	towering
boring	during	lowering	paring	soaring	wearing
caring	fearing	luring	pouring	stirring	withering

(5) Practice the words in each column below, in the same manner as above. What you will be saying as the second half of the "broken" word is not a real word, but a nonsense syllable which is spelled in IPA symbols above that column. Be sure that /ŋ/ sounds the same and is articulated the same in each word when recombined as it was in the split word.

/gɪŋ/	/zɪŋ/	/fɪŋ/	/vɪŋ/	/ðɪŋ/	/ɪŋ/
begging	brazing	coughing	having	bathing	agreeing
flagging	dozing	golfing	loving	breathing	being
gagging	easing	laughing	moving	scathing	bowing
lagging	pleasing	leafing	proving	seething	doing
nagging	raising	loafing	raving	sheathing	going
rigging	seizing	puffing	shaving	teething	owing
sagging	teasing	stuffing	striving	tithing	seeing
wagging	wheezing	surfing	weaving	writhing	sighing

B. If you are in the process of correcting a substitution of /n/ for /ŋ/ in words like **baking** and **having**, be careful not to apply this correction where it is inappropriate. **Chicken** should not be "corrected" to /tʃɪkɪŋ/, nor should **Evanston** and **Evansville** become /ɛvɪŋstən/ and /ɛvɪŋzvɪl/. When in doubt, let the spelling guide you.

C. Pronouncing /ŋ/ without adding a /g/ is a tenacious problem for some speakers. In English, when **ng** occurs finally in the root word, the correct pronunciation is /ŋ/, without a /g/ sound. The person who says /sɪŋg/ for **sing** /sɪŋ/ is reflecting the influence on his English of some other language in which /ŋ/ would not occur except before a /g/ or /k/. (The individual's speech can be affected by some other language or foreign dialect in his environment, although he himself does not speak a foreign language.) Eliminating the unwanted /g/ after /ŋ/ requires a period of careful attention to the articulation of /ŋ/. The articulation of /ŋ/ has two requirements: (1) the back of the tongue makes firm contact with the velum; (2) the velum lowers so that the voice is emitted through the nasal cavity. After the /ŋ/, if the velum is raised while the back of the tongue is still contacting the velum, the breath is stopped up behind the tongue contact;

then, when the tongue pulls away from the velum, the air is "exploded" in a /g/. The secret of preventing the addition of /g/ after /ŋ/ is to separate the back of the tongue from its contact with the velum *before* raising the velum. How do you control this required sequence of movements? Remember that as long as you *hear* a nasal sound, your velum is lowered to let the breath pass through the nasal passage. You can feel the back of the tongue touching the velum. This means that if you pull your tongue away from the velum *while you are still making a nasal sound*, you will not add a /g/.

(1) In the following words, /ŋ/ should not be followed by /g/. Pronounce each word with careful attention to the /ŋ/, easing the tongue away from its velar contact while you can still hear the nasal consonant continuing.

along	fling	king	rung	sprang	thing
among	flung	long	sang	spring	throng
bang	gang	lung	sing	sting	tongue
belong	gong	prolong	slang	string	wing
bring	hang	rang	slung	strong	wrong
cling	hung	ring	song	stung	young

(2) When a word ending in /ŋ/ adds a suffix, or a noun which makes it a compound noun, still no /g/ should be pronounced. After /ŋ/, pull the tongue away from the velum while you still hear the nasal sound.

banging	gangway	kings	ringlet	songs	tongues
belonging	hangar	longing	rings	springing	wingless
bringing	hanger	lungs	ringworm	stinging	wings
clinging	hanging	ringer	singer	stringing	wronged
flinging	kinglike	ringing	singing	things	wronging
gangs	kingly	ringleader	sings	thronging	youngster

(3) Practice the following phrases, making a careful transition from final /ŋ/ to the next word without inserting a /g/.

a long way	hang on	the song is
among ourselves	long arms	the thing is
bring us	sing out	wrong way
gang of boys	strong leadership	young ones

D. The two words **length** and **strength** are sometimes mispronounced by substituting /n/ for /ŋ/. The correct pronunciation can be achieved by thinking of the ending of these words as **–nkth**: /lɛŋkθ/, /strɛŋkθ/.

E. When **nk** or **nc** ends a syllable, it is pronounced /ŋk/. Practice /ŋ/ in the following words.

bank	blinking	ink	rink	sinking	trunk
banking	drank	plank	sank	spanking	winking
blank	drinking	rank	shrinking	thinking	zinc

F. Sentences for /ŋ/ practice.

1. The Earl of Bingham brings greetings to the king.
2. Both speaking and singing require a discriminating use of the English language.
3. He flung the junk into the trunk angrily, and banged the lid shut.
4. A gang of youngsters is bringing some things to the trading post this evening.
5. Congressman Kingston walked down the gangway with an anguished look on his face.
6. He had too little strength to hang on for even a minute longer.
7. Long ago a strong young king ruled this kingdom.

G. Reading selections for /ŋ/ practice.

1.   A very merry, dancing, drinking,
         Laughing, quaffing, and unthinking time.

                                    JOHN DRYDEN

2. From *Chicago* [11]

Come and show me another city with lifted head singing so proud to be alive and coarse and strong and cunning.
Flinging magnetic curses amid the toil of piling job on job, here is a tall bold slugger set vivid against the little soft cities;
Fierce as a dog with tongue lapping for action, cunning as a savage pitted against the wilderness,
    Bareheaded,
    Shoveling,
    Wrecking,
    Planning,
    Building, breaking, rebuilding,
Under the smoke, dust all over his mouth, laughing with white teeth,
Under the terrible burden of destiny laughing as a young man laughs,
Laughing even as an ignorant fighter laughs who has never lost a battle,
Bragging and laughing that under his wrist is the pulse, and under his ribs the heart of the people,
    Laughing!

                                    CARL SANDBURG

[11] From "Chicago" from *Chicago Poems* by Carl Sandburg. Copyright 1916 by Holt, Rinehart and Winston, Inc. Copyright 1944 by Carl Sandburg. Reprinted by permission of Holt, Rinehart and Winston, Inc.

3.   There was a rustling that seemed like a bustling
        Of merry crowds justling at pitching and hustling;
        Small feet were pattering, wooden shoes clattering,
        Little hands clapping and little tongues chattering,
        And, like fowls in a farm-yard when barley is scattering,
        Out came the children running.

ROBERT BROWNING

4.   From *The Cataract of Lodore*

     The cataract strong
          Then plunges along,
          Striking and raging
          As if a war waging
     Its caverns and rocks among;
          Rising and leaping,
          Sinking and creeping,
          Swelling and sweeping,
     Showering and springing,
          Flying and flinging,
          Writhing and ringing,
          Eddying and whisking,
          Spouting and frisking,
          Turning and twisting,
             Around and around
          With endless rebound
          Smiting and fighting,
          A sight to delight in;
          Confounding, astounding,
             Dizzying and deafening the ear with its sound.
             Collecting, projecting,
             Receding and speeding,
          And shocking and rocking,
          And darting and parting,
          And threading and spreading,
          And whizzing and hissing,
          And dripping and skipping,
          And hitting and splitting,
          And shining and twining,
          And rattling and battling,
          And shaking and quaking,
          And pouring and roaring,
          And waving and raving,
          And tossing and crossing,
          And flowing and going,

And running and stunning,
And foaming and roaming,
And dinning and spinning,
And dropping and hopping,
And working and jerking,
And guggling and struggling,
And heaving and cleaving,
And moaning and groaning,
And glittering and frittering,
And gathering and feathering,
And whitening and brightening,
And quivering and shivering,
And hurrying and skurrying,
And thundering and floundering;
Dividing and gliding and sliding,
And falling and brawling and sprawling,
And driving and riving and striving,
And sprinkling and twinkling and wrinkling,
And sounding and bounding and rounding,
And bubbling and troubling and doubling,
And grumbling and rumbling and tumbling,
And clattering and battering and shattering;
Retreating and beating and meeting and sheeting,
Delaying and straying and playing and spraying,
Advancing and prancing and glancing and dancing,
Recoiling, turmoiling and toiling and boiling,
And gleaming and steaming and streaming and beaming,
And rushing and flushing and brushing and gushing,
And flapping and rapping and clapping and slapping,
And curling and whirling and purling and twirling,
And thumping and plumping and bumping and jumping;
And dashing and flashing and splashing and clashing;
And so never ending, but always descending,
Sounds and motion forever are blending,
All at once and all o'er, with a mighty uproar,
And this way the water comes down at Lodore.

ROBERT SOUTHEY

/h/ as in he

h

Spellings of /h/: **h** as in **he**; **wh** as in **who**; **j** as in **Navajo**.

Description of /h/: This phoneme is a voiceless, glottal fricative. To articulate this consonant, no movement of tongue, jaw, or lips is required, the formation being entirely at the glottis. The vocal folds are separated enough that the outgoing breath stream does not cause vocal cord vibration (vocal tone), but they are held closely enough together so that the breath stream passing through the glottis produces a sound of friction. Since no articulation in the mouth is needed for /h/, the mouth articulators anticipate the articulation of the vowel or diphthong which follows.

EXERCISES

A. Omission of /h/ preceding the diphthong /ju/ is an occasional error. Pronounce /h/ initially in each of the following words.

hew	huge	humanism	humanly	humidor
Houston	Hugh	humanitarian	humerus	humiliate
Hubert	human	humanity	humid	humility
hue	humane	humanize	humidity	humus

B. There is some confusion about whether or not to pronounce /h/ in words derived from French. No rule can be laid down. One simply has to learn each word individually.
   (1) /h/ is correctly pronounced in many French-derived words, such as the following (some of which are repeated from Exercise A):

| heretic | hospital | hotel | Huguenot | humid |
| horrible | host | huge | human | humility |

   (2) Silent *h* occurs in a few words of French origin.

| heir | honest | honor | hour |

   (3) Alternate pronunciations, one with silent **h** and the other with /h/ pronounced, are in current approved usage for the following words. Choose the pronunciations which sound more familiar to you.

| herb | homage | hostler | humble | humor |

C. The **h** which begins a medial or final *unstressed* syllable in a word is correctly silent. In **shépherd** the **h** is silent; but in **shéep-hérder** the **h** is pronounced. In **prohibítion** the **h** is silent; but in **prohíbit** the **h** is pronounced. In **philharmónic** the **h** is silent; but in **dishármony** the **h** is pronounced. In **véhicle** the **h** is silent; but in **vehícular** the **h** is pronounced.

D. The **h** which begins an unstressed word occurring medially or finally in a phrase may be either silent or pronounced, depending mostly on the rate of speech. In conversation, particularly, the omission of initial /h/ in unstressed words (except at the beginning of a phrase) is entirely acceptable, as in the following phrases.

thóught he léft	Jóhn has fínished
if he cómes báck	ít has been próved
sáw him yésterday	the bóy has góne hóme
gíve him some cándy	shé had alréady léft
chánged his mínd	théy had tóld us
bórrowed his bóok	áll thése have been dóne
hélped her dó it	théy have góne
cálled her to dínner	wé have fínished

E. Foreign students may have difficulty pronouncing /h/ if their native language has no /h/ phoneme (e.g., French). Sometimes they attempt to make an /h/ by constricting the breath passage with the back of the tongue raised to the velum or hard palate. (This sound, whose IPA symbol is [χ], is often erroneously identified as /h/ in Greek, Hebrew, Japanese, and Spanish.) The /h/ in English has no articulation in the mouth. It is simply breath released from the glottis, preceding a vowel sound. English /h/ *always* occurs before a vowel sound. If you shape your mouth for the vowel to follow and silently breathe out before beginning to sound the vowel, you will produce /h/ before the vowel.

(1) First, practice /h/ initially in these words.

habit	has	help	hog	host	humid
had	head	Henry	hole	hotel	Humphrey
hand	hear	here	hold	house	who
handle	heart	heretic	hope	how	whole
hang	heat	his	horrible	huge	whom
happy	hello	history	hospital	human	whose

(2) Medial /h/ will probably be more difficult. As you practice the following words, first "split" each one just in front of the **h**. To hear the /h/ pronunciation, say the part of the word beginning with **h**. Then say the word all together, slowly, to allow time for attention to the /h/. Finally, say the word at normal rate, listening for the medial /h/.

adhere	behave	exhalant	foghorn	unhappy	unhurried
adhesive	behead	exhalation	preheat	unhealthy	unhurt
ahead	behind	exhale	prehistory	unheated	unwholesome
anyhow	behoove	exhume	reheat	unholy	withhold

F. Sentences for /h/ practice.

1. Hold your hands over your head while you exhale.
2. Ask him to hunt for the hose behind the house.

3. Get behind and push the horse while I pull him.
4. Uriah Heep had a very humble attitude.
5. Hubert is the happiest human being I know.
6. It seems horrible to have made an exhibition of beheadings.
7. A heretic adheres to no belief in deity and hence has no hope for the hereafter.
8. Our host was heir to a small inheritance from his half brother.

G. Reading selections for /h/ practice.

1.   He has half the deed done, who has made a beginning.

HORACE

2.   There is no more miserable human being than one in whom nothing is habitual but indecision.

WILLIAM JAMES

3.   "Home is the place where, when you have to go there
They have to take you in." "I should have called it
Something you somehow haven't to deserve."

ROBERT FROST

4.   On horror's head horrors accumulate.

WILLIAM SHAKESPEARE

5.   My heart is a lonely hunter that hunts on a lonely hill.

WILLIAM SHARP (FIONA MACLEOD)

6.   No house should ever be on any hill or on anything. It should be of the hill, belonging to it, so hill and house could live together each the happier for the other.

FRANK LLOYD WRIGHT

7.   The human heart has hidden treasures,
In secret kept, in silence sealed; —
The thoughts, the hopes, the dreams, the pleasures,
Whose charms were broken if revealed.

CHARLOTTE BRONTË

8.   The mind is its own place, and in itself
Can make a heaven of hell, a hell of heaven.

JOHN MILTON

VOCABULARY EXERCISES

A. Pronunciation of Common Words. The following familiar words are sometimes mispronounced. Check your own pronunciation to be sure it is correct.

	Correct Pronunciation [12] (*in IPA*)	Incorrect Pronunciation (*in IPA*)	Error (*in IPA*)
1. adjective	ˈ/ǽdʒəktɪv/	ˈ/ǽdʒətɪv/	/–/k/
2. children	ə/tʃíldrɪn/	/tʃíldɚn/	/ɚ/ri/
3. chiropodist	aɪ ó /kərapədɪst/	ó /ʃərɑpədɪst/	/ʃ/k/
4. chiropractor	/káɪropræktɚ/	/ʃáɪropræktɚ/	/ʃ/k/
5. chore	/tʃor/	/ʃor/	/ʃ/tʃ/
6. comfortable	/kə́mfɚtəbəl/	/kə́mptəbəl/	/p/fɚ/
		/kə́m̩ftɚbəl/	{/m̩/m/ {/tɚ/ɚtə/
7. congratulate	ə ʊ /kəngrǽtʃulet/	ə ʊ /kəngrǽdʒulet/	/dʒ/tʃ/
		ə ʊ /kəŋgrǽtʃulet/	/ŋ/n/
8. diphthong	/dífθɔŋ/	/dípθɔŋ/	/p/f/
9. dormitory	ˈ/dɔ́rmətori/	á ˈ/dɔ́mətori/	/–/r/
			ə /ɑ/ɔr/
10. escape	/ɛskép/	/ɛkskép/	/ks/s/
11. etc. (et cetera)	/ɛt sétərə/	/ɛk sétərə/	/k/t/
12. floor	ə /flor/	/flo/	/–/r/
13. hundred	ə /hə́ndrɪd/	/hə́ndɚd/	ə /ɚ/ri/
14. particularly	ˈ/pɚtíkjulɚli/	ˈ/pɚtíkjɚli/	/–/ul/
15. probably	ó ˈ/prɑbəbli/	ó ˈ/prɑbli/	/–/bə/
16. recognize	/rékəgnaɪz/	/rékənaɪz/	/–/g/
17. shrink	/ʃrɪŋk/	/srɪŋk/	/s/ʃ/
18. shrivel	/ʃrívəl/	/srívəl/	/s/ʃ/
19. terrible	/térəbəl/	/téəbəl/	/–/r/
20. united	/junáɪtɪd/	/junáɪntɪd/	/n/–/
21. veterinarian	/vɛtərənérɪən/	/vɛntərənérɪən/	/n/–/
22. wash	ə ɑ /wɒʃ/	/wɔrʃ/	/r/–/

[12] Alternate correct pronunciations are indicated by symbols written one above the other.

B. Pronunciation of Less Common Words.[13] Many words in the following list will be familiar to you, but some of them may not be in your speaking vocabulary. Learn the correct pronunciation of each word. If a word is unfamiliar, you should also learn its spelling and definition, experiment with using it in practice sentences, and make a conscious effort to include it in conversation several times immediately.

1. **accede** /æksíd/ (verb) to agree or assent; e.g., I accede to your wishes; he acceded to the request.

2. **archipelago** /ɑrkəpélǝgo/ (noun) a string of small islands; e.g., the Aleutian Islands comprise an archipelago extending from the coast of Alaska.

3. **attaché** /ætəʃé/ (noun) member of the diplomatic staff of an ambassador or minister; e.g., he served as attaché to the American ambassador in Moscow; many businessmen prefer attaché cases to briefcases now.

4. **brusque** /brəsk/ (adj.) rough and abrupt in manner; e.g., a brusque, curt manner; a brusque reply; a brusque command.

5. **cache** /kæʃ/ (noun) a place for hiding or securing possessions; e.g., a fur cache; a cache of food.

6. **chagrin** /ʃəgrín/ (noun) distress because of being humbled or embarrassed; e.g., chagrin at his defeat intensified the pain of his beaten body; he was overcome by chagrin.

7. **chaise longue** /ʃez lóŋ/ (noun) a chair with a seat long enough to support the feet; e.g., she rests every afternoon on a chaise longue in her bedroom; sunbathing on a chaise longue.

8. **charlatan** /ʃárlətən/ (noun) a pretender to knowledge or ability, a quack; e.g., this charlatan successfully masqueraded as a physician for fourteen years.

9. **chancellor** /tʃǽnsələ/ (noun) the secretary to a monarch; head of a state or department of the state; sometimes the head of a university; e.g., the Chancellor of the Exchequer presented the budget to Parliament; he is the Chancellor of the University of Chicago.

10. **chassis** /ʃǽsi/ (noun) framework supporting an automobile, plane, radio, TV, etc.; e.g., the chassis of our car was warped in the collision; he has to remove the television chassis from the cabinet to make the repairs.

11. **chaste** /tʃest/ (adj.) virtuous; pure in thought and act; e.g., she is chaste and above reproach.

12. **chauvinism** /ʃóvənɪzəm/ (noun) exaggerated or vainglorious patriotism; e.g., all this speechmaking is chauvinism, not real patriotism.

[13] Each pronunciation is given in IPA, with alternate correct phonemes shown one above the other.

13. **cherub** /tʃérəb/ (noun) an infant angel; a child who looks angelic; e.g., at the bottom of the picture are two cherubs leaning against the altar rail adoring the Madonna.

14. **chicanery** /ʃəkénəri/ (noun) sharp practice, trickery, or deception; e.g., beware of him; he is a master of chicanery.

15. **clapboard** /klǽbɚd/ (noun) narrow board, thicker on one edge than the other, used for house siding; e.g., a white clapboard house with red trim.

16. **cogent** /kódʒənt/ (adj.) appealing to the intelligence or reason; convincing; e.g., a cogent argument; a cogent explanation.

17. **complacent** /kəmplésənt/ (adj.) self-satisfied; pleased with one's personal attributes or accomplishments; e.g., jolt him from his complacent attitude; complacent students are under-achievers.

18. **cortège** /kɔrtéʒ/ (noun) a train or procession of attendants; a retinue; e.g., the funeral cortège proceeded on foot from the Capitol to Arlington Cemetery.

19. **digit** /dídʒɪt/ (noun) a finger; any figure from 0 to 9; e.g., he broke three digits on his left hand; a three-digit number.

20. **docile** /dɑsəl/ (adj.) easily trained, taught, or managed; e.g., the beagle is a docile dog; she is a docile child.

21. **facetious** /fəsíʃəs/ (adj.) amusing, humorous; e.g., a facetious reply; don't be facetious (what you said can't be taken seriously).

22. **fission** /fíʃən/ (noun) a cleaving or breaking up into parts; e.g., atomic fission; the cells divide by simple fission.

23. **fusion** /fjúʒən/ (noun) melting, blending, combining of parts; e.g., fusion of sand to form glass; fusion of chemical elements.

24. **gestation** /dʒɛstéʃən/ (noun) period of pregnancy; e.g., the gestation period of large mammals is longer than that of small animals.

25. **gesture** /dʒéstʃɚ/ (noun) motion of body or limbs to convey or reinforce meaning or emotion; e.g., hand gestures should be high enough that attention is not drawn from the speaker's face.

26. **gist** /dʒɪst/ (noun) the essence or main point of an argument, story, etc., e.g., the gist of the matter is that management will not grant the union's demands.

27. **glazier** /gléʒɚ/ (noun) one who works with glass; e.g., call the glazier to replace this windowpane.

28. **gregarious** /grɪgɛriəs/ (adj.) fond of company, sociable; e.g., overly gregarious students in dormitories are tempted to talk rather than study.

29. **harbinger** /hɑ́rbɪndʒɚ/ (noun) a forerunner; e.g., the robin is a harbinger of spring.

30. **longevity** /lɑndʒévəti/ (noun) length of life; e.g., our family is famous for its longevity.

31. **loquacious** /lokwéʃəs/ (adj.) talkative; e.g., she is so loquacious that she monopolizes the conversation.

32. **machinations** /mækənéʃənz/ (noun) artful plots or designs; e.g., the machinations of Castro to seize power; her machinations to entrap a husband.

33. **malinger** /məlíŋɡɚ/ (verb) to feign illness to avoid doing one's duty; to shirk; e.g., malingering is seldom successful in the army; I suspect he is malingering to avoid the math examination.

34. **monsignor** /mɑnsínjɚ/ (noun) a title of honor bestowed on certain priests; e.g., Bishop Sheen was a monsignor when his TV series began.

35. **obsequious** /ɑbsíkwiəs/ (adj.) servilely attentive, fawning; e.g., Uriah Heep concealed his crafty plots behind an obsequious façade.

36. **officious** /əfíʃəs/ (adj.) offering help where none is requested; meddlesome; e.g., she bustled about in an officious flurry; who is that officious little man acting as a self-appointed host?

37. **ostentatious** /ɑstəntéʃəs/ (adj.) showy; pretentious; e.g., an ostentatious wedding, more financial than sentimental; wearing three rings on one hand is ostentatious.

38. **petulant** /pétʃulənt/ (adj.) peevish, fretful; e.g., he succumbs instantly to her petulant moods.

39. **placid** /plǽsɪd/ (adj.) undisturbed; peaceful; quiet; e.g., trees mirrored in the placid surface of the lake; her placid disposition.

40. **poignant** /pɔ́ɪnjənt/ (adj.) keen, piercingly effective, moving, touching; e.g., poignant tragedy; poignant beauty.

41. **prestige** /prɛstíʒ/ (noun) renown; commanding esteem; influence; e.g., his prestige as a judge; her prestige as a hostess.

42. **pretentious** /priténʃəs/ (adj.) showy, ostentatious; e.g., a pretentious house; a pretentious car.

43. **querulous** /kwérələs/ (adj.) complaining, fault-finding, peevish; e.g., a querulous attitude; she tends to be querulous when criticized.

44. **quixotic** /kwɪksɑtɪk/ (adj.) idealistic but impractical; e.g., a man as quixotic as he needs a practical wife.

45. **regime** /riʒim/ (noun) prevailing governmental or social system; e.g., the Socialist regime; the Roosevelt regime; the Tory regime.

46. **regimen** /rédʒəmən/ (noun) a systematic course of diet, medication, etc.; e.g., this regimen will prevent a major heart attack; under this regimen you should lose two pounds a week.

47. **reticent** /rétəsənt/ (adj.) inclined to keep silent; e.g., he is a shy, reticent child; I am reticent about mentioning such an unpleasant subject.

48. **suite** /swit/ (noun) a set of furniture, rooms, or musical compositions; e.g., a bedroom suite; a hotel suite; a suite for piano and violins.

49. **taciturn** /tǽsətɚn/ (adj.) inclined to silence; reserved in speech; e.g., is he devoid of ideas or simply taciturn?

50. **tangible** /tǽndʒəbəl/ (adj.) can be touched, perceptible to touch; e.g., tangible assets; tangible evidence.

51. **tenacious** /tənéʃəs/ (adj.) holding on tightly; e.g., a tenacious mother who will not let her children grow up.

C. Words Relating to Clothing and Personal Grooming. Many of the words in this list derive from French. **Bolero** comes from Spanish. **Dacron** is a concocted word. **Waistcoat** is an English word with an unpredictable pronunciation.

1. **barrette** /bɑrét/ (noun) a clasp or bar for holding a girl's hair in place.
2. **beret** /bəré/ (noun) a soft cap without a brim.
3. **bodice** /bɑ́dɪs/ (noun) the blouse part of a dress.
4. **bolero** /boléro/ (noun) a short, unbuttoned jacket.
5. **bouclé** /buklé/ (noun) a nubby, heavy fabric.
6. **brooch** /brotʃ/ (noun) an ornament with a pin on the back.
7. **challis** /ʃǽli/ (noun) a soft, printed fabric.
8. **chambray** /ʃǽmbre/ (noun) a fine gingham having different colors of thread running the two directions of the weave.
9. **chamois** /ʃǽmi/ (noun) soft, pliable leather.
10. **chemise** /ʃɪmíz/ (noun) a loose-fitting dress or undergarment.
11. **chenille** /ʃəníl/ (noun) material embroidered with close-cut loops of thread.
12. **chiffon** /ʃɪfɑ́n/ (noun) a soft, sheer, silk material.
13. **chignon** /ʃínjɔn/ (noun) a coil of hair; a "bun."
14. **chintz** /tʃɪnts/ (noun) crisp cotton fabric with a glossy surface.
15. **coiffure** /kwɑfjúr/ (noun) a hair style; a manner of dressing the hair.
16. **corsage** /kɔrsɑ́ʒ/ (noun) a flower arrangement to be worn.
17. **couturier** /kuturié/ (noun) a dressmaker.

18. **Dacron** /dékrɑn/ (noun) a synthetic fabric resembling silk.
19. **décolleté** /dɛkɔləté/ (adj.) low-cut at the neckline.
20. **Empire** /ámpɪr/ (adj.) a high-waisted style of dress or gown.
21. **ensemble** /ɑnsámbəl/ (noun) items of attire which belong together.
22. **faille** /faɪl/ (noun) a corded silk fabric.
23. **frieze** /friz/ (noun) a heavy, napped woolen cloth.
24. **gingham** /gíŋəm/ (noun) a cotton material woven in stripes or checks of two or more colors of yarn.
25. **lingerie** /lɑnʒəri/ (noun) feminine underwear or night clothes.
26. **massage** /məsáʒ/ (verb) to rub; (noun) a rub-down.
27. **masseur** /mæsɚ́/ (noun) a man who gives massages.
28. **masseuse** /mæsɔ́z/ (noun) a woman who gives massages.
29. **matelassé** /mætləzé/ (noun) a material woven with a raised design resembling quilting.
30. **moiré** /mwɑré/ (noun) a silk material of a taffeta type which reflects light in a watery pattern.
31. **negligée** /nɛgləzé/ (noun) a loose-fitting robe or dressing gown for a woman.
32. **peignoir** /pɛnwár/ (noun) a negligée; a dressing gown or robe for a woman.
33. **percale** /pɚkél/ (noun) a finely woven cotton material, often with a printed pattern.
34. **suede** /swed/ (noun) leather with a nap surface.
35. **tulle** /tul/ (noun) a sheer fine netting.
36. **waistcoat** /wéskət/ (noun) a fancy vest.

D. Words Relating to Foods and Cooking. The following list includes some of the most common words relating to food which may cause difficulty in pronunciation. It is not intended as a complete lexicon of menu French.

1. **anchovy** /ǽntʃovi/ (noun) a tiny pickled fish used in salads and canapés.
2. **au gratin** /ogrɑtǽn/ or /ográtn̩/ (adj.) with a covering of cheese sauce or buttered bread crumbs.
3. **au jus** /o ʒús/ (adj.) served with its own juice.
4. **buffet** /bufé/ (noun) a piece of furniture used to store linens and silver; a meal served from the buffet or a table.
5. **caviar** /kæviár/ or /kɑviár/ (noun) salted fish eggs often served for hors d'oeuvres.
6. **chives** /tʃaɪvz/ (noun) green tops of an onion-like vegetable used for seasoning.

7. **crouton** /krutɔ̃/ [14] (noun) a small cube of toasted bread served with soup.

8. **cuisine** /kwɪzín/ (noun) the kitchen or its products.

9. **demitasse** /démitæs/ (noun) a small cup of black coffee served usually at the end of dinner.

10. **draught** (beer) /dræft/ (adj.) drawn out of a barrel.

11. **endive** /ɛndaɪv/ (noun) a salad green with curled leaves, related to chicory.

12. **entrée** /ántre/ (noun) the main course, such as the meat, fish, etc.

13. **filet** /filé/ (noun) a strip of meat or fish with bones removed.

14. **filet mignon** /filé mínjɔn/ (noun) steak cut from the rib "eye," without bones.

15. **gherkin** /gɚ́kɪn/ (noun) a small cucumber made into crisp pickles.

16. **giblets** /dʒíblɪts/ (noun) liver, gizzard, and heart of a fowl, used in gravy, etc.

17. **guava** /gwávə/ (noun) a fruit from tropical America used for making jelly, jam, etc.

18. **hors d'oeuvres** /ɔrdɚ́vz/ (noun) relishes or fancy tidbits of food served ahead of a meal, between courses, or with drinks.

19. **maraschino** /mɛrəskino/ (adj.) the red or green preserved cherries used to decorate desserts and certain drinks.

20. **mayonnaise** /meənéz/ or /méənez/ (noun) thick salad dressing made of oil, egg yolks, seasonings, and vinegar or lemon juice.

21. **meringue** /mərǽŋ/ (noun) fluffy topping for pies, etc., made of beaten egg whites.

22. **muskmelon** /mə́skmɛlən/ (noun) a melon with aromatically sweet flesh, either yellow, white, or green.

23. **parfait** /pɑrfé/ (noun) dessert of fruit and whipped cream served in a tall dish.

24. **petit fours** /péti fórz/ or /pəti fúr/ (noun) little sponge cakes or pound cakes individually frosted in a decorative design.

25. **pizza** /pítsə/ (noun) a large flat pie of bread dough spread with spiced tomato paste and cheese, sausage, anchovies, or mushrooms, thoroughly baked.

26. **ragout** /rægú/ (noun) a highly seasoned stew of meat and vegetables.

27. **sherbet** /ʃɚ́bət/ (noun) an iced dessert made of milk and fruit or juices.

28. **soup du jour** /súp du ʒúr/ (noun) the soup of the day.

---

[14] /ɔ̃/ is a nasalized vowel. The **n** is silent.

29. **thyme** /taɪm/ (noun) an aromatic plant whose crushed dried leaves are used for seasoning.

30. **tortilla** /tɔrtíjə/ (noun) Mexican unleavened pancake made of corn meal.

E. Names of Colors. Designations of colors can often be confusing. Pronunciations in this list need to be noted also.

1. **azure** /ǽʒɚ/ the blue of a clear sky.
2. **beige** /beʒ/ light tan.
3. **cerise** /sərís/ bright cherry red.
4. **cerulean** /sərúliən/ very deep sky blue.
5. **chartreuse** /ʃɑrtrúz/ light yellowish-green.
6. **ecru** /ɛ́kru/ very light brown with a slightly yellow hue.
7. **magenta** /mədʒɛ́ntə/ reddish-purple.
8. **mauve** /mov/ pale bluish-purple.
9. **mocha** /mókə/ the color of coffee, dark brown.
10. **ochre** /ókɚ/ usually yellow but sometimes orange or orange-red.
11. **puce** /pjus/ dark purplish-brown.
12. **sepia** /sípɪə/ very dark blackish-brown.
13. **taupe** /top/ dark brownish-grey.
14. **umber** /ə́mbɚ/ dark, dusky brown; sometimes dark reddish-brown.
15. **vermilion** /vɚmíljən/ very bright yellowish-red.

BIBLIOGRAPHY

Books

Anson, Barry J. *An Atlas of Human Anatomy*, 2nd ed. Philadelphia: W. B. Saunders Co., 1963.

Ballenger, Howard, and John Ballenger. *A Manual of Otology, Rhinology, and Laryngology*, 4th ed. Philadelphia: Lea and Febiger, 1954.

Bard, Philip, ed. *Medical Physiology*, 10th ed. St. Louis: C. V. Mosby Co., 1956.

Black, John W., and W. E. Moore. *Speech: Code, Meaning, and Communication*. New York: McGraw-Hill Co., Inc., 1955.

Bloch, B., and G. L. Trager. *Outline of Linguistic Analysis*. Baltimore: Linguistic Society of America, 1942.

Brackett, J. P. *An Analysis of the Vibratory Action of the Vocal Folds During the Production of Tones at Selected Frequencies*. Unpublished Ph.D. Dissertation, Northwestern University, Evanston, Illinois, 1947.

Brash, James C., ed. *Cunningham's Text-book of Anatomy*, 9th ed. London: Oxford University Press, 1953.

Coates, George Morrison, Harry P. Schenck, and M. Valentine Miller. *Otolaryngology*. Hagerstown, Maryland: W. F. Prior Co., Inc., 1947.

Culver, Charles A. *Musical Acoustics*, 4th ed. New York: McGraw-Hill Co., Inc., 1956.

DeWeese, David, and William Saunders. *Textbook of Otolaryngology*. St. Louis: C. V. Mosby Co., 1960.

Fairbanks, Grant. *Voice and Articulation Drillbook*, 2nd ed. New York: Harper and Brothers, 1960.

Fletcher, Harvey. *Speech and Hearing in Communication*, 2nd ed. Princeton, New Jersey: Van Nostrand, 1953.

Fulton, J. F., ed. *A Textbook of Physiology*, 16th ed. Philadelphia: W. B. Saunders Co., 1949.

Gleason, H. A., Jr. *An Introduction to Descriptive Linguistics*, rev. ed. New York: Holt, Rinehart and Winston, Inc., 1961.

Goss, Charles Mayo, ed. *Gray's Anatomy of the Human Body*, 27th ed. Philadelphia: Lea and Febiger, 1959.

Gray, Giles Wilkeson, and Claude Merton Wise. *The Bases of Speech*, 3rd ed. New York: Harper and Brothers, 1959.

Hanley, T. D., and W. L. Thurman. *Developing Vocal Skills*. New York: Holt, Rinehart and Winston, Inc., 1942.

Heffner, Roe-Merrill S. *General Phonetics*. Madison: University of Wisconsin Press, 1950.

Hockett, C. F. *A Course in Modern Linguistics*. New York: The Macmillan Co., 1958.

Hoops, Richard A. *Speech Science*. Springfield: Charles C. Thomas, 1960.

Houssay, Bernardo A. *Human Physiology*, 2nd ed. New York: McGraw-Hill Co., Inc., 1955.

Jackson, Chevalier, and Chevalier L. Jackson, eds. *Diseases of the Nose, Throat, and Ear*, 2nd ed. Philadelphia: W. B. Saunders Co., 1959.

Jacobson, E. *Progressive Relaxation*, 2nd ed. Chicago: University of Chicago Press, 1951.

Kantner, Claude, and Robert West. *Phonetics*, rev. ed. New York: Harper and Brothers, 1960.

Kenyon, J. S. *American Pronunciation*, 10th ed. Ann Arbor, Michigan: George Wahr Publishing Co., 1958.

Ladefoged, Peter. *Elements of Acoustic Phonetics*. Chicago: University of Chicago Press, 1962.

McNaught, Ann B., and Robin Callander. *Illustrated Physiology*. Baltimore: Williams and Wilkins Co., 1963.

Moses, Paul. *Voice of Neurosis*. New York: Grune and Stratton, Inc., 1954.

Negus, V. E. *The Mechanism of the Larynx*. London: Wm. Heinemann, Ltd., 1929.

Pierce, J. R., and E. D. David, Jr. *Man's World of Sound*. New York: Doubleday & Company, Inc., 1958.

Pike, K. *Intonation of American English*. Ann Arbor, Michigan: University of Michigan Press, 1945.

Potter, R. K., G. Kopp, and H. Green. *Visible Speech*. Princeton, New Jersey: Van Nostrand, 1947.

Quiring, Daniel, and John Warfel. *The Head, Neck and Trunk*, 2nd ed. Philadelphia: Lea and Febiger, 1960.

Russell, G. Oscar. *Speech and Voice*. New York: The Macmillan Co., 1931.

Sobotta, Johannes. *Atlas of Human Anatomy*, 7th Eng. ed. New York: Hafner Publishing Co., Inc., 1957.

Spalteholz, Werner. *Atlas of Human Anatomy*, 5th Eng. ed. Philadelphia: J. B. Lippincott Co., n. d.

Stewart, John P., ed. *Logan Turner's Diseases of the Nose, Throat and Ear*, 6th ed. Baltimore: Williams and Wilkins Co., 1961.

Thomas, C. K. *The Phonetics of American English*, 2nd ed. New York: The Ronald Press, 1958.

Trager, G. L., and H. L. Smith, Jr. *An Outline of English Structure*. Washington: American Council of Learned Societies, 1957.

Travis, Lee Edward. *Handbook of Speech Pathology*. New York: Appleton-Century-Crofts, 1957.

Van Riper, Charles. *Speech Correction: Principles and Methods*, 3rd ed. Englewood Cliffs, New Jersey: Prentice-Hall, Inc., 1954.

Van Riper, Charles, and John Irwin. *Voice and Articulation*. Englewood Cliffs, New Jersey: Prentice-Hall, Inc., 1958.

West, Robert, Merle Ansberry, and Anna Carr. *Rehabilitation of Speech*, 3rd ed. New York: Harper and Brothers, 1957.

Wise, C. M. *Applied Phonetics*. Englewood Cliffs, New Jersey: Prentice-Hall, Inc., 1955.

Wolf-Heidigger, G. *Atlas of Systematic Human Anatomy*. New York: Hafner Publishing Co., 1962.

Articles and Films

Berg, J. van den. "Myoelastic-aerodynamic Theory of Voice Production," *Journal of Speech and Hearing Research*, I (1958), 227–243.

Berg, J. van den. "Subglottic Pressures and Vibrations of the Vocal Folds," *Folia Phoniatrica*, IX, Fasc. W (1957), 57.

Bloomer, Harlan. "A Roentgenographic Study of the Mechanics of Respiration," *Speech Monographs*, III (1936), 118–124.

Bloomer, Harlan. "Observations on Palatopharyngeal Movements in Speech and Deglutition," *Journal of Speech and Hearing Disorders*, XVIII (1952), 230–246.

Bogert, B. P., and G. E. Peterson. "The Acoustics of Speech," Chapter 5 in *Handbook of Speech Pathology*, ed. Lee Edward Travis. New York: Appleton-Century-Crofts, 1957.

Darley, F. L. "A Normative Study of Oral Reading Rate," Master's Thesis, State University of Iowa, Iowa City, Iowa, 1940.

Draper, M. H., Peter Ladefoged, and D. Whitteridge. "Respiratory Muscles in Speech," *Journal of Speech and Hearing Research*, II (1959), 16–27.

Fairbanks, G., and L. Hoaglin. "An Experimental Study of the Durational Characteristics of the Voice During the Expression of Emotion," *Speech Monographs*, VII (1941), 85–90.

Fairbanks, G., and W. Pronovost. "An Experimental Study of the Pitch Characteristics of the Voice During the Expression of Emotion," *Speech Monographs*, VI (1939), 87–104.

Franke, P. "A Preliminary Study Validating the Measurement of Oral Reading Rate in Words Per Minute," Master's Thesis, State University of Iowa, Iowa City, Iowa, 1939.

Gray, G. W. "Regional Predominance in Respiration in Relation to Certain Aspects of Voice," *Louisiana State University Studies*, No. 27. Baton Rouge: Louisiana State University Press (1936), 59–78.

Hanley, T. D. "An Analysis of Vocal Frequency and Duration Characteristics of Selected Samples of Speech from Three American Dialect Regions," *Speech Monographs*, XVIII (1951), 78–93.

Hollien, H. "Some Laryngeal Correlates of Vocal Pitch," *Journal of Speech and Hearing Research*, III (1960), 52–58.

Hollien, H. "Vocal Pitch Variation Related to Changes in Vocal Fold Length," *Journal of Speech and Hearing Research*, III (1960), 150–156.

Hollien, H., and J. F. Curtis. "A Laminagraphic Study of Vocal Pitch," *Journal of Speech and Hearing Research*, III (1960), 361–371.

Hollien, H., and G. P. Moore. "Measurements of the Vocal Folds During Changes in Pitch," *Journal of Speech and Hearing Research*, III (1960), 157–165.

Hoshiko, M. "Sequence of Action of Breathing Muscles During Speech," *Journal of Speech and Hearing Research*, III (1960), 291–297.

Huyck, E., and K. Allen. "Diaphragmatic Action of Good and Poor Speaking Voices," *Speech Monographs*, IV (1937), 101–109.

Idol, H. "A Statistical Study of Respiration in Relation to Speech Characteristics," *Louisiana State University Studies*, No. 27. Baton Rouge: Louisiana State University Press (1936), 79–98.

Jacobson, R., C. G. M. Fant, and M. Halle. "Preliminaries to Speech Analysis, the Distinctive Features and their Correlates," *Technical Report No. 13*. Cambridge: Massachusetts Institute of Technology, Acoustics Laboratory, 1952.

Joos, M. "Acoustic Phonetics," *Language Monographs*, XXIII, XXIV (1948), 1–137.

Kelley, J. C., and M. D. Steer. "Revised Concept of Rate," *Journal of Speech and Hearing Disorders*, XIV (1949), 222–226.

Lynch, G. E. "A Phonophotographic Study of Trained and Untrained Voices Reading Factual and Dramatic Material," *Archives of Speech*, I (1934), 9–25.

Moore, G. P. "Voice Disorders Associated with Organic Abnormalities," in *Handbook of Speech Pathology*, ed. Lee Edward Travis. New York: Appleton-Century-Crofts, 1957.

Moore, G. P., and H. vonLeden. Film: "The Larynx and Voice: The Function of the Normal Larynx," January, 1957.

Moore, G. P., and H. vonLeden. Film: "The Larynx and Voice: Physiology of the Larynx Under Daily Stress," Laryngeal Research Laboratory, William and Harriet Gould Foundation, Northwestern University, Chicago.

Moore, G. P., F. D. White, and H. vonLeden. "Ultra High Speed Photography in Laryngeal Physiology," *Journal of Speech and Hearing Disorders*, No. 27, II (May, 1962), 165–171.

Murray, E., and J. Tiffin. "An Analysis of Some Basic Aspects of Effective Speech," *Archives of Speech*, I (1934), 61–83.

Pronovost, W. "An Experimental Study of Methods for Determining Natural and Habitual Pitch," *Speech Monographs*, IX (1942), 111–123.

Rees, M. "Some Variables Affecting Perceived Harshness," *Journal of Speech and Hearing Research*, I (1958), 155–168.

Rubin, H., and C. Hirt. "The Falsetto. A High-Speed Cinematographic Study," *Laryngoscope*, LXX (1960), 1305–1324.

Sallee, W. H. "An Objective Study of Respiration in Relation to Audibility in Connected Speech," *Louisiana State University Studies*, No. 27. Baton Rouge: Louisiana State University Press (1936), 52–58.

Sherman, D., and F. Goodwin. "Pitch Level and Nasality," *Journal of Speech and Hearing Disorders*, XIX (1954), 423–428.

Sherman, D., and E. Linke. "The Influence of Certain Vowel Types on Degree of Harsh Voice Quality," *Journal of Speech and Hearing Disorders*, XVII (1952), 401–408.

Smith, S. "Remarks on the Physiology of the Vibrations of the Vocal Folds," *Folia Phoniatrica*, VI, Fasc. 3 (1954), 166.

Snidecor, J. C. "A Comparative Study of the Pitch and Duration Characteristics of Impromptu Speaking and Oral Reading," *Speech Monographs*, X (1943), 50–56.

Snidecor, J. C. "An Objective Study of Phrasing in Impromptu Speaking and Oral Reading," *Speech Monographs*, XI (1944), 97–104.

Snidecor, J. C. "The Pitch and Duration Characteristics of Superior Female Speakers During Oral Reading," *Journal of Speech and Hearing Disorders*, XVI (1951), 44–52.

Snidecor, J. C. "Temporal Aspects of Breathing in Superior Reading and Speaking Performances," *Speech Monographs*, XXII (1955), 284–289.

Stetson, R. H. "Speech Movements in Action," *Transactions of the American Laryngological Association*, LV (1933), 29–41.

Stetson, R. H., and C. V. Hudgins. "Functions of the Breathing Movements in the Mechanism of Speech," *Arch. Néerlandaises de Phonétique Expérimentale*, V (1930), 1–30.

Thurman, W. L. "Frequency-Intensity Relationships and Optimum Pitch Level," *Journal of Speech and Hearing Research*, I (1958), 117–123.

Tiffin, J., and M. D. Steer. "An Experimental Analysis of Emphasis," *Speech Monographs*, IV (1937), 69–74.

Timke, R., H. vonLeden, and P. Moore. "Laryngeal Vibrations: Measurement of the Glottic Wave," *American Medical Association Archives of Otolaryngology*, LXVIII (July, 1948), 1–19.

Timke, R., H. vonLeden, and P. Moore. "Physiologic Variation," (Part II of "Laryngeal Vibrations"), *American Medical Association Archives of Otolaryngology*, LXIX (1959), 438–444.

vonLeden, H., and G. P. Moore. "Mechanics of the Cricoarytenoid Joint," *Archives of Otolaryngology*, LXXIII (1961), 63–72.

Wiksell, W. M. "An Experimental Analysis of Respiration in Relation to the Intensity of Vocal Tones in Speech," *Louisiana State University Studies*, No. 27. Baton Rouge: Louisiana State University Press (1936), 37–51.

Williamson, A. B. "Diagnosis and Treatment of Eighty-four Cases of Nasality," *Quarterly Journal of Speech*, XXX (1944), 471–479.

Williamson, A. B. "Diagnosis and Treatment of Seventy-two Cases of Hoarse Voice," *Quarterly Journal of Speech*, XXXI (1945), 189–202.

Index